WITHDRAWN

The Dream We Lost

COPYRIGHT, 1940, BY THE JOHN DAY COMPANY, INC.

All rights reserved. This book, or parts thereof, must
not be reproduced in any form without permission.

MANUFACTURED IN THE UNITED STATES OF AMERICA

Van Rees Press, New York

I pondered all these things and how men fight and lose the battle, and the thing they fought for comes about in spite of their defeat, and when it comes about it turns out not to be what they meant, and other men have to fight for what they meant under another name.—William Morris

Preface

THIS BOOK is in part a record of my personal experiences in the U.S.S.R. during the five and a half years I lived there, and in part an account of the new system of exploitation developed in Russia by the Communist dictatorship. This new system is one which not only orthodox Communists, but a whole host of socialists, liberals, and so-called progressives of various kinds, call "socialism," and regard from afar as a beacon light of hope for a crisis-ridden and war-torn world. Perhaps this new system *is* socialism, but anyone who knows what life is like in Russia must recognize that this new society has nothing in common with the society of the free and equal which socialists believed would follow the breakdown of the capitalist system. I hope that those socialists and Communist fellow travelers who still reason, and whose humanitarian impulses have not been entirely destroyed by "religious" zeal and scholastic dogma, will have the patience to examine the facts here presented, and to listen to the experiences of one who once also believed that the Communists would emancipate mankind.

Not only do Stalin and his henchmen wield a power more absolute than any despot of past ages, but it is obvious from an examination of official Soviet figures of wages and production under the Five Year Plans that the Russian people are worse fed, housed, and clothed than before the Revolution. There is grave doubt as to the accuracy of the Soviet Government's statistics, but if the true state of Russia's national economy is even worse than I have depicted it in Chapters VI, VII, and VIII of this book, the picture revealed by a careful analysis of the official data is dark enough to disillusion all those who do not refuse to see. It should also now be clear to the plan-mad liberals of the Western world that Russia's reputedly planned economy is a myth, and that production and distribution are in a far more chaotic state in the U.S.S.R. than under the capitalist system in its periods of worst crisis.

I shall, perhaps, be accused of being prejudiced by my personal experiences. So also, no doubt, have the victims of all tyrannies been prejudiced, whether they were slaves in the ancient world, or heretics persecuted by the Inquisition, or victims in Nazi concentration camps.

My disillusionment did not, in any case, come suddenly as the result of my husband's arrest and imprisonment without trial in 1936. It was a disillusionment which had begun in 1930 and had become more absolute with each month and year I lived in the U.S.S.R.

Disillusionment is, however, a negative process. Unless one is to abjure life itself one must endeavor not only to learn from experience but also to face disagreeable realities. Because the hopes of one's youth are dimmed, because history has not worked out in the way one expected, and because certain basic changes are taking place in the world which are distasteful or hateful, one should not ignore them or think one can halt them by force. We can perhaps moderate present historical trends, and to some extent control our destinies, by a fearless examination of what is occurring. But we cannot bid the world stand still because we dislike its evolution. For this reason I have not confined myself in this book to an account of the Soviet way of life, but have added some chapters dealing with the lessons of the Bolshevik Revolution and comparing Nazi Germany and Bolshevik Russia.

My thanks are due to the authors or publishers who have given me permission to quote from the following books:

Stalin's Russia, by Max Eastman (W. W. Norton); *Stalin,* by Boris Souvarine (Alliance); *Proletarian Journey,* by Fred Beale (Hillman-Curl); *World Communism,* by Franz Borkenau (W. W. Norton); *Vingt Ans au Service de L'U.R.S.S.,* by Alexandre Barmine (Albin Michel); *In Stalin's Secret Service,* by W. G. Krivitsky (Harper and Bros.); *The Voice of Destruction,* by Hermann Rauschning (G. P. Putnam's Sons); *The Vampire Economy,* by Guenter Reimann (Vanguard); *The United States of Europe,* by Alfred Bingham (Duell).

My particular thanks are due to Professor Vladimir Tchernavin for permission to reproduce in Chapter IX a long passage from his personal account of life in a Russian concentration camp, published in the *Slavonic Review.* I have made a number of references to the valuable work done on Soviet economy by Mr. L. E. Hubbard, author of *Soviet Trade and Distribution,* and other works published in England. I have also referred to data supplied in Professor Florinsky's well-documented *Toward an Understanding of the U.S.S.R.*

FREDA UTLEY

New York
July, 1940

Contents

PART I

I	Prologue to Disillusionment	3
II	The Miscarriage of Bolshevism	33
III	Learning the Soviet Way of Life	59
IV	Life in Moscow—1932-1936	94

PART II

V	What Is Socialism?	125
VI	The Servitude of the Peasants and Taxation of the People's Food	147
VII	Servitude of the Workers	172
VIII	The Cost of Soviet Industrialization	196
IX	The New Method of Exploitation	218
X	Arrest	260

PART III

XI	Nazi Germany and Soviet Russia	277
XII	Making the World Safe for Stalin	312
XIII	Can National Socialism Be Tamed?	335
	Index	365

PART I

CHAPTER I

PROLOGUE TO DISILLUSIONMENT

I FIRST VISITED the U.S.S.R. in the summer of 1927, at the time when Lenin's "New Economic Policy" was still in force, Trotsky not yet exiled, although already eliminated from the political scene, and the people of Russia enjoying a measure of material prosperity and a degree of liberty unknown three years later. Although there was still a society which might be called semisocialist, the signs of degeneration were already perceptible if one had the wit to see them. But I came as a delegate, an enthusiastic and youthful Communist recently emerged from the chrysalis of the Labour party, ready to believe most, if not all, that I was told, and without any previous experience of a police state to teach me that no one would dare speak his mind to a foreigner. The days when I was to live in Moscow as an ordinary citizen were still far off; and such Russian friends as I had in Moscow, although not all of them Bolsheviks, still fervently believed in the "good society" being created in the U.S.S.R.

"One's character is one's fate," and one's character is no doubt mainly the product of environment. But it is only as one approaches middle age that one can look back and see how the influences of one's early youth determined the course of one's life. Those influences in my case were both socialist and liberal. It was a passion for the emancipation of mankind rather than the blueprint of a planned society or any mystical yearning to merge myself in a fellowship which led me to enter the Soviet Union and to leave it six years later with my political beliefs and my personal happiness alike shattered.

I came to communism via Greek history, the French revolutionary literature I had read in childhood, and the English nineteenth-century poets of freedom; not as a revolté against a strict bourgeois upbringing, nor on account of failure to make a place for myself in capitalist society, but profoundly influenced by a happy childhood, a socialist father, and a Continental education. For me the communist ideal seemed the fulfillment of the age-long struggle of mankind for freedom and justice. I was, perhaps, mainly attracted to communism by its internationalism and its anti-imperialism. The Labour party in England had alienated me by its participation in the exploitation and oppression of the conquered races of Africa and Asia. My studies both of ancient history and modern economics made me abhor slavery in any form, and the Communists were the only socialists whose ideal was a world-wide equality and liberty. The same influences of my upbringing which by 1925 had turned my hopes toward the U.S.S.R., were to make it impossible for me to accept the Soviet regime once I came to know it intimately. I was, in Stalinist phraseology, a "rotten liberal," a "petty bourgeois intellectual"—one who foolishly desired social justice, freedom, and equality, and had imagined that socialism meant an end to oppression and injustice.

My father, whose influence over me was profound, had known William Morris in his youth, had been a friend of Marx's daughters and an associate of Bernard Shaw, the Webbs, and other Fabians. He had taken part in the great labor struggles of the late eighties and nineties, had been arrested with John Burns in a demonstration in Trafalgar Square, and had spoken from the same platform as Friedrich Engels in Manchester. Although he had retired from politics soon after I was born, I had been brought up in the socialist tradition.

My mother, daughter of a radical North Country family, had met my father at the age of sixteen when Aveling (the famous translator of Marx's *Capital,* who married Eleanor Marx) had brought him to my grandfather's house in Manchester. My grandfather, although a "bourgeois," being a manufacturer, was a free-thinker and a republican, and boasted of how his wife's mother, when very ill, had hidden the great Chartist leader, Feargus O'Connor, in her bed when the police were searching the house for him.

My mother, one of nine children, had shown an unusual independence by leaving her comfortable home to train as a nurse in London, and had there secretly married my father against the wishes of my grandfather. For in spite of his radicalism he considered marriage to a poor journalist most undesirable. When my mother left the hospital to live with my father, he was both leader-writer and musical critic on the *Star,* most famous liberal newspaper of the time.

My father's Marxism, like that of many English Socialists, was colored and humanized by the nineteenth-century liberal atmosphere, and he early implanted in my mind those libertarian values which have consciously or unconsciously motivated me all my life.

The favorite tales of my childhood were Greek legends and Norse sagas, and when I first started to read history my heroes were Pericles and the Gracchi. From an early age I loved the poems of Shelley, and in my teens I could recite long passages of Swinburne and the choruses of Euripides by heart. Swinburne's love poems I rejected as incomprehensible aberrations from the glorification of freedom and the denunciation of tyranny which I loved. I thrilled to such lines as

> *Pride have all men in their fathers that were free before them,*
> *In the warriors that begat us freeborn pride have we;*
> *But the fathers of their spirit, how may men adore them;*
> *With what rapture may we praise who bade our souls be free.*
> *Sons of Athens born in spirit and truth are all born free men;*
> *Most of all, we, nurtured where the North wind holds his reign.*
> *Children all we sea-folk of the Salaminian seamen,*
> *Sons of them that beat back Persia, they that beat back Spain.*

Brought up to be an atheist and to consider religion as the root of tyranny and cruelty, freedom of the spirit appeared to me as an indispensable condition for the economic and political emancipation of mankind. At the outset I failed to perceive the religious side of communism, but later it was my deeply rooted distrust of idolatry and superstition which finally made it impossible for me to accept Stalin as a god, and impelled me to recoil in horror from the degradation and enslavement of the human mind which are the predominant features of Stalin's Russia. The rationalism of my upbringing and its antireligious and international emphasis made it impossible for me to persuade myself that "socialist brotherhood" justified the imposition of torture and death on millions of innocent people, and the excommunication of those who questioned a single act of the self-appointed Communist "Leader."

Max Eastman, in his illuminating analysis of the motive patterns of socialism, has distinguished the "fraternal passion" impulse as the one which finds satisfaction in Stalin's totalitarian state capitalism. Socialists motivated by the "thirst for co-operative emotion, for the sense of membership in a totality" can excuse the crimes and cruelty and hypocrisy of the U.S.S.R. and find nothing wrong with a society in which not only is human freedom dead, but the very concept of freedom has become "counter-revolutionary." Hence the Dean of Canterbury praises Soviet Russia from the same unconscious motives as impelled the Dominican friars to uphold the Church of Rome in the days of the Inquisition. The Russian Bolshevik party to him, as to the Webbs, the editors of the *New Republic,* and scores of other "socialists" in England and America, is—or was—a "brotherhood" which they uphold as Catholics and Protestants upheld the religious fanatics who drenched Europe in blood during the Wars of Religion.

To these so-called socialists and liberals, Stalin's bloodstained tyranny, which has enslaved the whole Russian people, is a "classless" society to be praised, lied about, and imitated. They have been as ready to condone the crimes of the Soviet Government as sincere Christians on either side were to glorify the devastating wars and the persecution inflicted to ensure entry into Paradise for the converts to the "true faith."

Those, on the other hand, whose motive pattern is the emancipation of mankind, cannot accept tyranny, cruelty, and oppression as good, merely because a new set of people are inflicting them upon the mass of the people in the name of a new ideal. Lenin himself saw human freedom as the goal of the class struggle. The tragedy has been that in confining the conception of freedom to a minority and in inflaming the hatreds of mankind, he laid the foundations for a worse tyranny than the world had yet known.

Looking back at the influences which shaped my political thought in early years, I realize that the experience of going to an expensive boarding school in England helped to lay the psychological foundations in my unconscious for the militant communism which in my twenties supplanted the vague and academic socialist outlook of my early youth.

From the age of nine to thirteen, I had lived on the Continent, first traveling with my parents and then, at the age of eleven, being sent to boarding school on the Lake of Geneva. Those two years at school in French Switzerland among German girls "finishing" their education, was one of the happiest periods of my life; the four succeeding years at boarding school in England among the most unhappy. In Switzerland I was at first the only English pupil, and later one of two. I was also the youngest. The atmosphere was not unlike that of my home—studious, tolerant, kindly, and healthy. We skated, skiied, and tobogganed in winter, bathed in the Lake of Geneva, and rowed and walked in the summer. But sport was regarded as a pleasure, not as a duty, and study—real hard study—was demanded of us all. My brother was at school a quarter of a mile away across fields, and I had the run of his school as well as of my own. There were boys there from at least a dozen countries and of all ages from twelve to eighteen. I went there for fencing lessons, and my brother and I also had riding lessons together. One summer I went climbing in the mountains for a fortnight with the boys of his school, dressed as a boy and climbing the same mountains as boys of seventeen and eighteen. In that period of my life I had no feeling that boys and girls were so very different; and, mixing with English, Germans, French, Swiss, Italians, and other nationalities, speaking French fluently and German almost as well, I was little aware of national barriers and was imbued with an international outlook which neither my father's influence nor theoretical socialist teaching alone could ever have given me.

From those pleasant and educative days in Switzerland, I was plunged into the frigid, mentality-destroying atmosphere of an English boarding school for girls which aped the British "Public Schools" for boys. There was no fagging and physical brutality as in the boys' public schools—being physically very strong I should have been able to cope with that. But there was mental, or perhaps one should call it social, bullying of the worst kind. The greatest offenses against the social code which ruled the school were to study hard, or to show any originality in dress or behavior. I was handicapped from the start by having a slightly foreign accent—my r's were French r's—and I offended constantly. I can still remember being made to stand up in class to say "stirrup" over and over again, unable to pronounce the r in the English way.

I worked hard and I refused to be dictated to as to whether I should wear a black or a colored ribbon in my hair. I tried to avoid the disciplined games which bored me to go for walks instead. My sins against the social code were at first unconscious, then deliberate. The spirit of rebellion now, for the first time, had been awakened in me. Dimly I began to feel that the social hierarchy and the social code which governed the school were precisely that "capitalist system" which, as a socialist, I thought was the cause of all social injustice. The girls at my school came in later life to symbolize "the imperialist English bourgeoisie" in my unconscious mind: class-conscious, sublimely self-confident and scornful of learning. (The profound change brought about by the World War in the outlook of the English upper classes has since those days transformed the atmosphere of English private schools as of English ruling circles.)

Of course I made some friends, but they were rebels like myself. I was a favorite pupil of the head mistress, who imagined I was going to reflect glory on the school by future academic distinctions. She lent me books, gave me special facilities for study, in particular a room to myself. But in the end she did more to awaken my budding revolutionary outlook than anyone else. When the war came in 1914, my father was ruined. I was sixteen and had already passed my Little Go (entrance to Cambridge University). The head of my school, still thinking I would go to the University and win laurels for the school, gave me a year's scholarship. I began working for a scholarship to Cambridge, but it soon became clear that when I got it I should not be able to go to Cambridge, because my father was becoming more and more ill of tuberculosis and I should have to start earning money as soon as I left school. The head mistress began to make it very clear to me that my presence at the school was no longer welcome. Instead of arranging for me to go to London University—where, as I learned years later, I could have obtained a scholarship sufficient to keep me altogether—she cast me off, as no longer of any interest or value to the school. She let it be known that I was in the school free and that my people were now almost destitute. My home world had fallen to pieces, my brother was in the army, my father becoming so ill that we knew he would soon die. I left school with no regrets, and with personal experience to teach me that the social system could fling one into poverty from security, and prevent one from having an education even when one had proved one's mental qualifications.

At school I had been earnest, wary and distrustful of my fellow creatures, purposeful, and, I imagine, sadly lacking in a sense of humor. Life was serious, life was earnest, and one must struggle without ceasing against one's environment. As soon as I began to earn my living in an office, I began to find the world as friendly and decent a place as I had thought it when I lived in Switzerland, or traveled in France and Italy with my parents. I found the lower middle-class clerks I worked among at the War Office friendly, kind, and pleasant people. I even learned to laugh.

The death of my father in January 1918 brought me the first great grief of my life. I had loved him very dearly, and I had thought him the most wonderful person in the world—wise, tolerant, kind, never ill-tempered, and until the last absorbed in the course of history rather than in himself. He had died in extreme poverty in a tiny cottage in Cornwall, so primitive that my mother had to fetch water in a bucket from a pump across the fields. I was eighteen, and I had seen him choking to death as his exhausted heart could no longer pump blood through his diseased lungs. Half unconscious at the end, he had murmured Shakespeare's words about the bourne from which no traveler returneth, and said to us he was now only curious to know whether he was right in thinking that death was nothingness.

My brother was in Mesopotamia, and I brought my mother up to London. We lived in a small flat on the £2.5.0. which I was then earning as a clerk in the War Office. Fairly soon I earned more; but with a rent of 16/- and war prices for food, we had a fairly hard time.

During these war years I was too busy coping with the economic difficulties which had overwhelmed us, to think much about socialism; but, although I had gone to work as a clerk in the War Office early in 1917, my father's teachings and my Continental education prevented my ever becoming a "patriot." I never thought of the Germans, among whom I had been at school from the ages of eleven to thirteen, as any worse than the English, although I had some slight prejudice against the French as the most chauvinist and military-minded nation in Europe. This was probably due to the overdose of French literature I had swallowed while at school in Switzerland, which had given me a conception of the French as a nation eternally seeking *la gloire* and honoring the Napoleonic tradition above the revolutionary one.

At the War Office I soon became a branch secretary of the Association of Women Clerks and Secretaries, then endeavoring to organize women "black-coated" workers. Through this trade-union I obtained, in 1920, a Bursary to study at London University. My brother Temple, wounded for the second time in France in 1918 and demobilized early in 1919, was already at London University on a grant from an officers' fund. Once at college I began to take an active and prominent part in the socialist movement, becoming secretary of the King's College Socialist Society, and later chairman of the London University Labour party. I joined the Independent Labour party and devoted all the time I had over from study and from teaching in the evenings, to political activity.

Since my brother and I were supporting my mother, our Bursaries were not sufficient for us to live on. We both gave lessons in English to foreigners, helped by our knowledge of French and German. My brother had pupils at the Czecho-Slovak Legations—his checks, we called them—and I had Russians. Teaching English to the Soviet employees of the Trade Delegation first brought me in contact with Bolshevik theory. From the beginning I had been a defender of the Russian Revolution; but I had no more knowledge or understanding of communist theories than the Parlor Bolsheviks of today have of Marx. Nor did my first pupils enlighten me, for they were high Party officials out to enjoy life in the "capitalist world" after the rigors of Moscow, and confining their "propaganda" to jokes about England. Then I met Plavnik, an old Bolshevik who had lived long years in exile in Germany after the revolution of 1905. To him Bolshevik theory was the breath of life. He was honest and sincere, although extremely vain. His "English lessons" usually became my German lessons and lessons in Marxian theory, from which, however, I might have benefited more had he been a little less philosophical, dialectic, and involved, and a little more concrete. For I was by this time an ardent and active member of the Independent Labour party, admiring the Soviet Union, convinced that the official British Labour party was too "reformist" ever to establish socialism, and in revolt against the underlying imperialist concepts of the British Labour movement.

Plavnik was the most humane of men, and later on in Moscow where he remained my friend, he sank more and more into his shell, unable to defend, but unwilling to condemn outright, the atrocities committed by Stalin; unable to face up to the fact that the revolutionary movement to which he had given his whole life had failed and degenerated into Stalin's tyranny. We saw less and less of him because meetings were too painful between friends who dared not speak out their thoughts to each other. Plavnik was lucky enough to go into an insane asylum just before the great purge began; at least that is where he was supposed to be early in 1936, and we knew his mental faculties had been failing since the death of his wife a year or two before.

As early as 1923 I was a passionate defender of the U.S.S.R. In that year I was the college speaker in a debate on Russia, together with H. N. Brailsford. Our opponents were C. H. Driver, a fellow history student, now a Professor at Yale, and Sir Bernard Pares. When next I met Pares twelve years later, he and I had changed places. He had become the defender of the U.S.S.R. and I was back in England, holding my tongue for my husband's sake, but hating Stalin's Russia. The change, I believe, was in Russia, not in us.

From 1925 onwards I was drawing ever closer to the Communists. I stood with them against the Right Wing in the London University Labour party, and in the University Labour Federation. I began to read their literature. The only influence which held me back for a time from joining the Communist party was that of Bertrand Russell, and unfortunately it was insufficient. I had met him first when he came to speak for the King's College Socialist Society in 1923, and this had led to a friendship which has been one of the most precious and valuable things in my life. In the Easter vacation of 1926 I spent a month with him and Dora Russell in Cornwall, teaching his young son in the mornings, walking, talking, and bathing in the afternoons, reading aloud in the evenings. B. R. tried hard to convince me that the Marxist theory was untenable in the light of modern physics. I wrote to my mother in April 1926:

> Tell Temple I have been driven to try and understand relativity in order to understand what Russell thinks about Russia! I am reading the A.B.C. of Relativity, with Russell sitting near me to explain what I don't understand. He is most awfully kind to me.

Unfortunately, I never understood the theory of relativity. In spite of Russell's patience and the time he was prepared to waste on my education, my mind could not grasp either the theory or the basic connection between Marxism and Newton's theory of gravity. Nor would I accept the truth of his *Theory and Practise of Bolshevism*. This book, written in 1920, is uncannily prophetic of the Russia I was later to know. Bertrand Russell was one of the very few who, in those early days of the Revolution, was able to perceive what manner of tree would grow from the seed which Lenin planted.

Although only experience could teach me the truth of Bertrand Russell's philosophy, and he failed in 1926 to prevent my making a mess of my life, his teaching did at least help to prevent my becoming a Trotskyist when I revolted against Stalinism.

When I came back to England for a few months in 1931 and stayed at his house, I was still convinced that the horrible society being created in Russia was Stalin's fault, and that if Lenin had lived or if Trotsky's policy had been followed, all would have been well. Bertie would bang his fist on the table and say, "No! Freda, can't you understand, even now, that the conditions you describe followed naturally from Lenin's premises and Lenin's acts? Will you never learn and stop being romantic about politics?"

The General Strike of 1926 was the turning point of my earlier political development. The high hopes then raised and the "betrayal" of the workers by the T.U.C. and the Labour party led me finally into the communist fold. I became convinced of the reality of the class war, and of the fact that socialism could not be obtained "gradually"; that there was no solution for unemployment and low wages under the capitalist system; and that only the "overthrow" of the capitalist system and the "unity of the workers of the world" could save humanity from poverty and imperialist wars.

The General Strike stirred all my emotions, the more so as I was then living at Westfield College * as a research student among the most

---

* A woman's college in London; part of London University.

conservative set of University teachers I had ever met. My crude, somewhat childish, but I believe sincere, revolutionary reaction is expressed in the following letter written to my mother in Devonshire on May 10, 1926:

> I have never lived through such a terrible week. I feel all hot inside and trembling all the time. It is such an unequal fight for us, and I want so much to help. I am speaking tonight at Edgware, I am glad to say. I wish I could speak all day—never was there a more unjust issue and more lies told by a government. Yet the Government is so ruthless it may win. It is parading armored cars about and soldiers are all over the place. The buses are running with two policemen on each and volunteer O.M.S. labor. Everything is quite safe for ordinary people like me—I almost wish it were not! I cannot write properly, dear, I am too worried and upset. It is so dreadful not to be able to help and to have to listen to the misrepresentations of the capitalists. Westfield is impossible except for a few students. I spent last night with the Boothroyds.* I saw Wilmot,** who is half expecting to be arrested for sedition. Anything almost can be called sedition. The Archbishop of Canterbury and the churches proposed terms of peace: withdrawal of both lockout and strike. The Government would not allow the proposal to be broadcast! It would be acceptable to us and not to them.
>
> I am sending you a *British Worker* [organ of the T.U.C.]. Will you ask Cole [a Labour man in Sidmouth] to stick it up in Sidmouth . . .

A few years later I was to realize that the behavior of the British government was like that of a loving mother in comparison to that of the Soviet government toward the Russian working class. But I still remember the passionate anger I felt in 1926 against the "capitalist government" and its most ruthless member, Winston Churchill, who was responsible for the show of armed force and who was prepared to have the workers shot at if the strike went on. Ten years later Winston Churchill was to be the darling of the Communists and their fellow travelers; to me he has remained the prototype of a Fascist.

Today I also realize how tolerant were the Principal of Westfield College and even the staff members whom I hated and despised. No one interfered with me, even when I took a group of the undergraduates to T.U.C. headquarters to offer our services. Nor when I

---

* Boothroyd, whose pen name today is Yaffle, is the well-known Socialist and pacifist, humorous writer and cartoonist.
** Today a Labour M.P.

went off to Cornwall with A. J. Cook, Secretary of the Miners' Union, and other speakers.

The day I was invested with my M.A. degree was the day the General Strike was called off. After bicycling across to the Senate House at South Kensington and sitting impatiently waiting in a borrowed cap and gown to receive my scroll, I tore off to T.U.C. headquarters. The bitterness of defeat and the long agony of the miners which was to follow the end of the General Strike have quite obliterated from my mind any feelings of satisfaction I may have had at the time at having got an M.A. degree with distinction.

A year later I was invited to visit the Soviet Union as representative of all the Labour and Socialist clubs in British universities (the University Labour Federation). My writings had attracted the attention of Ivan Maisky, then Counselor of the Soviet Embassy in London, and I was by that time well known, not only to the British Communist leaders, but to the chiefs of the Soviet Trade Representation. Moreover, I had met Petrovsky, the Comintern representative in England during the General Strike, and had become very friendly with him and his wife. I was regarded, I suppose, as a promising young "intellectual" whose complete "conversion" would be useful, and who had shown some understanding of Bolshevik theory in the articles I was contributing to the *New Leader,* the *Socialist Review,* and the *Labour Monthly.* I intended to join the Party as soon as I returned, since it was considered desirable that I should wait until then. The propaganda effect would be greater if I joined after, not before, I saw the U.S.S.R.

My excitement at the coming trip to the Land of Promise knew no bounds. My brother, then as for a year past lying in bed in a tuberculosis sanitorium in Surrey, wrote me a few last words of caution:

MY DEAR FREDA:
This is just to wish you luck in your adventure. I think in one way you are quite right. I would do the same thing if I wanted to, I expect. After all, one must follow after one's own thinking and one's own desires. It is an adventure, but I do not expect for a moment that you will find what you are seeking for intellectually. Men are much of a muchness everywhere, and they behave much in the same way whatever they profess to believe.

Of course you will see the country and the people and society as you wish to believe they are, at first. But later, your skepticism will re-assert itself.

But don't join the Communist party. It seems to me a terrible thing for any intelligent person to adhere to any creed or dogma. To have to say that you accept any empirical generalization as an article of faith. I do not see why you should not work for them and with them and yet reserve your opinion about their fundamental propositions.

These sweeping generalizations are to be distrusted. Even when you are dealing with a subject like Physics—a subject by which human desires and fears are little affected in its findings, as more and more is discovered and its fundamental premises examined you are all the time modifying and modifying.

And what a phrase that "materialistic conception of history" is: "Matter"—the word is not really used in Physics. Bodies have mass and the mass of a body is its weight divided by the acceleration due to gravity. That is all Physics knows about it.

Matter psychologically is one's sense of resistance—pushiness—quite different. Matter is also a "banner word," a symbol with emotions attached to it used by various sects to throw at one another.

But I must end half finished or I will lose the post. I need another four pages to explain myself.

The best of luck, my dear. All my love—

TEMPLE.

But my actions were not guided by science or philosophy; I brushed aside my brother's arguments as I had those of Bertrand Russell. I couldn't see that they had anything to do with the question of how to get socialism. They were all too abstract, and mine was then a concrete world. Or perhaps I was disregarding all appeals to reason in much the same way as a convert to Catholicism. I had faith and I must lose myself in the body of the church. The truth of my beliefs was not a matter of philosophical argument.

I replied to Temple from Moscow: "In spite of what you say, I must join the Communist party. I cannot live without feeling I am doing worth-while work, and I see no hope in the Labour party. I think the communist thesis is right."

I traveled with Maisky from Berlin to Moscow, together with another Russian and J. W. Brown, Secretary of the Clerical Association, one of the most militant trade-unions in England. Two days after our arrival we stood in the Red Square in Moscow to witness the funeral of Voikov, murdered in Poland. This was the first demonstration I saw in the "socialist fatherland"; and I still remember vividly the exaltation, triumph, and excitement which filled my heart and mind as I stood close to Lenin's mausoleum in the sunlight under a blue sky and saw the Red Army parade and the thousands upon thousands of demonstrators. My mind in those days was full of romantic libertarian images, and I wrote my mother after the demonstration: "People in the street look well fed enough though poorly clothed, and there seems to be such vitality and purpose among the people one meets. ... The soldiers in the demonstration especially looked so splendid—more like the Greeks of Xenephon must have looked than like the usual wooden soldier...."

Visitors to the U.S.S.R. in those days were comparatively rare. There was no Intourist, and only invited delegates from trade-unions and Labour parties got the chance to travel over Russia. One was lapped around with kindness, hospitality, and good fellowship. Nor were outward signs of prosperity lacking. The market places of Moscow and other towns were overflowing with vegetables, dairy produce, milk, and other foods. New apartment houses and office buildings built in the severe but pleasing style introduced after the Revolution were much in evidence. There were no queues for bread and other foods at the state and co-operative shops, and one could buy the most delicious pastries in the world for only five kopeks. There was a shortage of manufactured goods even in the cities, but it was not to be compared to the shortage which came a few years later after the "gigantic successes on the industrial front."

One is tempted to imagine what Russia might have become if the N.E.P. had been continued. Lenin was dead and his influence dying out. As early as 1924 the "Scissors Crisis" (the disproportion between the price of manufactures as against agricultural produce) had split the Central Committee into Left and Right factions. The disagreements in the Party began concerning the question of how much to take from the peasants for industrial development, and ended in the bitter controversy over collectivization. With the aid of Bucharin, Tomsky, and the others on the Right who maintained that any attempt to force the pace of industrialization would destroy the stimulus to labor, Stalin had just overcome Trotsky and was soon to exile him and the rest of the Left Opposition. Once quit of the Trotskyists, Stalin, in 1929, was to wipe out the Right Opposition and embark upon an ultra-Left policy of forced collectivization and intensive industrialization. Soon the U.S.S.R. was to become a country of starved peasants and undernourished workers cowed and whipped by fierce punishments to toil endlessly for a state which could not provide them even with enough to eat. But, unfortunately for my own future, I saw the U.S.S.R. during the brief period of prosperity which began in 1924 and ended in 1928.

In September 1927 I returned to England full of enthusiasm and prepared to tell the world of the wonders of the socialist fatherland. I left the L.L.P., joined the Communist party, and addressed meetings all over England. I admitted that the standard of life in Russia was still lower than in the Western capitalist countries; but I explained the need to accumulate capital for industrialization and demonstrated how, because there was no capitalist class to exploit the workers, the burden of saving was borne equally by all. I said that there was therefore no such acute misery as in the era of Britain's industrialization in the early nineteenth century, and that all Russians were enthusiastically collaborating in constructing socialism. And I really believed it. I felt that the gates opening upon the road to Paradise had been unlocked to mankind, and all one had to do was to convince the workers of one's own country of the need to overthrow the capitalist class and join up with the U.S.S.R. Looking back on that distant time, distant not so much on account of the years between then and now, as on account of my bitter experience later, I wonder, did I really believe it. I suppose I did, or I should never have thrown up my job in the capitalist world and gone off with my husband to take our part, as we thought, in the construction of socialism.

Arcadi Berdichevsky, who became my husband in 1928, had worked from 1920 until 1927 at Arcos* or at the Soviet Trade Representation in London. He was a Russian Jew, who had studied at Zurich University and emigrated to the United States in 1914. In 1920 he had thrown up a very good job in New York to work for the Soviet government in London. He was not a Bolshevik, but had been a member of the Jewish Social Democratic party in Poland (the Bund), where he had lived until he went to study in Switzerland about 1910. He knew less about Soviet Russia than I did, since he had spent his whole time in England since 1920. He was a sincere Socialist, and although he was too much of a Jew and knew the old Russia too well not to perceive the naïveté of the picture I painted of the U.S.S.R., he believed as I did that a new and better world was being created in Russia. He, like me, wanted to take part in the building of that new socialist world. We knew that material conditions of life would be hard, that "living space" was difficult to obtain, and that the conveniences of life, the comforts and the pleasures, which he had for many years enjoyed abroad, were not obtainable in Russia. We also

* Arcos was the Russian trading organization established in London before diplomatic recognition of the Soviet Government enabled a Trade Representation to be established.

knew that, since he was not a member of the Communist party, he could never rise to the higher positions in the Soviet state.

In 1923 Arcadi had been asked to join the Party, but he had the typical intellectual's feeling that as he had played no part in the Revolution, he could not join now that the fighting was over, and being a member of the Party meant merely rising in the world. Also, he had something of my brother's feeling about adherence to a creed or dogma. He worked with and for the Bolsheviks, but he was not prepared to subscribe entirely to their philosophy. He was as convinced as I was, however, that a new and more satisfying life awaited us in "socialist" Russia than in the "decaying" and "degenerate" bourgeois world.

At the time I met Arcadi he had reached a stage in which neither his personal life nor his comfortable "bourgeois" existence in London as a well-paid Soviet "specialist" satisfied him. He had a wife and a young son, having years before in New York married the daughter of a well-to-do Jewish family of Russian extraction. They had first become estranged when he gave up an income of $600 a month in the United States to work at Arcos for $150. By the time I knew him his salary had been increased to $500; but his wife, Anna Abramovna, had neither understanding nor sympathy for his political views and could not see why he was not satisfied by a comfortable home, a pretty wife, and a secure job. To the last she never understood why he had left her for me since, as she told her friends, I was not pretty and would never make him comfortable.

Arcadi and I knew that we loved each other after only a few meetings, but his separation from Anna Abramovna was a long and painful business. In January 1927 he asked her to divorce him, but she begged him to wait until she could join either her brother in New York or her sister in Paris. She said she could not bear the thought of their friends in London knowing he had left her. Subsequently it became clear that she hoped all along that his feeling for me was a temporary infatuation and that if they continued to live in the same house he would return to her. Arcadi tried without success to obtain a visa for her to go to the United States but eventually secured a French one for her. However, by that time he himself was being expelled from England, and unfortunately for her own future she insisted on following him to Moscow. Since I had remained in England to finish my work, she continued to hope he would change his mind. When I finally came to Moscow they were divorced.

I had been too inexperienced fully to appreciate Arcadi's difficulties.

At times I had rebelled at his long delay in freeing himself to be with me. I had felt that he should either leave her at once or give up the idea of living with me. I knew that leaving his son was very difficult for him, but I had failed to understand that the ties between a man and a woman who have loved each other are hard for a sensitive man to break when the woman tries with every means at her disposal to maintain the old relationship. Moreover, in leaving his wife Arcadi was making a break with the "bourgeois" life he had lived since finishing his studies in Switzerland. For him I was a symbol as well as the companion in the new life in socialist society which we both expected to lead. Nearly ten years later the O.G.P.U. was to deprive me of all the letters Arcadi had written to me. But by some strange chance one he wrote to me during this difficult period of our relationship remained hidden within the pages of a book. I quote from it here as revealing a little not only of Arcadi's state of mind at the time, but also as showing his attitude toward the Communists with whom he had decided to throw in his lot:

DARLING FREDOCHKA,

I suppose you are right in your own way, your "brutal" way, and that I shall never be able to satisfy you as to the validity of my reason for acting in the way I do.

I shall not pick a quarrel on what you say about my "playing about with the idea of living a different sort of life"; "desiring to go on the same way as before" and a number of other things "read at the bottom of my heart." There is no use to argue about things on which we can never agree, and I shall not appeal to you to reverse your decision until I can tell you that the way is clear for my giving you as much of myself as you can desire. I love you and I cannot and shall not believe that everything is over until you refuse to come to me when I shall ask you to do so on the strength of changes in my family life. There are for me two possibilities only in the future: either I shall embrace fully to the extent of 100 per cent the creed which will keep me going and make me forget you, or I shall accept it partially as I have done until now and you will be my beloved comrade in fighting all doubts which will arise. Nothing else is possible and the "desire to go on the same way as before" is death, which I do not feel I am ready to accept.

In September 1927, while I was still in the U.S.S.R., Arcadi had been suddenly told by the British Home Office that he must leave England at once. He thought his expulsion was due to the indiscreet and fervent letters I had sent to him from Russia, but it may have been due to the fact that, as a trusted "specialist," the chairman of Arcos had detailed him to be one of the few Soviet employees allowed to remain on the premises when the British Home Secretary, Joynson Hicks, raided the Arcos offices in June 1927.

Although at the time I was flattered to think that I was regarded as a dangerous revolutionary by the British Home Office, it was a great blow to have Arcadi expelled. I was very much in love, but I never for a moment thought of giving up my work in England to go with him to Berlin where he was stationed for the next nine months. I visited him there in the 1927 Christmas vacation but, so seriously did I take my political work that when, in February 1928, he was allowed to come to London for ten days to represent Arcos in a lawsuit, I did not give up one single evening to him. As it happened, I was then standing as the Communist party's candidate in the London County Council Elections and was speaking either to indoor meetings or at street corners every afternoon and evening.

Meanwhile I was earning a living, with the indulgence of C. M. Lloyd, my Director of Studies, as the holder of the Ratan Tata Research Fellowship at the London School of Economics. I also took Workers' Educational Association Classes, reviewed books, and wrote articles. I was by now making a good living, and my mother had inherited a small income from her father. We were better off than we had been for many years, and a successful academic career was open to me. Although being a Communist in those days was a handicap, my academic distinctions and the tolerance which distinguishes most English universities ensured me a secure and pleasant career. But by this time I scorned the fruits of past years of hard study and never paused to regret the life I was leaving. The study of history could not satisfy. I yearned to take part in making it.

My Fellowship came to an end in June 1928; and, since Arcadi was by that time in the U.S.S.R. but expecting to be sent to Japan, I joined him in Moscow. Japan was the one country I particularly wished to visit, since my research work at the London School of Economics had concerned Eastern competition and the Lancashire cotton industry. This may sound a dull subject, but for me it meant a study in modern imperialism. I had chosen the subject immediately after having written a M.A. thesis on the trade guilds of the later Roman Empire, because I thought there was a parallel between the effects of slave labor on the conditions of free labor in the ancient world and the effect of colonial labor on Western labor standards in the modern world. In the course of my studies I had become interested in Japan and wished to see that strange semifeudal, semimodern imperialist state. If we could not yet live in Moscow, I was glad to get a chance to go to the Far East.

This time no smiling delegation met me at the Moscow station, and no luxurious quarters at the New Moscow Hotel awaited me. Arcadi took me to a tiny room, not more than fifteen feet by twelve feet, with a single bed, a chest of drawers, and two straight chairs. We had not even a table, and I used to cook and iron and write on the window sill. But the flat was clean, and there was only one family in each of the four rooms. For Moscow that was not too bad. Unfortunately the room was not ours, but only lent to my husband for a few weeks. During the three months we lived in Moscow we moved twice.

Arcadi's salary was only 300 rubles a month; and, since we were expecting to leave for Japan, I could not take a job. We just managed to live. Our rent was 50 rubles, meals at a cheap restaurant cost a ruble each. But bread was still cheap; and butter, when obtainable, about the same price as in England, with the ruble stabilized at 2s. Cigarettes were our greatest extravagance and difficulty. At the end of the month I used to cart bottles out to sell, or rake through our pockets for forgotten kopeks, to raise the price of a meal. We were very happy. Discomfort and comparative poverty do not matter much so long as one has faith. And we both still had faith. Arcadi never regretted his house in London, and I had been poor most of the years since 1914. I wrote to my mother:

> I feel sometimes that having found Arcadi is too good to be true. ...I feel that the fact that we have been able to be happy together in these conditions argues well for the future. We have begun life together in the worst material conditions instead of the best.... All the same, we both look forward to the day when we have a bed each and spoons and knives, and a bath and toilet of our own.

I was kept busy for a time finishing a translation from the German, begun in England, of the *Illustrated History of the Russian Revolution,* but I found it very hard to work that summer.

I attended the sixth Congress of the Comintern as a translator; listened to Bucharin from the visitors' gallery; saw Borodin walking in the corridors, already disgraced but still a romantic figure; thrilled at the sight of delegates, white, black, brown and yellow, from every corner of the world assembled in the socialist capital, visible witnesses of the "Unity of the Workers of the World."

Even in those days I had some slight deviations. I thought of Trotsky as the greatest leader, and my communism was essentially internationalist. But I never dreamed that Stalin would have the power to destroy all that Lenin and Trotsky and the other old Bolsheviks had created. Nor had I any inkling of the fundamental canker at the root of the Marxian doctrine. One believes what one wishes to believe, until experience bangs one's head against the wall and awakens one from dreams founded on hope, a misreading of history, and ignorance both of human psychology and science.

At last, after the O.G.P.U. had fully satisfied itself concerning my husband, he obtained his passport to go to Japan for the Commissariat of Foreign Trade. We left early in October, in the chill wet Russian autumn, with the first signs of coming hardships already visible in Moscow. For some weeks I had been spending more and more time chasing after food supplies from one shop to another. Rationing had not yet been enforced, but the peasants were already refusing to sell their produce in return for money which could not buy them the clothing and other manufactures they required. Russia was on the eve of the Calvary of forced collectivization.

At Chita, in Siberia, I left my husband—he to proceed alone to Japan, I to China. To my great delight the Comintern in Moscow had entrusted me with secret papers to take to China. I was to travel across the Russian border into Manchuria and on to Shanghai alone, so that I should not be suspect. For a day before I left Moscow I had hunted in the shops for a corset so that I could hide the papers in approved Secret Service style. I was extremely uncomfortable all through that journey, but the thrill of conceiving of myself as a real revolutionary, helping to fan the flames of the world revolution and liberate the "oppressed colonial workers" sustained me even through the ordeal of being corsetted for the first time in my life.

All I remember of Chita is the intense cold, and the memorials of the Decembrists, the 150 exiled revolutionaries of 1825 who had dreamed of liberty, equality, and fraternity under the Iron Tsar, Nicholas I. Only later was it to be borne in on me how mild had been the tyranny of the Tsars compared to that of Stalin. All those nineteenth- and early twentieth-century revolutionaries whose lives were spared and who were allowed to live in Siberia with their families were in exile, it is true; but for the most part not in chains nor herded in concentration camps, and able to escape with ease if they were so minded. Today such humane and civilized treatment of political opponents is unheard of.

I was looked after in Chita by a little O.G.P.U. man who had formerly been a sailor on American boats, and whom I was to meet years later in Moscow at the Comintern. He was the sort of man who loves being conspiratorial for its own sake, and his manner of putting me on the train two days later, from the tracks instead of the platform, into a specially reserved compartment, should have aroused the suspicion of the Japanese or Chinese spies, if there had been any.

I went through a bad half-hour at the Manchurian border. A German with whom I had got friendly on the train remarked to me at the passport and customs-control office, that the system was to watch the faces of the travelers rather than to search their baggage carefully. A row of huge White Russian guards stood behind the Chinese customs officials watching the passengers. I have an innocent face and a British passport, and they would need to have been very suspicious to search the person of a British subject. My papers remained safe "in my bosom," as the old novels would have said.

The Comintern, with the inefficiency characteristic of all Russian institutions, had been unaware that the fighting going on in North China had stopped all passenger traffic on the railway to Peking, and that I would therefore have to get to Shanghai by sea from Dairen. The money I had been provided with for my journey was insufficient to meet the extra expense of waiting in the hotel at Dairen for passage on the crowded boats, and I had hardly a cent of my own. So in order to preserve enough to exist on in Shanghai for the ten days I planned to stay there, I economized in Dairen by eating only one meal a day. I took the table d'hôte midday dinner at the Yamamoto Hotel and ate all through every one of its six or seven courses under the astonished and amused eyes of the Japanese waiters.

Eventually I got a ship to Shanghai and delivered my documents. To do this I had to go to the Palace Hotel and telephone to a certain business office, ask for a gentleman with a German name, and tell him I had brought the samples of silk hosiery. I enjoyed it all immensely, especially as I was allowed two days later to come and meet some of the Comintern agents in Shanghai, who plied me with questions about happenings in Moscow which, in my innocence, I was unable to answer. Probably the men I met, Americans and Germans, were, if not Trotskyists, at least extremely unhappy revolutionaries, who had witnessed Stalin's callous and cynical sacrifice of the Chinese Communists, and were watching with dismay the beginnings of his transformation of the Comintern into a mere sub-office of the Russian National State.

For a couple of weeks I lived a double, or rather a treble, life in Shanghai, spending part of my time as a serious academic investigator of conditions in the cotton industry, other hours as the guest of "British Imperialists" at luxurious dinner parties and dancing or going to theaters with them, and yet other hours in the secret meeting places of the Comintern's agents. It was part of the game that I should mix with the "bourgeoisie," and appear quite innocent of revolutionary activity; and my cotton industry investigations were in any case absolutely genuine. However, I am afraid I should not have been much good as a conspirator if any hard task had been assigned to me, for I was too anxious to testify to the "capitalists" concerning the rottenness of their system and the wickedness of their exploitation of the colonial workers. Thinking on one occasion to kill any doubts they might have about me, I told a Shanghai dinner party that I was doing some correspondence for the *Manchester Guardian*. This was true, and I thought it should establish my *bona fides* in the capitalist world. However, all values are relative. To my mind the *Manchester Guardian* signified the capitalist Press, but to my compatriots in Shanghai it was "that Red rag," the paper for which "that awful fellow Arthur Ransome" wrote.

This book is not one about my adventures in the Far East, so I will pass over the year I spent in Japan with my husband. It was the happiest year of my life. We were in love; we had no money worries, for my husband was earning the to my mind princely salary of £100 a month; and I was investigating labor conditions, calculating costs of production in the cotton industry, studying Japanese economics and politics, doing a series of well-paid articles for the *Manchester Guardian Commercial*, and writing my first book, *Lancashire and the Far East*.

Japan, however, gave me my first experience of a police state. Happy as I was under its blue skies, enjoying for the first time in my life a harmonious companionship with a man I loved, the shadow of the tyranny under which the Japanese lived kept my revolutionary fervor alive. Moreover, what my brother used to call my Puritan conscience soon made me restless. I had a deep conviction that it was wrong to be living comfortably and enjoying the greatest happiness which life can give, life with someone one loves more and more dearly as the days pass.

My letters to my mother from Japan are full of these inner misgivings:

I am living in the present for the first time in my life and I know it is dangerous ... that I am becoming "decomposed." *

In January 1929 I wrote:

Life now is altogether a different thing, more complete and wonderful than I ever imagined it could be. Even the love I felt for Arcadi a year ago seems a small thing now I love him so much more. There really is complete understanding between us and sometimes I feel my happiness is too great to last. You know I have always felt, like the Greeks, that the Gods are jealous of human happiness. But anyhow life is worth having lived for this alone. So you see how I feel, dear, in answer to your birthday letter and whether I am glad I was born. Life seems a wonderful thing now and also I can see that my childhood made this happiness possible. That in me which made me so unhappy five or six years ago is what has given me such great happiness in the end. The memories I have always had of you and Dada which made the substitutes, the second-bests, of no use to me and kept me lonely for so long, have now given me Arcadi and our happiness together. So I love you, Mother dearest, more and more for the happiness you have given me.

On June 25, 1929, I wrote:

Ten years ago I could not have believed that life would give so much. Only sometimes I know this happiness is too great to last, especially if I cease to do anything to deserve it. I must come home and do some work for what I believe.

Of course, no one knows his real motive. Perhaps it was not really my feeling that no one has any right to great personal happiness so long as the majority of mankind starve and toil without joy. It may have been love of power or the desire to make one's mark on the world, which is the same thing as love of power, which impelled me to leave Arcadi and return to work in the Communist party in England. Also, it may have been the feeling I expressed in another letter to my mother, the feeling that Arcadi's love for me was founded upon his conception of me as a revolutionary, an intellectual, an independent woman, not a "mere wife." I felt that if I lost myself in

* This was my husband's translation of the Russian adjective *razrucite* applied to Communists whose revolutionary energy was sapped by residence among the bourgeoisie. The word implies a general softening and giving way to the desire for an easy, comfortable life.

his love I might lose it, that I must somehow continue being what I had been when he began to love me. The extent to which it was ambition which impelled me to leave him is suggested in the following letter I wrote my mother soon after my arrival in Japan.

I wish I could go yachting with Temple ... perhaps some day. But of course I don't know how to sail a boat properly, I have just a rudimentary idea from the fishing boats in Devonshire. As regards what he says about my being turned into a "bloody intelligent," God forbid—yet already I feel "decomposed" in many ways. I am less inclined to strive and sometimes I feel that the days of my achievements, such as they were, are past. On the whole I am taking life much less strenuously, though I am trying now to work hard on my book. Somehow I don't get quite so agitated and worried as I used to about the things I do. You and Temple may say this is good but I don't think so. Perhaps I shall never do anything worth while again. I have also discovered about myself that beautiful things, especially beautiful colors, appeal to me much more than in the past. I can sit and look at a beautiful design on silk and just enjoying looking at it. Thus I can waste time instead of sitting down to write articles, etc.

The spirit to sit up all night and work at top pitch to finish a piece of work and do it well somehow, the spirit which used to carry me through the hardest tasks, was lacking last summer in Moscow and may be gone forever. Only I hope that my languidness was due to conditions in Moscow, not getting enough food and the new way of living, which is possibly exhausting at first. But things in Russia won't be so difficult in a year's time. I must have got pretty run down because this vaccination business would not have developed such complications otherwise. It is 7 weeks since it was done and the ulcers have only now begun to heal. Also I have had a lot of toothache. This is not to worry you, dear, it is only my feeble way of trying to console myself for having become lazy....

I have begun to think that in the end Temple will go much further than me. He has gone on steadily doing better and better in his line instead of frittering himself away on a multitude of activities as I have. I feel I have attempted too many things in the past instead of doing one thing really well. And now, at 30, I have really got to begin all over again in a new world where my past academic attainments count for little. Even this cotton business is difficult for me because, of course, my background should be economics, not ancient history! Temple will be a famous scientist one day and I shall be nothing at all. You remember too that Arcadi said Temple would never be "decomposed."

Looking back on things I realize that my unhappy love for Walter made me put all my energies into work whereas now . . . I have just received a letter from Walter, by the way. You might tell him what I say. If he admires my brain and capabilities as he says, tell him that he helped me to achieve things by refusing to love me. I can look back on it all very casually now and genuinely say to Walter, "Peace be with you." Tell him there is something in Russell Green's favorite saying: "The hobbyhorse of one's discontent becomes the Pegasus of one's ambition." And yet I am still ambitious only not so vividly so. I enjoy the present too much.

I begin to understand why Christian priests had to be celibate, why Venus was banished to a cave. And yet I hope that in union I may in the end achieve more than alone. Or is this also only an illusion?

I seem to have rattled on for a long time. I wish I could talk to you and Temple tonight. Should like to be sitting with you over a bottle of wine at Bertorelli's.

Today I regret nothing more in my life than not having savored my happiness to the full and lived out the brief period Arcadi and I might have had together before we were engulfed in that hell of disillusionment and suffering in Soviet Russia. Today, I not only know that the gods are jealous gods, but that the way to cheat them is not to be afraid of them. Euripides was right in those choruses in the *Bacchae* which I knew so well by heart in my youth, but whose meaning and truth only loss and unhappiness could teach me:

> *What of man's endeavor*
> *Or God's high grace*
> *So lovely and so great.*
> *To stand from fear set free*
> *To hold a hand uplifted over hate*
> *For shall not loveliness be loved forever?*
> . . . .
>
> *No grudge hath he of the great,*
> *No scorn of the mean estate,*
> *But to all that liveth*
> *His wine he giveth;*
> *Griefless, immaculate.*
> *Only on them who spurn joy*
> *Does his anger burn.*

Happy he on the weary sea
Who has fled the tempest
And found his haven,
But who'er shall know
As the long days go
That to live is happy
Has found his heaven.

To be alive at all is wonderful, and to have known, even for only a short while, the greatest happiness which life can give—to love and be loved utterly—gives life a savor even after it has all vanished with the snows of yesteryear.

Although he knew he would be terribly lonely when I had gone, Arcadi encouraged me to go. For he, even as I, believed in those days in what the Webbs call the Vocation of Leadership—i.e., the duty of the Communist to sacrifice personal happiness to political work. And yet we had already learned something in Japan of what Soviet society is really like. The intrigues, the calumnies, and the factional struggles which went on in the small Russian colony of employees at the Trade Representation and the Embassy should have taught us what to expect in the U.S.S.R. But we thought this was because the Russian colony was composed of "intellectuals" and that in Russia the proletarians ensured a cleaner atmosphere. Moreover, both the Ambassador, Tryanovsky, and the Trade Representative, Anikeev, were decent men and the same could be said of Maisky, later to become Ambassador to Britain but then only Counselor of the Embassy in Tokio. True that his wife and Madame Anikeev were at daggers drawn, and a telegram once had to be sent to Moscow to settle the delicate question of precedence at Embassy dinner parties and Japanese state functions: who came first—the wife of Maisky, the Embassy Counselor, or the wife of Anikeev, the Trade Representative. As far as I remember, the question was settled in Madame Anikeev's favor, but the whole Russian colony was split into factions by the antagonism between these two women. They were fairly evenly matched, because although Maiskaya was a member of the Party and Anikeeva was not, Maisky had not joined the Bolsheviks until 1924, whereas Anikeev was not only an old Bolshevik but also of proletarian origin, having once been a factory worker. Anikeeva being both a beautiful woman and an intelligent one, became a sort of First Lady, in spite of Maiskaya's qualifications. Tryanovsky's wife, an unassuming lady, played no part in the faction fights of "Red" society. Tryanovsky's first wife had been a Bolshevik when he was a Menshevik, and the story told was that during the civil wars she had condemned her husband to death when he was brought before her as a prisoner. Lenin himself had talked Tryanovsky over into joining the Bolsheviks and saved him from the death sentence imposed by his wife. I cannot vouch for the truth of this story, as whispered to me in Tokio; but at least it explained Tryanovsky's choice of a nonpolitical, rather colorless lady as his second wife. It is more pleasant to have a wife not liable to shoot one on account of one's political beliefs.

These dissertations are not entirely frivolous, for Soviet society as it really is could not properly be described without some account of the human factors. Russian women are just as prone to social discrimination, pride in their social status, love of fine clothes and admiration, as women in "bourgeois" society. Soviet society has its hierarchies and its jealousies and is *not* composed of simple-minded, ardent revolutionaries with red cotton handkerchiefs on their heads, intent on constructing socialism regardless of personal advancement and the material comforts such advancement brings. The simply dressed men and women who march in the demonstrations of the proletariat, to the admiration of foreign tourists, are most of them longing to change places with the "boyars of the bureaucracy" who watch them from the reserved seats in the Red Square.

Back in England I threw myself into the work of the British Communist party, and tried to bury in my subconscious the suspicions concerning Soviet "socialist" society which had been engendered by the year I had spent in Tokio and by the fortnight I had spent in Moscow on my way home at the end of 1929. I campaigned for the British Communist party among the textile workers in Lancashire. I campaigned for the Communist candidate at the bye-election in Sheffield. I became a member of the Industrial Committee of the Party in London. I wrote articles for the Communist publications, and I did a pamphlet for the Party on "What's Wrong with the Cotton Trade!" My husband sent me money to live on, and I never took a penny from the Communist party, even for my articles and pamphlets. I read the works of Marx and Lenin, conscientiously and thoroughly, and tried to explain in simple language the basic tenets of Marxism, which, if one could make them clear to the workers, *must* make them see that only through the unity of the workers of the world could living standards be improved and unemployment eliminated.

In speaking to the Lancashire cotton operatives and writing for them, I first came up against the basic dilemma of the Marxist revolution, and also against the obstacle of the Comintern's indifference to the troubles of the working class, or its fate outside Russia.

How could one convince the Lancashire cotton operatives that they should refuse to allow the cotton industry to be rationalized, refuse to work more looms, and go on strike for higher wages, when they knew as well as I did that the immediate result of such action would be more unemployment through the loss of more markets to Japan and other competing countries? To my mind it seemed clear that the basic need was to explain Marxist theory to them, to make them understand the meaning of "workers of the world, unite" by showing that if all textile workers in all countries got together in one organization they could establish higher wages for all; to make them understand that the capitalist system based on production for profit inevitably doomed them to increasing poverty now that other countries besides England were industrialized, and workers in the East with lower standards of life competed against them.

But now I came up against the Comintern, which was then pursuing an ultra-Left policy and insisting that agitation, agitation alone, was the task of the Communist. No theoretical explanations, no waste of time or energy in exposing the dynamics of capitalism; just tell the workers to strike and strike whatever the consequences. The Comintern, in fact, was not concerned with the livelihood of the workers; it wished only to weaken the capitalist states by continual strikes and the dislocation of economic life. Its only objective was the safety of the U.S.S.R., and it recked nothing of the interests or sufferings of the workers.

One day in Blackburn, the great weaving center of Lancashire, an elderly textile worker complained bitterly to me of the fact that it was all very well for the paid officials of the Communist party to get themselves arrested for deliberately and unnecessarily holding meetings where they obstructed the traffic, but how could we expect men with families to do so, especially since it was an utterly useless performance? Of course, he did not know how proud Communist party members were if, when they went to Moscow, they could boast that they had gone to jail in the class struggle. Such an accomplishment might be held to wipe out the stigma of their nonproletarian origin.

Finally I got myself into trouble with the Politbureau of the Party in London on account of an article of mine which the editor of the *Communist Review* had inadvertently allowed to be published. I had been reading Lenin's writings of the "Iskra period" and had discovered that he had condemned the "economists" who maintained that the intellectual has no role to play in the Party and that the socialist idea can spring "spontaneously" out of the experience of the working class. Lenin had insisted that the ordinary worker, by the experience of his daily life, develops not a full revolutionary class consciousness but only that of "a trade-unionist." Clearly, to my mind, in this period of declining markets for Britain, the workers' trade-union consciousness was likely to impel him to accept wage reductions and join with the bosses in attempting to recapture their markets. I did not, of course, foresee that this would lead Europe to a fascist development, but I dimly perceived that, unless the Marxist conception of international working-class unity could be put across to the workers, they would unite with their employers against other countries. Today we see how Hitler and Mussolini can rouse their people to fight under the slogan of the proletarian nations against the pluto-democracies.

Although my article was buttressed by quotations from Lenin, I was held to have deviated seriously from the Party line by maintaining that theory was of primary importance and that the intellectual, accordingly, need not play at being a proletarian, since he had an important part to perform in bringing knowledge of socialism to the working class. I was not directly accused of Trotskyism, but I was held to be slightly tainted with heresy.

Even at this stage of my communist experience I had not the sense to see that nothing good would come out of the U.S.S.R. and that the foreign Communist parties were already corrupted and impotent. I had a great respect and liking for Harry Pollitt, Secretary of the British Communist party, who had encouraged me and backed me up, and prevented the little bureaucrats in the Agitprop department from sabotaging my pamphlet and my Party work. To this day I find it difficult to understand how this British working-class leader of Nonconformist traditions came to subordinate his conscience and sacrifice his personal integrity to become a stooge of the Stalinists. The fact that Pollitt led the British Communist party deluded me into thinking that it was still a revolutionary working-class party.

Late in September I left for Moscow, expecting that my husband would join me there that month from Japan. Before leaving England I had spent a few days with my brother on the yacht in which he was preparing to sail across the Atlantic and on to the South Seas. He wanted me to come with him, at least as far as Spain; but I was, as usual, driven by that sense of urgency which has so often made me miss the greatest pleasures in life. I expected Arcadi soon to reach Moscow from Japan; and, much as I loved sailing, I felt one could not just dash off like that to no purpose. My brother and I were more intimate those last days, sailing down the English coast to Cornwall, than since our childhood. His skeptical outlook on life, his avowed lack of any exalted motives, and his insistence on both the joyousness and futility of life, now seemed to me less reprehensible than a few years back. The Norse sagas and Greek legends which had inspired me to dreams of human liberty through the economic reorganization of society, had led him to throw up his job in London to sail to the South Sea Islands, of which he had dreamed since childhood. Perhaps his dream was as worthy and no more futile than mine. This I could not yet acknowledge, but at least I had grown tolerant enough not to reproach him.

In the night watches, sitting together on deck under the stars, Temple warned me of the certain disappointments which awaited me. He knew the motive forces of my life better than I knew them myself. For me, as he realized, the concept of human freedom formed the axis of my socialist beliefs. I was in revolt against tyranny and oppression—not, as in the case of so many of those who have accepted Stalin's tyranny, a craving to lose myself and my reason in a universal brotherhood. In my mind Pericles' funeral speech, Shelley's and Swinburne's poems, Marx's and Lenin's writings, were all part and parcel of the same striving for the emancipation of mankind from oppression.

Temple foresaw that I would not be able to accept and condone a new kind of oppression, even if tyranny wore the mask of socialism. "You will probably end up in a Siberian prison, my dear," he said. "But so long as you don't deceive yourself, they will not break you. Only don't ever be a hypocrite to yourself; that is the only real sin against the Holy Ghost."

These words stuck in my mind. One can preserve one's inner integrity anywhere, even in the U.S.S.R., if one does not deceive oneself in order to be comforted.

Temple sailed away from Newlyn Harbor toward the setting sun one golden September evening. He waved to me from the deck of the *Inyala,* steering with the other hand. We never saw each other again, for he died five years later in Fiji. During those five years we were about as far away from each other as one can be on this earth.

Two weeks later I was on the boat going to Leningrad. I wrote from Hamburg to my mother:

I am beginning dimly to realize how blind and how much in a rut most people are. You see even people like Henry [a friend in the Party who knew a little of my doubts about the Comintern] do not want to see everything—it is too dangerous and too windswept and too awful. One must have courage, above all one must have courage, mentally as well as physically.

How much courage I was to require in the future was unknown to me, but I was to learn that it is not courage, but love, which can enable one to endure even the death of one's hopes and the loss of love itself.

CHAPTER II

THE MISCARRIAGE OF BOLSHEVISM

LENIN IN HIS youth was perhaps clearer sighted than when, in 1917, the opportunity to establish the dictatorship of his party proved too great a temptation to the great revolutionary strategist. In 1905 he said:

> Anyone who attempts to achieve socialism by any other route than that of political democracy will inevitably arrive at the most absurd reactionary deductions, both political and economic.

Lenin, "sleeping by Scamander's river," is luckier than Trotsky, who lived to witness the truth of this prophecy fulfilled; but who, even today, refuses to see the development of the U.S.S.R. under Stalin as inevitable from the premises on which it started out.

When, following the Revolution of 1917, Lenin perforce abolished Soviet democracy and established the dictatorship of the Bolshevik party, he thought that the "reactionary deductions" could be avoided. Perhaps if he had lived they might have been. But to think that one man could affect the course of history to the extent of changing its direction is un-Marxist. The Marxist must perforce believe that history, in broad outline, would have taken the same course had Lenin lived. If he had lived he might have shared Trotsky's fate. But if he had lived it is unlikely that Stalin would have been able to carry out the counter-revolution so unobtrusively. There would have been a split in the Bolshevik party and Stalin's victory would not have been won without an armed clash. It would then have been obvious to the whole world that the Bolsheviks had been defeated, and Stalin would not have been able to win influence over the radical movements of the West. The revolution would have been buried instead of its corpse poisoning the air of a whole generation of progressives in Europe and America.

As it was, Stalin was able to camouflage his counter-revolution, to accomplish it piecemeal, and to confuse socialists all over the world by his zigzags from Right to Left and back to Right until these terms have lost their meaning. He has divested socialism of its humanitarian content and its original nobility and strength, and left only a whited sepulcher to warn the world against all hope of a juster social order than the capitalist.

To understand the miscarriage of Bolshevism, one must summarize the views expressed by Lenin and Trotsky both in 1917 and when the New Economic Policy was introduced in 1921. One must also glance back at the profound and contradictory changes in the policy of the Soviet Government over the past two decades.

In the summer and autumn following the February Revolution of 1917, Lenin saw with that political clear-sightedness which was his peculiar genius, that in Russia the choice was one between a return to reaction or an advance to *social* revolution. Kerensky's government was powerless to solve the agrarian problem, to reorganize the collapsing national economy, to wage war or to make peace. Either Russia would lapse into anarchy or the old ruling class would return to power. There was no strong middle class capable of leading the "bourgeois democratic revolution"; i.e., solving the agrarian problem and establishing a democratic capitalist social and political order. Therefore, as Lenin saw it, "the proletariat" must take the lead. It would be "a crime" if the only new class capable of seizing power on the collapse of the old social order failed to do so.

"We must perish or go forward," was Lenin's constant refrain. Kerensky's government had begun to crush the peasant rebellion; and this meant "to lose the whole revolution forever and beyond recall." The proletariat alone could accomplish nothing; the peasants must be the motive force of the revolution. If their insurrection were once crushed, the motive force would be destroyed. Hence, as Lenin reiterated over and over again in October 1917, "waiting becomes a crime." He was also convinced that the world revolution was at hand, so that to wait was to betray not only the Russian Revolution but that of the workers of the world.

In his "Letter to the Petrograd and Moscow Committees of the Bolshevik Party" * in October 1917, he writes:

> The agrarian movement is developing, and the government is repressing it more and more savagely.... In February, the beginning of the revolution is doubtless at hand. The elections at Moscow have given 47% of the votes to the Bolsheviks. With the Left Social Revolutionaries we have obviously a majority in the country.
>
> . . . .
>
> The railwaymen and postal workers are in conflict with the government.... In these conditions, to wait is a crime.

* *On the Road to Insurrection.*

The Bolsheviks must take power immediately. In so doing they will save the world revolution (for it is to be feared, especially after the executions in Germany, that the capitalists of all countries will compose their differences and unite against us). They will also save the Russian revolution (for if we delay, perhaps the rising wave of real anarchy will be too strong for us) and they will save the lives of hundreds of thousands of men at the front.

"To wait is a crime.... It is to betray the revolution."

In Lenin's mind it was absolutely clear that Russia faced either a return to reaction or anarchy. The tide was at the flood; the Bolsheviks must ride out upon it before it ebbed.

From all his writings at this period it is clear that he was *certain* of the coming world revolution. "Doubt is no longer permissible," he says over and over again. "We are on the eve of the world proletarian revolution."

Thus, at the decisive moment, Lenin gave no thought to what would happen in Russia should the Bolsheviks, having seized power, find that the world revolution was delayed. He gave no thought to this problem in 1917 because he was quite certain that it would not arise.

When he found out his mistake, he retreated and instituted the New Economic Policy, but where this was to lead he never clearly stated.

It has been truly said that all Lenin's activities were stretched between two extremes: Russia and his political instinct on the one hand, the West and his theoretical convictions on the other. In the endeavor to reconcile the two, he twisted Marxist doctrine out of all recognition and outraged the convictions of the Social Democrats. For in the conflict between theory and instinct it was always theory which went to the wall. An opportunist of genius for whom *the revolution* was the primary objective, and what was to come afterwards dependent upon circumstances and opportunity, Lenin appears to have originally believed, like the Mensheviks, that the overthrow of the Tsar's autocracy must be succeeded by a "bourgeois democratic republic"; but to have shared Trotsky's belief that the proletariat alone was capable of leading such a revolution. Realizing to the full that in a predominantly peasant country such as Russia only an alliance with the peasantry could give victory to the proletariat, he had not hesitated to enlist that support by telling the peasants to take the land, knowing that by so doing he was laying the foundations for a capitalist, not a socialist, society. It would be more correct to say that he decided to go with the tide and proclaim as Bolshevik policy what was occurring spontaneously: the seizure of the estates of the landowners and church by the peasants.

This inevitably meant either the creation of a satisfied peasantry, surest bulwark of a capitalist state, or deceiving the peasants as to their future under the Soviet regime. The Bolsheviks could in fact only ensure the victory of the revolution at the cost of the future certain and final defeat of their attempt to set up a socialist state, since either they must abandon the attempt to create a socialist state, or do it by force against the wishes of the majority of the population. In either case, their course could not lead to socialism within the original meaning of the term: *communal* ownership and direction of the productive forces.

In thus sacrificing ends to means, Lenin laid the foundation of the economic and social problem which wrecked the Bolshevik party after his death, and eventually led to the establishment of Stalin's totalitarian tyranny. Stalin cut the Gordian knot of the insoluble problem of the contradiction between the desires and interests of peasantry and proletariat by enslaving both alike to his personal despotism.

Trotsky, who was Lenin's inferior as a practical revolutionist, was perhaps his superior as a theoretician. Whereas Lenin subordinated everything to his immediate aim and twisted the theory to fit his actions, Trotsky insisted that action conform to theory. To the Social Democratic argument that socialism could not be constructed in a backward country, and that Russia must therefore pass through a stage of capitalist development, Lenin replied that the Bolsheviks would establish a *smytchka* ("alliance") of proletariat and peasantry, presumably with the conviction in his mind that with himself to guide them the seemingly irreconcilable interests of workers and peasants could be harmonized. Lenin thus took refuge in what one can consider either a typical Russian and mystically vague conception of what was to follow the Bolshevik seizure of power, or a sublime belief in his power to defeat the materialistic interpretation of history. But Trotsky took the bull by the horns and proclaimed that the problem of the Russian Revolution was in fact insoluble so long as the revolution did not spread to other, more advanced, countries, in particular to Germany. If Germany joined up with Russia, the problem of Russian industrialization could be solved, the conflict of interests between workers and peasants resolved, and socialism made possible in Russia.

Both he and Lenin were at first convinced that their revolution would spread from country to country and that this would relieve the beleaguered fortress held by the small Russian proletariat. This was Trotsky's famous theory of "permanent revolution." From this theory it followed logically that the main energies of the Russian Bolsheviks should be devoted to inciting and assisting revolutionary movements in other countries, since alone they could not construct socialism in Russia.

Lenin, intent on the practical problem of getting an economy of any kind to function after the disorganization and destruction which was the legacy of the World War, the Bolshevik Revolution and the Civil War and intervention, left much of the theorizing to Trotsky. But it was Lenin who stated that he would willingly sacrifice all the gains of the Russian Revolution for the hope of revolution in Germany. In 1918 he stated at the First Congress of the Supreme Economic Council that: "We must not forget that we alone cannot achieve a socialist revolution in one country only, even if it were a less backward country than Russia."

The partnership of Lenin and Trotsky can be said to have been based largely upon Lenin's leaving points of theory to Trotsky and upon Trotsky's submitting to Lenin on all organizational questions, and when immediate courses of action had to be decided upon. The difference between the two men can in some sort be compared to the difference between those Englishmen who are now (1940) busy discussing war aims, and those who, like Churchill, insist that winning the war is what matters at present. Since Lenin was a great statesman, and states can be run best without a logical theory, he could do without Trotsky; but Trotsky, the schematic thinker, could neither retain power nor form a party without Lenin.

Marx, although rather vague concerning the "dictatorship of the proletariat," had had no doubt that it was to be absolutely democratic, for in his view socialism was to come after capitalism had reduced all but a small minority to the condition of "proletarians." For him, seizure of power by the proletariat meant the overthrow of a small group of capitalist exploiters by the overwhelming majority of the people. Socialist society was to be the only truly democratic society since socialism alone could deprive an exploiting class of its economic and political power. Engels, commenting upon Marx's vindication of the Paris Commune of 1871, had proclaimed that absolute democracy was the natural form of the dictatorship of the proletariat. As we have seen, Lenin himself in 1905 had declared that without democracy there could be no socialism.

Nevertheless, Lenin, in his insistence from 1907 onwards that the Social Democratic party should be composed of professional revolutionaries, was denying the democratic basis of Marxian socialism. This was realized by the minority of the Russian Social Democratic party (the Mensheviks) and also by Trotsky, who did not join the Bolsheviks (the majority party) until 1917. In effect, Lenin saw what the Social Democrats failed to see, that the working class did *not* naturally desire socialism, and that if one waited for it to become revolutionary by itself, one might wait until the Greek Kalends. Marx had believed that the course of capitalist development would of itself turn the working class into revolutionaries. Lenin saw before 1914 that it wouldn't, and after 1914 that the workers were patriots first and a class-conscious proletariat second. He did not on that account reject Marxism, but carried Engels' thesis of the corruption of the British working class through imperialism, to the further hypothesis that the working class in all European countries had been corrupted. His solution was a revolution, led by professional revolutionaries who knew better than the workers what the latter needed for their own good—viz., socialism. All along he distrusted "the masses" and saw "the Party" as necessary to prevent their falling away from the revolutionary path.

This transmutation of Marxism was the easier for Lenin because he was a Russian. The belief in democracy was inherent and deep-rooted in the minds of the Marxists of western Europe; and it was the rational side of Marx, not his mystical belief in the inevitability of progress, which appealed to them. But Lenin was a Russian, and his ideas were unconsciously affected by the fanaticism and naïveté of his country and his people. For him what one may term the religious side of Marx, the bedrock belief that history was "inevitably" leading mankind to a better social system, was fundamental. To him Marxism was a creed and a body of dogma which he could interpret according to the practical needs of the moment. This made him far more resolute and immediately successful than the hesitant, tolerant, and essentially humanitarian leaders of the western Social Democratic parties; but it also made possible the later grotesque distortions of the aims of the revolution under Stalin.

Marx had deliberately refused to consider "utopian schemes." He had stated that the workers had "no ideals to realize" but needed only "to set free the elements of the new society which the old society carries in its womb." So Lenin had little to go upon when once the revolution had been accomplished. This was his strength and his successors' weakness. He approached the problem of how to organize the new society realistically and disinterestedly as regards immediate policy, but with vagueness as to the future. Did Lenin consider the distant future at all in 1917? Did he imagine that the "reactionary deductions" which he himself had said must follow from the attempt to achieve socialism by tyranny could be avoided? He may have believed it because he thought he himself and his comrades in the Bolshevik party would be strong enough and incorruptible enough to steer Russia against all the contrary winds of its internal contradictions. This belief was founded on faith, not upon political philosophy. It was in fact in direct contravention of the Marxist philosophy, and showed the tremendous power of ideas over the material world, to have even attempted to establish a socialist economy in Russia.

As Franz Borkenau has expressed it:*

> On his native Russian soil his naïveté and fanaticism hampered Lenin as little as it had hampered Mohammed to be, at the same time, a visionary and the shrewdest politician. On the contrary, inconsistencies and adaptations which would have broken the resolution of any less deeply convinced man did not distress Lenin: he could take every liberty with the principles he confessed because something deeper than intellectual formulae guaranteed him against becoming what he called a "traitor," against losing sight of the ultimate aim, *"the* revolution."

As a politician and a practical revolutionary, Lenin was bound to recognize in 1917 that democracy, as ordinarily understood, doomed the Russian proletariat and its "vanguard," the Bolshevik party, to impotence. Following the February Revolution, all organized parties in Russia were for continuing the "war of defense" against Germany, although it was clear that the mass of the people had no interest in the war and that the peasant soldiers wished only to get home and get their share of the landowners' estates. Until Lenin's return from exile, even the Bolshevik party in Petrograd, led by Kameniev and Stalin, supported the war. The Constituent Assembly, which up to then the Bolsheviks had demanded equally with the Mensheviks and the liberals, if elected would probably have given the Bolsheviks only a few seats. So Lenin abruptly switched over to championship of the Soviets, which he had rejected in 1905 and which up to 1917 Trotsky alone had viewed as the organ of the new political order. Lenin now perceived that the Soviets (the elected representatives of the workers in each factory and of the regiments and villages) which had come into being more or less spontaneously, could be utilized to overthrow bourgeois democracy, or, as Lenin saw it, to establish the democratic dictatorship of the workers, peasants, and soldiers. Since the Soviets were directly elected by the "toilers" and excluded the "exploiters," the establishment of a Soviet state should ensure the victory of the proletariat and

* *World Communism. A History of the Communist International.*

yet preserve democracy. But when it was found after the experiences of war communism that not even a majority of the workers were Bolshevik in sympathy and aim, Lenin's conception of "democracy" had to be narrowed yet further: the dictatorship of the Bolshevik party was established over the Soviets. This was done by the simple method of proscribing all other parties, and so preventing the Soviets from expressing any opinions but those of the one legal party—the Communist party.

Thus was Soviet democracy abolished and the Soviets converted into mere administrative organs and rubber stamps for the ukases of the Party.

The Cheka, inheritor of the powers and methods of the Tsarist Okrana, was created in the days of the Civil War to discover and stamp out the counter-revolutionaries. It was converted into an instrument for terrorizing not merely the old bourgeoisie but all workers and peasants who expressed opinions unfavorable to the Bolshevik regime. In Lenin's day its powers were kept within bounds and exercised mainly against the remnants of the "exploiting classes," though also against the Social Revolutionaries and Mensheviks, i.e., against the now proscribed parties of the peasants and working class. Under Stalin, its successor, the O.G.P.U., became an instrument of terror exercised not only against the proletariat in whose name the dictatorship was exercised, not only against the peasants without whose support the Bolsheviks could never have won power, but also against those members of the Party who disagreed with Stalin.

In 1920 the dissatisfied workers were still permitted to voice their opinions although already excluded from the Press. The following statement made to the visiting delegation of the British Trade-Union Congress and Labour party by the Russian Printers' Trade-Union, is amazingly prescient of what was to come. Although the statement is so sharply critical of the Bolshevik dictatorship, it is important to note the immense change in the status and rights of the workers then and ten years later. Under Lenin the workers could still dare to make such protests; under Stalin they were deprived of even that privilege:

> All Russian socialists are convinced that the triumph of Socialism in Russia is possible only if there is a socialist revolution in the West. All endeavors to force Socialism upon one backward country alone will give no positive results. They will only lead to endless sufferings of the working population. That is why the Russian working class insists on the independent fight against its class enemies and

on the independence of the labor organizations contrary to the wishes of the present ruling power.

Our present government is not only a workers' government; it is a worker-peasant government. The interests of workers and peasants are not always identical. The Russian working class must therefore be on its guard against any attempt of the present government to go beyond necessary concessions to the peasantry and in any way to harm labor interests.

Utopian endeavors, on the other hand, to enforce the immediate introduction of Socialism in Russia, meet with desperate opposition from the peasantry; they increase civil war and deepen the chronic disorganization of the country resulting from four years of civil war. The economic policy of the Soviet Government in introducing all-round nationalization leads to a further disorganization of the whole economic life of Russia.

The national economy of Russia cannot be improved by methods of violence against workers, by the militarization of labor, by miserable rates of pay and long hours of work.... It can only be saved by the free and independent labor organizations. The heroic efforts of the working population will be crowned with success if the Government itself adopts a rational economic policy at home and abroad.

A system of reconstruction based on the compulsory labor of hungry and enslaved workers and on the destructive policy of the Government with its grotesque, parasitic, administrative machine kept going out of the earnings of the working masses, will lead to further economic decay and the breakdown of the Revolution and of Socialism.

The system of reconstruction brings into opposition to the Government not only the peasantry but the workers themselves. The working class in Russia is decaying and losing its power and influence: it is dying out physically through hunger and ill-health; it is degenerating morally and politically, for the *worker is on the one hand being converted into a bureaucrat in the factory, and on the other being subject to constant supervision exercised through the communist "cells" and commissars.*

The Communist party has set itself up as the dictator not only to the enemies of the working class, but to the working class itself. The Communist party, which embraces only a small part of the working population and makes use of the state machinery and the country's resources, is imposing its will on the majority of the population and depriving the working masses of the right to have independent free organizations.

Freedom of the press and of election do not exist even for the workers themselves. The Communist party alone may issue daily papers, journals, print pamphlets and books, giving no chance for the opposition to let itself be heard. All the socialist parties work underground, in constant fear of being arrested, sent into exile, or deprived of their right of citizenship. Many workers have been shot for their political views and for criticizing the Communist party....

There are only a few trade-unions left whose council or Praesidium has been properly elected; and those trade-unions whose officers have managed to keep in touch with the working masses are under constant watch and suspicion....

The Soviets in Russia represent only to a small extent the views of the workers and peasants. *All non-Communist Soviets are usually dissolved....*

In spite of all this we are against foreign intervention or the intervention of the old Russian bourgeoisie in our quarrel with the Communist party. We admit only the intervention of the international proletariat in our affairs. We hope that the working class of other countries will bring moral pressure to bear on the Communist party to give a chance to the Russian working class to fight for the economic regeneration of Russia, for their rights, for their liberation, and for Socialism.*

During the years of civil war and foreign intervention which soon followed the October Revolution, the consequences of Lenin's abandonment of democracy were still hidden. In those years of confusion, war, and pestilence, discussions as to future Bolshevik policy were largely academic. The all-absorbing problem of the Bolsheviks was how to save the revolution in face of the Allied intervention, and how to keep the Red armies supplied when the whole economic mechanism of the country was breaking down. This was the period of military communism when the war industries were the only ones to which any attention could be paid. The original conception of workers' management of the factories inevitably gave place to rigorous state control.

In 1919, at the second Trade-Union Congress, Lenin declared: "It is inevitable to give a state character to the trade-unions, inevitable to merge them with the organs of state power."

The question of peasant ownership or state ownership of the land became a question of little moment when the exigencies of war forced the state to requisition grain from the peasantry to feed the army and the towns. War drove the Bolsheviks to apply their theories in an extreme form, not because it was considered theoretically the best policy to abolish the market and for the state to undertake the collection

* Verbatim Report of the General Meeting of the Printers' Union, Moscow, 1920.

and distribution of food, but because there was no other way. Industrial production of consumers' goods sank almost to zero, and the peasants were hiding their grain because there were no goods to exchange it for. At least so the war communist period was represented later by Lenin and by Trotsky, who called it "the systematic regimentation of consumption in a besieged fortress." Nevertheless, in those years of starvation, degradation, suffering, and terror, it was believed by many of the Bolsheviks that "socialism" could spring full-grown from their minds like Athena from the head of Zeus.

The retreat from war communism in 1921 was therefore regarded by many, not as a return to normal after the cessation of civil war and intervention, but as the abandonment of the attempt to set up a socialist economy.

Nineteen twenty-one was the year of the great famine, more terrible than any Russia had known. The Soviet Government was forced to retreat or to collapse. Russia had sunk down almost into that savage state when every man's hand is against his fellow. There were reports of cannibalism in some villages, and the whole population starved. There could be no hope of instituting a "planned economy" by the methods of forced collections with industry almost at a standstill and agricultural production lower than ever before in Russia's history. Nor was there any longer any expectation of the proletarian revolution in Germany, which, until 1921, had been expected to solve Russia's problems. A Soviet Germany would have enabled the U.S.S.R. to obtain German machinery and manufactures, skilled workers and engineers to build up Russia's shattered productive forces. But without an alliance with an advanced industrialized country, socialism in Russia could not be.

The Bolsheviks had triumphed, but Russia was becoming a desert. The protests of the Kronstadt sailors, although drowned in blood, showed that both workers and peasants could stand no more.

Lenin did not hesitate. He introduced the New Economic Policy. The peasants were no longer forced to give up their produce to the state. The market was reconstituted in place of state distribution of goods. By heroic efforts industry began to produce manufactures for sale to the village in exchange for bread.* Private trading was again permitted and even industrial production on a small scale for private profit. The "commanding heights," as Lenin called them: large-scale industry, transport, communications, power stations, banking, and foreign trade, remained state monopolies; but outside these, private en-

* For a graphic account of this period read the novel *Cement* by Gladkov.

terprise was permitted and encouraged. Freed of the strait jacket of enforced communism, the almost defunct national economy was set functioning. The machine which had slowed down almost to a standstill began to gather momentum. Shakily and uncertainly at first, the wheels of industry and trade began once more to revolve. Industrial production doubled in 1922 and 1923, and by 1926 had reached its prewar level. Meanwhile, the harvests were increasing now that the peasant had not only got the land but had been given an assurance that he could work it for his own profit; he brought production of grain up to and beyond the prewar level. For a few years the Russian peasant enjoyed a prosperity he had never known before; he no longer paid rent, his taxes were comparatively light, and he was encouraged to produce for profit and told to "get rich." Manufactured goods being very scarce, and the seizure of the great estates having increased the number of peasant landholders from sixteen to twenty-five million, the peasants did not bring the same proportion of the harvest to market as in the past. *The peasant ate more himself and brought less to market.* For the first and last time in Russian history the peasants had enough to eat and were not forced to starve to support either an aristocracy or a bureaucracy.

This fact was the great obstacle to industrialization. The peasant could not be induced to sell more so long as industry could not produce more goods for him to buy. But industries could not be expanded and new ones developed unless more produce could be obtained from the peasants to feed the workers engaged on new construction, and to export in exchange for machinery. In other words, the only source of capital accumulation in the U.S.S.R. was the peasantry; yet, unless the peasants were coerced, they would not finance industrialization. If they were coerced, as the years 1918-21 had proved, they would sit back and produce no more than they themselves consumed.

Lenin was an opportunist, but he was not prepared consciously to sacrifice end to means. The idea of deliberately starving some millions of peasants to death to teach them a lesson, and transforming the whole peasantry into serfs of the state, was not one which Lenin could for a moment have envisaged. In his mind the problem was to be solved by controlling the country's economy, not by war upon the village by the state.

Other undeveloped countries could borrow from the advanced capitalist countries; could, that is to say, get machinery and construction goods on credit and pay for them when they began to produce goods. This had been the method of industrialization of the United States,

Canada, Australia. But the U.S.S.R., which had expropriated the former capitalists and refused compensation to foreign bond-holders, could not get loans abroad. It is probable that in the course of time she would have been able to, if she had finally repudiated the world revolutionary aim of the Bolsheviks and liquidated the Comintern. At this stage such an idea was inconceivable; Lenin had introduced the N.E.P. in Russia as the policy to be pursued while awaiting the communist revolution in other countries, which alone could solve the problems of the U.S.S.R.

N.E.P., then, for Lenin, constituted a strategic retreat while awaiting reinforcements—not the abdication of power by the proletariat but concessions to capitalist tendencies. But he apparently relied as much upon the gradual development of Russia's productive forces as upon reinforcements from abroad. His idea was for the proletariat to hold the fort—state power—either until revolution occurred in Germany or until Russia herself was sufficiently industrialized to make socialism possible. In answer to the Social Democratic argument that Russia lacked the objective economic premises for socialism, he said: *

> If the creation of socialism demands a definite level of culture, then why cannot we begin by winning with a revolution the premises for that definite level of culture, and then afterwards, on the basis of the workers' and peasants' power and the Soviet structure, set out to catch up to the other peoples?

Lenin died too soon to instruct the Party as to what should be done if reinforcements never came, if no other communist revolution occurred, and if Russian agriculture failed to provide the means to industrialize Russia. But we know that he envisaged state capitalism for Russia, not socialism, should the world revolution be indefinitely delayed. (See Chapter V.)

For the Right wing of the Party, for men like Bucharin, who had perhaps at heart always been Mensheviks, N.E.P. was a permanent change. For Trotsky it was a breathing space, a strategical retreat as the preliminary for another attempt to establish socialism.

To Stalin the whole discussion was purely of personal interest. He saw that by setting the Right wing of the Party against the Left he would be able to destroy both and obtain absolute power himself. So all through those years 1921-26 he was busy in the background spinning the web in which both the Right and the Left oppositions were to find themselves helplessly enmeshed. Securing the key positions in

* Quoted by Max Eastman in *Stalin's Russia*, New York, 1940.

the Party for his own men, getting control of the whole Party apparatus from local to regional party secretaries, he put himself in a position to destroy both the Left and the Right.

After Lenin's death in 1924, the hope of revolution elsewhere grew ever fainter. The capitalist world which Lenin had believed to be breaking down was recovering from the war. In 1923, even before Lenin died, the revolutionary movement of the German proletariat had been defeated and the acceptance of the Dawes Plan had sounded the death knell of proletarian revolution in Germany. There was still some prospect of revolution in the colonial and semicolonial countries until Chiang Kai-shek's defeat of the Comintern in 1927. But even a victorious "socialist" revolution in another backward country such as China could not have helped to solve Russia's problem. Only a proletarian revolution in an advanced, industrialized country, in particular Germany, could have enabled the Soviet Government to escape from the dilemma: how to acquire capital for industrialization without either oppressing and alienating the peasantry or permitting a restoration of capitalism.

Bucharin and the Right wing of the Bolshevik party said carry on with the N.E.P.; don't expect we can industrialize the U.S.S.R. rapidly, but bit by bit industry can be expanded, can produce more and sell more to the peasants so that capital accumulation will be gradually accelerated. These Right wing Bolsheviks also undoubtedly hoped to get credits from the capitalist world. They were apparently prepared to abandon the aim of world revolution, and Bucharin went so far as to develop the thesis that capitalism would reorganize itself and not go smash as orthodox Communists insisted. Unfortunately for the Russian people, Bucharin, although a great theoretician, was completely deceived by Stalin. He could not from his very nature compete with Stalin's gangster methods and was as putty in his hands. Stalin used him only so long as his arguments were needed to destroy Trotsky.

The Left opposition, headed by Trotsky, pointed to the widening of the scissors—i.e., the growing disparity between industrial and agricultural prices as industry failed to keep pace with mounting agricultural production. Handicraft industries, revived in the villages and financed by the richer peasants, threatened to create a self-sufficient village economy. If, said Trotsky, industry continues to lag, there will be a break between city and country. Already the free market has intensified the differentiation of classes in the village, some peasants growing rich and others becoming landless laborers. The growth of the

Kulak class, said Trotsky, is creating a new capitalist class in the village: the wealthy peasant who exploits the other peasants. While Bucharin told the peasantry to "get rich," Trotsky insisted that this slogan meant the enrichment of a minority of the peasants at the expense of the great majority and the gradual emergence of a "bourgeoisie." True that only thus could the surplus produce of the village be sold to the state in the Soviet condition of scarcity of manufactures; for if all were independent farmers, consumption of food in the village would be much higher than if a comparatively small number of peasants owned most of the land and many worked as their hired laborers for a low wage which did not permit of their eating as much as they needed.

In its desire to increase agricultural production and ensure the delivery of grain to the market, the Soviet Government in 1925 had legalized the hiring of labor power and the renting of land. Ah, said the Left opposition, here you are creating a new capitalist class; soon we shall be back in a capitalist state. As Trotsky expressed it:

> The peasantry was becoming polarized between the small capitalist on one side and the hired hand on the other. At the same time, lacking industrial commodities, the State was crowded out of the rural market. Between the Kulak and the petty home craftsman there appeared, as though from under the earth, the middleman. The State enterprises themselves, in search of raw material, were more and more compelled to deal with the private trader. The rising tide of capitalism was visible everywhere. Thinking people saw plainly that a Revolution in the forms of property does not solve the problem of Socialism, but only raises it.*

Trotsky and his followers were absolutists. They were determined that the U.S.S.R. must become a completely socialist state, and that any small capitalist blossoms must at once be struck down. And yet they themselves held that "socialism in one country" was an impossibility. Preobrazhensky, the most honest of the Left opposition group, stated openly that only by treating the Russian countryside as a colonial area could the necessary super-profits be obtained to finance the industrialization of the U.S.S.R. Such plain speaking was too much even for the Left opposition and brought ruin to the author once Stalin was in control and busy carrying out Preobrazhensky's policy in an extreme form.

By 1926, nearly 60 per cent of the grain on the market was being

---
* *The Revolution Betrayed*, p. 23.

sold by a mere 6 per cent of the peasants, the Kulaks. These Kulaks were selling to middlemen; and a new "petty bourgeoisie" of shopkeepers, restaurant-keepers, and small industrialists had cropped up like mushrooms after the rain. The state could no longer lay its hands on enough grain to export even a small quantity for the import of machinery. Handicraft industries were reviving to serve the needs of the village. The peasants were creating their own self-subsistent economy outside the sphere of control of the Soviet state. The working class in the state industries suffered, and the Soviets came more and more to represent the interests of the peasants. Stalin went with the tide; and, anxious to secure his own power by enlisting the support of the Right wing of the Party against Trotsky, he contemplated in 1925 giving each peasant a forty-years tenure of his land. As against this "denationalization" of agriculture and stagnation of industry, which in truth must have led to the U.S.S.R. becoming a semicapitalist state, Trotsky proposed collectivization—not the collectivization at the point of the bayonet which Stalin was later to enforce, but gradual collectivization through the grant of state credits and the supply of machinery by the state to those poorer peasants who would voluntarily join a collective farm. This could, however, only be accomplished if the richer peasants were more heavily taxed to finance the collective farms and to allow the state to import machinery for industrialization and the production of tractors and other machinery, and for the erection of power stations. Heavier taxation of the Kulaks would not only stunt the growth of the new "capitalist" class, but would enable the state to produce more manufactured goods, lower prices, and break the "strike" of the peasants, who were replying to the shortage of industrial goods by working less, consuming more of their own produce, and disposing of the rest to the Kulak middlemen, who, instead of selling it to the government, used it to support local handicraft industries. But, said the Right opposition, if you bear too hardly on the Kulaks we shall have war between town and village.

Trotsky's plans for collectivization and industrialization were called fantastic, and scorned as "industrial romanticism," "poor peasant illusions," and so forth. It would be sufficient, said the Right wing of the Party, if the growth of industrial production *declined* yearly from a 9 per cent increase to a bare 4 per cent increase.

The difference of opinion between the Right and Left wings of the Bolshevik party on the policy to be pursued was distorted by the struggle for power. The problem which faced the Soviet Government was never calmly considered and soberly discussed as it might have been if Lenin had been alive, or if Soviet democracy had been allowed to function. Polemics took the place of serious argument; the implications of both a continuance of N.E.P. and of the Left wing policy of pressure on the Kulaks and nascent capitalist class were never considered by the Bolshevik party as a whole, simply as an economic and political problem. Nor did the working class participate in the discussion of its fate. Stalin had little theoretical knowledge, and in any case was not in the least concerned with the rightness or wrongness of either policy. He wanted absolute power, and he saw his way to get it by crushing Trotsky and the Left by the aid of Bucharin and the Right, and then eliminating the Right opposition by pursuing a policy far more "Left" than Trotsky's. The final result was that the worst features of the policy of both sides were adopted by Stalin as the "party line": super-industrialization on a scale never dreamed of by the Left opposition, accompanied by the destruction of the elements in the Bolshevik party most capable of carrying out such a policy; accumulation of capital for industrial construction by robbing the peasants, accompanied by the liquidation of the technicians and administrative personnel who alone could have made the new industries function efficiently.

By the end of 1927 the truth of Trotsky's arguments had become so obvious that he and his followers had to be eliminated if he were not to take Stalin's place. The decreasing food supplies in the towns were convincing the proletariat that Trotsky was right in prophesying the return of capitalism. The workers of Leningrad appear to have been behind Trotsky almost to a man. The Kulaks were by now holding up the cities to ransom to force a rise in the price of grain. Trotsky and the Left opposition leaders were arrested by the O.G.P.U., which Stalin controlled, and imprisoned or exiled.

Stalin was able to do this because he had the support of Bucharin, Tomsky, Rykov, Kalinin, and the rest of the Right wing of the Party. These men had no conception of Stalin's real intentions until it was too late. They were sincere, and none of them were anxious for personal power. They were probably right in thinking that Trotsky's policies would have led to civil war between town and country and a revival of the horrors of the period of war communism. They did not dream that Stalin was planning a civil war far more bloody than anything Trotsky had desired, and to be carried out in such a fashion as to destroy all hope of socialism in Russia. In July 1928, Stalin was still insisting that individual cultivation of the land must be supported, and collectivization would be a mistake. By October, Bucharin, Rykov, and Tomsky were being condemned as bourgeois liberals who desired the restoration of capitalism, and Stalin was preparing to sponsor an adventurist policy of super-industrialization, complete collectivization, "liquidation" of the Kulaks, and savage coercion of the peasantry. Trotsky's prophecies were being fulfilled. The Kulaks were holding the government to ransom; less and less food was procurable in the towns, and the workers began to suffer. In 1927-28 grain stocks were seized from the Kulaks and even from the "middle peasants." Those they had employed found themselves without work, since the Kulaks naturally saw no point in cultivating large farms if the produce was to be confiscated.

In 1928 the grain harvest had sunk to 73 million tons from the pre-war level of about 90 million. By December 1928 the food shortage was making itself felt even in Moscow, the most favored of the cities. Bread cards were introduced, unemployment increased, and real wages fell. Forced buying from the peasants at an unremunerative price and heavier taxes on the Kulaks could not solve the problem. The peasants hid their grain or refused to sow it. There were murders by the peasants of the Party functionaries who seized their grain. Military force could seize the food in the villages; but it could not, so long as individual farming persisted, coerce the whole peasant population to work for the benefit of the state. The expense of coercion and intimidation was too great unless and until the peasants could be herded together like the workers in the factories. Collective farming was therefore ordered by decree—not the voluntary pooling of resources by the poorer peasants, encouraged by state credits and able to produce more than individual farms by being supplied with machinery, which Trotsky had advocated—but collectivization by the knout. Not collectivization with the purpose of immediately increasing the productivity of the land by means of machinery and modern methods of production, which obviously could not be introduced on small individual holdings, but collectivization with equipment suitable only to small-scale farming, with the object of getting all the peasants together under the control of the O.G.P.U. so that they could be forced to labor.

In November 1929, Stalin announced the end of individual farming, ordered the "liquidation of the Kulaks as a class," and the establishment of collective farms everywhere and for everyone. Stalin had decided to solve the agricultural problem "in a socialist sense" by violence and terror. If collectivization had been accompanied by a rapid increase in the supply of manufactured goods to the village the peasants might perhaps have been reconciled to the new system. But Stalin had simultaneously inaugurated the Five Year Plan for industrial development, which concentrated all the resources of the country on the production of capital goods and armaments. The peasants were expected to work practically for nothing since the state could not supply them with clothing and other manufactures of prime necessity.

There began that terrible murder of the Kulaks by the state, which is almost unparalleled in history for its cruelty. I use the word murder deliberately, for although the Kulaks were not lined up and shot, they were killed off in a manner far more cruel. Whole families, men, women, children, and babies, were thrown out of their homes, their personal possessions seized, even their warm clothing torn off them; then, packed into unheated cattle trucks in winter, they were sent off to Siberia or other waste parts of the Soviet Union. A few of the men survived to start life again and build farms in the waste lands into which they had been exiled. The women and children perished. Hundreds of thousands of other peasants were herded off to the timber prison camps in the Arctic regions, to die like flies from hunger and cold and exhausting labor, whipped by the O.G.P.U. guards and treated like the slaves of Pharaoh or some other Asiatic tyrant.*

When the father of the Kulak family alone was arrested, this was hardly more merciful, since all food in the house was confiscated, down to the last sack of flour. Wife and children were left to starve to death. Mothers sometimes killed their children to save them from the worse slow lingering death from famine. The story reported by Malcolm Muggeridge, correspondent of the *Manchester Guardian* in the U.S.S.R. at that time, is typical of many of the gruesome tragedies of that terrible time. A woman in a Cossack village in the Caucasus, whose husband had already been arrested and taken off to forced labor as a Kulak, had her last sack of flour confiscated by the O.G.P.U. officer, Comrade Babel. When he had left she looked at her three children fallen asleep by the stove. There was no food and no hope of securing food. She fetched an ax and killed the children as they slept. Then, after tying each one up in a flour sack, she went to the town and reported to Comrade Babel that she had decided she ought no longer to defy the Dictatorship of the Proletariat, and confessed that she had three more sacks of flour hidden away. Comrade Babel went back to

* Veressayev, the author of a famous book on the civil war called *Deadlock*, was allowed to write one last book before he was "purged." In this book, *Two Sisters*, he describes how young Comsomols dragged the felt boots off the feet of small children of the Kulaks so that they died of frostbite.

her house with her along the snowy road. She took him up to the loft and showed him the three bulging sacks. As he bent under the rafters to see, she killed him with the ax.

Of course the woman was shot, and Comrade Babel's death "on the class-war front" was reported in Moscow. *Pravda* spoke of the "plots" of the class enemy, of the need to "root out mercilessly all hostile elements in the villages," and of the need for "increased severity on opportunists" (i.e., on those whose humanity was not yet so dead as to allow them to murder women and children of the "class enemy"). The case was reported as one in which

> a notorious counter-revolutionary, wife of an exiled kulak, lured Comrade Babel to her house with false promises and murdered him in the loft with an axe. Three soldiers downstairs suspected of complicity... symptomatic of new tactics of kulak elements... apparent submission used as a cloak for sabotage and other treasonable activities... work sometimes from within collective farms; sometimes even from within Party organizations.... New propagandist campaign and sterner measures against class enemies are needed to root out this evil.*

Fear of reprisals by the desperate, starving, expropriated peasants drove the Party to attempt to exterminate all their victims. "We must destroy our enemies until not one is left," was the cry. An orgy of cruelty raged in the countryside. One must go back to the days of the Mongol hordes who swept across Asia and eastern Europe in the thirteenth century, or to the massacres by the Assyrians in biblical times, for an historical parallel with the communist "class war" on the Russian peasants.

Many motives, fanatic faith, fear, sadism, revenge, played their role in this horrible massacre of the innocent by famine and the firing squad. Jews who remembered old pogroms in the Russian villages, workers who had suffered under the Cossack whips in Tsarist times, gave vent to dusty and dim hatreds sanctified under the banner of the class war. Earnest young men and women whose best instincts were perverted by the orders given them by the Party, convinced themselves that in depriving the peasants of their last stores of food they were helping to build a socialist society. O.G.P.U. and Red army officers sent to carry on the "war on the agrarian front" feared that if they were not absolutely merciless they would be stabbed in the back on dark nights by desperate peasants.

* Quoted in *Winter in Moscow*, by Malcolm Muggeridge.

Who were the Kulaks now declared enemies of the state? In theory they were the exploiting peasants, those who rented extra land and employed hired labor, or who advanced money or seed at high rates of interest to the poorest peasants. Kulak means a fist, and the word meant an exploiter and a usurer. Under Stalin the word came to mean any peasant who dared to oppose collectivization.

Long before the period of forced collectivization, the Bolsheviks had endeavored to break the solid front which the villages presented to the towns and the Soviet state, by instituting a class war in the villages. It was hoped that if some peasants could be set against others, it would be possible to break the solid opposition of the peasants to what they viewed as the exploitation of the agricultural population for the benefit of the working class and the furtherance of industrialization. So in the N.E.P. period the state, which was encouraging the Kulaks with one set of decrees to "get rich" by producing more, was discouraging them by treating every prosperous peasant as a social outcast and inciting the poorer peasants against them. It was little wonder that the peasants brought less and less grain to the market.

In order to stimulate class warfare, the peasants were registered in three classes: Kulaki, Seredniaki ("middle peasants"), and Bedniaki ("poor peasants"). In villages where there was a dead level of poverty, the Soviets were nevertheless ordered to find Kulaks even where none existed. Some families must be designated as such even if there were no exploiters or usurers. Dr. Calvin B. Hoover relates how, in one village which he visited, the local chairman of the Committee of the Poor exhibited to him a family of Kulaks quite in the manner of showing one a family of lepers on whom the judgment of God had fallen. "He regarded them," relates Dr. Hoover, "with hopeless pity and said that all the troubles in the village dated from the time when the villagers had been compelled to divide themselves into the three classes." When the query was put as to why the family was regarded as a Kulak one, he replied that someone had to be a Kulak, and that this family had many years before owned a village inn. They no longer did so, but there was apparently no hope of their ever losing their status as a Kulak family. If they did, there was no other family to take their place as Public Enemy, and for some reason unknown to anyone, the Soviet Government insisted that each village must produce at least one Kulak family to be oppressed. These Kulaki had no electoral rights, had to pay 40 per cent of their miserable income to the state, and their children were not allowed to go to school.

In practice, since in many parts of the country real Kulaks who "exploited" other peasants were hard to find, the designation was applied to every peasant who was a little better off than his neighbors, to anyone who owned two horses and two cows, or had managed in some way to lift himself a little above the miserably low general standard of life in the Russian village. It meant that hard work and enterprise were penalized wherever they were found. What Tartar invasions and long centuries of feudal oppression had begun, the Soviet Government consummated. The Russian peasant sank further into slothfulness and hopelessness. Since to raise himself above the level of his beasts of burden was now accounted a crime against the state, he worked as little as possible, and ate and drank whenever possible without thought of the morrow, which was almost certain to be worse than today. The fecklessness of the Russian character was the result of Russian history, but it was left to the Soviet Government to make laws penalizing all who worked hard and took thought for the morrow. Its treatment of the best and most progressive elements among the peasantry might have been expressly designed to prove the truth of the old arguments against socialism.

Precisely those peasants who had the knowledge, skill, and industry to raise Russian agriculture above its medieval level were liquidated. The collective farms were deprived of the men who could have made them function efficiently. And yet the army of city workers sent down to coerce the peasants and manage the collectives took far more from the villages in the shape of wages than the Kulaks had taken as profit. If, by allowing them a larger share of the produce than the other peasants, the Kulaks had been persuaded to run the new farms, instead of being killed off or imprisoned, the new system might have worked. It was, of course, argued that they were irreconcilably hostile to the Soviet state. But they had never been given a chance to be other than hostile. The government discriminated against them, reviled them, and instigated everyone to loathe them. Naturally they hated the Soviet Government. But to argue that they were irreconcilable enemies of the Soviet state is like saying that the Jews in Germany deserve what they get because they hate the Nazi Government which oppresses them.

It was not only the Kulaks who were expropriated, exiled, or imprisoned. Except for the minority of landless peasants, all regarded collectivization as expropriation. Ordered by the state to pool all their property—i.e., give everything up to the Kolkhoz ("collective farm"), and faced with exile or the concentration camp if they refused to join the Kolkhoz, the peasants naturally killed their pigs, their sheep, their cows, and their chickens, and ate them or sold the hide and the meat for money, which could be hidden. In 1934 the number of horses in Russia was half what it had been in 1929, and the sheep and pigs less than half.

Although Trotsky calls it "liberal twaddle" to assume that collectivization as a whole was accomplished by naked force, he himself has described it in the following words:

> Twenty-five million isolated peasant egoisms which yesterday had been the sole motive force of agriculture—weak like an old farmer's nag, but nevertheless forces—the bureaucracy tried to replace at one gesture by the commands of 2000 collective farm administrative offices, lacking technical equipment, agronomic knowledge, and the support of the peasants themselves.

Trotsky, with justice, called this a blind, violent gamble. The Left opposition had never advocated anything so drastic, so rapid, and so unprepared. It had envisaged gradual collectivization over a period of fifteen years. Stalin, having at last decided upon collectivization, thought he could force it through by a terror exercised against the whole peasant population. He did it, but in doing it he laid waste the countryside and caused the death of millions from starvation. The total grain harvest fell from 835 million *centners* in 1930 to 696 million in 1932, sugar production from 109 million *poods* to 48 million. Since even in 1930 there was hunger in the towns, this fall, combined with the previous slaughter of livestock, meant famine in many parts of the country and near-starvation for the workers in the towns. Between five and ten million peasants are estimated to have died of starvation.

Soviet morale has never recovered from those terrible years which were my first years of residence in the U.S.S.R. The Communist party and the Comsomols ("Young Communist League") became the expropriators of the people, an army of occupation in the countryside. Decent young men and women sent down to the villages were persuaded that it was their duty as Socialists to stifle all humanitarian scruples while driving the bewildered, sullen, and resentful peasants into the collective farms, and levying grain, milk, and meat from men and women whose children were to starve to death in consequence. Those who could not perform the terrible deeds expected of them were expelled from the Party as "rotten liberals." Both duty and hopes of a career compelled the Party member and the Comsomol to utter ruthlessness and inhumanity. Many of the young people became hardened and cynical careerists prepared to commit any atrocity commanded by Stalin. The war on the peasants was more brutalizing than war against another nation, for the peasants were unarmed and defenseless. Whereas in Germany only a minority of Nazis have tortured Jews and political prisoners, in Russia a whole new generation of the Communist party was degraded and brutalized in the war against 25 million peasant families.

Meanwhile the workers in the factories found themselves suffering almost as great a degree of privation as in the years of civil war. Not only was Stalin's violent agrarian policy drastically reducing the amount of food produced in Russia; his equally senseless industrialization plans were causing food and manufactures to be exported from Russia to pay for machinery imports. Butter and eggs disappeared from the worker's table and were dumped abroad. Meat and even herring became a rare luxury. The conditions of life in the towns are described in other chapters, as also the servitude of the working class, which soon became as absolute as the servitude of the peasants.

During my first winter in Russia (1930-31) it was believed that if once the peasants could be forced into the collective farms, the food problem would be solved. But, although by 1931 most of the land had been taken over by collectives, the peasants had not yet been forced to work for the profit of the state. Since they now no longer owned the land, since intensive industrialization and concentration on the production of capital goods meant that the state had even less to sell them than before in the way of manufactured goods, and since the state virtually confiscated the grain by taking it at nominal prices, the collectivized peasants worked less than ever before. They opposed to the government the same passive resistance as before the N.E.P. had been introduced, and sowed and reaped just enough to feed themselves. This fact, coupled with drought in the Black Soil region, reduced the harvest to a much smaller amount than in previous years. But the government nevertheless enforced its full demands, telling the peasants that it was their own fault if they were short of food, and leaving them to die of starvation. A terrible famine set in, especially severe in the rich corn-bearing lands of the Ukraine. This time there was no relief from abroad, since the Soviet Government denied that there was a famine and deliberately left the peasants to die of starvation.

Foreign journalists were not allowed to visit the South. All Russia knew what was happening; but the hacks of the foreign press, obedient to Stalin for fear of losing their jobs, sent out no word. Only a few brave and honest foreigners like Eugene Lyons of the United Press and Malcolm Muggeridge of the *Manchester Guardian* told the truth and were expelled from Russia, or put in a position in which they were forced to leave. The others followed the lead of Duranty of the *New York Times* and denied the existence of a famine, until years afterwards.

Foreign visitors, carefully shepherded by Intourist, and given huge meals in the hotels of the starving land, went home to deny the rumors of famine. I well remember the delegation from England in 1932 which included Mrs. G. D. H. Cole and various professors from London University. One of them, a lecturer at the London School of Economics, told me as we ate a wonderful meal at the New Moscow Hotel (at his expense) that it was all nonsense about the famine, for at Kiev he had been given caviar, butter, eggs, and coffee for breakfast! I had to let him talk, for I knew if I told him the truth and he repeated it, my husband would be sent to prison.

Stalin's utter ruthlessness won the day. The resistance of the peasants was broken. Since 1932 they have known that they will starve unless they produce the quota taken by the government and enough to feed themselves. They have been forced to work on the government's terms. They have become serfs of the state whose labor on the collective farms is forced labor, and corresponds to the labor service rendered to his overlord by the serf in medieval times. Since 1935 the peasant has been allowed a small allotment of his own to grow vegetables and sometimes a little grain. On this allotment he works after hours for his own profit. His labor on the collective farm produces a minimum for subsistence in good years. But since he knows that the government will always cheat him if it can, he has no incentive to increase the productivity of the land. He knows that should the "communal" land be made to yield more, the state collections will be raised, or the amount set aside for capital improvements increased. Bitter experience has taught him that he cannot raise his standard of life, since a jealous government will in one way or another deprive him of the profit of his labors. Hence the veritable stagnation of Soviet agriculture over the past five or six years.

Collectivization has never surmounted the original scissors crisis of the twenties. The shortage of consumption goods remains acute, and has since 1936 been intensified by the diversion of industry to the supply of armaments. The disparity between the prices of industrial goods and the prices at which the agricultural population is forced to sell its produce to the state has grown much greater, not smaller, during the past decade. What collectivization has done is to make the collection of the forced grain deliveries to the state much easier. A small detachment of O.G.P.U. soldiers in each district can terrify the collectives into giving up the greater part of the harvest, whereas an enormous number of troops would be required to terrorize each individual peasant cultivating his own farm.

All the much-vaunted use of modern farm machinery imported or produced at tremendous sacrifice in the U.S.S.R. has not increased the yield of the land or lowered the real cost of production. The tractors and other modern farm implements have not compensated either for the destruction of livestock in 1930 and 1931, or for the lost incentive of the peasant to labor. The machinery paid for by the blood and sweat of a whole generation of Russians is often entirely useless because it has broken down and cannot be repaired, or partly wasted because it is not used to its full capacity. Neither the peasant nor the state has reaped any real benefit from the modernization of agriculture concerning which the Soviet Union boasts so extravagantly. (A more detailed account of the agrarian system is given in Chapter VI.)

If the N.E.P. had been continued, the U.S.S.R. today might have been a prosperous country with the land yielding 50 per cent more than in Tsarist times, and the urban workers as well as the peasants enjoying a decent standard of life. All that the Five Year Plans have accomplished in agriculture is to enable the peasants to produce about as much as before the Revolution, while transforming them into bitter enemies of the Soviet Government.

CHAPTER III

LEARNING THE SOVIET WAY OF LIFE

WHEN I GOT to Moscow late in September, 1930, I found that my husband had been ordered to make a trip to China before coming to Russia, so that he did not join me until January 1931. I had three months alone in Moscow, three months during which I was at last made aware of what manner of society and government was being created under Stalin, but yet did not have the sense to dash off to China to stop my husband from entering the country. How often in future years was I to regret my stupidity! Or was it some last lingering hopes which led me to allow him to walk into the spider's web from which he could never again be extricated? For it was soon made clear to me that if he once entered the Soviet Union he would never get out again. Already almost all the "non-Party specialists" had been recalled from abroad and no passports were any longer issued to go abroad except to those of unimpeachable proletarian origin or to Party members of long standing. The first great purge had begun, the purge which was to kill off so many of the old "intellectuals"—the engineers, technicians, scientists, and administrative personnel who had been educated under the Tsarist regime, but had not run away after the Revolution, and had been working loyally for the Soviet state ever since the introduction of the New Economic Policy.

The Commissariat of Foreign Trade, anxious to keep a few qualified men abroad, wanted my husband to go to the United States to work at Amtorg.* They cabled him to proceed straight to America from Shanghai, and offered to pay my fare to join him in New York via Hamburg. He refused to obey their order and insisted upon coming to Moscow. As he wrote to me then, he was determined to settle down at last in Russia. He was sick of life abroad and wanted to play his part after his long exile in the great creative work going on in the U.S.S.R. I realized later that he wanted to drown his doubts in work and to merge himself in the collective human effort with a subconscious desire to atone for his long years of divorce from the socialist movement, and for the individualism of his nature. He was an acutely sensitive person, reserved and somewhat unsocial by nature. For him

* The Soviet Trading Organization in U.S.A. which corresponds to Arcos in London.

social contacts were always something of an effort; he concentrated his love and affection upon a very few individuals and rarely lowered the barriers of his reserve to any human being. For that reason perhaps he desired in a way which I often found difficult to understand to merge himself in the stream of humanity, and to share a fraternal passion with those who, as individuals, repelled his fastidious standards of behavior. A keen sense of humor and a quick wit saved him from being considered a misanthrope; he could always ward off threats to his privacy by a joke and, although his wit could be sharp and cutting, he directed it too frequently against himself for it to arouse rancor.

He had become convinced that he suffered a moral disadvantage as a privileged intellectual working in comfort abroad and ought to come back and suffer with the mass of the people. Although a Jew, he was also a Russian; and Russians more than other people appear to have a kind of mystical urge to immolate themselves, to castigate and humble themselves. They seem to be the least individualistic of peoples and the most prone to servility and a kind of mystical masochism. Arcadi was essentially Western in education and ideas, but even he suffered for a while from the Russian martyr complex. His tragedy was that, although he shared the Russian intellectual's desire for self-immolation upon the altar of an ideal and the Russian desire to merge his individuality in a totality, he did not share the Russian aptitude for servility and sycophancy. He was unable to fawn upon the great or wheedle favors from the Party bosses. Thus he could never adapt himself completely to Soviet conditions of life; yet he would not, or could not, break away from Russia. He preferred working at a low salary without privileges to abasing himself sufficiently to obtain food supplies, a flat, and other perquisites. He was too much of a Westerner to fawn and beg; too much of a Russian to cut loose and escape.

Narcomveshtorg* thought so highly of his capacities and knowledge, and was so certain that if he once came to Moscow they would never be able to send him abroad again, that they eventually offered me my full fare to China, and thence to the United States, if I would go and persuade him to sail for San Francisco. But by that time I had become convinced that it was hopeless to try to change his decision. No one, not even the woman a man loves, can persuade him to go against his convictions; and by now I knew that one can learn only through experience. Perhaps also my English capacity for straight thinking had been dulled by the gray and leaden Moscow atmosphere; and the terror, of which by now I was cognizant, prevented my

* Commissariat of Foreign Trade.

writing to him fully and frankly by post. Even if I could have got a letter out to be posted in England, I had no other address than the office address in Shanghai where my letters might be opened. If I told the truth as to conditions in Russia, he might not believe me; and to do so would endanger his life if after all he decided to come to Russia.

Although I was aware in my subconscious that the dream was already lost, I clung to my illusions. I could not as yet admit even to myself that the U.S.S.R. had no longer any resemblance to the socialist ideal which for so many years had ruled my life, and that Russia had already gone too far along the road to bureaucratic tyranny for there to be any hope of her turning back to the ideals of the October Revolution. Nor could I, being English, really accept the fact that if later we wished to leave Russia my husband would not be able to do so. I sent telegrams, but I did not go to China. I waited in Moscow hoping against hope that he would not come, yet not daring to admit, even to myself, how fearful I was of the future should he come.

During this period I wrote two letters to my mother in England. In the first, dated September 29, 1930, I wrote:

> Even P— [an old Party member whom I had known in London] says it is just as well for Arcadi to spend the coming year in America. The fact of the matter is that the economic position is so strained that there is no confidence in anyone, and the conditions of work for all "intellectuals" are very difficult indeed. Arcadi is one of the very few competent people left in whom they still have confidence.

A month later I knew it was dangerous to give a hint of conditions in letters sent through the post, and I sent a letter through the hand of E. F. Wise, the English adviser of Centrosoyus.* I was fairly confident he would not read my letter or show it to anyone, but I was not quite sure. So I wrote guardedly, but my words conveyed my state of mind:

> Only workers from the factory or men of proletarian origin are now allowed to go abroad. Whether Arcadi realizes the position or not I do not know.... The way business is now being run is hopeless. They put absolutely useless people into leading positions just because they are of proletarian origin. I suppose it can't go on and there will be a reaction soon, but in the meantime it means the

---

* The Central organization of the Russian Co-operatives, which at that period, had some employees abroad. E. F. Wise had previously been a Labour M.P. He died soon after I went to live in the U.S.S.R.

most terrible waste and inefficiency. *Things are very different from two years ago.* Perhaps, dear, in the end I shall go back to being a historian. Only now am I beginning to learn a bit about mankind and its queerness. To understand a little what one means by *Menschen sind Menschen*. To understand that life is not so simple, so to speak. I am still pretty certain of my main ground but the carrying out of what is wanted is not so simple.

I added a postscript, whether to reassure myself or my mother I am not sure.

Dear, you know, apart from anything else it is the most interesting country in the world to be living in, and one must be philosophical enough to take the bad with the good, so long as one believes that in the end there will be far more of the latter.

Life in Russia consisted in learning the painful lesson that there was far more bad than good, and that the good was disappearing so rapidly that there was soon nothing but bad. Soon I was aware that the road to socialism, along which Lenin in 1917 thought he was leading the working class, had become the road to a totalitarian tyranny so cruel and destructive of human life and dignity that Nazi Germany appears in comparison an enlightened tyranny.

While awaiting Arcadi's arrival from the Far East I lived with his sister and her two sons in their tiny two-roomed apartment in the Dom Politkatajan on Pokrovka. This was the House of the "Political Hard-Labor Prisoners"—i.e., of those who had done hard labor in Siberia under the Tsar. Vera, my sister-in-law, had been sent to a Siberian prison from Lodz in Poland while still in her teens. First, like Arcadi, a member of the Bund (Jewish Social Democrats) she had become a Social Revolutionary in Siberia but had joined the Bolsheviks in 1917, and had herself fought against the Japanese in the Intervention. She had been imprisoned by them but had escaped. Her whole life had been one of adventure, hardship, and sacrifice; but now she had a good job and was full of confidence in the future. She radiated happiness. Her first child had died as a baby on the long trek in the snow across Siberia to the prison camp. Trying to shield it from the cold, she had suffocated it in her arms. Her second son, Shura, had somehow survived the rigors of prison and exile, and was now a youth of eighteen studying engineering at the Moscow University. Vera also had an adopted son, Grischa, whom she had taken in infancy from a poor peasant family in Siberia which had so many children it could not feed Grischa. The two boys were devoted to each other and to their mother. Their relations were entirely comradely. They called her Vera and treated her as an elder sister. Vera's husband had died fighting in the Red Army, but I gathered he had been a bit of a ne'er-do-well, and little love had been lost between them.

Vera and my husband had been very close to each other in their youth. They had had a stepmother who treated them cruelly, and they had both become revolutionaries at about the same time. Curiously enough, the cruel treatment they had experienced in childhood and which had made Arcadi so distrustful of individual human beings had not affected Vera. She was very sociable and trustful of others and almost childlike in her faith. Arcadi, being the elder, had taught Vera and instructed her. This she always remembered even though now she was a member of the Communist party and he had no such distinction. When they had met in Moscow in 1928 they had not seen each other for twenty-two years. It was typical of that meeting that, whereas Arcadi, when he saw Vera approach his office desk, merely said: "Hello Vera, how are you," she had tears in her eyes and embraced him in front of everyone. During those twenty-two years Arcadi had studied in Zurich, worked in business in England and the United States, and acquired a Western manner and a truly English reserve. Vera's life had been entirely different. She had had hardly any education, had participated in the revolutionary struggles of two decades, had known hunger and cold, and in general lived a life of great hardship. She had often been in danger, but she had always lived among "comrades," never struggled on her own in an alien new world. They felt a great affection for each other, and Vera took me to her heart at once as his wife. Her attitude toward Arcadi retained something of the flavor of their youth; he was the educated clever elder brother who had instructed her in Marxist theory long ago in Poland. Although he was not a Party member and she was, she felt no superiority. Her fate and Arcadi's were to be similar. She was arrested and disappeared in 1937, a year later than Arcadi, when most of the inhabitants of the Hard Labor House were purged because their revolutionary pasts made them suspect to Stalin.

Vera was very proud of Shura, who, in Siberia before they came to Moscow, had been elected representative of all the Comsomols of the Irkutsk region. But at the time I came to Moscow he was causing her much anxiety. He did not conform sufficiently at the university, was apt to ask awkward questions at Young Communist meetings, and was in danger of being expelled from the Comsomols. His mother's reputation and influence had so far prevented this, but she was always begging Shura to hold his tongue. Shura once said to me: "How simple life was in Vera's youth and how good it must have been. One was a revolutionary and one struggled against Tsarist tyranny. But now? ..." What Shura meant was what I often felt myself. Those very impulses of generous youth which in the old days had led so many of the students to become revolutionaries, now impelled them to protest against Soviet tyranny and injustice; but this today meant accusations of being *counter*-revolutionary. Vera still had absolute faith in the Revolution. She was a product of its romantic past; Shura was a product of its disillusioned present. And whereas Vera knew little of theory, Shura was being educated in it, and the writings of Marx and Lenin impelled him to see more clearly than his mother the difference between theory and practice in the Soviet Union. In those days the writings of Marx and Lenin were still available to all in unexpurgated editions. Later the government saw to it that the originals were hard to come by except for high Party members with a ticket to the Party Bookshop, and produced only extracts of Lenin for the "masses."

Long before I left Russia Shura had ceased to take any interest in politics and, like so many of the best elements among the Soviet youth, had become a cynical young man philosophically accepting life as it came and no longer yearning for the fulfillment of the forgotten hopes of his early youth. Intent only upon earning enough to keep his young wife and child in reasonable comfort, he had gone as an engineer to the Far North where the pay was highest.

With her Jewish sense of family solidarity and her Siberian tradition of hospitality, Vera unquestioningly gave me shelter and shared her food with me in those days. Having no job, I had no bread card and nowhere to get a meal. A job was open to me at the Marx Engels Institute, but since I had to contract myself for three years' work, and since I did not know whether or not we were going to America, I could not take it. I got translation and editing work to do and wrote some articles, but this did not produce a food card.

Those were cold and hungry days. In the morning we had a meal of potatoes, bread, and herring. Unable to swallow the raw salted herring which is the most nourishing food available to the poorer Russians, I subsisted on the bread and potatoes until 5 P.M. At that hour Vera and the boys returned from work, and we shared the dinner for three to which they were entitled from the communal kitchen of the apartment house. It cost 65 kopeks (32 cents) a head and consisted usually of cabbage soup and mince meat balls or pike, that heavy and unappetizing member of the shark family, which seems to have been the only fish to survive the revolution. We never tasted butter, but the two boys, who were classed as industrial workers, got a monthly allowance of a kilo of margarine. Twice a month Vera received the family's meat ration. She would then telephone to her friends, tell them the joyful news, and invite them to come and eat it with us. She would make delicious Siberian meat dumplings in soup; and for one evening we would eat to repletion. She never thought of making the meat last several days; she had the old exile's feeling that one shared all good things with one's comrades, and like most Russians she was generous and had no disposition ever to save anything.

There would be vodka and sweet Crimean wine, boiled sweets, and tea to follow, and we would sit round the table for hours talking and singing songs. For a while I had a glimpse of the kind of people and the atmosphere of the old revolutionary days. These men and women, Communists but not high functionaries, all of them formerly exiles and not yet corrupted by the privileged position the revolution had given them, were the salt of the Party. They were simply people, hearty and jolly, and full of faith. Times were hard, but this was only a temporary phase; mistakes were perhaps being made, but they would be rectified and socialism would soon be created. How could it not be so since "The Revolution" had been victorious? In contrast to the Communists of higher rank, they were comradely in their personal relations and were not acquisitive.

For all her revolutionary past, Vera was very house proud, orderly and feminine. Her little flat was as clean as a pin, she hung lace curtains at the windows, she looked pained if a single object were out of place, she dressed neatly, took great pains to arrange her flaming red hair becomingly, loved nice clothes although she had none, and told lies about her age. These lies were very naïve. If she had been only as old as she said, she would have been a prisoner in Siberia and mother of a child at the age of fourteen.

She was the soul of hospitality, emotional and tender, always full of vitality, good-tempered and sensitive to human suffering. Later I was to meet the type of Communist who would roughly turn a starving child from the door and warn me that one must on no account give anything to these little beggars since they were probably the children of Kulaks. But Vera would always give a piece of bread or sugar to the destitute, although she knew that as a "good Bolshevik" she ought not to.

Besides Vera, Shura, Grischa, and myself there was usually at least one other visitor in our tiny rooms. Siberian friends passing through Moscow, or temporarily homeless in Moscow, came to sleep on the floor or in one of the boy's camp beds. The boys then slept on the floor.

We ate in the kitchen, which was also the bathroom. Getting a bath was a matter of luck, since one never knew at what hour and on what days the water would be heated for the hundreds of flats in the building.

Vera and the boys spoke only Russian. Since I knew only a few words, we communicated at first largely by signs. I made more rapid progress in the language than at any later period and learned to make one word do the work of many. For instance, I can remember once wanting to convey to Shura the idea that I could see he was depressed. So I said to him "bad weather here" pointing to his head and heart. And he understood me and gave me the word *nastrayenia* for "mood."

Vera's greatest friend, Nina, was often with us, a woman of peasant origin, also a Party member but hard put to it to support her two little girls living with their grandmother in the village. Her husband had deserted her years before, and she received no alimony. Nina knew a few words of English to help out our conversation, and I got very friendly with her and later visited her village with her. Very plain in appearance and dressed almost like a man, she was gay and kind, full of enthusiasm and vitality, and particularly interested in the communist movement abroad.

Our life in the flat was jolly and friendly and had for me a little of the adventure and that precious atmosphere of comradeship which was so rapidly fading elsewhere. Evenings at the flat kept my spirits up, but my days were dreary. I wished I had stayed in England until Arcadi arrived from the East, wished even that I had first sailed with my brother across the Atlantic as he had begged me to do. Since my association with Russia began, I had continually been hurrying off somewhere and then been forced to wait weeks and months with nothing to do. It had been so in 1928, and now it was so again. I had rushed away from England without even waiting to arrange publication of the book I had written for the School of Economics; I had refused the joy of sailing at least as far as Spain with Temple; and here I was pacing the streets of Moscow with nothing to do. Early in November I spent a few days in Leningrad where Dementiev, a friend of Arcadi's just arrived from Japan, was working. From there I wrote to my mother: "Yesterday we went just outside the town to look at the sea—such a cold gray sea and such a flat shore—but the sea nonetheless. I wished I were with Temple on the Atlantic; after all I could have gone with him instead of waiting here so long."

Nothing is more depressing than autumn in Moscow. It rains and rains; the streets are half flooded, for the gutters don't work properly; it is cold; and there is only occasional heating of the houses. One is expected to keep the windows shut all the time and preserve the warmth for three days until the house management puts the heating on for another twelve hours.

As I walked the streets the sadness of the atmosphere, the drab, sad-faced crowds, the miserable peasants selling a few rotten apples or gherkins at the street corners, the homeless children, wet and hungry, depressed my spirits. I spent a good deal of time going to offices inquiring about the flat which had been promised to us, and for which we had already paid £100 in *valuta* and far more in rubles, seeing about the Russian translation of my *Lancashire and the Far East,* getting translation and other work, seeing English comrades working at the Comintern, the Marx Engels Institute, and the Lenin School. But already the world of these English comrades seemed far from mine. Most of them lived in the Lux Hotel and had no worries about food or shelter. They knew nothing of the life of the ordinary Russians, and spent their time discussing theory, organization, and foreign affairs, or gossiping about each other within their own closed-off world. Already I felt a barrier between them and myself, a barrier caused by the constant need to put a half-hitch on one's tongue, as they say in Devonshire. For them, all was for the best in the best of all possible worlds, the U.S.S.R. To doubt it even when the evidence was all to the contrary was heresy. The only man at the Lenin School who dared to express some doubt to me was a Yorkshire miner whom I had known in England. There he had been unemployed but had lived in a three-roomed house with his wife and one child. In Moscow no employed worker dreamed of owning more than two rooms, and felt himself very lucky if he had one.

I had other friends, Russians whom I had known in London at Arcos and at the Russian Trade Representation, now occupying high positions in Moscow. The old friendliness persisted, but I thought they must feel that I was no longer the naïve enthusiast of two years before. I even felt a certain embarrassment on their part at the difference between the idealized picture of the U.S.S.R. they had painted for me in London and the stark reality of the Soviet *Byt* ("way of life"). My conversation was guarded, but probably I failed to display the required enthusiasm when they held forth about the sacrifices "we are making" for the industrialization of the Soviet Union. They were not fools, nor was I; and they must have known that already I perceived that these high Party functionaries were getting the best of everything and that all the sacrificing was being done by the dumb crowds, the dragooned peasants and the helpless workers. The very first week I had discovered that my old friends the Plavniks had supplies of good food when they invited me to dinner. Plavnik and his wife were old Socialists, had spent a large part of their lives in exile in Germany, and were essentially Europeans with a civilized outlook and standard of personal behavior and honor. They were therefore ashamed of receiving more and better food than the workers. But others were not ashamed at all.

In fact, a year or so later one heard wives boasting of the "distributor" they enjoyed since this showed the high rank of their husbands. I learned first then, in 1930, of the existence of these "closed distributors" for high Party officials where foodstuffs and clothing were sold which were unobtainable at all elsewhere, or only to be purchased on the "free market" at exorbitant prices. Later, in 1931, other closed distributors were opened for other grades in the social hierarchy: for second-class Party functionaries and non-Party specialists and for the workers in heavy industry. There came to be, roughly speaking, the following grades: First the "Kremlovsky" people: Commissars, chairmen of big trusts, members of the Central Committee of the Soviets and of the Party—all the leading Party members. Next the O.G.P.U. shops which served food almost as good and as plentiful as the shops for the Kremlovsky people. Then, Gort A, for high officials—all Party men—and for a very few specially favored scientists and engineers. Next, Gort B, for the "middle class"—i.e., Party men of lower rank and highly qualified non-Party specialists. In addition there were the well-stocked shops for the Red army officers. There were also the various closed distributors for the factories producing capital goods. These varied greatly from place to place. In some the workers could obtain the official ration of butter and milk and meat; in others none of these "luxuries" were ever on sale. But the Kremlovsky shops, Gort A, and the Foreigners Store, Insnab, were always supplied with butter and meat whoever else went short. My husband eventually received a book for the Gort B shop, receiving a kilo of meat and a kilo of butter a month; but this was not until more than a year after his arrival. His rations from Gort B were about the same as Vera later received in her "Political Hard Labor Shop." The kind of joke that went about Moscow in those days was the one about Vera's shop where there was said to have been jam on sale one day, but a notice over it read: "For sale only to regicides." As my husband once remarked, the Party people and the other ex-revolutionaries were now drawing their dividends on their investment in the revolution years before.

Gradations of social rank in those days went according to one's food ration as in the ancient Byzantine Empire where the salaries of imperial officials and generals were reckoned in measures of corn, wine, and oil.

In those early months of my life in Moscow it was only the tip-top people who were favored by special food supplies. This device of Stalin's, which ran directly counter to Lenin's institution of the Party maximum, and Marx's injunction that the official was to be paid no more than a worker, was designed to keep Party men loyal to him personally. Any deviation from the Party line involved expulsion from the Party and the loss of these precious food supplies. It meant as well the loss of many other privileges awarded in kind not in money: use of an automobile, the pick of the housing accommodation, special hospitals, and an excellent medical service reserved for the new aristocracy alone, and so forth. The closed distributors also enabled the government to reserve for the aristocracy the scarcest goods of all, such as fruits, fresh vegetables, cocoa, chocolate, as well as butter, eggs, and milk. It enabled the Soviet Government to tell the world that C. P. members never received salaries higher than the Party maximum of 300 rubles (later 350), while actually their salaries were worth ten or twenty times as much as those of the non-Party specialists, who in theory were supposed to be getting more, and than those of the workers, who in theory were supposed to be paid about the same as the Party functionaries.

I soon came up against the snobbishness of the Party members. Old friends from London who had known my husband there as well as myself would try to ask me to parties without him. Or if he were invited and went he was made to feel a social inferior. Although I had been very poor in England, I had never in my life before felt a social inferior, and although I myself was treated as an equal because I was a member of the British Communist party, I was infuriated at the attitude taken up toward my husband, who, as I knew, did work of far greater value than most of the Party functionaries and took far less than they did from the "Socialist" state for doing it.

Before Arcadi arrived, Mrs. Khinchuk, wife of the Soviet Trade Representative in Berlin, whom my friend Jane Tabrisky and I had known in London, asked her one day how I, a Party member, had come to marry beneath me. Not that she was a Party member herself, but any Soviet woman not too unattractive or of too bad social origins endeavored to secure herself a Party man for a husband. Just as a "bourgeois" woman in capitalist society is expected to marry into her class and not into the working class, so in Soviet Russia one was *déclassé* if one married outside the Party. One was debarred from entry to the "best society" if one were not oneself a member of the Party or married to a member.

Mrs. Khinchuk was the perfect example of the Soviet snob and hypocrite, but she was only one of many. She did no work, she shopped and visited in an automobile which she did not "own," but which was at her disposal day and night. And she loved to hold forth about the sacrifices "we" are making. Jane Tabrisky, who was staying at the Khinchuk's flat while awaiting the room promised her by the Marx Engels Institute, got so disgusted that she often came to Vera's in order to get away from the society of the privileged. Khinchuk himself was decent and hardworking, but as I had already perceived in Japan, it was the wives of the Bolsheviks who led the way in the degeneration of the Party and showed so obviously the characteristics of the *nouveau riche* society then coming into being.

Jane, who had been a member of the British Communist party since she was sixteen, who had been secretary of the London University Labour party when I was chairman, who had also been in the same Communist party local with me in North London, had arrived in November to take the job at the Marx Engels Institute which I had had to refuse. Her arrival in Moscow was my greatest joy in those days of waiting. She was an old and real friend to whom I could speak freely, and in Moscow this was a blessing above all others. We learned rapidly. Collectivization of agriculture, and the Five Year Plan in Four Years, were no longer matters of abstract theory to be discussed *ad infinitum* in Party meetings in the comfortable bourgeois world. They had become realities of our existence and of the existence of those around us. They meant, as we could not help seeing, starvation for many and near starvation for the majority; and they meant the formation of a privileged aristocracy as cut off from the masses of the people by the conditions of their lives as any noble of the *ancien régime* in France. Our lives were spent mainly with ordinary "middle class" Russians and what was going on could never again be for us just a remote social experiment. It was a terrible and moving reality involving untold suffering for millions of human beings of flesh and blood like ourselves. We could not regard them as rabbits in a laboratory, as did the "Friends of the Soviet Union" abroad.

Nor were we long in Moscow without sensing the terror then in full operation against the non-Party intellectuals. This terror was not nearly so all-pervading and inclusive as the terror of a few years later. Party members still felt themselves comparatively safe; they were not likely to hear the fatal knock at the door in the night which meant that the O.G.P.U. had come to claim a victim. But I heard of some of the victims from an old non-Party friend of my husband's whom I will call E, since he may still be alive. Every "specialist," however loyal and long his service had been, feared arrest, for the government was attempting to lay the blame for the food shortage brought about by its agrarian policy upon the wretched non-Party engineers, agronomists, technicians and administrators, scientists and professors. A scapegoat must be found for the masses, so that they would not blame the Bolsheviks for the shortage of food and clothing and houses to live in, for the universal misery and disorganization of life. They must be made to believe that "wreckers" were responsible, and lay the blame for their ever-increasing misery upon agents of the "foreign bourgeoisie" and Tsarist elements inimical to the proletariat and to the construction of socialism. Hence the continual arrests of the non-Party "specialists," a term which included not only engineers, professors, and scientists, but all the educated: accountants, technicians, teachers, doctors, and those with administrative experience, or experience in trade and finance. Stalin, whose pathological hatred for the educated was as yet restricted in its operation to those outside the Party, was doing his best to "liquidate the intellectuals as a class." This senseless terror, which struck down or demoralized the men essential to any successful industrialization of the country, was perhaps as fundamental a cause for the failure of the Five Year Plan to raise the standard of life of the Russian people, as the forced collectivization of agriculture.

I remember the case of an old man called Kipman, which illustrates both the cruelty and stupidity of the O.G.P.U. He was arrested that winter of 1930-31 on his return with his wife from London, where he had worked for several years at the Soviet Trade Representation, and was accused of having embezzled £10,000. My friends who knew him were certain that he was absolutely honest, and it was moreover obvious that if he had taken the money, he and his wife, who were both over sixty years old, would have stayed in London and lived on it for the rest of their lives. However, he "confessed" to the crime and was sent to a Siberian prison for five years. His wife, in spite of her age and failing health, struggled valiantly for years to get him out of prison. She appealed, she made representations, she

There had developed a "new and higher form of economy" under the Soviets whereby the peasants produced milk for the townspeople in exchange for bread to produce that milk. Whereby also hundreds of thousands of peasants near the towns of Russia spent at least half a day traveling to and from the towns and standing in the market or at street corners selling milk or a few miserable vegetables. To arrange that one of their number should do the selling while the others worked on the land was forbidden; the seller would have been punished as a middleman, a speculator. Stalin had found a novel way to banish unemployment by forcing each peasant with milk or other produce to sell to spent the greater part of the day selling it.

Shortly before my husband's arrival from the East, I had managed to rent a room in a new flat on Novinsky Boulevard. The owner of the flat, once a sailor on the famous ship *Potemkin,* whose crew had mutinied in 1905, was working at the Soviet Consulate in London. His two daughters let me a room at the "commercial price"—i.e., I paid for the one room more than they paid for the whole flat. This was usual in Moscow at the time, although the subletting of rooms and country houses by the Party members had not yet become the source of *rentier* income it later became. Subletting was also done by non-Party people; but, since it was the Party members who secured most of the new flats, they were predominantly the landlord class.

Jania, the elder daughter, was a nice girl. Very unpolitical, she was typical of the daughters of the new aristocracy. She dressed well, she enjoyed life, and she had a job. The job, however, did not provide her with half her income. She not only let a room, but she sold at commercial prices the very large ration of eggs, butter, and other "luxuries" which it was her father's privilege to receive as a member of the Moscow Soviet. The fact that he was working abroad and had Jania's stepmother with him in London, did not mean that his ration was cut off. Jania drew five kilos of butter and a large number of eggs every ten days. Sold at commercial prices (about five times as high as the price she paid) these supplies produced an income equal to more than half her monthly salary as a clerk in an office.

The flat was always full of young men in the evenings, and when I once remarked to her how popular she was, she replied seriously, "Oh, no, it isn't that; they just all want to marry me because we have a flat."

Jania was a decent sort and honest. She made no pretense of admiring or believing in Soviet policies and eventually married beneath her. She was then already in love with a young engineering student who was not a Comsomol and could never be a member of the Party, since his father was a highly qualified engineer. Years later I met Jania for the last time before leaving Russia. She was working in the Intourist office in Moscow where I bought my ticket to England. Very pale, very thin, all the gaiety and youth gone from her face, she was dying of consumption and knew it. Because she had married outside her class, her father no longer had anything to do with her; and she and her husband and child all lived in one room. She had, of course, no hope of getting to a sanatorium, since neither she nor her husband were members of the Party.

This flat, on Novinsky Boulevard, was one of an ultra-modern block completed in 1930. It was built on supporting pillars like a lake-dwelling, and a broad covered way ran along the front of each story. One side of the house was all glass, and no doubt it would have been very healthy and hygienic and comfortable if there had been sufficient heating, or if only one family had inhabited it. But to house several families, as most Russian flats do, it was most inconveniently built. There was a large room below, the second room consisted of a kind of balcony above, and only the third room had both a door and a ceiling, and so some privacy. At first I slept in the hall-like room below, overlooked by Jania's sister above and unable to go to bed or to work when the latter entertained her boy friends. When Arcadi arrived, I persuaded Jania to let us have the enclosed room with the door. The floors were of stone and we had no carpet. The only furniture we had was a single bed I had brought from England, a small table I had managed to buy, and three hard chairs. We kept our clothes in our trunks and our books and toilet articles on the window ledge. Nevertheless, our conditions of life in Novinsky Boulevard were the best we were to know for many a year. There was a bathroom with a hot-water heater, and there was a gas stove in the kitchen. Also, this being a house occupied by important officials, there was a communal kitchen where one could buy much better dinners than at Vera's.

Unhappily, Jania's father returned to Moscow in the summer of 1931 and we had to move. I was at that time in England arranging the publication of my first book, *Lancashire and the Far East,* which, originally accepted for publication by the School of Economics, had been turned down by Sir William Beveridge, the Director of the School, after my departure from England. C. M. Lloyd, Director of the Social Science Department, had written to me that it could only be published by the School if I would modify my chapters on India. Rather than abate by a jot my indictment of British imperialism, I had gone to England to arrange publication myself, with the assistance of C. M. Lloyd.

When I returned to Moscow in September, 1931, Arcadi had moved into a very small furnished room near the Sukharevsky Market. For this room and a share of the kitchen and bathroom, we paid 100 rubles out of Arcadi's salary of 300 and mine of 275, although the monthly rent for the whole three-roomed flat paid by our landlord was only 45 rubles. The room was cheap as rooms went; many people had to pay more for a room. It was a "co-operative" flat. This meant the landlord had acquired it by paying monthly into a co-operative building society for several years. When he finally secured his flat, he, like most other owners of flats, let out one of his three rooms and so secured a return on the capital he had invested for years past. Being non-Party, he had had to wait years and pay several thousand rubles before getting his flat. Party men, if not already in possession of a decent apartment built before the Revolution, and taken possession of during its early years, often secured a new flat without payment, or by only a year or so of membership payments to the Co-operative. In any case, the Party men always had priority in the allocation of flats, and so could secure the precious capital which a flat represented without previous investment or by only a small investment. All owners charged a super-profit on renting rooms, but whereas the Party member charged anything the market would bear, which often meant 200 rubles, the non-Party man was more afraid of doing this, for he might be accused of "speculating."

It was here in our room on Trubnaya Ulitsa, near the Sukharevsky Market, that I first witnessed the terrible exploitation of servants. Jania had done the work of the flat herself, and so did I. But our landlord and landlady here had a "domestic worker." She was, like nearly all Moscow servants, a peasant girl. She worked from 7 A.M. until 11 or 12 P.M., cleaning, cooking, washing, and standing in line at the shops. The latter occupation was the most strenuous part of her labors and the most painful. For to stand in line in the cold Russian winter when you have neither proper footwear nor a really warm coat is agony. This girl had neither. Nor did she eat the good meat meals she prepared. She lived on soup, black bread, and cereals, with an occasional bit of herring. At night she slept on the floor of the kitchen. The *Kazaika* ("house mistress") cowed her, bullied her, and drove her. The girl was often in tears and always sad and miserable. When we asked her why she did not leave, she said she would be treated just the same anywhere else, and she couldn't go to work in a factory since she had no room to live in.

In other flats all through my stay in Moscow I found the same conditions for servants. In some of the old apartment houses one found as many as five or six families living, all sharing one kitchen. (One young Russian whom I had formerly known at the London School of Economics, and who lived in one room with his wife and child, shared a toilet and kitchen with 35 other people in the flat.) Several of the families would have a servant, and it was not uncommon for three or four servants to sleep together in the kitchen side by side on the floor or on the kitchen table. Bugs ran over them at night, and the atmosphere was so fetid and foul that one hesitated to go in and boil water at night for tea or to wash.

The employers of these girls were often little better off than they. A family of four to a room, feeding poorly themselves, would employ a servant mainly in order to have someone to stand in line at the shops for food. Even the limited rations obtainable on the food cards could not be obtained without a long wait; and this, together with foraging around for unrationed food occasionally obtainable in the shops, was almost a full-time occupation.

The waste of labor entailed in the "socialist fatherland" by the hopelessly inefficient distribution system, and by the shortage of food and clothing, was such as to make it easy to believe that there could be no unemployment problem. If husband and wife both worked at a large enterprise and there were no children, a maid could be dispensed with since both could eat a dinner in the *stolovaya* of the factory or office. But if there were children, food must be procured for them somehow. Party men of high standing kept maids to spare their wives labor, but the great majority of the families who employed "domestic workers" did so in spite of their poverty, or because of their poverty. Enough food for the children could be bought only if both parents worked; but someone must do the shopping. Hence the servants.

The terrible exploitation of domestic labor was in part due to the poverty of the employers, and in part to the exodus of peasant girls from the hunger-stricken villages. To be allowed to live in the towns and get some sort of a meal every day was to be incomparably better off than in the village, even if they had to work sixteen hours out of the twenty-four. Work in the factories (even if obtainable without close probing into why they had left the village and as to whether their parents were "Kulaks") could not secure them a shelter. So they went to work as servants.

Servants were consequently easy to get and, being entirely unprotected by law or custom, could be exploited mercilessly. There was no alternative for them except starvation, and they were practically slaves. On the other hand, they naturally had no moral sense. Their village world had been destroyed, they or their neighbors had been expropriated and robbed by the state, and their religion vilified and reviled. To be religious was tantamount to being counter-revolutionary. So they stole whatever they could lay their hands on, and all Russian housewives locked up every bit of food and kept a strict watch upon their scanty wardrobes.

It was typical of the relation between mistress and maid in the U.S.S.R. that the German Communists who wanted their servants to sit and eat together with them found the servants took this as a proof of their meanness. "The *Kazaika*," they said, "is so afraid of our eating too much that she forces us to sit with her at table to keep an eye on how much food we consume."

Servants were still treated like serfs by the Russians even when their conditions of life allowed of their giving some elementary comforts to their dependents. Party men who secured large flats very rarely gave their domestic workers a room of their own to sleep in. Even a family with four or five rooms at its disposal made the servant sleep in the kitchen, or at best in a kind of open cupboard constructed in the modern flats over the front door especially for servants to sleep in.

For me the servant problem was at first insoluble. I could not drive people to work, and, being what the Russians called a "petty bourgeois idealist," I felt it was indecent to lock up our bread, sugar, and butter in a cupboard, and periodically to search through the domestic worker's basket or suitcase for stolen goods. So after a couple of months during which a large part of my precious foreign clothing was stolen and our food supplies mysteriously disappeared, I went back to doing the work myself. The difficulty was that we could never be sure whether the servant or the landlady had stolen the stuff. Each accused the other. I thought it was quite likely to have been the landlady, but, since she was already eager to turn us out of our room and we had nowhere to go, I could do nothing.

We were paying "only" 100 rubles for our room, and by this time it was becoming easy to let rooms for 150 or 200, so we were no longer welcome. Arcadi was making only the 300 Party maximum, but had no Party privileges; I also was now earning 300, having become a "textile specialist" at Promexport. Out of this sum we had to support Arcadi's divorced wife and his son, so there was little left to feed ourselves after 100 rubles for rent. As yet we neither of us had a "closed distributor" but we had first category food cards like industrial workers. So we got two pounds of bread each a day, half of which we exchanged for milk from the peasants on the street corner. We also got enough sugar and a kilo of meat a month each. Everything else had to be bought on the free market at high prices. The only solution was extra work. Editing and translation work was easy to come by, but Arcadi worked late at the office every evening, and I couldn't do Russian translations without him. Luckily, I got an advance of 2500 rubles for the Russian translation of *Lancashire and the Far East,* but we paid 1600 rubles of this into the Housing Co-operative I had joined in 1928.

In October we had managed to buy *putofkas* in a Rest House at Gagri in the Caucasus. Here in the Land of the Golden Fleece, where Jason found Medea, we enjoyed our first restful time together since Japan. Gagri is one of the loveliest places in the world and by its blue sea with the Caucasian mountains rising behind us we could almost forget the pushing crowded petty life of Moscow. Here there were few signs of the construction of "socialism." There were the ruins of a castle of Mithradates whom Great Pompey conquered and who had fled from the Roman legions to die in the Armenian mountains to the south. Here also was a small Byzantine church of the fifth century which had withstood the ravages of all the many races which had passed to and fro along this land bridge between Europe and Asia.

It was a hungry holiday but a very happy one. We used to supplement the meager food supplied by the Rest Home by eating large quantities of walnuts, the only reasonably cheap food obtainable in the few shops of the small town. Occasionally we bought grapes but they were very expensive. The sea was still warm enough to swim in and the mountain walks were very beautiful and gave us a feeling of release.

Back in Moscow securing a flat was again our main preoccupation. Since Arcadi's hopes of getting the one long since promised, and long since paid for, were fading, we began to concentrate on one in my name instead. Since I was a Party member, I had a better chance of securing one. Unfortunately, however, I had joined the Railway Worker's Housing Co-operative up in Grusynski Val near the Alexandrovsky Station, and railway workers at that time were not a favored category. I had joined it originally in 1928, through M.O.P.R. (International Class War Prisoners Aid) with which it was affiliated. The apartment house this co-operative was building progressed very slowly on account of lack of materials, labor, and money. I had a friend on the board of the co-operative, a certain Polish Party member called Lofsky, whom I had made friends with when a delegate to Russia in 1927, and who had since been off on secret Comintern work in South America. He advised me to present the Chairman of the Co-operative with an English woolen cardigan and promised to keep an eye open in my interest. The art of securing the flat to which one's payments entitled one consisted in haunting the premises of the co-operative at the time when a certain number of flats were being completed and about to be allocated. If around and about at the time, one might get one. Otherwise, one was always left out, whatever one's rights or one's membership stage, unless one were a high Party official.

Unfortunately, Arcadi was always working so hard at the office that he couldn't hang around his co-operative and kept on being missed out. My own hopes faded when Lofsky was again sent abroad. I never got my flat through all the succeeding years, nor was I able, when at last Arcadi got his, to secure the repayment of the 4500 rubles I had paid up years before.

Every letter I wrote to my mother in 1930, 1931, and 1932 refers to the flat problem—the hope for it in the spring, then in the autumn, then for the following spring. At first I believed the promises; but by November 1932 I was writing that I had given up having any confidence in promises.

The first lesson the Soviet citizen has to learn is that promises and contracts mean nothing at all. The government cheats its citizens all the time in big things and little, and every official behaves in the same way. Only the foolish foreigners think that the letter of the law, or the written contract, or the spoken promise have any meaning.

There stands out in my memories of life in the winter of 1931-32 a picture of the snowy street outside our apartment house along which I went to work. Some construction work was going on near by, and every morning I saw carts full of bricks or wooden planks drawn by thin, miserable horses. Often the carts got stuck in the ruts in the thick snow, and the drivers dressed in rags of sacking whipped the horses mercilessly. The breath of the struggling horses and men was a thick steam in the cold air. I used to hurry along trying not to see the sores on the horses nor to hear their panting. Horses and men were alike starved, and the sufferings of the animals were only one degree worse than those of the wrecks of human beings who drove them. It was said that on the collective farms the peasants deliberately drove the horses to death so that they might get meat to eat. An inhuman system made men treat their beasts as cruelly as the government treated them, and with as little thought of preserving life. Cold, snow, misery, and want were the background of one's life in Russia.

At the beginning of 1932 I had my first intimate experience of the free medical service and the hospitals which foreign visitors to the U.S.S.R. describe in such glowing terms.

I was pregnant, and was foolish enough, on New Year's Eve, to carry home ten kilos of potatoes which I had miraculously secured. The tram, as usual, was chock full and in the scuffle to get through it and out at the front I got my glasses knocked off. In my efforts to retrieve them, I got rather badly knocked about. I reached home exhausted and trembling but did not know I had injured myself. That evening we went over to a New Year's Eve party at Jane's. By midnight I was feeling rather ill, so we stayed the night in Jane's large room with her and Michael, another old friend, who had come out from England early in 1931.

Next morning, alone with Michael after Jane had gone to work, I had the miscarriage. Michael could not get Arcadi by phone, for there was only one line at his office and it was out of order. So he fetched Jane home and went off in a droshki for Arcadi. Arcadi tried for two hours to get a doctor and finally came with one he had secured "commercially." (The doctor to whose services my trade-union membership entitled me arrived about six hours later and was obviously not a doctor at all but a bedraggled, dirty, haggard young woman whom I would not have allowed to touch me. Her only use to me was to sign a certificate for my office that I was ill.)

By this time the pain had lessened and the real doctor said if it did not get worse again I need only lie still. If the pain returned, I must go to the nearest "abortion house" and be scraped.

Next day at noon I was in agony. Michael, having telephoned to Arcadi, sat beside me trying to soothe me until Arcadi managed at last to secure a taxi to move me to the hospital. There he had to leave me. I was strapped down upon an operating table and scraped by a "surgeon" who did not even wash her hands before operating, and whose whole painted appearance suggested a prostitute rather than a doctor. I was given no chloroform and the pain was excruciating. Then I was taken upstairs to a small room about twelve by twelve feet, with five beds in it. I was given an ice pack and left. No one came near me, no one washed me; there was no nurse or attendant of any kind. The other patients next day begged me for the loan of the piece of soap I had brought with me; I was the only one of the five patients who had any and none was provided.

At about eleven o'clock the following morning, after a breakfast of thin gruel, I was ordered to get up and come downstairs. I protested that I was bleeding and should not walk. No one paid any attention. Downstairs I was again put on the operating table, held down by four attendants, and scraped again. I yelled, "Why twice?" But no one paid any attention. After this I broke down and found myself weeping. I had been suffering for forty-eight hours, the pain was agonizing, the place was filthy, and I felt I was in a nightmare. When I asked for something to wipe away the blood, the "nurse" picked a dirty piece of wool off the floor and handed it to me.

I determined to get out of this terrible "hospital" before I caught some awful disease, and sent a note to Arcadi telling him he must get me out somehow. At first they wouldn't allow me to go, but after he had told them I was an English journalist, they got frightened. A doctor speaking French came up to see me. It then came out that the first "doctor" had forgotten to write down on my case sheet that I had already been operated upon; hence the second ordeal.

Jane offered to nurse me, and I got back to her room that evening. I remember very vividly the joy of being back with her and Michael and Arcadi in her clean room after that terrible hospital. For a week I lay there in bed, Arcadi coming in the evenings for the dinner which Jane cooked for us all. Poor Arcadi never got away from the office for dinner till eight or nine in the evening, and afterwards still had to get home by tram. He looked far more ill and exhausted than I did, and my experience had upset him very badly.

It was as well I did not have that baby, although I was very disappointed at the time. We did not secure a room of our own until 1933, and what we should have done with a baby on our constant removals from room to room I do not know.

The companionship of Jane and Michael that winter of 1931-32 lightened our hearts. Arcadi did not easily make friends or give his confidence to anyone, but Michael and he liked each other immensely. Michael, like Arcadi, had had an unhappy childhood, and like him had learned at an early age to hide his feelings from a hostile world, and to take refuge in humor for the hurts which his sensitiveness would otherwise have found intolerable. Where I would boil with rage and indignation at the divergence between Soviet professions and Soviet practice, Michael and Arcadi would make a joke of it. Whereas

I hated Stalin as the brutal and callous oppressor, Michael and Arcadi saw him not as the bloodthirsty despot, but as an historic phenomenon. If there had been no Stalin, there would have been someone else like him. I had leanings toward Trotskyism and was at that stage convinced that if he had led the Bolshevik party instead of Stalin there would have been no famine, and no perversion of the revolutionary movement. They assured me that Trotskyism was sheer romanticism, and that the course which history was taking in the U.S.S.R. followed logically from Lenin's foundations. Since this was so, it had to be accepted as socialism; and one could only hope, and work, to make it a little more tolerable. Life might be a tragedy to those who felt, but one must keep sane by seeing it as a comedy.

Michael had gone into the army in the World War at the age of sixteen and nearly died afterwards of consumption. He had something of my brother's cheerful skepticism and good humor, and like Arcadi had no great hopes that the world was at all likely to be run rationally and intelligently or justly. To Michael Marxism was a tool not a dogma; an aid to the understanding of history, past and present, not a revelation. What was happening in Russia must be accepted as the consequence of the socialization of the means of production and distribution by a minority in a backward country. Here was no society of the free and equal, nor was it likely to become so; but it was no use getting indignant because the new society was so very different from what men had hoped for.

His view of the U.S.S.R. was very close to that expressed years later by Max Eastman in *Stalin's Socialism*. Since this was the society which had come out of the socialization of land and capital it *was* socialism. The fact that it bore no resemblance to the society which socialists had envisioned and that there was even greater social and material inequality than under capitalism did not prove that it was not socialism. Michael and Arcadi were extraordinarily impersonal in their judgments. They saw men as moved by forces they themselves could not understand, and the ills of the Soviet world as due more to the stupidity of its rulers than to their malignancy or wickedness. I could not for a long time accept their view that under Lenin or Trotsky it would have been essentially the same. But because they taught me not to view Stalin as a personal devil but rather to see him as the result of Russia's past history and of the Bolshevik Revolution, not as a cause in himself but as a result, I have similarly understood that Hitler is no personal devil, but the product of historical circumstances.

Friendship is a very precious thing in an uncertain, savage, and strange world, where everyone's hand is against his neighbor, and fear and the struggle for bare subsistence drive even decent men and women to spy upon one another and denounce one another. Life is endurable only if one has at least one human being to whom one can speak one's mind freely and without fear. To come home, close the door, and shut out the world in which life is one continual pretense, a perpetual licking of the hand which smites. A little freedom of expression, honesty of thought and speech, are as necessary as air. Without them one would suffocate in the foul Moscow air. The glaring contradictions between theory and practice, between what was supposed to be and what was, and the constant effort to say and look the opposite of what one thought, were by no means the least strain in Soviet life. One understood why so many men sought escape in drink, why the vodka shops were never empty, and why men lay drunk in the snow by the roadside.

Such conditions draw one ever closer to the few people one loves and trusts. Like primitive man sheltering with his mate in a cave against the violence of the elements and the fear of wild beasts, so in Soviet Russia one shelters with one's family in one's room or corner from the storm of terror, hate, regimented sadism, hunger, cold, and wretchedness and the nauseating cant and hypocrisy of Soviet life.

Arcadi is lost to me, but to this day Jane in England and Michael in America remain friends with whom the ties forged in that period of disillusionment and horror are stronger than the ties of friendship with anyone else in my life.

We three were together most evenings, and this saved me from what would otherwise have been intolerable loneliness and long hours of brooding. For Arcadi was working literally twelve or thirteen hours a day. He came back late at night so tired out after a day at the office practically without food, that my one care and interest was to feed him and get him to bed. Breakfast was the only meal at which we had much chance to talk. He often worked even on his free day.

When I had returned in September 1931, after my three months in England arranging publication of *Lancashire and the Far East,* I had found him so thin and pale and worn out I was frightened. It was almost as if he wished to kill himself with work. On the other hand, conditions of work for the non-Party men were such that most of his time and energy were wasted. Whatever he did to improve efficiency would be undone by someone else; and he, like the other specialists, was in constant danger of being arrested as the scapegoat for the mistakes of his Party supervisors.

Toward the end of the year we received a visit from C. M. Lloyd, head of the Social Science Department of the London School of Economics, who had directed my research there. He was also Foreign Editor of the *New Statesman*. Lloyd was a friend, and discreet; and I talked to him freely. Arcadi denied the truth of what I said, or modified it. He convinced, or almost convinced, Lloyd that a socialist society *was* being created in the U.S.S.R. The privileges of the Party members, the suffering of the people, would pass, were not important, or were inevitable. Since Arcadi cared very little whether or not he shared those privileges, he dismissed them as unimportant; whereas I was convinced they were the basis for all the corruption and distortion of the socialist idea. Lloyd went home and wrote a series of articles in the *New Statesman* which, although cautious in their optimism, showed his confidence in the Soviet system.

After Lloyd had gone Arcadi and I had our first, and I think our last, real quarrel. For weeks we were estranged. Arcadi, in fighting me, as he later acknowledged, was fighting his own doubts. He almost hated me for a while. I was miserable, but I could not recant. I still saw the English papers and the trickle of information there about the ghastly conditions in the timber prison camps, and about the famine in the Ukraine, was confirmed not only by rumors in the capital, but by the sight of the starving peasants. Our friend G, who was working on timber export and often went to Archangel, described the merciless driving of the prisoners hewing the timber in the Far North. (See Chapter IX.)

The food position in Moscow that winter of 1931-32 was far worse than the winter before. By this time Arcadi had Gort B and I had Insnab, which meant we were infinitely better off than most people. Many of our acquaintances were half starving and were grateful for the gift of a pound of cereal from my rations.

My visits to the textile districts in the course of my work had shown me the condition of the working class which was supposed to be the ruler of the country. At Ivanovo Vosnysensk I had seen wretched men and women striving to "fulfill the plan" on a diet of black bread and mush. In the textile factory *stolovayas* the dinner consisted of millet with a little sunflower-seed oil. There was no herring even to be had in the shops. True that a meat dish of sorts could be had for 2 *Rs.* 50 in a restaurant, but the average monthly wage was only 70 or 80 rubles.

I was receiving two kilos of butter, six kilos of meat, and thirty eggs a month, besides cheese, flour, millet, buckwheat, semolina, and even one pound of rice—most precious cereal in Russia. I could buy milk if I arrived at the Insnab store at the right time, and quite often I could obtain sour cream (*smetana*) and sour milk. Arcadi's ration was a good deal smaller, but compared to that of the workers, and that of the office clerks, we were rich. We could also buy cigarettes and soap, which had become almost as great a luxury as butter.

Arcadi finally broke down when he went on a *Komanderofka* to Odessa in April 1932. He came back white and miserable and shaken. Down there he had seen the starving and the dead in the streets. At each railway station en route there had been hundreds and hundreds of starving wretches, emaciated women with dying babies at their milkless breasts, children with the swollen stomachs of the starving, all begging, begging for bread. In station waiting rooms he had seen hundreds of peasant families herded together waiting transportation to the concentration camps. Children dying of starvation and typhus, scarecrows of men and women pushed and kicked by the O.G.P.U. guards. It sickened even those who were hardened to the sight of suffering in the Far East.

Arcadi had relatives in Odessa. From them he heard the facts of the Ukrainian famine. The picture he painted for me, a picture which had seared him to the soul and shattered the optimistic view he had until then insisted upon preserving, bore out all the rumors we had heard—was in fact worse. What perhaps shocked Arcadi most of all was to find that the train guards, conductors, and attendants were all speculators. They were buying food in Moscow, always better provided for than other cities, and selling it at fantastic prices down in the stricken southern land.

Starving children are the most pitiful sight on earth. There were enough of them in Moscow to make one's heart ache, but in the Ukraine they were legion.

Bodies of the starving lay in the streets, and pitiful wrecks of humanity, with great watery blisters and boils on their feet, legs, and arms, dragged themselves from place to place till they died in the vain quest for work and food.

In the summer of 1932 we went on a holiday to the Crimea, taking with us my mother, who had just come from England. We left Moscow well provided with food for the long journey. But by the end of the first day my mother had given it all away to the starving wretches at the country stations. With tears streaming down her face she called my attention to one wretched beggar after another, especially to the pitiful children. That journey was an ordeal I shall never forget. It was a sea of misery which the few bits of food we had could do nothing to assuage.

Totia dai Kleb, Totia dai Kleb ("Auntie, give bread"), will always ring in my ears as the national song of "socialist" Russia.

As in China, so in Russia, one hardened oneself to the sight of suffering in order to live. But at least in China the government does not hold it a crime to give aid to the starving. In Russia it tells you that the starving are Kulaks or counter-revolutionaries not to be aided, whereas in reality they are bewildered, ignorant, powerless wretches sacrificed to the insensate ambitions and fanaticism of a man and a party.

It was the contrasts which were always so appalling. The fat officials in the dining car, the well-fed callous O.G.P.U. guards, and the starving people. We and they, we and they, rulers and ruled, oppressors and oppressed.

In the Rest Home in the Crimea, where we had got places, there was abundant food. So abundant that bread and fruit, ices and cake were thrown away when left on the plates of the guest, or when too much had been provided. This place belonged to the Central Committee of the Soviets of the Crimean Republic, and we were there by the grace of Berkinghof, whom we had known in London and who was a prominent Bolshevik who belonged to this part of Russia. It was so very "upper class" that we really had no business there, but it gave us an insight into the life of the Party aristocracy. The sight and sound of the starving was shut out from these former palaces and country houses of the Russian nobility, now as in the past. Only now there was a new aristocracy. That seemed to be the main difference.

This new aristocracy and its hangers-on were even more grasping, cruel, and ruthless than the old aristocracy which had lived in conditions of less general want and misery. The bureaucracy and their employees felt themselves like those in a shipwreck who have managed to get into the few lifeboats not smashed to pieces. If one helped the drowning wretches in the sea into the boats, all would drown; so the lucky ones beat back the masses of the unfortunate with their oars. The few who did not starve in the U.S.S.R. thus aided the government in repressing the masses who did, and denounced as counter-revolutionaries starving wretches who had once followed the Bolsheviks as their leaders, believing the latter would establish a just social order and a prosperous economy.

There was, of course, a convenient theory to justify the terrible social and material gulf between the rulers and the ruled. The rulers were "indispensable" as the "builders of socialism." They were so important that they must always be well fed and enjoy comfortable holidays in luxurious sanatoria and rest homes, else they would be unable to bear the great burden of their responsibilities. The wretches dying of starvation and the ill-fed workers and peasants were just cannon fodder in the battle for socialism; if there were not enough food to go around, the officers of the socialist army must have enough even if everyone else went short. In the future everyone would have plenty if the rulers were ruthless enough now to see millions die in the cause of industrialization.

This theory did not explain why the survival and comfort of the wives and children and mistresses of the Party bureaucracy were also essential to the Revolution, but I suppose it could be argued that the peace of mind of the rulers must also be preserved.

Thus have aristocracies in all historical periods justified their privileges. The Soviet aristocracy was no exception.

Life in the U.S.S.R. might be uncomfortable and saddening, tragic and repulsive; but it educated one politically as no other experience could have done. Michael, Jane, and I felt this even when the process of being educated was most painful. We learned to recognize reality under appearances and were cured of political illusions; or at least cured of the propensity to fall for slogans, facile panaceas, and hypocritical pretenses. Ever since I lived in Russia it has been almost impossible for me to accept professions and declared aims at their face value anywhere. Perhaps I have gone too far to the other extreme, being now inclined to think that those who profess least virtue are likely to have most. In any case I am, I believe, forever cured of the Western intellectual's preoccupation with forms and labels.

Life in the U.S.S.R. also made one realize that some absolute standards of behavior are essential to mankind if we are not to return to the life of the brute. Voltaire's saying that if God did not exist, He would have to be invented, needs restating in new terms. Even if one does not believe in God one must have a moral code, must accept certain social values as absolutes, and allow some freedom to the individual conscience. How can a just and humane social order be created if we root out our own humanity in the process of destroying the old society? After long years of bitter experience I have come to accept Bertrand Russell's social philosophy. I have learned that absolute power will corrupt any minority, that more evil is caused by fanatics than by wicked men, that no movement or individual can be certain enough of the effect their actions will have to subordinate means entirely to ends, and that democracy for all its inefficiency is likely to secure more justice than any despot, however benevolent he may be or may profess himself to be.

The coalescing of political and economic power which is taking place everywhere and has reached its consummation in the totalitarian states, confronts mankind with new problems in urgent need of solution. A new set of principles and a new morality are needed to secure order, social unity, liberty, and the rational use of the vast productive forces science and technology have created. Yet instead of seeking for a way to combine order and control with individual liberty, most of our "progressive" intellectuals of recent years have taken refuge under the mantle of Stalin's cruel despotism. Their critical faculties have become atrophied together with their liberalism; and, while barricading the front door against Brown National Socialism, they have opened wide the back door to the Red variety.

Whether or not we can ever deepen and widen our democracy to control economic as well as political power, and thus cope with the problem of an over-ripe capitalism without destroying the liberties to which capitalism gave birth, is perhaps doubtful. But there would be a little more hope of our doing so if our one-time liberals had not been lured along the totalitarian path by the blood-red light of Stalin's "socialism."

One also learned in the U.S.S.R. how slight are the differences between men, between the "good" and the "bad." I remember one evening how Michael said to Jane and me: "Can't you realize now that you and I, all of us, everyone we know, is capable of deeds at which we now shudder?" What seems to differentiate men most is their greater or lesser degree of courage—in particular the moral courage to face the fact that they have been mistaken in their beliefs. This was particularly obvious in Russia where the decent and humane and altruistic types of Communist too often recoiled before the realization that they had wasted their lives, sacrificed their personal happiness, and endured prison and exile to accomplish the opposite of what they desired. Rather than face up to so terrible a realization they buried their heads in the sand and drowned their doubts in work or even in excessive cruelty to others.

But even men of high courage and integrity can be broken by an inhuman system. Men who can face hunger and prison and even torture for themselves cannot endure starvation for their children. That breaks the hardiest spirit and enslaves the boldest. The workman who goes on strike can endure to see his children starve if there is some hope of victory. But few men can face the prospect of their wives and children being thrown out into the snow to die of starvation and cold, when they know there is no hope of winning out against the state which is employer, policeman, and judge.

Often in Russia I used to remember the words which Euripides put into the mouth of Andromache when, after the fall of Troy, they take her little son away to be killed: "Oh, ye have found an anguish to outstrip all tortures of the East, ye gentle Greeks." The Soviet state had found a better method of breaking human beings than the crude physical tortures inflicted by the Nazis on their victims. It had learned that the surest way to break resistance to tyranny was by getting at men through their wives and children. How can the Russian worker strike when he knows that not only will he be imprisoned but that his family will be thrown into the street immediately, and his wife refused employment? How can the intellectual refuse to write or speak the lies demanded of him, when the O.G.P.U. tells him that if he will not his wife will also be imprisoned and his children left to become homeless waifs? Only the peasants, too brutish and too tough, still sometimes defy the Soviet Government by passive resistance.

The Soviet Government had also learned that, whereas some men can face torture and death and even the reprisals inflicted on those they love, provided their sacrifice will inspire others to revolt, few men can bear to die behind closed doors without the opportunity to testify to the world what they are dying for. When Christian martyrs faced the lions in the arena, or when in the religious wars Protestants were burned at the stake, they could face death knowing that they had lighted a torch which others would carry on; they could endure tortures because they were convinced the sacrifice would not be in vain. But would they have endured to the end unflinchingly if they had been shot without trial in some dark cellar, knowing that they would be accused, not only of crimes they had never committed, but at having aimed at the overthrow of what they were trying to save?

An open counter-revolution in Russia might have left Communists and Socialists believing in their cause and prepared to start the struggle for social justice and liberty over again. But Stalin's counter-revolution had been a long, secret, and disguised process. Men were not expected to repudiate the old aims; they were instead expected to mouth the old slogans and to testify to their belief in the old faith while the meaning of the old slogans, theories, and words had been completely changed. The result necessarily was a mental, moral, and political confusion in which men could no longer see the road clear before them. Even when most revolted by the cruelty of the Party and its perversion of the Revolution, there remained a doubt as to whether there was any alternative to Stalin's "socialism." Those who were convinced that the gravest mistakes had been made were unsure how they could ever now be remedied.

Deprived of faith and of hope, the Russians sank into apathy and skepticism, or made up their minds to do the best they could for themselves in this new anarchic, cruel world in which pity was a crime and fraud and hypocrisy the qualities needed for survival. The struggle for bare existence absorbed the minds and energies of the masses, while the struggle for position and affluence absorbed those who were fortunate enough to belong to the Party.

The best way, in fact the only way, to preserve your integrity and your life if you were an intellectual in Soviet Russia was to give up all expectation or desire for advancement and honor, and never to talk about anything but trivialities even to your closest friends. There were men of education who took jobs selling newspapers and books or cigarettes at street kiosks, happy to have found a niche where they were likely to be let alone; where no one would envy them or suspect them and they could call their souls their own. Specialists known to have high qualifications could not thus hide themselves. The state insisted upon their working in factories, mines, and offices, on the railways and communications. Here they were always in danger of being made into scapegoats, but if they could secure a Party patron likely to be "permanent" (the Soviet expression for a Party bureaucrat so well connected as to be unlikely to fall from favor), and work loyally and unselfishly for him, letting him take the credit for their cleverness and hard work, they could hope to survive. It was rather like the old Roman system of senators and clients. The word "protection" was openly used in the U.S.S.R. "So and so," it would be said, "has a powerful 'protection'; he's likely to be all right." If a non-Party man could marry his daughter to a high Party official he felt very secure, but this was difficult unless she were particularly attractive, for Party men naturally wished to ally themselves to those who could be of use to them, not to non-Party specialists. Of course, in the holocaust of Party members from 1936 to 1938, the protection of the highest often came to mean disaster to his clients. When a powerful man was purged, a whole row of small skittles was knocked down with him. It was a storm in which the highest trees as well as the lowest were struck by the lightning, and no one felt safe.

Sometimes I am asked about the Soviet educational system; questioned as whether at least a great deal has not been done for the children. And I remember the homeless kids who slept in the loft above our flat in Ordinka and begged for crusts and hot water. I remember the pale children of the textile workers at Ivanovo-Vosnysensk, living crowded together in the tenements without beds to sleep upon. I remember the charwoman at Promexport who lived in a corridor with her two young children and considered that a soup made of bones was a great luxury. I remember the babies at the *Consultazia* for mothers, where in 1934 I took my son each week to be weighed. The mothers could get free medical advice, but they could not afford milk, and had to feed their babies on black bread soaked in water. They took a photograph there one day of my son to exhibit because he was almost the only baby who did not have rickets.

And I remember the children in the queues at the prison where I went with food after my husband's arrest. There was a boy there one morning with a sack of food for his mother, who could not have been more than nine or ten years old. When I showed my ignorance of the procedure he asked me with astonishment: "Is this the first time you have been here?" There are brave children in Russia inured to "eating bitterness," as the Chinese say; children sometimes left alone in an empty room when their parents are both arrested, and who sell up all the small possessions of the family to take food to their parents. If there is no relative to shelter them and neither parent comes home, they join the hordes of homeless children and learn to beg, to thieve, and to live like little wild animals in the savage world. That is one kind of Soviet education.

Of all the cruel acts of Stalin the most horrible is the provision for the liquidation of the older homeless children. In 1935, when by decree the death penalty for theft was made applicable to children from the age of twelve, the police were given the power to rid Soviet society of the unwanted children of the unfortunate.

If your mother and father are docile, careful never to breathe a word of criticism of the government, and work hard, you can get a different sort of education. You can learn how wonderful socialism is, how many tons of iron and steel the Soviets can produce, and how many more they hope to produce; and how terrible is the life of the working class in the capitalist world. You will be taught to sing patriotic songs and do military exercises and to worship the great Stalin. You may even get the chance later to study to be an engineer or a pilot, or be trained for some other profession if your social origins are all right and if you have carefully conformed throughout your school life.

If you are the son or daughter of a prominent Party member, the way will be made smooth for you all along, as it is made smooth for the children of the rich under capitalism. You will go to a select school with airy classrooms and the best teachers. At home you will have a room of your own to study in and plenty of books instead of trying, like the children of the workers, to do your homework in a small room occupied by your father and mother, brothers and sisters. You will sleep in a good bed, not on the floor or in the same bed as your brother and sister, you will eat the best food and have long holidays in the country instead of feeding on black bread, cabbage soup, and gherkins and spending the hot summer in the city. You will have servants to wait upon you instead of having to stand in line yourself at the shops when you come home from school.

Equality of opportunity in the Soviet Union is a myth. There are different schools for the masses and for the aristocracy, and in any case there can be no equality in educational opportunity where some children are undernourished and housed little better than pigs, while others live in comparative luxury.

CHAPTER IV

LIFE IN MOSCOW 1932-36

My search for some useful function to perform in Soviet society had caused me to change my job almost as frequently as we had changed rooms. My first work, that of a "referent" in the Anglo-American section of the Comintern, had been utterly futile and nauseating. True that part of my job was to read and mark the newspapers, and this at least kept me in touch with foreign affairs. But for the rest, I spent my time participating in futile post mortems on the work of the British and American Communist parties, and in assisting to draw up memoranda and "directives" which were supposed to tell the English comrades what they ought to do. The "directives" were drawn up mainly with an eye to self-insurance, so that whatever happened the blame would not be placed on us; and for the rest consisted mainly of a lot of Party platitudes and abstract principles. Consequently, these "directives" were worse than useless as guidance to the British party and were probably never read. Instructions as to the "party line" at any given moment came from much higher sources, and they were all the foreign parties had to pay keen attention to.

Fed up with the futility of my work, and fearing also that if I remained in so-called political work, I should soon be discovered to be a heretic, I took advantage of an offer to work as a "specialist" on textiles upon my return to the U.S.S.R. after a visit to England in the spring and summer of 1931.

After six months work at Promexport (see Chapter IX) I had accepted an offer to work at the newly created Commissariat of Light Industry. In the summer of 1932 I was invited to work at the Institute of World Economy and Politics at the Communist Academy. Here at last I found more satisfying work, and I remained there until I left the U.S.S.R.

All through 1932 our struggles to secure our flat, or at the least a room of our own, had continued. For some weeks in the spring we lived at the New Moscow Hotel, our room paid for by Lecterserio, the export organization of which Arcadi had been made vice-chairman. This room cost 25 rubles a day, which we could not, of course, have paid ourselves. The manner in which it was secured for us revealed to me something of the corruption now rife in Soviet life. Being without a room of any kind, Arcadi was living with Jane and Michael in Jane's room at the Marx Engels Institute, while the Anikeevs were kindly putting me up. Anikeeva (see Chapter I) was a dear, and never became a Soviet snob. In spite of her husband's high position, they both remained our friends. However, this situation was impossible. So Arcadi and I more or less camped down in the office of the man at Narcomveshtorg who was supposed to secure rooms for employees of this Commissariat. We spent a whole day there, from 10 A.M. to 7 P.M., refusing to budge until something was done for us. By now we understood a little of the Soviet way of life and only a kind of sit-down strike of this kind was likely to secure to Arcadi his rights. For Narcomveshtorg had promised him a room many weeks before if he would take the chairmanship of Lecterserio, and in so doing give up the room he would have received from Promexport in February. The Party member in charge of rooms had over and over again promised Arcadi this room or that, only to give it to someone else. Arcadi had been absorbed in his work and was always passed over. Now we were determined to force the Commissariat to honor its contract.

Finally, in the late afternoon, Comrade X got on the phone to the manager of the New Moscow Hotel. A long conversation ensued. The manager of the hotel wanted a *quid pro quo*. He had been trying to get a Gort A book for one of his assistants not really entitled to it. If Comrade X would secure this for him, he would let us have a room at the hotel. But Comrade X only had a limited number of Gort A books to give away, and he wanted them for his own cronies. Getting a room for a non-Party man was a small return for the Gort A book, since a non-Party man had no patronage with which to pay for a room to live in. Arcadi went off to Rabinovitch, ex-chief of Arcos in London, now almost a Vice-Commissar. Rabinovitch phoned Comrade X and told him to come up and talk to him. Finally we were saved. Reluctantly, Comrade X agreed to give the precious Gort A book to the Intourist manager's assistant in return for a room for our humble selves. Triumphantly, we presented ourselves at the New Moscow Hotel.

Food was now our greatest problem. I had Insnab and Arcadi had Gort B, but how could we *cook*? In the hotel dining room a dinner cost about 20-25 rubles, and was accordingly out of the question. However, Arcadi had brought a little electric saucepan and an electric kettle from Berlin in 1928, and with these I managed to make meals of a sort. Disposal of the rubbish was the greatest problem, since cooking in our room was forbidden. We solved this problem by carrying out potato peelings and other refuse in neat brown paper parcels which we disposed of in the street dustbins on the way to work.

We were better off than many other people in the hotel. A few doors away lived Soermus, the well-known Finnish violinist who had played in the streets in England to collect money for the miners in 1926. His wife, an Irishwoman, had nothing to cook on except an electric iron. Ingeniously, she turned this upside down, put a saucepan on it full of vegetables and meat, and left it to cook all day.

Once or twice a month we treated ourselves to a real dinner in the hotel dining room, and very occasionally a friend or acquaintance from England out on a trip to Russia would give us some of his Intourist meal tickets entitling us to a free breakfast, lunch, or dinner.

The manager of the restaurant, a Caucasian, spoke perfect English and said he had been the headwaiter at the Ritz in London. I discovered this through a casual reference to horse racing as the "opium of the people" in England. This man remembered the name of every Derby winner for goodness knows how many years, and he was so delighted to find someone who at least knew what horse racing meant, that he treated me to real coffee several times.

Coffee—even now, years afterwards, I remember the delight with which one drank coffee in Moscow. Rarest of luxuries, greatest of joys. Whenever anyone one knew came out to Russia, one asked them to bring coffee, coffee above all else, and secondly, toilet paper.

Even in this Intourist Hotel toilet paper was unknown for a long time. Then one afternoon, returning from work, the floor manageress took me by the arm, marched me triumphantly into our douche room and toilet, and, pointing towards a few sheets of thin gray paper, exclaimed, "Look—Kultur!" However, this concrete evidence of Soviet "Kultur" was a fleeting phenomenon. The gesture made, the supply soon gave out.

In this hotel I also got an inkling of the luxurious lives lived by the O.G.P.U. officers who occupied many of the rooms in the hotel. Enormous meals were sent up to the next room to ours, and the sounds of drinking and song and laughter came through the wall late at night, when our O.G.P.U. neighbor entertained his friends. The diners in the restaurant were either foreigners or O.G.P.U. officers, with a very occasional couple of ordinary citizens blowing a quarter or half a month's salary on a "bust."

I wrote to my mother in February 1932:

> I leave the office usually at about 4:45 or 5 o'clock, and rush up to the Insnab shop to buy bread, etc., and milk if there is any—which is very seldom now. I get home about seven o'clock and have some kind of a meal. Then I try to do some work—translation or editing. Or Jane and Michael come around and we talk or play cut-throat bridge. Then Arcadi comes home much later and I make tea for him and something to eat. You can have no conception how complicated life is and how much time one wastes over simple things like buying bread.... I am sorry if I sound depressed, dear,—I am not unhappy only I have never before in my life had work to do which was rather dull, and did not have to exercise my faculties to the full and felt that I was making no progress of any kind.... I suppose that most of all I miss the very full political life I had in England: speaking, writing, and so forth. I feel I am rusticating and losing all my mental faculties.

Our semiluxurious existence in the New Moscow Hotel came to an end late in April. May Day was approaching, and we were told that all Russians (except, of course, the O.G.P.U.) must clear out to make way for the *valuta*-paying foreigners.

Again we were homeless. This time we both went over to Jane's room. For a few days we lived four together. Eventually we secured, temporarily, the use of two rooms on Ostojenka Street in the flat of Gavrilov, an old Party member, whom we had known in England and who was again working abroad. For the first time since we came to Moscow we had *two* rooms in a modern flat. I at once brought my mother out of England. I could not send her any money, owing to the impossibility of exchanging rubles into foreign currency, and her own income was very small indeed. So the only solution was to have her out to live with us for a time. Her coming was in any case a great pleasure. At sixty-two she was still young, and the novelty of life in Russia pleased her. She loved the Russians, who are, in fact, a kindly people when not driven to be brutal by the government and economic difficulties. Our Russian friends, for their part, thought Mother a wonderful woman, for her vitality, youthful appearance, and zest for living were unknown among old people in Russia.

I got a servant, a nice clean German girl from the Volga. Her village had been devastated—no other word can convey one's meaning—by the liquidation of the "Kulaks." In the German Volga Republic the peasants, who had been settled there two hundred years before to set an example to the Russians, had been better farmers and so enjoyed a higher standard of life than most peasants in Russia. Consequently, the greater part of them were classified as "Kulaks" and liquidated. What had been a region of model farming became almost a desert, for more than half the population was exiled or sent to concentration camps. The young people left the villages if they could, the boys to go to the factories if they could get jobs, or to become vagabonds if they couldn't. The girls came to the towns to work as servants, and were highly prized, since they were more competent, cleaner, more honest and self-respecting than the Russian peasants. Curiously, they were the most purely Teutonic Germans I had ever seen; Germans like the pictures in Hans Andersen fairy tales: blue-eyed, with long golden plaits and lovely, fair skins. Being Protestants, and regarding the Russians around them as little better than barbarians, they had intermarried little and retained a racial purity which would no doubt have delighted Hitler.

An echo of the tragic fate of Russia's German population reached the world when the "Mennonites" flocked to Moscow and sought permission to leave the country. Some of these Germans had tried to obey the government and had formed collective farms, only to have them liquidated as Kulak collectives. Being first-class farmers, they had committed the crime of making even a Kolkhoz productive and prosperous. Others had been quite simply expropriated from their individual holdings. All were in despair. Few were allowed to leave Russia. They were sent to Siberia to die, or herded into the concentration camps. The crime of being good farmers was an unforgivable one, and they must suffer for this sin.

My Hilda seemed a treasure. She could cook, she could read and write, she kept herself and the rooms clean and looked like a pink and flaxen doll. I could treat her as an equal without finding this led to her stealing my clothes and doing no work.

The servant problem in the U.S.S.R. for me and Jane consisted in our inability to bully and curse and drive, which was the only treatment the Russian servant understood. It was quite natural that this should be so, since Soviet society, like Tsarist society but to a far higher degree, was based on force and cheating. Cheat or be cheated, bully or be bullied, was the law of life. Only the Germans, with their strong religious and moral sense—the individual morality of the Protestant as opposed to the mass subservience demanded by the Orthodox Church and the Soviet Government—retained their culture and even some courage under Stalin's Terror. I used to be amazed at the outspoken way in which Hilda and Sophie (another German girl who worked for Jane) voiced their hatred and contempt of the Soviet Government. Sophie, one of thirteen children of a *bedniak* (poor peasant) would shake her fist and say: "Kulaks! The Kulaks are up there in the Kremlin, not in the village." The word "Kulak" originally signifying an exploiter and usurer, her meaning was quite plain.

After a few months of civilized existence on Ostojenka Street, the Gavrilovs returned, and we were once more homeless. I sent my mother back to England with Jane, who was about to leave for a holiday. Michael had left the U.S.S.R. for good a short while before. Arcadi and I once again got a room at the New Moscow Hotel. This time we had Hilda also in the room with us, and Hilda had to manage the secret cooking on the electric stove.

There was a young American called Clark Foreman living in the New Moscow Hotel who, years before, had been a friend of Jane's when they were both students at the London School of Economics. He was in the U.S.S.R. studying the social services for the Julius Rosenwald Foundation. Thanks largely to Jane and myself and to a Russian friend of ours I will call M, he was one of the very few foreign visitors to learn something of the realities of Soviet life. A cheerful and intelligent young man with progressive views and few prejudices, he did not take the socialist tragedy as seriously as we did, but neither did he fail to see it. His American lightheartedness relieved the atmosphere in which we lived, and through him we were brought into somewhat unwilling contact with other foreigners. We met Bernal, the Cambridge scientist who was to become an ardent Stalinist, and others like him in whose presence we had the greatest difficulty in keeping our mouths shut. Clark was very loyal to us all, both at this time and later.

Occasionally we went to those parties of the foreign colony in Moscow which Malcolm Muggeridge has described with such biting irony in his *Winter in Moscow*. At these parties one found foreigners trying to recreate the London and New York Left Bohemian atmosphere of hard drinking and easy loving. But it was no longer youthful and harmless; it had been poisoned and become rather loathsome against the starvation and misery of the Russian background, and by the cant and hypocrisy of the Communists and the fellow travelers. Moscow's Bohemia was not that of struggling writers, journalists, poets, artists, and students, but consisted of the fortunate, the doctrinaire, and hard-boiled foreign Communists and those foreigners of various kinds working in Moscow because they were failures at home, and enjoyed favors as foreigners which their own merits could never have secured to them. They dined and wined on the produce bought at Insnab, while most Russians were starving. Michael professed to find it all a huge joke, but he did not relish this society any more than Jane and I. Arcadi was far too busy for such parties, and anyhow had no liking for drink or salacious stories and songs.

An English newspaperman who in his youthful revolutionary days had been a member of the I.W.W., now a debauched, fat little man, would lead in the singing of songs which might sometimes be funny but were usually just nasty. He was known to be a homosexualist, and was later expelled from the Soviet Union for corrupting young men. His immorality was, however, more honest than that of many who, under the guise of being Marxists, had come to the Soviet Union in order to find a society without restraints. In this they were mistaken, for Russian society was not for the most part sexually licentious except perhaps in its upper ranks. Most Russians were far too busy struggling to live at all, to have time or energy to imitate the vices of Western "progressives," and marriage was usually a serious partnership, not a light liaison.

I remember leaving a party at the Foxes * in the early hours of a spring morning with Jane and Michael, and Temple's friend Rab, who had come out to visit us. They walked home with me up Kropotkin Street. Outside one of the stores a long queue of weary men and women had already formed waiting for it to open at 9 A.M. These people were waiting to receive a small ration of food, but we had left a party where caviar, hors d'oeuvres, ham, wine, vodka, chocolates, and fruit had been consumed in abundance, and where as we left they had been singing revolutionary songs in drunken voices. They may of course have been forgetting their carefully hidden disillusionment in this way.

Clark studied it all with admirable objectivity. When he went back to the United States and later became an important New Deal official in Washington, he was never tempted to join the Communist fellow travelers. He had stanch views concerning the need for a planned society, but no illusions concerning the Soviet Union or the foreign Communists.

All this time, in spite of our housing difficulties, our standard of life was far above that of the majority of workers and employees. We did not rank with the aristocracy, but we were upper middle class. I

---

* Ralph Fox, later killed in Spain; then Jane's chief at the Marx Engels Institute, and his wife, Madge Palmer.

myself, with my Insnab food book, could in fact be counted as an aristocrat insofar as food was concerned. But, although our conditions were far better than a year or two before, life for most people, that winter of 1931-33, was more miserable than ever before. The scanty meat and butter rations which the industrial workers were supposed to be able to buy were usually unobtainable. Most if them subsisted on black bread, millet, and buckwheat.

That winter "commercial shops" began to be in evidence in Moscow—i.e., state shops where meat, butter, eggs, vegetables, and clothing could be bought by anyone at prices ten times or more higher than those paid for the rations available for the privileged. Butter, which cost us *Rs*.3.50 a kilo could be bought in the commercial shops for 40 rubles; meat for 10 rubles a kilo against the ration price of 2 rubles; sugar at 15 rubles a kilo instead of the 1 ruble we paid. Gradually the commercial prices were lowered to nearer five times the ration prices as a preliminary step to the derationing of food and clothing in 1935.

These "commercial shops" benefited the "middle classes" most, those specialists and employees who had no closed distributor, but whose salaries of 400-600 rubles enabled them to buy some food at commercial prices. They also benefited the small and select group of writers, dramatists, actors, and musicians, some of whom earned very large sums of money and could now buy as much as they needed of all essential foods. Previously they had bought on the restricted free market direct from the peasants, at prices higher than those in the new "commercial shops." Those who, like ourselves, could earn extra money by translation work or writing, could enjoy more food than allowed on our ration books. Money again came to have some value, and men often took on two jobs to earn enough to buy at the new shops.

There was a story told that winter of a Russian who returned from several years' work abroad and went around seeing his friends. Each in turn told him of his difficulties. One had a salary of 600 rubles, but since he got only bread and sugar on his food card and had to buy everything else at commercial prices, life was very difficult. Another with a salary of 500 had the same tale to tell: only bread and sugar on the food card, and everything else to be bought at commercial prices. "We hardly ever taste meat, and butter is our greatest luxury." After questioning many people and always receiving the same answer, he met a girl who used to be his secretary.

"And how are you?" he said. "You must be finding life very hard."

"Oh, no," she replied, "I'm doing fine. My salary is only 120 rubles, but that provides me with a food card and so with bread and sugar; for the rest I undress at commercial prices."

Incidentally, this story illustrates a fact ignored by the tourist, who believed what he was told about the disappearance of prostitution in the U.S.S.R. It had only disappeared in the sense that every prostitute needed some kind of a job to ensure possession of a food card; the job need not be the main source of income.

There was also a joke in those days about giving to Mikoyan, the Commissar of Internal Trade, the task of liquidating prostitution. "Why Mikoyan?" "Well, because everything else he controls disappears!"

Even the commercial shops were not supplied with abundant quantities of essential foods. Queues formed there to secure milk, butter, eggs, and meat, even at the fantastically high prices at which they were sold.

The other new shops which now opened up in one district after another were the Torgsin shops. Here one could buy better and more abundant supplies than anywhere else except in the Kremlovsky distributors—if one had gold or foreign currency. Prices for food at Torgsin were not much higher than world prices, and less than double prewar Russian prices. Everyone who had the tiniest bit of gold—a ring, a bracelet, or jewels—could exchange them for Torgsin tokens and secure food. The only snag was that the O.G.P.U. was also on the lookout for possessors of gold, and might at any moment arrest you and force you by torture to disgorge any hidden wealth you had for nothing. So people went in fear and trepidation to Torgsin, driven by hunger but fearful of the O.G.P.U. Torgsin was, in fact, an outstanding example of the mixed system of terror and reward by which the government was by now seeking to increase its revenues.

The greatest source of revenue of the Torgsin shops was remittances from abroad. Jews, in particular, often had relatives abroad—in Poland, in Germany, and above all in the United States—who would send them a few dollars a month to save them from starvation. The percentage of Jewish people standing in the Torgsin queues—there were queues even at these shops since there were never enough shop assistants—was very high. Anti-Semitism, although officially condemned, took a new lease on life when the Russians saw their Jewish neighbors in the apartment kitchens cooking good food which they never had a chance to buy. A few years later, in the great purge, countless Jewish families suffered for their past enjoyment of a little food bought with money sent from abroad. By 1936 it was held a crime to have relatives abroad; the Torgsin shops had been closed down, and many Jews were arrested and sent to concentration camps for the "crime" of having corresponded with relatives abroad. But from 1932-1935, the Soviet state was anxious to secure *valuta* at any cost and Torgsin served to produce a large *valuta* revenue.

There was a story told in those years of two Jewish women friends who met after many years. One asked the other, a widow, how she was managing to live. "Oh, I'm all right," she said. "My son provides for me."

"Oh," said the other, "is that your eldest son Boris, whom I remember as a lad?"

"No, not Boris; he's an engineer in Sverdlovsk earning 500 rubles, and since he has a wife and child he can't, of course, spare me a kopek."

"Is it your son Ivan, then?"

"No, Ivan is chief accountant at an Export organization, and of course he can't allow me anything out of his salary of 400 rubles."

"How, then, do you live?"

"I'm all right because my youngest son, Grischa, is unemployed in America!"

It was in fact the case that even two or three dollars a month could ward off starvation; could enable the recipient to buy a little flour and fat at prices one-fifteenth or one-tenth below the prices paid for the same foods in Russian currency.

Life that winter of 1932-33 became almost as hard for the majority of the people as in the famine year of 1920. As the Plans became more and more grandiose, and as the plaudits for the "gigantic successes of Soviet industrialization" of the tourists and Communist parties swelled into a paean of praise, so did the conditions of life for workers, peasants, and employees become more and more terrible. One came to dread reading in the newspapers of great "successes" or of the "approach of socialism" because such announcements almost always heralded some new measure of oppression, some new sacrifice.

A little Italian Communist from Trieste, who worked with Michael at the State Publishing Office, one day graphically expressed what we all felt. At 11 or 12 o'clock one had a glass of "tea" at the office, and a piece of bread and cheese if one could afford it. (Dinner in Russia is eaten in the late afternoon.) One morning the "tea" was not even faintly yellow; it was just plain water. Michael looked at it in disgust, and the Italian grinned.

When I first came to the U.S.S.R., he said, we were served with real tea with lemon and sugar in a glass on a saucer with a spoon. A year or so later there was no more lemon. The following year they started to give us *Ersatz* tea made of dried carrots. Next there was no more sugar. Then there were no more spoons. Now, apparently they have run short of the *Ersatz* tea. But, Michael, cheer up, it's still hot. We haven't got socialism yet!

Since the worker could not be induced to welcome Stalin's brand of "socialism"; since the peasant fled his village and the worker migrated from village to town in the search for a job with sufficient food, or a room to live in, the state began to exercise a greater and greater degree of compulsion. Early in 1933 the passport system was introduced to rivet the worker to the factory and to force the peasants back to the desolate countryside. There was also the Work Certificate, a sort of criminal dossier of each worker and employee, wherein was written down his social origins, any fines he had paid, any "crimes" he had committed, and the reasons for his dismissal or for his leaving the factory. If he could not show good cause for having lost his job, he was not to be allowed work elsewhere. The workers were now reduced to the same serfdom as the peasantry.

The introduction of the passport system caused terrible suffering. One of the objects of the system was to clear out of the towns all the unemployed and those whose "social origins" rendered them unfit to enjoy the privilege of living in Moscow and Leningrad, where the food position was a little better than elsewhere. Among the unemployed were the hundreds of thousands of peasants who had come to the large towns from the starving villages in hope of work.

Passportization brought governmental repression close home to us. Both Jane and I had Volga German girls working for us, and it was specially decreed that all the German peasants should return home. My Hilda had no parents and Jane's Sophie was one of thirteen children of a poor peasant. We both moved heaven and earth to keep them from the death by starvation which they assured us awaited them at home. In Hilda's case the decree was particularly brutal since the spring floods had cut off her village from the nearest railway station forty miles away. Hilda wept and wept, and each day we tried to get her a permit to stay in Moscow. I spent hours at the Militia station, and hours at the Public Prosecutor's, pleading, begging that at least she be allowed to stay with me until the spring floods subsided. All ordinary avenues of appeal proved useless.

Hilda's aunt worked for Max Hoelz, the famous German Spartacist leader. One morning we went to him to ask his help. Although I did not then know it, Max Hoelz was already bitterly disillusioned with the U.S.S.R. and early that year he tried to return to Germany, after he had perceived that the Comintern had deliberately sacrificed the German Communists in the hope of an understanding with Hitler. He was then murdered by the O.G.P.U. That morning, in his room at the Metropole Hotel, I talked to him at some length. He told me he was quite helpless; that he had no influence at all, having tried in other cases. A tall, handsome man, a former hero of the German working class, he sat disconsolate, sad and suffering at the universal misery, not attempting even to pretend that there was any justification for the cruelty of the Soviet Government.

Finally, I went to a friend of ours, a certain Z, who had been and probably still was, in the O.G.P.U. He was a decent little man, very fond of a good joke and relishing my husband's wit. Completely cynical, a *bon vivant,* a beautiful singer and a strong drinker, he was also kindhearted and he had heaps of friends. He gave me a note to a friend of his, a high Militia official. At last I had secured the right patronage. Hilda was saved.

The sad end to the story of Hilda is that she was demoralized by fear and idleness. During the month I had struggled to save her life, she had done no work; she had wept and stood in queues and wept again. Slowly she degenerated in the atmosphere of the New Moscow Hotel, and I am afraid eventually became "one of those of whom we know there are none," as E. M. Delafield describes the prostitute she saw in the Metropole Hotel in Moscow.

Jane left Moscow for good early in 1933 and I took over her Sophie, for whom she had finally also won the passport battle. Sophie was a treasure; but I lost her, too. She went home to her village a year later for a holiday, and being cleaner, better dressed, and generally far more "cultured" than the peasant girls, succeeded in marrying the catch of the village, the tractor driver Party member. Presumably by now having joined the village squirearchy, Sophie has forgotten her former hatred of the Soviet Government.

We also had an anxious time securing a passport for Arcadi's former wife and her son. She had a job by this time, but her social origins were exceedingly bad. Her father had been a merchant and her brother was an engineer with the General Electric Company in New York, where Arcadi had met and married her. Partly out of fear that his son would be sent away from Moscow, and partly because they had no room of their own but were sharing one with relatives, Arcadi and I gave them one of the two rooms which we at last secured in February

1933. Her passport was secured as Arcadi's dependent living under his roof.

The position of ex-wives and mistresses under Soviet law as interpreted by the courts was very peculiar, for although it was expressly stated that bigamy was illegal, it was also forbidden to a man to turn out of his apartment or to refuse to support any woman by whom he had had a child, whether the child had been born to married people or was born to a man who already had a wife. A case referred to by N. V. Krilenko when Commissar of Justice, in an article written in the *Bolshevik* in September 1936, illustrates the position. He wrote:

> We shall give below several examples showing the influence of the old social order on Soviet family relationships, and the revolutionary effect of Soviet law as it protects the family and teaches those who still follow the old customs.
>
> Here is the case of Citizen and Citizeness Gentschke, who dismissed their servant Lebedeva and ordered her to leave their flat. Lebedeva had worked for Gentschke as a servant from 1927 to 1929. In 1929 Lebedeva ceased to be a servant and became a housewife—in other words, she ceased to receive payment for her work, for Citizen Gentschke started to have sexual intercourse with her. In the year 1935 the Gentschkes terminated the labor contract with Lebedeva and told her to clear out. Lebedeva appealed to the Court and said she was not a servant but in fact the wife of Gentschke. In her passport, which had been obtained for her by Gentschke, she was shown as his dependent, and this is why she had a right to live in his flat. Lebedeva, an illiterate young woman, proved that she had been violated by Gentschke and had lived with him from 1929 to 1935. The higher court to which the case was eventually transferred, did not recognize her as Gentschke's wife because Soviet law only recognizes a marriage if a common life together has been declared, differing only from a registered marriage by the fact that no registration has been made. If the Court had recognized Lebedeva as a legal wife it would have meant recognizing a double marriage, which is not permissible in our law. Gentschke's behavior from the point of view of civil rights deserved criminal punishment for deceit and exploitation.*

It is nevertheless implied that Citizen and Citizeness Gentschke had to allow Lebedeva to continue living in their flat. In another case of which details were given in this article, a servant called Rakitnikova, who had been the servant of a Dr. Levinson and had had two children by him, won her case in the Courts when the doctor wanted to turn

* From a translation done by the author for the English *Political Quarterly*.

her out. It was decided that he must give up to her a third of his flat. In the case of a mistress who has had children by a man, he must allow them all to live in his flat and must help to support them, or support them entirely if the woman is not working.

Anna Abramovna, having been Arcadi's wife before he divorced her in 1928 and having in addition had a son by him, had a legal right to obtain a passport as his dependent.

Marriage and divorce prior to the tightening up of the laws in 1936 entailed merely a visit to *Zaks* for registration, or, in the case of marriages, it was enough to register with the House Committee of the apartments as husband and wife jointly occupying a room or flat. This constituted a common law marriage, and by it the wife secured the same rights as if the marriage had been registered at the *Zaks*. Arcadi and I were thus married in common law, but we had never registered at the *Zaks* because I was afraid of losing my British citizenship if I did. Originally I had wished to retain my British passport in order to return home when I wished and in order to be able to travel freely abroad, for Russian citizens had the greatest difficulty in obtaining visas to enter foreign countries. Later it became a question, not of the value of my British passport in entering other countries, but of its value in permitting me to get out of the Soviet Union.

Divorce in the U.S.S.R. until 1935 required only a statement at *Zaks* by either husband or wife that the marriage was annulled. Today it is harder for one of the parties to obtain a divorce without the consent of the other, and the cost of divorce has been made almost prohibitive for the mass of the population. It used to cost only a ruble or two; now it costs very much more and rises to 400 or 500 rubles for the third divorce.

Most of the cases brought before the courts arise from the difficulties caused by the housing problem. Even when both husband and wife wish to separate, it is almost impossible for them to do so because neither can find a room to move into. One couple of our acquaintance who had twice divorced each other always got together again because they had to go on living in the same flat. Since most families have only one room to live in it is almost impossible to separate, just as young people are often unable to get married and therefore have "light affairs" instead because they cannot get a room to live in away from their parents. Often again married couples have to share the one room occupied by mother and father and brothers and sisters. A girl I had known in London lived with her mother and husband (who was also her uncle) in one very small room for years. The Soviet Government, however, ascribes all the misdemeanors of its citizens as due to the "remnants of bourgeois ideology," and to the "rottenness of the old world, which still continues to poison the Soviet atmosphere." Krilenko cites a number of cases in which men had tried to turn their former wives, or even their children by a former wife, out onto the street in order to make room for a new one. He gives the following example of a wicked worker whom bourgeois ideology had caused to behave in a most shameless way:

> To illustrate the influence of old traditions, even among working class people, we will cite the case of Alexander Maloletkin, a worker in a machine tool factory in Moscow. He looked on woman as a chattel. He showed an unbounded cynicism in his sexual intercourse. Maloletkin met a woman working in the same factory. He swore that he loved her and promised to marry her. Two days later he told her that he did not intend to marry her and did not want to see her again. He did the same thing to another woman in the same factory, and to another woman in a different factory. He had sexual intercourse with all these women and then mocked them and abandoned them. These women took the matter to Court.... Unfortunately the judge then officiating had the same conceptions as Maloletkin. Maloletkin explained that he could not have married any of these women because in the first place they were "light" women, and in the second place because he had no room of his own. In the third place he said that he was married already and had a wife in the village. All these excuses were due to the strong influence on his mind of capitalist conceptions of woman and the family.
>
> In the sentence of the Court it was written:
>
> "O. knew perfectly well that Maloletkin had no room and could not get married. Therefore if he made a promise of marriage, the woman should have understood that a man may promise a lot of things at a moment of sexual excitement and should not have taken the promise seriously."

This Court decision, which is impregnated with conceptions and a morality alien to us, was quashed in the Higher Court and the judge was dismissed.

As Marx had said, the cultural level cannot be higher than the material conditions on which it is based, and the Soviet theoretical conception of marriage has no reality in the absence of the material conditions—in particular housing accommodation—which would make a "new and higher morality" possible.

The abolition of legal abortions since 1935 has, of course, made conditions for Russian women very much harder, and intensified the housing shortage. The upper classes, as elsewhere, are little affected by the change; they can buy contraceptives or they have a high enough "cultural level" to avoid excessive childbearing. But the women of the working class and the peasants now either have to resort secretly to unqualified abortionists, or maintain families of five, six, seven or more children in one room. Contraceptives are very rarely available for sale to the majority of the population.

For five months we lived under conditions unbelievable except in Moscow. We shared kitchen and bathroom with Arcadi's divorced wife and child, and with another family of three persons (mother, father, and boy of fourteen) occupying the third room in the flat. Anna Abramovna hated me so much that she always left the kitchen when I entered, and she forbade Arcadi's son to come into our room. If he wanted to talk to his father, he had to stand on the threshold. Her hatred did not prevent her accepting the share of my munificent Insnab rations which I regularly sent in to her; but never once in those five months did we speak to each other, although inevitably we saw each other every day. I was quite willing to be friendly, but she nursed her hatred and sought to make Arcadi's son hate him as well as me. In her indeed what the Soviet Press termed "the remnants of bourgeois ideology" were very strong.

At last she secured a room elsewhere and for a few weeks we had our two rooms to ourselves. Then I went to England to fetch my mother.

My most lasting memories of life in Moscow concern the three years we spent in our two rooms on Ordinka near the Moscow River. They were our first home together and our last, for we did not secure our long-promised flat until three months before Arcadi's arrest in April, 1936. Badly built, with doors and windows of unseasoned wood which would not shut properly, unpapered and thinly whitewashed, they were home. They were ours, not a temporarily secured shelter out of which we must move when the owners returned. The Barskis in the third room were pleasant "cultured" people who had lived for some years in South America. Sharing the small kitchen and the bathroom and toilet, we rarely quarreled and could keep things decently clean co-operatively. We even managed to get the flat clear of the bugs which haunt most apartment houses in Moscow. This can only be done by scrupulous cleanliness and constant paraffining of floors and woodwork. In the flats where we had occupied only one room the bug plague could not be coped with since one's neighbors' bugs could always invade one. Even in Ordinka we could not avoid occasionally bringing home bugs on our clothing after standing in the crowded street cars. I considered myself an expert bug-catcher. They bite you at night in bed and the art of catching them consists in switching on the light and turning down the bedclothes all in a second. You then catch the bug in the act of retreating at top speed into the darkness under the mattress.

At the beginning we had a geyser to heat water for the bath, and this in itself was a rare luxury in Moscow. Unfortunately, one morning a month or so before my son was born, the geyser blew up while I was waiting for my bath. A shower of bricks fell around me, and Mrs. Barski rushed off for smelling salts, expecting at least a premature birth. We could never get the geyser repaired, so in future baths could only be taken by boiling kettles of water.

One of the minor annoyances of Soviet life was the impossibility of getting repairs done. The state provided none, and any individual who set himself up as a tinker, tailor, or whatnot, was classed as a capitalist and an enemy of the state. So naturally there was never any way of getting things mended.

This flat was one in two new stories built on top of an old house. We were on the top floor and above was a great loft with beams which barely kept out the rain and snow. Up in that freezing cold loft at night, there would be dozens of starving peasants or beggars—mostly children. These wretched little waifs, the *bezprizornii,* came daily to plead for crusts. Shivering with cold, they held out conserve tins for hot water. If one gave a piece of sugar to these poor children, an ecstatic smile would break over their pale faces. Periodically the militia would hound them out of their wretched shelter into the street, but after a few days there would be others.

The most terrible and pitiful sight I saw was one late afternoon in November 1933. Looking out of the window I saw militia men driving some wrecks of humanity down into one of the cellars. More and more people were brought in as the evening fell. Going down into the courtyard I was told by other occupants of the apartment house what was happening. The militia were rounding up all the beggars and the homeless in the city prior to the November Revolution celebrations. The foreigners must not see the starving, homeless hordes, so they were all to be dumped outside Moscow. Our cellar was one of the depots. Late in the evening lorries arrived, and the beggars were pushed into them. Some were sick, others lame; many were children. They were to be taken 40 or 50 miles outside Moscow and dumped on the road to die. If the stronger ones managed to straggle back to

Moscow the celebrations would be over by the time they got there. We all watched that pitiful exodus from our windows. A thin rain was falling and the air was damp and chilly. Although by that time I should have been conditioned to brutality, I was pregnant and it made me feel sick. Those mothers down there with their cold and hungry children being driven out into the desolate countryside must be suffering unbearable anguish. It would have been more merciful to shoot them outright.

I thought with icy foreboding of the world into which I should soon bring a child. But I am blessed, or cursed, with a sanguine temperament; and, although I knew with my mind that one could not escape from the U.S.S.R., I still went on believing in my heart of hearts that some day, somehow, we might get out. In my daydreamings I imagined Temple, back from the South Seas, sailing his yacht to the Black Sea and rescuing us. My mind played around with the idea; could one pretend only to be going for a sail, or could I teach Arcadi to swim well enough to reach the yacht at night through the warm Crimean Sea? Fantastic dreams which I never told Arcadi about. He would have laughed at such romantic fantasy, and we hardly ever spoke of the desire to get out of the Soviet prison house. It was too painful and too dangerous to think of. Arcadi had resigned himself to life in Russia, and still got some satisfaction and comfort out of doing his job. He still worked very long hours and came home too tired to think very much. I had less strenuous work and too much time for thinking. Since Jane's and Michael's departure I had felt myself cut off entirely from my old life in England, and had felt keenly the loss of the two friends with whom I could talk freely in the long evening hours when Arcadi was still at work and I sat at home waiting for him. In those first years in Moscow I had still believed that one day we should all get out into the free world again; now I knew that the past was utterly past and the long vista of years in Russia stretched ahead of me.

I wrote to my mother at this time:

> A baby will perhaps stifle my recurring regrets at the loss of all the things—career and work and politics—which I have, I now realize, lost and got to lose. Arcadi makes up for 80% and perhaps the baby will make up for the rest.... On the whole I am happy. Happy in my personal life—that should be a great deal and is. I have found such a deep love. Only I have had to tear myself away from all the other things which used to fill so large a part of my life. I suppose one cannot have everything.

Arcadi and I loved each other dearly and were together and soon we should have a child. After all, that was more than most people ever got out of life even in the free world outside. Our love knew neither jealousy nor antagonism. We were comrades in a real sense, helping each other, considering each other, and so close in thought and feeling that we had little need of words to reassure each other of the depth of the affection between us. Arcadi had a boyish playfulness which sweetened our relationship and kept him young, although he worked so hard. Illusions and false political beliefs had originally brought us together; disillusionment, trouble, and hardship, the need each of us had of the other, and an attraction which the years had welded into a oneness of body and spirit, had firmly united us. We had lived so long in one small room, adapting ourselves the one to the other and never quarreling over small things as so many people with whole flats to live in do. I still felt, and I know Arcadi felt it too, that to be in the U.S.S.R. together was infinitely better than not being together in the free world. He would every now and again tell me to save myself, leave him and go back to England. But he knew I never would. I had wept when I left England after the few months I spent there in the summer of 1933; I would have given up almost anything in the world, except Arcadi, to get out of the U.S.S.R.; but I had at long last adapted myself, learned to hide my thoughts and feelings in public, learned to avoid any political subjects in conversation, and to talk only about food or rooms or scandal, except to one or two intimate friends.

In March 1934 my son was born, and I began the happiest period of my life in Moscow. In any society at any historical period men and women have the same fundamental needs and satisfactions, and perhaps children are the greatest of these. With my son's birth I began to accept life, to be more restful and more calm. I could forget even politics for long periods and become absorbed in his needs and his development. In fact, I became far too absorbed and was abruptly awakened one day by M saying to me that it would matter far more to Jon in the future what his mother was and had done than the fact that I myself had attended to all his wants. M, an "intellectual" of the type one rarely finds outside Russia, considered me far too much "of the earth earthy" and resented both my love for my husband and the fact that I had been so human as to have a child at all. But he was good for me both as stimulant and irritant. Without his suggestion and encouragement I should probably never have written *Japan's Feet of Clay* and thus failed to keep my link with the Western world outside. It may even have been the case that this book saved me from being arrested with my husband two years after my baby was born.

Jon's birth was a long and painful business. I was thirty-six and he weighed nine pounds. I spent two days and nights in a ward with nine other women screaming most of the time. I had arrived about 4 a.m. after waiting two hours for Arcadi to find a taxi to get me to the birth house. The doctors and nurses, working 12-hour shifts, had no time to pay any attention to us except at the actual moment of birth. Three times in the second night I was brought into the delivery room, only to be taken back to the ward when I failed to give birth. No one gave me any advice or help, and no relief was given for the pain. Narcotics of any kind were ruled out, since the birth house had none. During the time I spent in the delivery room I saw many children born, for there were no screens and one just lay in pain watching the babies of others being born.

Finally at about 9 o'clock on the second morning at the changing of the shifts a doctor examined me and decided that my baby's heart might soon cease to beat. He gave me an injection to revive my strength, and he and another doctor threw themselves in turn upon my chest and abdomen. Meanwhile another doctor cut me a little, and at last my son was born. I lay and watched my screaming baby being cleaned and dressed, and then a ticket with his number was tied around my wrist. I was given a bowl of soup where I lay flat on my back on the padded table, and I wrote a note to my husband waiting anxiously downstairs. I was then left where I was until 3 p.m. before anyone had time to stitch me up. This was finally done without an anesthetic. After that I was moved into a comfortable bed in a ward for eight persons, clean, but with windows tight shut. There I remained eight days without seeing Arcadi or my mother, since no visitors were allowed into the hospital for fear of infection. I was in one of the best birth houses in the U.S.S.R., the Clara Zetkin, having secured a place there months beforehand by a combination of wangling and money. It was clean, and the food was ample; but I nearly suffocated for lack of fresh air. Our babies were brought to us to be fed all swaddled up, but my son was allowed to have his head uncovered because he had so much hair. I longed to relieve him from the weight and discomfort of his swaddling clothes, and did so at once when I got him home.

A few days after I came home Arcadi got terribly ill; they feared he had typhus, but in the end he hadn't and recovered. The Russian servant I had then, Masha, left us abruptly when Arcadi got ill, and with my mother nursing him I had to get up. However, having a child agreed with me. I felt well, I looked years younger, and I had plenty of milk. Soon I acquired Emma, the last and best of the Volga German girls I employed. She became a devoted friend, who was the one human being besides Arcadi's sister who still dared to correspond with me after he was arrested. Emma had red hair and a quick temper, and she horrified our Russian friends by thouing Arcadi and me and in general behaving like one of the family. She loved my son and she loved us, and, although I had to teach her everything, she was intelligent and quick to learn. I myself had to bring my boy up on a book and with my mother's help, for Russian ideas about babies were almost medieval. Babies were all swaddled both when they went out and in their cradles, windows were never opened, and the doctors at the Consultazia said one must on no account hold them out till they were six months old. It was taken as normal that a baby should either be constipated or have diarrhoea. I had to trust to the advice in the Truby King book I had and to such advice as I could get by air mail from a friend in England.

However, since I was able to nurse Jon entirely for six months and partly for nine, he was a healthy, happy baby and nothing ever went seriously wrong. There were, of course, no baby foods to be had in Russia; if one could not nurse one had to give plain cow's milk and water. Luckily some Australian Communist friends of ours, the Baracchis, were then living on *valuta* at the New Moscow Hotel, but had an Insnab food book as he was working in Moscow. They gave me their rations for four months, and this enabled us to live so well that I kept up my strength even when I went back to work and had to rush home at twelve and climb five flights of stairs to feed Jon. We had plenty of money, for my *Lancashire and the Far East* had at last, after many delays, been published in Moscow.* I had received several thousand rubles in royalties, and it lasted a long time.

Since the autumn of 1932 I had been working at the Institute of World Economy and Politics, and my work there demanded no regular hours of attendance, although I had to spend a good deal of time away from home in the library.

---

* The vicissitudes of publication in the U.S.S.R. are well illustrated by what happened to this book. Translated originally in 1931 and an advance on royalties paid to me, it was first held up because an introduction praising it had been written by Safarov, who fell into disgrace. Next the MS. was lost when the Party publishing office moved to new premises. Finally in 1933 Radek discovered the English edition, sent for me, praised it very warmly, and arranged for its immediate translation and publication. I got a new contract and was paid over again.

When my son was nine months old I paid a flying visit to England to make a contract for my projected book on Japan.

Soon after my return, in March 1935, my mother left us. She had been with us a year and a half, and now that we had Jon, life in Moscow in two rooms for us all had become very difficult. I was trying to provide English hygienic conditions for Jon, which meant his sleeping with the transept open in winter in a dark room. So in the evenings we all had to share the other room. The evening my mother left I got a cable from Temple's friend, Rab, in London that Temple had got blood poisoning in Fiji and might die. My mother was already on her way to England, and there was no way of stopping her. She had to face the news of his death alone ten days later. That was in April, just a year before I was to lose Arcadi as well.

Temple's death brought home to me the passing of the years and of the hopes which had gone with them. I remembered our happy childhood together, our college days after the war when the world had seemed to me a place of infinite promise, a progressive world on the way to the establishment of a just society. Temple had never believed this. Romance for him had not lain in politics but in the South Seas, in getting away from civilization, not in remolding it nearer to the heart's desire. He had died in the warmth and beauty of the tropics, but for him too the dream world in which he sailed freely for a while had become, after his second marriage, the humdrum provincial world of Suva where he had settled down as a general practitioner. In one of the last letters he ever wrote he said to my mother: "Freda's letter to me was in tone and spirit very sweet. We neither of us quite seem to have found our new world. Moral—do not read your children romantic tales in their infancy. However hard-boiled they may become afterwards, the original taint remains. Tell Freda to teach Jon to list the maxims of La Rochefoucauld as his first primer. Freda, at 11, and I, at 14, learned them too late."

That last summer we took a *datcha* in the hot summer months because of Jon. Life at the *datcha* was wearing because in these wooden houses in the villages outside the city everything was primitive. Cooking had all to be done on oilstoves, water had to be fetched in buckets, and food obtained mainly from town and carried the long distance from the local station. One servant could not possibly do everything and look after a young child. So I had to do a great deal myself as well as traveling to Moscow once or twice a week to the Institute and back and endeavoring to write *Japan's Feet of Clay*. Arcadi could not get to the *datcha* every evening, as he worked too late and an hour standing in a railway carriage packed to capacity was too exhausting after at least ten hours of office work. But he was always with us at the week end, and I sometimes stayed a night in town.

The *datcha* we lived in was a large house which the Chairman of Promexport got from the Soviet for the summer for about 600 rubles and let out in separate rooms at 500 apiece. This was the normal practice. We had two rooms and a terrace. The other three families living in it had only one and Kalmanofsky kept two for himself, his beautiful wife, a well-known actress, and his brother, who was a non-Party engineer whom I happened to have met in the Caucasus in 1927.

The other women in the *datcha* thought me very bold because I dared to walk alone in the dusk from the station along the narrow path through the forest. It was true that murders were reported with disquieting frequency, murders committed merely for the purpose of securing the victim's clothing. But, as I wore only a *sarafan* (cotton dress cut like an evening dress at the neck) in the hot summer, I felt pretty safe. Russian women are usually very timid, as I had learned long before in Tokio, where they had been afraid to go alone down the lonely lane behind the Trade Representation building. Emma feared neither men nor governments. Superbly built, with arms strong enough to knock a man down, she had a scornful contempt for the pretty delicate *Kazaikas* who neither toiled nor spun, but even when their husbands earned little spent their time in idleness.

In late August and September when the weather was really chilly, we longed for wood to make a fire. But one could not buy wood in the village, although there was forest all around. One day there was a mighty thunderstorm, one of the most magnificent I have ever seen. Three trees in the *datcha* garden were struck by lightning, one falling over the terrace and just missing the house. We were delighted. Here was some wood at last. It was forbidden to cut trees—they belonged to the village Soviet—but one might take the branches. So we started to work, and Emma and I filled our terrace with enough wood to burn for many days. The other wives sent their servants and looked upon me with disapproval because I demeaned myself by such physical labor. Surely, one of them said, you, a writer, shouldn't go out with the servants to cut wood! Five years before, no such remark could have been made; but already the Soviet upper classes had developed their caste theories. Moreover, since Russian men for the most part preferred ultra-feminine women, all who could lived up to this ideal. They prinked and painted, wore the highest heeled shoes they could buy, would go without food to buy the fantastically expensive materials now on sale at a few shops, and considered me a hopeless blue-stocking and far too democratic in my behavior. The fact that Emma called me and Arcadi by our Christian names quite shocked them, and they really objected to Emma's status in my household because it made their own servants discontented.

Russian summers are usually lovely and warm and fine, but that summer on the *datcha* it was rainy and cold. Having spent so much money on the *datcha* so that Jon might have air and sunshine, we found it very disappointing. I was working hard and getting very little sleep as I used to get up at 6 o'clock with Jon, and we were now much shorter of nourishing food than at any time since 1931. Bread had been derationed and doubled in price in January 1935; then Insnab was closed down in the early summer. Gort closed at the end of the summer. Everything had to be bought in the commercial shops or on the peasant markets at high prices. Arcadi's salary remained at the same level of 600 rubles which he had been earning for two years past, and while working on my book I was earning only my minimum salary of 300 rubles. We sold some old clothes, and Arcadi got one month's extra salary as a premium. I had a few English pounds' advance on my book, which we spent gingerly at Torgsin. We managed to feed Jon well and to live, but we went rather short and I twice went down with 'flu. Temple's death had saddened me, and I felt ill and old and depressed. I wrote to my mother that I realized that the best of life is over before one knows it has begun.

Finally after we returned to Moscow, I had a breakdown which the doctor called a heart neurosis or something like that. The Institute sent me to a very good sanatorium for five weeks—a sanatorium reserved for "scientific workers" of high qualifications—where the food was excellent and I had a beautiful room to myself. From there I wrote to my mother on November 11:

> The life I am leading reminds me of the past—skating and talking French most of the time. I have memories of La Combe. How life has flown on and here I am 37—nearly 38—and no longer a jeune fille, and somehow it has all happened so rapidly. I suppose that is the way life takes everyone. I am reading Anatole France again and enjoying it much more than when I was young....

When I returned to Moscow I felt well again and the depression had lifted from my spirits. I settled down to intensive work on my book. This work and the previous work I had done at the Institute of World Economy and Politics had given me a good deal of satisfaction. The Institute was about the best place I could have found in the U.S.S.R. to work in. As a "senior scientific worker" in the Pacific Ocean Cabinet, I had for three years past done research work on Japan in particular and the Far East in general. I got a regular salary and was paid in addition for every article or report I wrote. We "scientific workers" had our own individual plan to fulfill and worked very much as we liked. One had to attend meetings of various kinds, but otherwise one spent just about as much time at the Institute as one pleased, or as one's work required. The head of the Institute, the well-known Hungarian Marxist, E. Varga, was a very decent, kindly, and intelligent old man. He always toed the Party line and has, I believe, survived all the purges; but he was a real worker and tried to keep out of his Institute unqualified Party men looking for a cushy job. Some attention was paid to scientific exactitude; figures might be twisted to have various meanings, but the figures were accurate. The Institute contained many sections, a statistical section producing a *Konjunktur* journal; and various other sections dealing with economic conditions in every part of the world. Since my work concerned Japan, and since, luckily for me, Japan remained unfriendly to the U.S.S.R. all the time I worked at the Institute, I could do honest research and honest writing. We had a wonderful library containing practically every book, old or new, one needed or desired to read. We had the newspapers from all countries and an excellent press-cutting department for reference purposes. It was, in fact, a first-class research institute, which, because it was occupied in making reports on economic and political conditions and developments abroad, did real work. The Comintern, the Central Committee of the Party, and the Commissariat of Foreign Trade, which all used the material we produced, might make some queer uses of it; but that did not directly concern us nor greatly affect the quality of our work.

There was a good story told about Varga which illustrates the little value the political side of our work had. While in Berlin Varga received a telegram from the Central Committee of the Party in Moscow demanding that he should at once prepare a report on economic conditions in Europe. A few days later he wired back, "Analysis ready, telegraph at once what *perspectives* should be given." In plain English Varga was asking for instructions as to what he was required to prove by his figures. The story was perhaps an invention, but it illustrated perfectly the fact that nowadays Communists use economic facts to prove a political thesis decreed from above, instead of deducing the political developments from the economic conditions, as Marxists are supposed to do.

I imagine the Institute must have greatly changed since my day. For already in 1936 the great purge was seriously affecting our work. When the great fell they dragged down many lesser men with them. For instance, when Madyar, who had been the chief theoretician of the Chinese revolution, was disgraced and imprisoned after Kirov's murder at the end of 1935, there began a strenuous heresy hunt. The "Red professors" and "scientific workers" all started thumbing through each other's old books and articles to discover Trotskyist deviations or signs of Madyar's influence. Since Madyar's word had been law to us, this was not difficult. Everyone in the Pacific Ocean Cabinet felt imperiled and everyone tried to denounce his neighbor to show his loyalty to Stalin and escape being denounced. The situation was rendered all the worse because Voitinsky, the chief of our department, had played a prominent role in the Comintern in 1927 and had then been made a scapegoat together with Borodin for the tragic fiasco of the Chinese revolution. He had only a few years before come back into favor, and it was always those who had "deviated" and been disgraced in the past but had been reinstated who were most unscrupulous to others. He started accusing almost everyone who worked under him and those who worked on China all feared for their lives or their jobs.

Soon the whole Institute was affected by the purge. Varga had to dismiss his brilliant Vice-Director, Melnitskaya, a woman of great intelligence and force of character and a real scholar. She managed to survive by taking an obscure position helping to produce the Encyclopaedia then being completed, but she has probably been liquidated by now. The other women Party members were very jealous of her. She had been a Trotskyist many years before; and her husband, who worked at the Marx Engels Institute, was already under suspicion.

I left the U.S.S.R. before the storm had reached its height, so the fate of most of the men and women I worked with for three and a half years is unknown to me. But by noting the names of those who still write for the publications of the Institute I perceive that the non-Party men have fared best.

At the Institute I knew many decent and intelligent men and women, and there was a somewhat cleaner and less hypocritical atmosphere than in most other places; a little less frantic pushing and denunciation in the careerist battle; a little more interest in work and knowledge; generally a "higher level of culture," as the Russians would describe it. One never discussed things openly, but one felt with many of one's co-workers that they knew that one knew that they knew what was the real state of the U.S.S.R. and of research work under Stalin's tyranny.

I was in and yet not of the life of the Institute. I was a foreigner and English. English and Americans were the most favored foreigners in Moscow, since this was the period of the Popular Front line in Comintern policy, and every effort was being made to conciliate British and American public opinion. I spoke Russian very badly, and this saved me from the necessity of making speeches at meetings—saved me, that is, from the necessity of lying and being a hypocrite. I did my work well; I had some sort of a reputation as an author, and I am naturally of a friendly disposition so that people did not dislike me and were in fact very nice to me. I never sought to acquire a higher position by calumniating others, and I suppose that most of my fellow scientific workers felt I was harmless and might as well be left unmolested.

Upon one occasion when it was reported to me that I had been criticized behind my back, I took the bull by the horns, marched in to Voitinsky, and demanded, in what Jane used to call my best British imperialist manner, for an investigation of the accusation. This reaction was so unexpected and unusual that it took Voitinsky aback, and the attack on me was quashed. One of my friends at the Institute was highly amused. He said that the normal Russian way of dealing with the kind of accusation leveled at me behind my back, would have been to start a counter whispering campaign against the man who had accused me. But my English lack of finesse and method of direct attack was so unexpected as to have disarmed my enemies. However, I fully recognized the fact that only my British passport had enabled me to act in this way; no Russian could have risked it.

The Germans at our Institute, and at the Marx Engels Institute near by where Jane had worked, were in the most unhappy situation. Their very zeal and sincerity got them into trouble. They worked hard to learn the language and to become an integral part of Soviet society. They religiously studied their *Pravda* and *Izvestia* and all the Party resolutions. They took the "Party line" seriously, and tried to understand it; and in consequence they often rushed in where angels feared to tread. They were happy and proud to be able to make speeches and to show how thoroughly they understood Party "doctrine." Since the "Party line" and the interpretation of the sacred texts varied from season to season, this was a very dangerous way to behave. My complete withdrawal from politics, my indifference to the whole sorry game, and my poor knowledge of the Russian language enabled me to sit or stand through the meetings in safety, my thoughts miles away. But the Germans wanted to testify, and this often brought them to disaster. The poor devils still believed and were bewildered, confused, and undone when the "Party line" changed overnight, or a new interpretation was given to last month's Party resolution which they had so carefully studied.

Also the Germans, many of them refugees from fascism, some of them escaped prisoners from German concentration camps, were utterly honest and painfully sincere. Nor had they lost their personal integrity; it was difficult, almost impossible, for them to lie and cheat. I remember the case of one German couple at the Institute. The husband was condemned to prison as a Trotskyist. The wife was told she could keep her job if she would publicly denounce him as a Trotskyist spy, etc., and repudiate him. She protested his innocence and refused to do so. So she was thrown out, to starve. However, there was a rumor that Varga, who was a very humane man, later secured her a job as a factory worker in a remote provincial town.

The spirit of many of the German Communists who had taken refuge in the Soviet Union was broken in time. Looked upon always as potential fascist spies, disliked or envied for their superior knowledge or intelligence or diligence, with no government to protect them, and persuaded or forced to become Russian citizens, they were completely at the mercy of the Soviet Government. Those who had been active revolutionaries in Germany were most suspect, and thousands disappeared during the great purge. Others became as shameless as the Russians in calumniating their comrades and saving themselves by lying, hypocrisy, and false accusations.

It is a singular proof of the *comparative* humanity of the Nazi government that of the two most prominent leaders of the Communist party in 1933, the one who stayed in Germany is alive although in prison, but the one who escaped to Russia was shot in 1937. I refer here to Thaelmann and to Neumann. Thaelmann may be dead by now, but the Nazis did not shoot him out of hand as the O.G.P.U. shot Neumann and countless other Germans in the great purge.

My work at the Communist Academy kept me in touch with the outside world, kept my intelligence alive, and enabled me to earn a living without selling my soul. It also gave me the opportunity to write *Japan's Feet of Clay,* which in the future was to save me and my son from destitution in England. The fact that I was writing a book for publication in England rendered me almost immune from attack, and the writing of it gave me immense satisfaction. My detestation of Japanese tyranny and hypocrisy was second only to my hatred of Soviet tyranny and hypocrisy, and it seemed to me that the world had almost as many illusions about Japan as about Russia. I could not do anything about the Russian illusions, but at least I could tear the veil from the face of the Japanese tyranny. At the Institute I had access to an immense quantity of material and time to do real research work, while the year I had spent in Japan gave me the necessary background. The fact that I had managed to make a contract for the book with Faber and Faber in England before I wrote it, so impressed the Institute that I was allowed to spend a year writing it without interference or supervision. I remember, though, that when it was finished and I had given some chapters to read to one of my few trusted friends, he advised me to take out what I had written concerning outward conformity to the state creed and expressions of enthusiastic loyalty under a tyrannical government. It was too obvious, he said, that I really meant the U.S.S.R. when writing about Japan!

PART II

CHAPTER V

WHAT IS SOCIALISM?

THE COMMUNISTS AND their sympathizers, when faced with the disagreeable realities of life in the Soviet Union, have one defense and only one. Since there are no capitalists in the U.S.S.R., and since all land and productive capital is state-owned, Russia is a socialist state. Capitalism equals private ownership of the means of production and distribution; socialism equals state ownership of these things. So if you object to anything in Russia, or to anything which Russia does, you are opposing "socialism." It is very simple, as simple as the view of the Catholic who may not have relished the Inquisition but condoned and made possible the infliction of tortures by the Roman Church because it was the "Christian" church. To object was not to be a Christian.

If state ownership of land is all one cares about, it would be easy to argue that Egypt under the Pharaohs, or the Congo under King Leopold II of the Belgians, was a "socialist" or near socialist state. If one is indifferent to the question, "Who owns the state?" one can count some of the most horrible forms of exploitation of man by man as socialist.

The apologists for the Soviet Union entirely ignore the basic question: who controls, or owns, the state? For them the question of political power apparently ceases to have any importance once the "capitalist system" has been destroyed. This attitude is largely the result of their lack of historical knowledge, and of their having for so long taken for granted the liberties won by their forefathers that they have forgotten what is the basis of liberty. They see no further back than the nineteenth century, and are therefore blinded by their obsession with economic power. They fail to understand that such power is derivative, not primary. The power of the Nomad hordes, who in the past periodically destroyed the river valley civilizations or settled down as conquerors to enjoy the fruits of the labor of the people they had subjected, was clearly not economic but military.

The feudal aristocracy which owned the land in medieval times had taken the land by the sword; and the state, in so far as it existed, was *their* state by virtue of their military power. Only in the nineteenth century, and then only in western Europe and the United States, can power be said to have been derived from ownership of land and productive capital. Even so, the ownership could not have been maintained if the mass of the people had not consented to the virtual monopoly of the state power by the capitalists and the landowners. Democracy and the capitalist system were compatible because the large majority of citizens consented to the private ownership of the means of production and distribution.

This blindness of the latter-day Communists to the all-important question, "Who has the power?" in the U.S.S.R., is all the more remarkable because no one was more vividly aware than Lenin that the question of political power was the primary one. In his *State and Revolution,* Lenin clearly defines political power as the basis of economic power. Hence, he demonstrates, the necessity for revolution to win control of the state and thereafter set about controlling economic power.

In the writings of Marx and Engels two conditions are held to be essential as the basis for socialist society: public ownership of land and productive capital, *and* political democracy. The Stalinists have no warrant at all in the doctrine to which they still pay lip service to regard the first condition as the only essential.

In Marx's and Engels' view, and in Lenin's theory, socialism was to be an extension of democracy; it was to make possible real democracy for the first time in history. They never defined "state ownership of the means of production and distribution" as socialism, as do their latter-day "disciples." For them *communal* ownership would be socialism; and communal ownership was impossible without political democracy. Socialism was to be a society of the free and equal because in establishing it the proletariat was to emancipate all mankind, not merely itself. Democracy in capitalist society could never, in their view, be real democracy because the bourgeoisie monopolized economic power. Substitute collective for individual ownership of land and productive capital, and democracy would become a reality. Socialism was to be an extension of civilized values, not a denial of them.

The transformation of capitalist into socialist society, according to Marx, was to come about as the consequence of the ever-increasing concentration of capital ownership and the consequent ruin of the middle classes, that is to say their "proletarianization." The working class would come to include the great majority of mankind; and its seizure of political power and establishment of its dictatorship was to mean the dictatorship of the great majority over the small minority of "exploiters." This "dictatorship" would need to be exercised only for a short time, since the process of suppressing the small minority of capitalists would be quick and easy. This once accomplished, the whole people would collectively own the land and capital, and collectively administer their property. The state as an instrument of coercion would cease to be necessary and would "wither away."

Lenin expressed this concept of the dictatorship of the proletariat simply and unequivocally in the following passage in his *State and Revolution:*

> In capitalist society we have a democracy that is curtailed, wretchedly false; a democracy only for the rich, for the minority. The dictatorship of the proletariat, the period of transition to communism, will, for the first time, create democracy for the people, for the majority, in addition to the necessary suppression of the minority—the exploiters....
>
> Under capitalism we have a state in the proper sense of the word, that is, a special machine for the suppression of one class by another, and of the majority by the minority, at that. Naturally the successful discharge of such a task as the systematic suppression of the exploited majority by the exploiting minority calls for the greatest ferocity and savagery in the work of suppression, it calls for seas of blood through which mankind has to wade in slavery, serfdom and wage labor.
>
> Furthermore during the *transition* from capitalism to communism, suppression is *still* necessary; but it is suppression of the exploiting minority by the exploited majority. A special apparatus, a special machine for suppression, the State, is *still* necessary, but this is now a transitory state; it is no longer a state in the proper sense; for the suppression of the minority of exploiters by the wage slaves *of yesterday* is comparatively so easy, simple, natural a task that it will entail far less bloodshed than the suppression of the risings of slaves, serfs or wage laborers, and it will cost mankind far less. *This is compatible with the diffusion of democracy among such an overwhelming majority of the population* that the need for a special machine of suppression will begin to disappear.

It is abundantly clear from all their writings that Marx and Engels never for a moment conceived of the future socialist society as other than a democracy, and would have recoiled in horror at the travesty of socialism in the U.S.S.R. today. Lenin, himself, when faced with the problem of what to do in a country like Russia where the proletariat was only a small minority, and the peasantry constituted the huge majority, preferred to call the new system in the U.S.S.R. state capitalism, not socialism. Stalin, who, to judge from his words and actions, must consider Marx and Engels as "rotten Western liberals," has not scrupled to call the U.S.S.R. a socialist state since 1935, although it is the most perfect example of a state in which an "exploiting minority" uses the "greatest ferocity and savagery in suppressing the exploited majority."

Since, according to Marx and Engels, socialism meant public ownership of land and capital *plus* political democracy, they specified that the people's control of the state was not to mean merely the right to elect representatives to govern them, but also the right themselves to share in the administration of industry, agriculture, and trade. The workers, they wrote, once having won the political power, would smash the old bureaucratic apparatus and put in its place a new one consisting of workers and employees. The measures to be taken to prevent the degeneration of the new officials into a bureaucracy were to be the following:

(1) Election and recall at any time.
(2) Payment no higher than that of the workers.
(3) Control and superintendence by all so that all shall become bureaucrats for a time and therefore no one can become a bureaucrat.

Marx and Engels were, in fact, not so blind to future dangers as one would suppose in listening to the Stalinists. They clearly appreciated the fact that unless the workers had the power to deprive the officials of their jobs (the recall) the latter might have little concern for the interests of the people.

Lenin's device of the Party maximum, abolished by Stalin, was meant to ensure that at least the second of Marx's premises should be adhered to. At the beginning he also tried to institute workers' control in industry, but when it was found that this produced anarchy he abandoned it, for he never let theory stand in the way of practical politics.

In general it is obvious that the whole Marxist conception of socialism was unrealizable in Russia from the beginning, since it was a backward agrarian country, since the proletariat was the minority, not the majority, and since even that minority were not unanimously in favor of socialism. As Marx had stated, "law can never be higher than the economic structure and the cultural level conditioned by it."

It is curious today to read what Lenin wrote in 1918 of the transformation of monopoly capitalism into state capitalism, and of the degeneration of Marxism. His words are so closely applicable to what has occurred in the U.S.S.R. under Stalin's leadership that they sound almost prophetic. Yet Lenin could not see that he was himself laying the foundation of the "monstrous oppression of the masses of the toilers by the State" which he saw developing in other countries during the World War. "The advanced countries," he wrote, "are being converted into military convict prisons for the workers." ... The trend to socialism in words, and chauvinism in deeds ... is distinguished by the base, servile adaptation of the "leaders" of "socialism" to the interests of "their state." What he writes of Marxism as interpreted by the Social Democrats, whom he scorned, was to prove far more true of the Bolshevik party which he was leading:

> What is now happening to Marx's doctrine has in the course of history often happened to the doctrines of other revolutionary thinkers and leaders of oppressed classes struggling for emancipation.... After the death [of great revolutionaries] attempts are made to convert them into harmless icons, to canonize them, so to speak, and to surround their *names* with a certain halo for the "consolation" of the oppressed classes and with the object of duping them, while at the same time emasculating the revolutionary doctrine of its content, vulgarizing it and blunting its revolutionary edge.

"The revolutionary soul of Marxist doctrine," he writes further on, "is obliterated and distorted." (*State and Revolution,* 1918.)

Yet Lenin never dreamed that this is precisely what would happen to himself. He has been canonized, and his embalmed body lying in the Red Square in Moscow is an icon for the duping of the oppressed masses in the cause of whose emancipation and enlightenment Lenin gave his life. Such are the ironies of history.

According to Engels, the state is a product of irreconcilable class antagonisms. In order that the classes with conflicting economic interests "might not consume themselves and society in sterile struggle, a power apparently above society became necessary for the purpose of moderating the conflict ... and this power, arising out of society, but placing itself above it, and increasingly alienating itself from it, is the state." The existence of the state, says Lenin (following Marx and Engels) proves that the class antagonisms are irreconcilable.

Yet Stalin, twisting Marxist doctrine out of all recognition, insists that the U.S.S.R. is already a classless society although the state has by no means "withered away" but become stronger than in any country at any time in history.

If one treats the writings of Marx and Engels, and particularly those of Engels, not as revealing absolute truths for all time, as the

"Marxists" do, but as penetrating analyses of developments in the world of their time, much truth is to be found in them. Their method of analysis retains value and can be used as a tool to dig out the truth of our own times. Economic and political developments since the nineteenth century render their conclusions inadequate or incorrect, but the bases of their analysis are often correct.

Engels, writing at the end of the century, could prescribe that "periods occur when the warring classes are so nearly balanced that the state power ostensibly appearing as a mediator, acquires, for the moment, a certain independence in relation to both." Such, he perceived, were the absolute monarchies of Europe in the seventeenth and eighteenth centuries, and the Bismarck regime in Germany.

But Marx and Engels lived too soon to foresee the growth of the great new middle class of executives, professional men, technicians, etc., and the consequent shrinkage in the relative numbers of the proletariat in capitalist society. Postwar Europe, in particular Germany, saw the development of society into a stage where "the warring classes" became nearly balanced, and where the state power therefore could acquire independence in relation to all classes. Absolute monarchy has returned to the world once more, only now the monarch is called a *Fuehrer* or a *Vozhd* or a *Duce*. What again Marx and Engels could not know was that modern science would give to the absolute rulers of the twentieth century coercive powers beyond the dreams of the old absolute monarchs. The machine gun and the airplane, the radio and the automobile, knowledge of psychology in breaking the human spirit and annihilating courage, make it possible for Stalin to maintain his power even when *all* classes are opposed to his rule. The same is true to a lesser degree in the case of Hitler. The German Fuehrer, enjoying more popular support, does not have to resort to the use of terror to the same extent as Stalin; but both their governments are based on force, not on consent and law.

As the quotation given above shows, Engels did perceive that the government of a country (the state power) might acquire independence of all the classes. He qualified this by inserting "for the moment"; but Engels could not know what great power science was soon to put into the hands of a minority. Most of our present-day Communists have, of course, never read Marx and Engels, although they may have learned a few quotations from the selected and expurgated versions of their works which the Great Father in the Kremlin provides for his obedient children. Thus they are blind to possibilities which Marx and Engels had in fact dimly perceived. Stalinists will insist that

Stalin's dictatorship *must* be one of the proletariat because it obviously isn't one of any other class. They think that no government can be other than a class government. They think there have been in the past only two kinds of society: the feudal and the capitalist. They know nothing of the ancient civilizations of Egypt and China, of that "Asiatic system" to which Marx directed passing attention: the system whereby a priesthood or a bureaucracy owned the state and took a profit from the labor of the people, not as a landowning military aristocracy, not as a "capitalist class," but as the administrators —i.e., *as the government.* The parallel with Soviet Russia is obvious, and it is not surprising that when a bright young man working at the Marx Engels Institute in Moscow proposed doing a thesis on Marx's writings concerning "The Asiatic System" he was stopped by the authorities.

The ownership, or control, of all means of subsistence by the state enables the dictator to wield a power over the lives of men undreamed-of in past history and unforeseeable by Marx and Engels. Moreover, they and Lenin himself were essentially humanitarian, and their age was an age when moral values were held even by those who decried them, or questioned their validity, or showed up their inadequacy. An amoral world, in which no kind of humanitarian or moral scruple held the hand of the ruler, was something beyond their ken. Lenin was so blind to the consequences of his own action in overthrowing the rule of law and smashing "bourgeois" standards of conduct, that he could confidently write as follows:

> Freed from capitalist slavery . . . people will gradually become accustomed to observing the elementary rules of social life that have been known for centuries and repeated for thousands of years in all copybook maxims. They will become accustomed to observing them without force, without compulsion, without subordination, without the special apparatus for compulsion which is called the State.

In this passage Lenin reveals himself almost as naïve an idealist as Rousseau, and entirely imperceptive of the fact that his party was throwing out not only the flower of bourgeois civilization but also the root of all civilization. He himself was so thoroughly civilized, so imbued with the Western world's ideals of personal integrity, honesty, tolerance of opposition, and regard for truth, that he never realized that the majority of his compatriots were not thus conditioned to observation of the "elementary rules of social life." He was aware before his death that Stalin was not to be trusted to observe these elementary rules, but he did not realize that Stalin mirrored in grossest form the barbaric nature of the Russian people and would therefore be the man most likely to succeed him.

It is, however, not only in the U.S.S.R. that the foundations of civilization have been weakened if not destroyed. The World War dealt a mortal blow to the moral standards which, although often sinned against and never fully lived up to, had not before been denied *in toto* even by the "intellectuals" who should have been their stanchest defenders.

An immense change has come over Europe since the World War. The origins of that change lie not in the war itself but in the conditions which led to the war. The denial by the European peoples of their own accepted ethical standards in their dealings with the colored people of Asia and Africa, combined with their failure to institute social control of production and distribution, led to imperialist expansion by the strong powers in the search for markets, raw materials, and secure fields for foreign investment. Imperialist rivalry led to the first World War, which gave the "barbarians in our midst" their chance to overthrow the civilized values of Western civilization in Europe itself. As Leonard Woolf has expressed it in his *Barbarians at the Gate:*

> All the life and energy which might have gone to developing civilisation and to making it, spiritually and materially, deep-rooted in society, were diverted into a civil war within the heart of European civilisation. This was the opportunity for which all the barbarians in our midst, unconsciously and instinctively, had been waiting. They flung themselves joyfully into the class war on one side or the other. They made the Boer War and Mafeking day. They sent Dreyfuss to Devil's Island and determined to keep him there, even though the heavens fall, for that is the justice of barbarism. They put on shining armour in Germany and sent the *Panther* to Agadir, and beat the cobbler in Alsace. They hanged the inhabitants of Devshane. They depopulated a considerable area of the Congo. They burnt the Winter Palace in Peking. They massacred the workmen before the Winter Palace in Petersburg. And then at last they made the World War.

Up to the World War the moral standards of civilization—standards which have come down to us from the City States of Greece and Rome, standards which have at times been denied in part and at times applied more fully, standards which the Christian Church for all its shortcomings preserved as an ideal in the anarchic world of the Dark

Ages, standards which are in fact the basis of our civilization—were not completely overthrown.

They were preserved, because the acts of aggression committed against weaker peoples were committed far away, and because the nations whose governments perpetrated them upon Africans and Asiatics neither saw nor heard what was being done. Those directly responsible evolved a theory that they were civilizing savages, and "bearing the white man's burden" when they founded colonial empires for the profit and glory of the motherland.

As yet the methods tried out upon savages by the savages in our midst who thought themselves civilizers were not applied to Europeans except to some extent in eastern Europe. But from 1914 onwards, the standards formerly held in abeyance only in Africa and Asia, were thrown over in Europe as well. The World War brutalized us all, drove those who had suffered most back to the law of the jungle, and conditioned everyone to atrocities. Today methods of government tried out upon the Negro and the Indian are being used by Hitler upon the weaker peoples of Europe, and by Stalin upon his own people.

It is perhaps not so much in the greater amount of cruelty, persecution, savagery, and suffering in the postwar and prewar worlds, as in the attitude of many Europeans and Americans to these phenomena that the advance of barbarism is to be measured. Before the war, cases of persecution, massacre, cruelty, and violence aroused great protest when exposed in the Press or in parliaments. Even the treatment of, and attitude toward, non-white peoples was diminishing in ruthlessness. Today little protest is made except when such acts are perpetrated by those we dislike or fear. Nazi persecution of the Jews arouses great excitement and is condemned by the outside world because Germany is feared. But Stalin's massacre of Kulaks, intellectuals, socialists, and of all who challenge his supreme power, has been condoned and excused, even praised, by men who call themselves liberals, socialists, progressives. Absolute standards of behavior by governments and people have been thrown over. Ends justify means, however vague and uncertain the ends and however terrible the means. If you have a religious faith in the end, all means are held to be justified. There is no longer any standard of absolute values because life itself has taught the people to think either that the old standards are a sham or that they are no longer valid in the present state of the world.

Both Stalin and Hitler have thrown out root and branch those ideals of liberty, justice, and humanity and those standards of honest and decent behavior between man and man which are the basis of civilized life—the life of the citizen as opposed to the savage. Stalin has done it in the name of a class, Hitler in the name of a race—that is the only difference. Hatred, fear, self-preservation, the lust for power, have become the rule of life in the Soviet Union far more completely than in Nazi Germany. But Stalin's Russia, at least until 1939, did not menace the security of the Western world, whereas Hitler's aim being a German empire, which would threaten Britain, France, and even the United States, the persecution of Jews was condemned. The fact that it is fear, not sympathy for the oppressed, which rules us, is proved by both the British Empire and the United States having refused to allow the persecuted Jews to enter their vast territories in anything but insignificant numbers.

Stalin, up to 1939, menaced no one but his own subjects. Therefore the "liquidation of the Kulaks," the condemnation of the intellectuals to concentration camps, the purge of 1936-38 which delivered fresh millions of victims to the prison camps, were regarded either with indifference, or with positive approval.

The difference was strikingly illustrated for me by a conversation I had in New York early in 1939 with Robert Dell, the well-known "liberal" English journalist. He is violently anti-Nazi, and also anti-German. After a long dissertation he had made about the Nazi persecutions and the iniquity of the Munich settlement, I asked him whether he felt the same way about the Soviet Government. "The Soviet Government!" he exclaimed. "Of course not!"

"Well," I said, "what about Stalin's liquidation of the Kulaks? That was a massacre on a far larger scale than anything which has occurred in Germany."

"Oh," he said, "that. You mean the peasants who resisted collectivization. How can you make such a comparison?"

It is this lack of any moral standard which must lead the world to barbarism unless we can adapt and revitalize the old civilized values to fit the changed condition of the world.

For many "liberals" of the Robert Dell, *New Republic, Nation* type, Stalin's massacres were excusable, because they believed Soviet Russia to be a socialist state. Only fascist massacres were wicked.

The result of the Bolshevik exposure of the shams of capitalist society, of the sham of "bourgeois democracy," and of the iniquities perpetrated against the colonial peoples has not been to substitute the reality of liberty and civilized values for the sham, but to destroy those values altogether. Tell the ordinary man and woman that capitalist justice is a mockery, that representative government cloaks merely a capitalist dictatorship, that social services are mere sops to the dispossessed to ward off revolution, that the so-called Christian standards of personal behavior are merely devices to keep the oppressed submissive and teach them that in the class war lies, cheating, and cruelty are not only permissible but necessary if freedom is to be won; and the result must be barbarism and the death of freedom.

It is fruitless to argue that all that has occurred in Russia since 1917 was due to historical backwardness. It is no doubt true, as Gorki said, that a people "tutored for centuries with blows of the fists, with rods and whips, cannot have a tender heart," and that "you cannot expect justice from those who have never known it." But it may also be true that only such a people will have the necessary contempt for civilized values to carry through a violent class war of the Bolshevik type. The tragedy of the Social Democrats, as distinct from that of the Communists, was that they waited for the day prophesied by Marx, which could never dawn: the day when the working class would have the conviction, the will, the numbers, and the strength to overthrow capitalism peacefully, and establish the socialist commonwealth.

Lenin was determined upon social revolution whether or not the people wanted it; determined that the Bolshevik party should dictate to the Russian working class what it should have, because he was convinced of the infallibility of his own doctrine. Only in Russia were the people barbarous enough and ignorant enough to be thus driven; only in Russia of the countries of Europe were there sufficient socialist intellectuals prepared to lead a ruthless, intolerant, cruel, and liberty-destroying revolution in the name of liberty, humanity, tolerance, and social justice; prepared to deny democratic rights even to those in whose name the dictatorship was established and to sacrifice the content of socialism for its outward appearance.

It may be true that it was Russian "barbarism," not Bolshevik theory, which transformed the Soviet state into the antithesis of what socialists the world over had meant by socialism; but it is no less true that Russian "barbarism" alone made the Bolshevik Revolution possible.

A revolution is of necessity brutal, cruel, violent, and indiscriminating as between the just and the unjust; it causes for a long time far more misery and injustice than the system it destroys. It suspends the rule of law and the standards of civilized behavior far more completely than wars between nations, though perhaps not more completely than religious wars. Prisoners are not taken, the wounded are not succored, reprisals are inflicted on the wives and children of the class enemy, men fight each other to the death in the belief that the enemy is altogether vile. As Lenin expressed it, "barbarism must be combated by barbarism."

So long as a revolution is quick, and the forces it releases strong enough to overcome the old state power and destroy the old economic and social system without much difficulty, civilized values can survive. The ideals of social justice, liberty, and humanitarian behavior need not then be overthrown, but only temporarily disregarded. The "easy suppression" of the "exploiting minority" was what Marx and Engels had envisaged by the "proletarian revolution" of the future.

But in Russia the social forces released by the Bolshevik Revolution were too weak to conquer, and the revolutionary party had too little social support to rule by consent. Russia was a peasant country, and the working class in whose name the dictatorship was established had many ties with the village, and in general, except for a small minority, was uncultured, uneducated, unaccustomed to responsibility. The Bolshevik party did not trust even the working class, and it therefore began at once to take all real power away from those organs of popular rule, the Soviets. Similarly it deprived the trade-unions of all power. The workers were treated as children who could not know what was best for them and must be led, disciplined, and cheated. Lenin, the wise and humane father, reasoned with them, and led them. Stalin, the Caucasian stepfather of the Russian proletariat, used force naked and unashamed to make them obey his will. Not even Lenin's genius could for long have persuaded the Russian people to follow a path not of their own choosing. Lenin had not envisaged the terror as a permanent instrument of government, but even he had found it expedient to prolong its use after the cessation of civil war.

Government by coercion was in fact essential if the U.S.S.R. were to be kept on the straight road to "socialism" and not wander off along the primrose path of free enterprise, peasant proprietorship, and enjoyment of the fruits of their toil by workers and peasants alike. If, in a word, Russia were not to follow the natural line of development to capitalism once feudalism had been liquidated. Since the peasants wanted only to possess the land in peace and work for their own profit, and since the workers were apt to inquire, "What did we fight for?" when told they must pull their belts even tighter and forego the necessities of life to finance industrialization, peasants and workers alike had continually to be coerced, threatened, terrorized into submitting to the burdens imposed upon them by the Party dictatorship. Conditions for government by consent continued to be absent. The rule of violence temporarily necessary during the revolution became permanent since the Bolsheviks were not "going along with" the tide of popular desires but against it, not releasing productive forces from the bonds of an outworn social economic system, but attempting to prove the incorrectness of Marx's materialist interpretation of history. They were seeking in effect to prove that an idea can force the material world to take its image, and to conjure into existence an economic and social system which, according to Marxist theory, could only exist in an advanced industrialized country. Since such a country did not exist in Russia, the Bolsheviks would create it even if they had to kill, imprison, and starve millions of workers and peasants in order to do so.

Thus the barbarous, repressive, cruel, and undemocratic methods of ensuring order and obedience, which can be held justified during the seizure of power by revolutionary means, were continued and from year to year intensified. The Soviet regime was stabilized as an authoritarian dictatorship, first of the party, then of one man. The mass of the people were deprived of all rights, judicial, political, economic. There is no social or political restraint of any kind upon the dictator and his party. He holds power by armed force, and can be deprived of it only by an insurrection. Lenin had set the goal of a "democratic" dictatorship of the workers and peasants, believing that he would be able to persuade the people to go in the direction he considered desirable. Under Stalin there was no longer even an attempt at persuasion; coercion became the systematized method of government.

In a fine passage Boris Souvarine * has shown the consequences of the denial of democracy in Russia:

> Bolshevism could not escape the psychosis of systematised murder. At the end of the Civil War it was soaked in it. Its principles, practise, institutions, and customs had been turned into new channels by the weight of the calamities it had endured. It was its misfortune rather than its fault. There is a remarkable disparity between Bolshevism conservative and Bolshevism triumphant. But in passing from "war communism" to communism in peace, the chosen few owed it to their doctrine, their culture, their socialist past and their revolutionary present, to move into the "more humane path" of which Lenin spoke. To renounce that path by adopting the dictatorship in opposition to democracy, instead of raising themselves to the height of a synthesis, was to compromise the future irremediably

* *Stalin. A Critical Survey of Bolshevism.*

and to make the boldest effort abortive. But by following out their own programme the Bolsheviks with the aid of the workers of other countries, could have made a reality of this Socialist Federal Republic of Soviets, which was neither republican, nor socialist, nor federal, and could have revived the Soviets which had virtually ceased to exist. Their impotence to attune speech and action, theory and practise, confirmed the truth of a prophetic saying of Rosa Luxemburg's:

"In Russia the problem may be posed: it cannot be resolved."

The Bolshevik argument is that if they had allowed the Soviets to function as the government of the country, if, that is to say, they had made a reality of Soviet democracy, the "bourgeois elements" would have won control. In other words, that, since the country was predominantly agricultural, its natural path, once the peasants had got the land, was toward capitalism. The party dictatorship was established to break the waves of historical necessity. Yet, since the state controlled the "commanding heights," banking and large-scale industry, and since the Soviet election system gave weight to the industrial workers far greater than their actual numbers, there was no very real danger of such a development. Never in history have scattered peasant households been a match for the towns. What the Bolshevik leaders were really afraid of was not a return to capitalism but their own loss of power. A democratic Soviet Russia would have had no need of them except insofar as they were intelligent and able beyond other Russians. Their privileged positions would have depended on merit, not upon their past investment in the revolution.

In fact the best revolutionary elements inside and outside the Communist party, those who had knowledge and ability and were prepared to work, not merely talk, for their living, were absorbed into the minor administrative posts and as engineers, technicians, etc. Unfortunately it was the incompetent, the "uncultured," who became the high Party bureaucrats and thus controlled state policy; and for them it was vital to preserve the Party dictatorship. Again, had the Bolshevik leaders not been doctrinaires, had they shared Lenin's common sense and his practical genius, they might have realized that a semi-socialist Russia governed by consent was infinitely more progressive and would offer a far more attractive example to the workers of the world, than a Russia outwardly completely socialist, and inwardly rotted to the core by the denial of political liberty and the poison of terrorism. "What we gain in a free way is better than twice so much in a forced, and will be more truly ours and our posterities'." Cromwell's dictum, reflecting as it does the whole Protestant tradition of the supremacy of the individual conscience, was the antithesis of the Catholic authoritarianism which Communists and Nazis alike have adapted to their own ends.

"Socialism" without political democracy is a tragic caricature of the society which Socialists have striven to create for a century. Stalin's "socialist state" merely intensifies and carries to hitherto unheard-of lengths the evils of capitalism, without its compensations: wage slavery, economic anarchy in spite of the pretense of planning, poverty in the midst of plenty, extreme social inequalities, even imperialist war. And to set against these neither political nor judicial liberty, nor the rule of law, nor the humanitarianism which to some extent modifies the "weak to the wall" theory of capitalist society.

Soviet democracy did not perish without a struggle. There was a minority of "class-conscious workers" who were not prepared to see the workers' power become a sham, and the working class reduced to the state of helots of the communist bureaucracy.

In 1920 there were many strikes in Leningrad, and workers' meetings demanded that they be given the "bread and liberty" which the Bolsheviks had promised. The revolt of the workers and peasants against the Communist party reached its height and was then extinguished when the Kronstadt sailors rebelled. This was the last occasion upon which those who had given power to the Bolsheviks dared to insist that the latter should implement their own October program, and put the Soviet Constitution into operation. After Kronstadt the O.G.P.U. prevented any repetition of such an occurrence. In the spring of 1921 the sailors of Kronstadt passed a resolution demanding: free election to the Soviets; liberty of speech; liberty of the press for workers and peasants, Left Socialists, anarchists, and trade-unionists; liberation of workers and peasants held as political prisoners; abolition of the privileges of the Communist party; equal rations for all workers; the right of non-profiteering peasants and artisans to sell their products.

Communists like to tell the story about the American who was jailed during the World War for reciting the Declaration of Independence, yet when Zinoviev imprisoned the leaders of the Kronstadt sailors and Trotsky bombarded the sailors themselves, they were treating as "counter-revolutionaries" those who repeated the Bolshevik program of October. However, neither Lenin nor Trotsky enjoyed what they had felt themselves forced to do. They did not glory in it as Stalin was to glory ten years later when he crushed the peasants, who, like the Kronstadt sailors, had made the mistake of thinking that the Bolshevik program of October 1917 was sincerely meant. Whereas Stalin in the future would simply liquidate popular opposition, Lenin bowed to it. The red light of warning from Kronstadt caused him to make a complete *volte face*. Rather than again turn the guns of the Revolution upon its sons, he instituted the New Economic Policy.

The trouble for Lenin's successors was that he had said such different and even contradictory things at different times. This meant that he learned from experience and never held himself bound by a rigid theory; but in the struggle for the succession after his death, his various pronouncements were quoted as holy writ, and both the Left and Right could with some justification claim that *their* policy was "Leninism." At one moment Lenin represented the N.E.P. as a strategic retreat, at another as a permanent retreat. He maintained in one place that war communism was an aberration imposed by the Civil War and the breakdown of production; at another he stated that it was a mistake.

> Our attempt to attain communism straightway has cost us a more serious defeat than all those inflicted upon us by Kolchak, Deniken and Pilsudski. . . . We have been defeated in our attempt to attain socialism by assault.

Most of the evidence goes to show that Lenin viewed N.E.P. as a "retreat toward state capitalism"; not a breathing space before the renewed "assault" to attain socialism, but the only possible line of policy to be pursued if the world revolution were indefinitely delayed. "If," he wrote, "revolution is delayed in Germany, we shall have to study German state capitalism, to imitate it as best we can, not to be afraid of dictatorial measures to hasten the assimilation by barbaric Russia of Western civilization and not shrink from barbarous methods to fight barbarism." Stalin could find much comfort and support in these words, although he, unlike Lenin, was not honest enough to call the system "state capitalism" but preferred to debase the word socialism by applying it to his totalitarian tyranny.

The fact of the matter was that Lenin never conceived of the Bolshevik party's becoming an instrument of a savage and barbarous Asiatic despotism. He did not envisage what "barbarous methods" could mean in the mind of a Stalin. Lenin thought in western and northern European terms, and with western European precepts in his mind. But giving such political precepts to the Russians was as destructive of civilization as giving modern arms to savages and teaching them how to use them. Only those for whom the rule of law is instinctive can afford to discredit the rule of law, not nations long ruled by force. State capitalism for Lenin meant, as he clearly stated, an advance over feudalism, and a capitalism which could and should be admitted because it was indispensable for the peasants. His argument ran: An economic alliance with the peasantry is necessary in Russia unless there is revolution in other countries, because only agreement with the peasants can maintain the socialist revolution. The only way to accomplish this alliance is to allow freedom of trade. This means giving rights and liberties to capitalism. But there is nothing else to be done. If we keep the party pure, develop electricity and hold the commanding heights, we shall be ready to switch over to socialism if and when the "world revolution" occurs, and to aid that revolution at the outset.

Before his death Lenin was probably aware that the aim of his whole life, the Bolshevik party and its socialist ideal, were being drowned in Russian barbarism. In 1922, when he temporarily recovered from his paralytic stroke, he exclaimed, "We are living in a sea of illegality." The general culture of the Russian middle classes, he said, was "inconsiderable and wretched," but in any case "greater than that of our responsible Communists." The Russians use the word culture in a far wider sense than we do. It means education, civilized behavior, and scientific knowledge. Lenin perceived that Russia was reverting to type, and referred to the state machine as "borrowed from Tsarism and barely touched by the Soviet world." He even foresaw Stalin's later "great Russion chauvinism" and castigated him for his treatment of the Georgians. On that occasion he said that he was disgusted by Stalin's brutality and remarked that "Russians by adoption are worse than native Russians when they become chauvinists." Lenin's last efforts to stem the tide which was sweeping the Russian workers toward a tyranny far more oppressive than that of the Tsars were unavailing. He could not command the waves to retire. He died with some foreknowledge of what was to come, but still hoping that Trotsky would be able to curb Stalin and remedy the abuses which he spent his last breath in denouncing.

When I saw Lenin's embalmed body in the Red Square it seemed to me that his lips were set in a sardonic and bitter smile. In his last hours he had no God to whom to cry, "Why hast thou forsaken me?" but his expression suggests the realization that his life's work had borne a bitter and unwholesome fruit.

Long before the Bolshevik Revolution, the issue of democratic versus authoritarian socialism had been fought out. The Mensheviks (minority) in the Social Democratic party had opposed Lenin's conception of a party of professional revolutionaries linked with the working class, not part of it. The Mensheviks in Russia and the Social Democratic parties in other countries being essentially European in thought and behavior, had conceived of the social revolution, as Marx and Engels had conceived of it—as coming when the working class perceived its necessity and desirability. They saw no value in a movement of professional revolutionaries who would impose socialism whether the working class wanted it or not. Rosa Luxemburg, Lenin's most brilliant opponent, wrote from her German prison in 1919 that the proletariat must learn by its own experience, and that the mistakes committed by a revolutionary working-class movement were historically more valuable than the infallibility of any "Central Committee of the Party" or of one man. Hers was the Protestant tradition of the northern European, and her words echo those of Cromwell's, which I have already cited: "What we gain in a free way is better than twice so much in a forced, and will be more truly ours and our posterities'."

Trotsky in the early years had, like Rosa Luxemburg, opposed Lenin's conception of a party of professional revolutionaries linked with the organizations of the working class. He had said that Lenin's conception of the Social Democratic party as the vanguard of the working class would lead not to a dictatorship *of* the proletariat, but to one *over* the proletariat. He had even foreseen that "the apparatus of the party substitutes itself for the party, the central committee substitutes itself for the apparatus and finally the dictator substitutes himself for the central committee." But Trotsky, who before 1917 had endeavored to bring about unity between the two wings of Social Democracy, the Bolshevik authoritarians and the Menshevik democrats, joined Lenin after the February Revolution and accepted Lenin's views on the organization of the Party. Tragically enough for the future of socialism, Trotsky ceased to believe in Trotskyism at the critical historical moment, and even after Lenin's death refused to recognize that he had been right in his youth and Lenin wrong. True that he had fought against Stalin for inter-Party democracy; but he refused to save himself, and perhaps also to save socialism, by not appealing to the working class over the head of the Party. He stubbornly adhered to Lenin's conception of the Party as the vanguard of the working class even when the Party apparatus had been captured by Stalin, and the Party was becoming one of counter-revolutionary bureaucrats. He would not trust the revolution to the mass of the workers by putting himself at their head to destroy the corrupted and tyrannical Party bureaucracy.*

It was Plekhanov, the father of Russian social democracy, and the man whom Lenin himself had reverenced next to Marx and Engels, who back in 1907 prophesied most exactly what Lenin's policy would lead to:

> At the bitter end, everything will revolve around one man, who will *ex providentia* unite all powers in himself.

This is precisely what happened in the U.S.S.R., and Lenin must be adjudged responsible before the bar of history equally with Stalin. He sought to challenge the laws of his own god, historical materialism; he thought he would be able to make men behave like demigods and thus create a world in the image of his ideal. Socialism was his aim, and he was determined to achieve it by any means—suiting his political theory to circumstances, dropping one method to adopt another as each in turn proved impracticable.

Having declared first for a "democratic dictatorship of workers and peasants" exercised through the Soviets, he abandoned this for the dictatorship of the proletariat when the peasants proved recalcitrant to the Bolshevik will. Later he frankly declared, "Yes, dictatorship of a single party, and we will not yield an inch." His fundamental thesis of 1917 was abandoned—Soviet democracy, abolition of the secret police, freedom of the press. Being honest, Lenin did not camouflage what he was doing. He admitted the existence of the dictatorship of the Party when he stated that the proletariat was organized in the Soviets *directed by* the Bolshevik party. He frankly acknowledged that "all the committees of the great majority of the trade-unions are composed of Communists and merely carry out Party instructions," and did not pretend that these committees had been freely elected by the workers. He even admitted that the Party itself did not dictate, but was dictated to by its Central Committee of 19, and more precisely, by its smaller committee, the Politbureau.† He admitted that the U.S.S.R. was ruled

---

* In his *Stalin's Russia,* Max Eastman contrasts Lenin's "underlying human wisdom" (which he considers was deeper than his programmatic ideas), with Trotsky's schematic thinking, and suggests that Lenin, if he were alive, would not, as Trotsky does, have ignored the close historic and practical connection between his scheme and that of the Fascists, nor failed to re-examine the basis of his own political thinking in the light of modern fascist developments.

† According to Souvarine, Lenin stated that the Party was under the complete control of "a Central Committee of 19, permanent work at Moscow being carried on by two still smaller committees, the Orgbureau and the Politbureau, of five members each elected in plenary session; a real oligarchy ... Not even the simplest question ... is settled by any of our republican institutions without instructions from the Central Committee of our Party"—i.e., from the "oligarchy."

by an "oligarchy" and he would probably have been prepared to admit that "everything revolved around one man."

Lenin himself was never corrupted by power. He preferred to be *primus inter pares* and to persuade, not to coerce by violence. Again and again, at the most critical moments, he would stop to argue and persuade his followers, and he never thought of expelling and shooting the Communists who opposed him. But the fact that Lenin himself was perhaps a little more than human does not excuse him for ignoring the nature of human beings. Everything was prepared for the tyrant when he died; he himself (or the force of circumstances which drove him once he had chosen his path) had laid the foundations for Stalin's one-man despotism.

It is indeed astonishing that Lenin, who so clearly analyzed the workings of history as regards the outside world, failed to perceive that they must also apply to Soviet Russia. It may be thought that, having seen the drift toward oligarchy, he was preparing to stem it, and would have done so had he not died. But Lenin could no more hold back the tides which were engulfing his doctrines and his purpose than Prometheus could withstand Zeus. Chained to the rock of men's weaknesses, fears, greed, and ambition, humanity still suffers the tortures imposed by those who have power.

Dictatorial government means a government based on force, and unrestricted by law in its dealings with the people. It is essentially the same type of government as an absolute monarchy, whatever its origins and its professions. The Party dictatorship which was originally conceived of as the dictatorship of the "vanguard of the proletariat," formed to destroy capitalism, has become a personal despotism, unrestricted by law in its relations with the working class as in its relations with the peasantry. But no despot of old could dream of wielding such absolute power over the lives and thoughts of men as Stalin, for he is not only head of the State and of the "Church," but also the super trust magnate, owner of all land and capital, able by a nod to deprive men not only of the right to live, but also of the right to work. The feudal overlord had similar power, but in the Middle Ages no one had such weapons of coercion and oppression at his disposal as those wielded by Stalin and those whom Souvarine terms the "boyars of the bureaucracy." The efficiency of the means of destruction and the impossibility of producing modern armaments except in large factories and with access to the raw materials which the state owns, plus the rapidity of communication and transport, give the dictator of the twentieth century powers undreamed of by the absolute monarchs of the past, or by the feudal aristocracy of the Middle Ages.

There is a close analogy between medieval feudalism and the modern industrial feudalism of Russia and Germany. The power of the feudal aristocracy depended on its monopoly of armed force. So long as the knight in armor could lord it over everyone else—i.e., so long as arms were too expensive for the majority of the population to own them— the landed aristocracy had the power. With the development of archery, and the victory at Crécy and Agincourt of English yeomen armed with bows over France's mail-clad chivalry, the "bourgeoisie" began to challenge the feudal aristocracy. With the invention of firearms the feudal aristocracy was doomed. The era of democracy was dawning. But with the advance of science and the development of the gigantic, expensive, and complicated armaments of our age, the democratic sun is sinking. It is no longer possible for "the people" to overthrow the tyrant with rifles and pistols, or for the workers to defend themselves behind street barricades. Governments now dispose of means of coercion which cannot be withstood by the people, even if a large majority wish to destroy the government. Airplanes, machine guns, tanks, cannot be manufactured in secret, nor used by untrained men. Moreover, since the state owns all the means of subsistence, there is no economic basis from which to prepare an insurrection. Dissident members of the ruling group who in past ages assisted or even led the forces opposed to the old order, are today as helpless as the majority of the people.

It would seem that today a small group can keep a whole people in subjection if it is ruthless enough, in much the same way as the imperialist powers have been able to keep the millions of Africa and Asia in subjection. Only an external force or the army and secret police can overthrow the dictator. Hence the special privileges given by the dictator to these forces upon whom the maintenance of his power depends. A new aristocracy, part military, part "clerical" (the "theoreticians" and administrators who are Party members), is being created in Russia in this age of totalitarianism.

As regards the "withering away of the state," one might argue that, in a sense quite contrary to what Marx and Engels imagined, the state has disappeared in Russia. In place of the state power founded on law, there is a government of gangsters who rule and oppress the whole people. There is no law, for the government arbitrarily decides what "the law" is to be; there is no sanctity of contract, for the people have learned from bitter experience that the Soviet Government's promises are worthless as the paper they are written on—good paper being a scarcity commodity in Russia. There is no security, for the peasant can be thrown out of his house and sent to a concentration camp, and the worker deprived of his job, his room, and his food, at three days' notice, all without "due process of law." In fact, none of the functions of the state are performed in the U.S.S.R. except the function of repression, and this repression is arbitrary, not according to law. There is no more state, in the original Greek sense, than in a jungle. All that is left of it is the "apparatus of suppression" of the majority by a small minority.

CHAPTER VI

THE SERVITUDE OF THE PEASANTS AND TAXATION OF THE PEOPLE'S FOOD

WHEN THE CARNAGE and wreckage of forced collectivization had been cleared away, there developed in the U.S.S.R. an agrarian system similar in many respects to that of the Middle Ages in western Europe. The great majority of the peasants are perforce members of the collective farms, but since 1935 they have been allowed to cultivate small plots or gardens for their own profit, and to own a cow and some pigs and chickens as private property. They have to labor a part of their time on the collective farm, just as the medieval serf had to labor so many days a week on his lord's land. But their real interest is in their own small plots and livestock. To these they have devoted real care and willing labor; whereas on the collective farm they are forced to work for a small return. Even if the collective farm produces a fair quantity of grain over and above that which the state takes as tax, or as payment to the machine tractor station, this does not help the peasant much. For it also must be sold to the state at a price only a little higher than the obligatory quota.

Moreover, the money income which it produces is of little use to the peasant. The shelves of the village shop rarely contain the salt, textiles, boots, and other manufactures which he needs. If he lives near a town, there is a little more incentive to work harder and make the collective farm yield more, for in the towns the shops are somewhat better supplied. The prices in all the shops are very high, but in the town there is a market where the collectivized peasants can sell their produce direct to the consumer at a far higher price than the state pays even for voluntary sales. This, however, does not apply to grain, since it is useless to the consumer unmilled, and of course the state owns all the mills. In the towns the peasants can, however, sell other produce at the "cost of production" plus a profit for themselves, whereas the peasants in distant regions can find only one buyer, the state, which itself takes a huge profit when it resells to the urban population.

Agrarian economy has gone through several phases since 1932, with slight relaxation of pressure on the peasant since 1934, but little general increase in prosperity.

Up to the end of the First Five Year Plan, the peasants, collectivized or not, were compelled to sell the whole of their "surplus" to the government at prices arbitrarily fixed. When the farms had no "surplus," they had to sell the food they needed to live on. The government's collections were theoretically based on contracts with the peasants for the delivery of a certain quantity of grain, but the contract was entirely one-sided, since the government decreed how much was to be sold and collected it by force if the peasants resisted. Naturally the peasants resisted these forced collections, paid for at the excessively low government prices, as they had resisted similar collections in the period of war communism. They refused to sow more grain than they needed for their own subsistence. But this time there was no Lenin at the helm of the "socialist state" to bow before the stubborn fact of the popular will. Stalin had no humanitarian scruples; and, in spite of the fall in the harvest in 1932, the government enforced its full demands upon the peasants, depriving them of their food and seed, and telling them it was their own fault if they starved to death. The resistance of the peasants to what they regarded as confiscation of their land and livestock, and then the confiscation of the produce of the collective farms by the government, was broken by the "artificially created famine" of 1932-33. The peasants henceforth knew that resistance was futile since the government would again calmly let them die of starvation.

However, the famine which killed off five to ten million peasants also affected the towns. Unless the workers were to become as bitterly hostile to the Soviet Government as the peasants, the harvest had to be increased. If repression alone were employed against the peasants—if, that is to say, the government were to rely entirely upon compulsory deliveries at nominal prices which gave the peasant no inducement at all to produce—there would be famine every year, and soon there would be no one left for the government to exploit. So a new system was introduced in January 1933 whereby the compulsory deliveries were reduced to a fixed quantity per hectare sown, and the collectivized peasants informed that they could henceforth dispose "freely" of the rest of their produce. This system, inaugurated in 1933, has continued until now, with certain modifications to be dealt with later in this chapter. An examination of that system in some detail is necessary, since Stalin's "socialism" is based upon the bread tax—i.e., upon the exploitation of the peasants as producers and that of the workers and employees as consumers.

By the end of the year 1934, the collective farms were cultivating three-quarters of the arable land. By 1939 93.5 per cent of the peasants were collective farmers, and hardly any land was left in the hands of individual peasant cultivators. Theoretically the Kolkhozi hold the land in perpetuity (according to the Collective Farm Charter of 1935) and enjoy its fruits free of rent. But in fact they pay a rent in kind to the state. This rent consists of a fixed quantity of grain per unit of land, not a percentage of the actual crop. The state is assured of the same quantity of grain whether the harvest is good or bad. The amount taken by the state varies from one part of the country to another, being highest in the most fertile regions, but taking no account of the amount of land and the number of cultivators in the individual Kolkhoz. These compulsory grain deliveries—one can call them either a rent in kind or a tax in kind—now amount to nearly 40 per cent of the gross harvest, according to a statement made by Molotov to the Communist Party Congress in 1939.

The government's quota up to 1940 was calculated on the *planned* area to be sown. When a Kolkhoz failed to fulfill the plan allotted to it, the government did not abate its demands, but when land in excess of the plan was sown, the government took its quota. The government therefore made the peasant bear the loss in years of bad harvest, but took more from him when he cultivated more land than was compulsory.

In December 1939 the burden on the peasants was increased by the state's shifting its tax in kind from the planned area sown to the total land owned by the collective farms. The Kolkhozi are now left to make their own grain-sowing plans, but have to produce a fixed amount of grain. This change was no doubt designed to force the peasants to clear and cultivate waste lands, but it would appear from foreign Press reports that in many cases wooded lands and other uncultivatable lands have been included in the government's assessment, thus rendering the tax burden on the acreage actually cultivatable impossibly high. The result, as might have been expected, has been passive resistance on the part of the peasants. This in large part explains the threat of a new famine in Russia in 1940.

When a Kolkhoz fails to fulfill its obligations, the case is referred to the Public Prosecutor. If the charge is proved, the penalty is a money fine equal to the value of the grain in dispute, at the higher "voluntary" purchase price, plus delivery of the deficit grain. Even if it is drought which has made the Kolkhoz fail to deliver its compulsory quota, this is not accepted as an excuse, although occasionally prosecutions are subsequently withdrawn when drought has been severe. The law of May 1937, which laid down the quotas and penalties, makes no mention of any excuse considered valid for nondelivery of the compulsory quota.

The compulsory grain deliveries, although they account for a third or more of the harvest, are not the end of the state's demands. There are in addition "voluntary" sales to the state of "surplus" produce. "Voluntary" as they are supposed to be, there is a plan for these, too, and the state has its organs of compulsion always at hand to force the peasants to fulfill this plan, too. In any case, there is no one except the state to whom the peasant can sell his grain; and, as regards other produce, it is only in the districts near the towns that the collective farmers have an opportunity to sell direct to the consumer in the free market.

The "conventional prices" paid by the state for the "voluntary" sales of the Kolkhoz (over and above the compulsory quota per hectare) are usually about 25 per cent higher than the compulsory delivery prices. This is, of course, several times less than the peasant would obtain on a free market in which the price of grain bore a normal relation to the price of bread. In 1935 "voluntary" sales, according to the calculation of Mr. L. E. Hubbard, who has done the most careful research work on Soviet economy,* amounted to only 3.6 million tons against 30.5 million tons compulsorily delivered.

The government being in a position of absolute monopoly as regards grain and industrial crops, and having a quasi-monopoly as regards other foods, the prices it fixes for purchases from the peasants are arbitrary. The only check on the government is the need to keep the peasantry alive and to give them some slight incentive to work. However, even this check does not always operate, since the birth rate is high and Russia has agrarian overpopulation, and since the soldiers and spies of the O.G.P.U. are always at hand to force the peasant to work.

Mr. Hubbard gives the average prices obtained by the Russian peasants in 1913, in 1927-28, and in the famine year, 1932-33, which show that they received only 75 per cent more for their grain in the latter year than in Tsarist times, although the retail price of manufactured goods in 1932 was five times higher.

Although the prices for compulsory and "voluntary" grain deliveries

* *Soviet Money and Finance.* London, 1936.

have been raised by 25 per cent—or possibly 50 per cent—since 1932-33,* the price of manufactured goods has risen by several hundred per cent (see page 193).

In addition to the compulsory and "voluntary" sales, the collective farms served by the Machine Tractor Stations have to pay "rent" in kind for the use of the machinery. This rent amounts to 7 per cent or 9 per cent of the grain for threshing, and to a fixed number of kilograms per hectare for plowing and sowing.

According to Mr. Hubbard's reckoning upon the basis of the payments to be made to the Machine Tractor Stations by decree of 1937, the Kolkhoz has to give about 12 per cent of a light crop to the M.T.S., 18 per cent of a heavy crop, and about 16 per cent from an average crop.

The peasants have no choice in the matter. They must "accept" the services of the M.T.S. whether or not they would prefer to do the work with their own hands or by animal power. Moreover, the Kolkhozi which are not served by an M.T.S. have to deliver about 45 per cent *more* grain to the state than those cultivated by machinery—viz., 30 per cent instead of 20 per cent of the *gross* crop. The higher taxation of nonmechanized farming than of the "modern" farms in itself constitutes an admission that mechanized farming, Soviet style, is more expensive than the old primitive methods of cultivation.

Hubbard calculated that in 1935, 30.5 per cent of the total grain harvest had been sold or delivered to the government, but at the March 1939 Congress of the Russian Communist party Stalin actually boasted of the fact that in 1938 about 40 per cent of the grain harvest had been "released" for the market, as against only 26 per cent in Tsarist times. Since the total harvest in 1938 was barely above the 1913 figure,† this constitutes an open admission of the fact that the peasants now have less to eat than before the Revolution.

* According to Mr. E. L. Hubbard's estimate, the peasant in 1932-33 was receiving on an average 6 kopeks a kilogram for rye. The same authority says the prices paid to the peasant were raised 20 per cent in 1934. According to my own information while resident in the U.S.S.R., the price paid to the peasants in 1935 for rye was 1.10 to 1.50 rubles a *pood* (16.38 kilograms) which equals 8 to 9 kopeks a kilo. According to foreign informants in Russia in 1938, the peasant was then still receiving only 8 or 9 kopeks a kilo for rye. There appears therefore to have been a 50 per cent increase since 1932-33.

† See table below, page 156. It must be taken into consideration that in Tsarist times, and also in the period of the N.E.P., there was a considerable handicraft village industry and that the consumption of the artisans came out of the nonmarketed grain. But since this handicraft industry supplied many peasant households with a subsidiary income, this fact cannot be taken to have any considerable effect upon my estimate of the conditions of the peasants now and before the Revolution.

Further proof of the lesser amount of food allowed the peasant for the nourishment of himself and his family since the collectivization of agriculture can be obtained from a statement made by Molotov in 1938. According to *Pravda* of January 16, 1938, Molotov stated that the state's grain procurements had increased 150 per cent over the 1928 figure. Since, according to the official figures, the 1937 grain crop was only 50 per cent higher than in 1928, it can be estimated that the proportion of the harvest taken by the state has increased 66 per cent. Of course, in 1928, under N.E.P., the peasants could and did sell to "speculators" as well as to the state; but, since they then got something in exchange—either locally produced manufactures or a higher money price than the state paid—it is true to say that the peasants as a whole are now very much worse off than in 1928. This is obvious to anyone who has seen a typical Russian village then and now, but it is important that the official figures bear out the impression of one's eyes. It has, moreover, been calculated that in Tsarist times the average peasant household sold only between a quarter and a third of the gross production of grain. This indicates that the Soviet state takes more in taxes than the Tsarist landowners and usurers took in rent and interest.

It must also be borne in mind that the nonmarketed produce retained by the peasants has today to provide for the support of the small army of managers, accountants, agronomists, and clerks who run the collective farms.

It is in considering the value of the peasant's money income that his worsened standard of life becomes most obvious. Mr. Hubbard has worked out a most enlightening comparison of the real income of the peasant in 1913 and in 1936 in terms of the quantity of indispensible manufactures:

One *pood* of Rye Flour would purchase 1913		One *pood* of Rye Flour would purchase 1936	
Sugar	4.1 kilo	Sugar	0.5 kilo
Household soap	3.3 kilo	Soap	1.3 kilo
Cotton print	6.4 meters	Cotton print	0.5 meters
Kerosene	27.0 liters	Kerosene	4.2 liters
And 7 *poods* would purchase a pair of ordinary leather boots.		And about 80 *poods* would purchase a pair of leather boots.	

(The further rise in prices of manufactured goods since 1936 has yet further worsened the condition of the peasants.)

Moreover, in the old days the peasants derived a considerable subsidiary money income from the sale of goods produced by handicraft cottage industries, which are now practically extinct; for, from 1930 onwards, peasants who indulged in such labor were accounted "capitalists" and became liable to liquidation.

According to prewar estimates, the average net money income for a peasant household was between *Rs.* 130 and *Rs.* 150, and *Rs.* 180-*Rs.* 200 per annum. If a household consisted of three adult workers, the average money income was around 60 or 70 rubles. Today it varies enormously from farm to farm, but appears to average between 120 and 300 rubles per adult collective farmer, according to such official figures as are available concerning total money income of the Kolkhozi. (No average figures of farm income for the whole of Russsia are published by the Soviet Statistical Bureau, and most of the information published in the Press concerns the Kolkhozi which are particularly prosperous.)

According to figures available up to 1935 in the Soviet Union's Statistical Year Book, the value of the agricultural output of the whole country was 16 billion rubles. Of this sum $3\frac{1}{2}$ billion represents the value (at state prices) of the produce left to the peasants for their own consumption. Hence the gross money income of the peasants in that year was $12\frac{1}{2}$ billion rubles. However, the peasantry is reckoned in that year to have spent only 7 billion on manufactured goods supplied to the rural areas. Allowance must be made both for the compulsory capital improvements, for the salaries of the directors, specialists, etc., of the collective farms, for payment of the milling charges of the government, and for loss of grain in transit. Some peasants also will have spent their money income in the towns, and others will have had to buy bread back from the state. All in all, the peasants' money income cannot have amounted to more than 9 or at most 10 billion rubles. This income divided among 26 million peasant families comprising on an average three adults, means between 116 and 130 rubles per head.

Whereas under the Tsar the peasant with 60 to 70 rubles a year money income could purchase each year, if he wished, two pairs of boots, eight meters of woolen dress cloth, and a pair of galoshes, and still have a few rubles over, in 1938 even the lucky collective farmer with an income of 200 rubles had to spend nearly half his yearly income to secure one pair of boots of inferior quality.*

Even if the peasants' money income has been trebled since 1913, as

* See prices of various manufactured goods on page 193.

the official figures make out, the purchasing power of the ruble is about one-twentieth. In 1935, when a larger proportion than before of the manufactured goods produced was made available in the village shops, less than 35 per cent of the total of manufactured goods was supposed to have been allotted to rural trade. But in that year the peasants spent 7 billion rubles on merchandise, which is only one-twelfth of the total of about 56 billion rubles of manufactured goods sold by the state to the whole population.*

All the evidence goes to prove, as shown above, that as regards both food and manufactures, most of the peasants are worse off than before the Revolution. The Soviet apologists will, of course, argue that the peasant now enjoys "social services" unknown before the Revolution. It is true that crèches for a very few children, a clubroom, and in some places primitive medical services, are now available to the peasants. *But these have all to be paid for out of the Kolkhoz income* as calculated above. The peasant even has to pay in additional money taxes for the education of his children where there are schools.

Nor is grain the only produce which the peasant is forced to deliver to the government, at nominal prices. A fixed quantity of milk per cow, a certain quantity of meat, of potatoes, of anything and everything which the collective farm, or individual peasant, produces, is demanded by the state and paid for at prices about 90 per cent less than the free market prices in the towns. A fixed quantity of milk is demanded from each cow, whether owned collectively by the Kolkhoz, or individually by the Kolkhozniki. This compulsory milk sale amounts to between 10 per cent and 25 per cent of the total milk produced according to the yield of the cow. The same applies to meat.

Lastly, the peasant has to pay to get the grain for his own consumption ground into flour at the state mill. This payment amounts to 10 per cent of the grain milled.

In 1936 the government, in an effort to stimulate, as well as force, the collectivized peasants to work harder, introduced a system of premiums on the "voluntary" grain and other sales. The larger the quantity sold to the state, the higher the price. These premiums favor the larger and more prosperous collective farms over the smaller, and have helped to produce that differentiation in the income and prosperity of the Kolkhozi, which is now a marked feature of Soviet agriculture.

* The cost to the state in 1935 of the total production of consumers' goods was 28 billion rubles. Since the state takes a profit of 100 per cent or more (in the form of the turnover tax) on manufactured goods sold to the population, it can be estimated that it sold the total of 28 billion rubles' worth of manufactures for 56 billion rubles.

Whereas the Kolkhoz "voluntarily" selling between 10 and 50 *quintals* receives only 10 per cent above the basic price, the large Kolkhoz able to produce a surplus of 1,000 *quintals* gets double the basic price.

All the measures of compulsion and stimulation have, however, failed to induce the great bulk of the peasants in the collective farms to produce more. The harvests remain very low. Although of course higher than in the terrible famine years, the average is little if at all higher than in the days before the Revolution. The peasant is even more severely exploited by the state than he was by the landlord and the usurer under the Tsar, and he has less incentive to work, since, even when he gets money, there is so little he can buy. He has less personal liberty, hates the government more, and feels himself worse treated. For the Soviet Government in its early years gave him the land and gave him hope, only to deprive him of both after a few years. Nothing the peasants suffered under the Tsar is comparable to what they suffered from 1930-33, and under the Tsar the peasant might starve but he was not continually watched, spied upon, disciplined, and threatened with exile or prison. Although from 1935 to 1939 the pressure on the peasants was slightly relaxed and that on the workers increased, the standard of life of the peasantry is certainly well below that of Tsarist times.

Working on the collective farm, the peasants are at the mercy of the chairman and the committee, who, although in theory his elected representatives, are in reality state officials. The chairman is almost always a Party member and is frequently a man appointed from outside with little or no knowledge of farming. Even if he is of peasant origin, his function is to ensure the fulfillment of the state's plan, and the delivery of the state's quota. Each peasant has to perform whatever task is allotted to him, and his individual share in what is left to the farm after deliveries to the state have been fulfilled, depends upon the number of days' work performed. But one day's work at some kinds of labor is reckoned as worth two days of other, simpler kinds of labor. Thus the farm, like the factory, has its aristocracy of labor in the person of the tractor driver, the plowman, etc. Obviously, also, the value of a man's labor on a farm cannot be so exactly estimated as in a factory, so that the number of "work days" credited to a peasant in the division of the farm income depends largely on the good or ill will of the chairman. On the land as in the factories, toadying, fawning, flattery, and slavish repetition of Party slogans are more likely to secure you enough to eat and clothes to your back than conscientious work.

The Machine Tractor Station serves also as an O.G.P.U. headquarters, and in every district soldiers of the "internal army" of the O.G.P.U. are at hand to quell peasant revolt and to arrest grumblers.

Legislation medieval in its ferocity punishes the peasant for the slightest misdemeanor. The *death sentence* is applied for small thefts, even to children. A hungry child who has stolen a few vegetables from the Kolkhoz, if twelve years of age or older, is shot "by due process of law."

Calculations as to peasant income cannot be made, because no one knows how large a share of the Kolkhoz's divisible fund is taken by the agrarian bureaucracy. In 1931 the number of officials in the villages was reckoned to be two million. Now that the peasants' resistance has been broken, the number is probably a good deal lower, but the cultivators still have to support a small army of managers, controllers, brigadiers, accountants, and other employees. Only the armed guards who prevent their "stealing" the produce of their own labor are paid by the state. Since the yield per hectare is at most only about 5 per cent above the prewar figure, there is no doubt that, taken as a whole, the costs of production (which must include the salaries of the parasitic farm bureaucracy) are far higher than before the Revolution.

Since collectivization, the grain harvests have been as follows:

In Million Tons

1913	94.1 *
1928	73.3
1932	69.6
1933	89.8
1934	89.4
1935	92.0
1936	82.7
1937	120.3
1938	95.0
1939	No definite information but estimated to have been at about the 1938 level.

* The net yield in 1913 was 80.1 million tons but the "biological yield" is calculated to have been 94.1. The biological yield as used in Soviet harvest calculations since 1933, is the quantity of grain estimated in the standing crops with a deduction of 10 per cent for harvest losses. Mr. Hubbard says that actual harvest losses in Soviet Russia are over 40 per cent. Even if this estimate of losses is too high, it is clear that the Soviet Government's method of assessing the amount of the harvest is designed to exaggerate them grossly in order to deceive the outside world and to pretend that the peasants are left with more to eat than is actually the case.

In 1939 Stalin reported to the eighteenth Congress of the Russian Communist Party that the total yield of grain in 1938 was 18.6 per cent higher than in 1913, while the area under grain had increased 8.5 per cent. This is not true if the same reckoning of "biological crops" is used for 1913 as for 1938. Even if it were true, since the population has also increased, or is supposed to have done, on the official Soviet figures the peasants are producing certainly no more, and probably less, per capita than before agriculture was "socialized." Thus the heavy sacrifices made to produce tractors and other machinery, the whole capital investment in agriculture over the past decade, has not increased the yield of the land. The sacrifices, the labor, the blood and tears of the expropriated peasant population have gone for nothing except to substantiate a barren claim on the part of their rulers to have "socialized" agrarian economy.

The national economy has been weakened, not strengthened, by collectivization and the boasted "mechanization of agriculture." Workers who might have been producing consumption goods to raise the general standard of living have produced tractors and other agricultural machinery which, owing either to its poor quality or to the lack of trained mechanics, has failed to increase the yield of the land. It would even seem from the statistics available that a larger number of peasants with tractors is producing less food per head of the population that a smaller number of peasants *without machinery* managed to produce before collectivization.

As we have seen, the Soviet Government in 1934-35 was forced by the incurable mismanagement of the collective farms, and by its failure to provide enough of the machinery upon which the success of large-scale agriculture depends, to make concessions to the peasants in an effort to increase the yield of agriculture. These concessions were given grudgingly; and the peasant, knowing they might be withdrawn at any moment, had not the necessary confidence to make him work harder and better. He is primarily a serf and he knows it too well to have the heart to make an effort to raise his standard of life. At any moment the state may raise the compulsory quota or decrease the price of grain; and bitter experience has taught the peasant that this is most likely to happen if he works harder and produces more. Hence the almost stagnant yield of basic crops.

On the other hand, even the minor concessions made have diminished the "socialized sector" of agriculture. This is true in particular of the concession of an individual plot and the right to private ownership of some livestock. This was a concession which, even if later annulled, cannot place the peasant who takes advantage of it in a worse position than before. He can eat the potatoes or vegetables or fruit which he grows with loving care on his *own* little plot, and the government can't take it back out of his stomach next year. Also, he can sell this privately produced produce to the urban consumer for cash which he can spend at once on a pair of boots, or trousers, or other clothing for his family. True that these manufactured goods are still scarce and very dear, but the prices he obtains for his produce on the free market are also high.

Naturally the peasant has spent as much time as he possibly could attending to his own plot, to his pigs, chickens, and cow, if he has risen that high. The return on the produce from these is sure, whereas the results of his labor in the Kolkhoz vanish into the clutches of the government or are allocated for capital improvements on the farm which hardly benefit him. In general, the distribution of the Kolkhoz income is designed to give the working peasant just enough bread to live on at a bare subsistence level. When the farm produces more, some means is found to cheat the members out of the increased income. It can always be decreed that the excess income shall be utilized for "capital improvements" on the farm, and the peasants often have grounds for the suspicion that the chairman and other officials put the increased income into their own pockets. No peasant is willing to risk his neck by demanding an inquiry into the doings of the all-powerful Party bureaucrats who administer the farm.

In short, the peasant gets a very small return for all his "work days" on the Kolkhoz, but he gets quite a lot in return for his labor on his own allotment. The analogy with medieval serfdom is obvious. The serf worked as lazily as he dared on the lord's manor, but with all his vigor on his own land.

The consequences in the Soviet Union have been far-reaching. The peasant is not allowed to own much land privately; but, intensively and carefully cultivated, this land yields far more per acre than the "collectively owned" farms. Similarly, the individual care given by the peasant to his privately owned livestock and chickens has increased their importance in the national economy. In 1936 about 40 per cent of the total area producing vegetables in the U.S.S.R. consisted of private allotments, gardens and individual farms. Chickens and eggs are supplied almost exclusively by private enterprise. In 1938-39 the percentage of the total livestock in the country owned by the collective farms was found to be as low as 20.6 per cent in the case of cattle,

26.5 per cent in the case of sheep and goats, and 21.4 per cent in the case of pigs.

The household allotment varied from region to region, but until 1940 was between 1½ and 2¼ acres exclusive of the garden around the peasant's house. This was about the same amount of land as most Japanese peasant households have to cultivate; but, of course, not being irrigated, it could not be made to grow crops like rice, of which the yield per acre is very high. Nor can the Russian peasant secure chemical fertilizers for his personal use. Nevertheless, he has of recent years been driven by the fearful mismanagement of the collective farms and by the small return he received for his labor on the communal lands, to subsist more and more off the produce of his individual allotment and that of his cow, pig, or sheep. Moreover, larger plots than those allowed under the law had been secured by many of the peasants. This was made clear in the preamble to a decree of May 28, 1939, which, taken in conjunction with a second decree issued in July of that year, virtually annuls the Collective Farm Charter of 1935, and severely curtails the amount of land privately cultivated and the number of livestock privately owned.

According to the decree and to articles in the Soviet Press, the right to private ownership of a plot of land and some cows, pigs, and chickens had come to be exercised to such an extent that many of the collective farmers had "virtually withdrawn from the Kolkhoz, and were spending all their time working on their own land." Not only this, but "in some cases they are even renting out a part of their illegally acquired holdings to others and becoming landlords." These "illegally acquired holdings" are shown to have been obtained by the Kolkhoz administrations' allowing members to take over a part of the land supposed to be cultivated collectively. Some of the fields and meadows belonging to the Kolkhoz had been turned over to the personal exploitation of individual peasant households. It seems probable that some of the harassed Kolkhoz chairmen had allowed this as the surest way to get enough grain or other crops produced to meet the government's compulsory collections. Individual farming is so much more productive than socialist production à la Stalin that this letting out of Kolkhoz land paid the peasant even if he had to pay the Kolkhoz chairman for the privilege as well as meet the government quota. The quota is high, and bribery charges might also be high, but at least he did not have to pay the Machine Tractor Station for use of its too often broken down machinery. Nor was he then subject to the arbitrary orders of an overseer, or forced to pay out a large part of the produce to support the whole administrative personnel of the farm, or to finance "capital improvements" which do not benefit him at all.

In fact, something of the same thing appears to have happened in the state feudal agrarian system in the U.S.S.R. as happened toward the end of the Middle Ages in Europe. The bailiff, finding it very difficult to force the serfs to work well on the lord's land, let out parcels of the manorial domain to the peasants for a fixed rent. Thereby he ensured to his lord a certain definite income. Similarly, from 1935 to 1939 the Kolkhoz manager who let the peasants take over a part of the Kolkhoz lands for private cultivation in return for a fixed rent in kind, was ensuring for his master, the Soviet Government, a definite quantity of produce.

Thus the failure of collectivization and mechanization to increase the yield of the land, or to raise the standard of life of the cultivators, caused a "relapse" to private cultivation. The economic forces pulling Russia back to individual farming have been too strong for even a government maintained by naked force.

The decree of May 1939 complains of a serious deterioration in the work of the collective farms due to shortage of labor. *Pravda* reported that at a certain collective farm the shortage of labor caused by so many of the members' being engaged in individual enterprise, had resulted in failure to erect barns, and in mown hay being left to rot in the fields. This farm had consequently been forced to spend 12,000 rubles to buy cattle feed for the winter. The result was that the "honest" collective farm members had received only 90 rubles each for a year's work. In contrast to this, one "pseudo collective farmer" earned more than this by a day's work "repairing someone's porch." *Pravda* does not mention the fact that this implies connivance on the part of some high official, but it is obvious that it does since no one but a well-paid Party bureaucrat could afford to pay 90 rubles to have his porch mended.

The May 1939 decree inaugurated a new drive against the peasants to deprive them both of the extra land they had acquired and of most of their privately owned livestock. It refers to the "illegal extension" of the norms of privately held garden plots "through the squandering and embezzlement of common collective farm land in favor of the personal enterprise of the collective farmers." This had occurred, it is stated, "either through fictitious division of families, when a collective farm household fraudulently acquires an additional parcel of private apportionment to members of the family, or by means of a direct allotment of individual plots to collective farmers at the expense of the common field area of the collective farm." This is held to constitute an "anti-Kolkhoz and anti-state practice" and the sacrifice of the interests of the Kolkhoz to "elements of private ownership and graft, who make use of the collective farm for purposes of speculative and personal profit." (It should be noted here that "speculator" in the U.S.S.R. is a term applied to anyone selling direct to the consumer instead of to the state—i.e., to any producer who tries to get a full return for his labor. The duty of the loyal Soviet peasant is to sell his produce to the state at about 1/10th of its market price.) The private plot, continues the decree, has been losing its subsidiary character and is sometimes turned into the main source of income of the collective farmer. Consequently there are a lot of "fictitious collective farmers" who either do no work at all on the Kolkhoz lands, or "only work for show, devoting the greater part of their time to their personal homestead." This has led to an "artificial shortage of labor" in the collective farms, although in most regions of the U.S.S.R. there is "a large surplus of labor" which ought to be "made available for the settlement of those parts of the U.S.S.R. where land is plentiful and there is an actual shortage of labor." Blame is placed upon the local Party and Soviet organizations for not having safeguarded the collective farms from "the attacks of private ownership elements" and to their having "left important decisions to chance and to grafters among the collective farmers." This clearly implies that many collective farms had been allowed to manage their own affairs, provided only that they paid up the compulsory deliveries to the state. What had occurred is designated as a "most outrageous violation" of the law, and is, of course, ascribed not to the natural working of economic forces, but to "the bourgeois tendencies of private ownership introduced by the remnants of the defeated Kulaks." (Since all the so-called Kulaks were liquidated long ago it must be concluded that it was their ghosts which had haunted and perverted the Russian villages.)

All these wicked and "anti-Bolshevik" "opportunistic" practices are put an end to by the decree. The Kolkhoz lands are declared "inviolable"; they are never to be decreased, only increased. Continuation of the old practices becomes a criminal offense. The penalty for subletting garden plots is to be expulsion from the collective farm and loss of the individual holding—i.e. complete pauperization.

The decree specifically forbids chairmen of collective farms to lease the hayfields and meadows for mowing by individual collective farmers or to individual peasants. This proviso is designed to force the collective farmers to sell their beasts to the Kolkhoz because they will no longer be able to feed them. (See below, page 163.)

A complete survey of all communal and private land had to be made by August 15, and all personal plots lying in the collective farm fields or in forest pastures are to be assessed to the common land. When the individual garden plot around the collective farmer's house is below the norm permitted, the amount is to be made up out of the land set aside for plots to new collective farm households—i.e., newly married couples wishing to set up a household of their own will often no longer be able to secure garden plots.

The maximum size of individual plots is to be limited henceforth to 1/10 of a hectare in irrigated cotton-growing districts; to ½ hectare in fruit, vegetable, and beet-growing regions; and to one hectare in all other parts of the U.S.S.R. The maximum amount of land to be allowed anywhere to individual peasants who are not members of a collective farm is to be only 1/5 of a hectare.

New officials, called Inspector-Surveyors, are appointed for the periodic checking up of the size of individually owned plots and to see that the Kolkhoz has not alienated any of its lands.

The decree lays down a minimum of work days to be spent by each collective farm member on the collective farm lands, as against the days allowed for private work. In most parts of the country this minimum is set at eighty days per year.*

This decree reveals how far the reversion to individual cultivation has already gone. Even as decreed, only a quarter to a fifth of the days of the year are now to be given to work in the "socialized sector" of agriculture. If free days are allowed for (1 in 6), the peasants are being forced to labor less than a quarter of their working days on the collective farms.

Expulsion from the collective farms is decreed as the penalty for performing less than the required amount of labor on the Kolkhoz. The government is threatening something in the nature of a repetition of the horrors of 1930-33, for it is stated in the Press, "This decree will fit in with the program that the government has already launched for transporting peasants to sparsely populated regions, especially the Volga and the Far East."

If "transporting peasants to sparsely populated regions" meant moving them from overpopulated regions with due provision for their settlement elsewhere, it would be a legitimate and wise method to

* Sixty days only in north and central Russia and one hundred days in the cotton-growing districts of the South.

solve the problem of rural overpopulation which the ambitious industrialization program has failed to solve, or to ameliorate. But in the U.S.S.R. such a measure is always brutally accomplished as a punishment and without provision of food, housing, and farm equipment to clear the waste lands and keep the peasants alive until the new land yields crops. It means, as in 1930-32, the death of the weak, in particular of the women and children of the expelled peasants sent off without food and water in unheated cattle trucks.

The May 1939 decree was only the first of the measures to curtail the little scope previously allowed the peasantry to exercise its "bourgeois instinct" to labor for its own profit instead of for that of the Soviet bureaucracy. A decree of July 1939 alters the method of computing the amount of meat demanded by the government from each collective farm and from each individual collective farmer in possession of livestock, in a manner calculated to force the latter to hand over their cows, pigs, sheep, or goats to the Kolkhoz. As from January 1, 1940, deliveries of meat are to be calculated, not as before on the basis of the number of animals actually in the possession of the collective farms, but upon its area of arable land. In other words, the collective farms which possess few or no cattle, sheep, or pigs have got to get them and to feed them. The only way they can get them is, of course, to confiscate those belonging to their members. To facilitate this, the decree doubles the amount of meat which every collective farmer individually has to "sell" to the government each year. The amount used to vary from 15 to 32 kilos live weight; by 1942 it is to amount to between 32 and 45 kilograms. (The great variation in the amount demanded in different parts of the U.S.S.R. is due to the greater quantity of meat which has to be supplied by the predominantly pastoral regions.) By the end of 1940 the amount demanded is already to be increased, although not to the full amount. Obviously many peasants will be unable to retain any livestock, while others will have to diminish the number of their privately owned livestock. Since the state had deprived them in May of the opportunity to feed their beasts on fodder obtained from the collective farm meadows and forests, few are likely to be able to keep a cow or more than one or two pigs.

The collective farms are instructed to buy the individually owned livestock at the state price—i.e., at about 1/10 of the market price. A very small consolation prize is given to the collective farmers by the provision that they are to be credited with from 10 to 20 work days for each animal thus "sold" to the Kolkhoz.

On the basis of the figures given in the decree it can be calculated that by the end of 1942 the collective farms on an average will be required to own one cow for every 25 hectares of arable land, one ewe for every 34, and one pig for every 61. This works out for the whole of the U.S.S.R. to at least 30 million cows—and presumably 60 million cattle *—as compared with the total of only 12.9 million cattle which they possessed in 1939. They will further be required to possess 22 million ewes as against the total of 27.2 million sheep and goats possessed in 1939. The number of pigs is to be increased from 6.6 to 12 million. Sixty per cent of these figures have to be owned by the end of 1940.

Thus, although it has been amply proved that the only way to ensure a steady increase in the number of livestock in the U.S.S.R. is to allow the private ownership which induces the peasant to take real care of the livestock, Stalin has decreed that this is not to be permitted. He would rather the Russian people continued to go short of meat, milk, and butter than have them eat enough by means of "capitalist" methods of production. They are, in fact, almost certain to have even less dairy products to consume than during the past few years. Already in the winter of 1939-40 and in the spring of 1940 the scanty consumption of the working class has been reduced. The shortage of meat, vegetables, and dairy products in the towns led the government to raise prices 35 per cent in January 1940, and a further 25 to 75 per cent in April 1940.

The ever-increasing reliance of the Soviet Government upon the bureaucracy to ensure fulfillment of its plans, and the abandonment even of a pretense of relying upon the willingness of the peasants to work "collectively" is shown by the kind of people who are exempted from the compulsory meat deliveries, and by the new system of bonuses introduced in 1939. The following are exempted from delivery of the compulsory meat quota per household: directors of state farms, livestock experts, directors of the M.T.S., agronomists, technicians, and engineers, teachers, doctors, and veterinarians. (Office employees, and old peasants who have no able-bodied member of their family working, and the parents of soldiers who have left behind wives and children below the age of seven, are also exempt.) These exemptions indicate increasing privileges for the ruling strata in the countryside. The same applies to the system of bonuses. An article by the Commissar of Agriculture published in *Pravda* on March 7, 1939, refers to bonuses equal to from one to three months' salary to be paid to directors and

---

* Since Soviet statistics give cows as constituting 40-50 per cent of the total head of cattle in the Soviet union.

assistant directors of Machine Tractor Stations, and to chief agronomists, head mechanics, and chief accountants for "exemplary fulfillment and overfulfillment of the annual agricultural plans, for those who have increased the yields in the collective farms which fall within the scope of their work, as well as for ensuring the delivery of payment of agricultural produce due from the collective farms."

It is abundantly clear from every measure taken by the Soviet Government that it is the managers and administrative personnel in general who are relied upon to drive the peasants, and that the latter are unwilling workers who loathe the whole collective farm system.

The above article by the Commissar of Agriculture is also of interest as showing the failure of even the proletarians on the farms; i.e., the tractor drivers, mechanics, etc., to perform the work assigned to them, and the need felt to punish them for scamping their work. He writes: "Tractor drivers who violate the rules regulating the depth of plowing are to be fined up to 50 per cent, and chiefs of tractor brigades up to 10 per cent, of the cost of the fuel used for this work." The same article specifies the detailed regulations made with regard to depth of plowing, number of harrowed furrows, dates at which sowing is to be begun, and other operations on the farm begun or completed, and so forth. It is further insisted upon that all aggregates are to work in two shifts with the tractors doing 20 hours of "smart, highly productive field work."

Whereas the Third Five Year Plan provides for only a small capital investment in agriculture, emphasis is laid upon forcing the collective farmers to work harder. Those who don't are to be expropriated and forced to become unskilled laborers in industry, or exiled to sparsely populated regions. In his speech to the Communist Party Congress in 1939, Molotov laid down as the main task in agriculture "intensification of the struggle against violations of the constitution of the agricultural artel" and "not to allow unlawful extension of the personal holdings, personal plots of land, title of individual collective farmers, which leads to a violation of the interests of the collective farm and hinders the strengthening of collective farm discipline." He also spoke of the need "systematically to release members for work in industrial enterprises, primarily those who are little employed upon work on the collective farm, have few days to their credit, and are therefore a burden to the collective farm." It is to be presumed that the type of labor for which the peasants are required is timber cutting, road and railway building, canal digging—the kind of work which is performed in the main by the victims of the O.G.P.U. in the concentration camps. It is to be surmised that the O.G.P.U. has been running short of labor for its vast enterprises, since the term of life in the concentration camps is short, and most of the so-called Kulaks must by now have died off.

Thus once again the peasants have been cheated by the Soviet Government, being now deprived even of the slight concessions made to them in the Charter of 1935. The consequent further disheartening of the peasants is bound to decrease the amount of food produced in the U.S.S.R. The Soviet Government refuses to learn the lesson that forced labor—virtually slave or serf labor—cannot be made as productive as free labor. The peasants are too cowed and their spirit too broken for open revolt, but their passive resistance makes it impossible to increase agricultural productivity except at a prohibitive cost. It would require almost as many guards as there are peasants to force them all to labor as hard and as conscientiously as is necessary to increase the yield of the land and of the livestock.

The growing shortage of foodstuffs and increased prices of all except bread in 1940 are to be ascribed to the renewed drive against the peasants rather than to the Finnish campaign and war preparations. For it is to be surmised that the peasants faced with a survey of their possessions in 1939, to be followed by virtual confiscation of their livestock, or on account of the impossibility of feeding them any longer, preferred to kill and eat them rather than sell them to the Kolkhoz at a price only a tenth of the market price. Where this seemed too dangerous an act to perform under the eyes of the O.G.P.U., they may have preferred to wait until the increased meat deliveries to the state gave them the right to kill their beasts. It is unlikely that many of the peasants would "sell" their animals to the Kolkhoz if there remained any way of killing and eating them which did not render them liable to imprisonment.

These latest measures taken to blast the revival of individual husbandry in Russia are but the latest example of the manner in which Stalin clamps down his iron heel to crush the first buds of prosperity whenever a slight revival in some form of private enterprise has produced some small increase in the well-being of the Russian people. It would seem that the more absolutely Stalin departs from the democratic and equalitarian concepts which were an integral part of the Marxist theory, the more rigidly does he adhere to the dogma that all means of production and distribution must be state-owned. The more unsocial the content of Stalin's Russia, the more socialistic are its economic forms.

The food shortage in 1940 has apparently not led to any modification of the 1939 decrees. On April 25, 1940, the newspaper, *Socialist Agriculture,* was complaining of the "criminal practice" of squandering the common lands of the collective farms not yet having been checked. Instances are cited of wicked peasants who have planted vegetables on plots previously taken away from them, and of cases such as that of two collective farmers at Krasnodar who dared to plant a tenth of an acre with potatoes. It is stated that the survey of private plots carried out in 1939 had shown that more than 6 million acres too much land had been found to be in the private possession of collective farmers.* Orders are given once again to "exclude hostile elements" from the collective farms. This indicates that many thousands of peasants are being herded off to the concentration camps.

The dissatisfaction of the peasantry is likely to have been one of the main causes for the extremely unsatisfactory accomplishment of the spring sowing plans in 1940. *Izvestia* on April 16 reported that the total acreage sown by April 10 was a mere 4.2 million hectares, only 5 per cent of the plan, and compared this with 12½ million hectares sown by that date last year when 15 per cent of the plan had already been fulfilled.

The breakdown of a large number of tractors and the failure to repair them, combined with a shortage of tractor drivers due to the Finnish war and a shortage of gasoline due to the same cause and to the poor showing of the Baku oilfields since 1939, have all contributed to the critical state of Russian agriculture in 1940. *Pravda* on December 12, 1939, reported that the plan for tractor repairs was being fulfilled only 30 per cent in the last quarter of the year. The organ of the machine-building industry reported on December 11, 1939, that there was an acute shortage of tractor parts, and that half of all the pistons manufactured at the Stalingrad plant had had to be scrapped. In January the same journal reported that only 63.5 per cent of the plan for production of tractor parts had been fulfilled in the last quarter of 1939.

On December 10, 1939, *Socialisticheskoe Zemledelie ("Socialist Agriculture")* carried an article by the Commissar of Agriculture referring to the slowness in the execution of the plan which called for the training of 100,000 women tractor operators by the end of 1939, and

* *New York Times,* April 26, 1940.

said: "We must successfully train an enormous number of women capable of operating various machines by the spring of 1940, in order that no complications in the international situation may disturb the normal course of the development of our socialist agriculture."

It is obvious that Soviet agriculture, both in respect of its mechanical equipment and skilled labor force, and the "morale" of the peasants, is in no condition to face the strain of war. It is even feared that a famine on something like the 1932-33 scale may threaten the U.S.S.R. in 1940.

In spite of its poor yield, Russian agriculture remains now, as before, the main source of capital accumulation in Russia. The Soviet Government's principal source of revenue is not nationalized industry, nor the oil wells and mines, nor the great forests, but the bread tax. Most of the "Giants of the Five Year Plan" remain expensive toys which have not yet even today paid the high cost of their construction. The Soviet Government relies still upon the heavy toil of the millions of peasants for its existence. Industrialization, insofar as it has progressed, has done so at the cost of excessive exploitation of the peasants and heavy taxation of the workers' food.

The buying of grain cheap from the peasants, and the selling of it dear to the urban population, constitutes the state's major source of revenue. This revenue is collected in the form of a "turnover tax" which amounts to several hundred per cent on sales of bread and flour. In 1936 the "turnover tax" on the sale of agricultural foodstuffs by the state amounted to the colossal sum of 32 milliard rubles out of a total budget revenue of 71 milliard. The state made a profit of 32 milliard since the turnover tax consists of the difference between the cost to the state and the selling price.

In 1937 the state's profit from the sale of bread and other foodstuffs came to an even larger figure: 44.5 milliard rubles, of which about half consisted of the profit on bread alone. If one adds the 6.2 milliard profit obtained from the sale of vodka and other liquor, one gets a total of over 50 milliard as the revenue of the state from the taxation of the people's food. This 50 milliard constituted two-thirds of the total turnover tax, and half of the total budget revenue. The tax on the sale of consumers' goods produced only 11.4 milliard in spite of the high prices at which such goods were sold. As against the colossal figures for indirect taxation, direct taxation (income tax) produced a mere 2½ milliard, and taxes on enterprises less than 1 milliard.

Thus, at the end of the Second Five Year Plan, Russia's much-vaunted industrialization had produced so little result that the peasants were still bearing the brunt of state taxation, were in fact still the sole source for any considerable accumulation of "capital." Or, put another way round, the bread of the people was still the main source of revenue of the "socialist fatherland."

As an illustration of the colossal ignorance of the Webbs concerning even the admitted facts of Soviet economy, one must cite their observation that indirect taxation centers on "undesirable luxuries and upon expenditures not much incurred by the masses of the people." In fact, peasants, workers, employees, the whole population, pay enormous indirect taxes. The following "turnover taxes" were levied in 1937: *

Sugar	85%
Salt	66-83%
Cigarettes	75-90%
Makhorka (low-grade tobacco)	68-75%
Cotton textiles	44-65%
Hoisery	15-65%
Knitted underwear	25-55%
Rubber overshoes	33%
Sewing machines	39%
Boots and shoes	17-35%
Soap	34-59%
Shaving cream, toothpaste	68%

It will be noted that "luxuries" such as sewing machines were taxed *less,* not more, than necessities such as sugar, for the simple reason that the high cost of production of sewing machines made their selling price, even without the turnover tax, so high as to render them inaccessible to all but the top social stratum of the population. The turnover tax has been increased since 1937 (see Chapter VIII).

The state acquires from the peasants food supplies for the towns, and agricultural raw materials for industry, at arbitrary prices; and as a monopolist middleman sells food to the town population at any price it likes. It can do this, not only because it monopolizes trade, but because it has the power to force the peasants to produce. At one time it may slightly relax its pressure on the peasants and increase its pressure on the workers by raising the price of grain and increasing the price of bread; at another time it reverses the process. The decision

---

* Figures taken from *Toward an Understanding of the U.S.S.R.*, by Florinsky.

is made according to whether peasant or working-class discontent is considered most dangerous at the moment.

For instance, in 1934, following on the famine of the winter and spring of 1932-33, it was so obvious that the peasants had no incentive to work, and agriculture was in such a desperate condition, that the prices paid for grain were raised 20 per cent, while the price of bread was doubled. This doubling of the price to the urban consumers, while increasing the price paid to the peasant by only 20 per cent, gave the state a much larger revenue. The measure was mainly due to the derationing of bread, which made it essential to increase its price unless the workers were to be allowed to eat more. The abolition of bread cards was quite definitely a measure designed to reduce the privileges of the working class and improve the relative position of the peasants, for the doubling of bread prices assured the inability of the workers to buy as many other goods as before, and so set free a larger quantity of manufactured goods for village consumption.

When bread was derationed in 1935, its price was again doubled; but the price paid to the peasants for their grain is now not more than 50 per cent higher than in 1933. That is to say, a 200 per cent increase in the selling price of bread has been accompanied by an increase of 50 per cent or less in the purchase price of grain.

There has been some increase in the amount spent by the rural population on industrial consumers' goods, but their share in the national money income has not risen, but steadily declined. In 1930 the contribution of agriculture to the national income was reckoned at a quarter of the total, in 1933 at one-fifth, and in 1935 at less than one-sixth. Later figures (except for the planned ones, which are practically valueless) are not available.

The collective farms receive between 1.10 and 1.50 rubles for a *pood* of rye from the state. At the higher figure, this equals 9 kopeks per kilogram. The state sells black (rye) bread to the people in its shops at 85 kopeks a kilo. Since it takes approximately one kilogram of unmilled rye to make one kilogram of bread, the profit taken by the state is colossal even if a liberal allowance is made for milling, transport, and distribution costs.

In the case of tea, the exploitation of producer and consumer by the government is even more glaring. Collective farms in Georgia receive 10 to 12 rubles per kilo of tea, and the state sells this tea at about 75 rubles a kilo.

In spite of the boasted industrialization of the U.S.S.R. over the past decade it is still the hard physical labor of the peasantry—not the new factories and blast furnaces—which forms the main economic support of the Soviet state. As in colonial countries the exploited and oppressed cultivators of the land toil for the profit of a small ruling group, except that in Russia the majority of the exploited and exploiters are of the same race.

CHAPTER VII

SERVITUDE OF THE WORKERS

The history of the U.S.S.R. has proved to the hilt Trotsky's contention, expressed in 1905, that Lenin's conception of the dictatorship of the proletariat would in effect mean a dictatorship *over* the proletariat. Under Stalin the working class has finally lost all the gains of the Revolution. Their trade-unions have been transformed into state instruments of pure compulsion; they have no longer the right to strike, which workers in the Western capitalist countries enjoy; there is no habeas corpus to protect them against summary imprisonment or execution without trial; and there is no longer even a pretense of workers' management or control of industrial enterprise. The "labor book" * and the passport system chain them to their jobs and place them at the mercy of the factory manager. Whereas they are not allowed to leave one job to seek a better one elsewhere, the factory manager can dismiss them at three days' notice without appeal, and write adverse reports upon them in their labor book, which makes it difficult or impossible for them to secure other jobs.

The same applies to office employees and "specialists," but in the case of the highly qualified specialists it is mitigated by the nature of their work. The chairman of an enterprise cannot force a man to use his brains in quite the same crude way as he can force a man to use his muscles. (The manner in which the technicians are exploited by the political power is reserved for treatment in Chapter IX.)

For a few months, in 1917, the workers did control, through their shop committees, the working of the factories and mines and other enterprises. According to a decree of November 14, 1917, signed by Lenin and the People's Commissar of Labor:

> The workers' control organs have the right to supervise production, establish the minimum output of the undertaking, and take measures to ascertain the cost of production of goods. . . . They have the right to control all the business correspondence of the undertaking, and supervise accounts. The decisions of the workers' control organs are binding upon the owners.

---

* Originally "work certificates," but replaced in 1939 by "labor booklets."

This was an attempt to practice the dictatorship of the proletariat according to Marx. But Marx had somehow never realized that the owners and a large number of the engineers and technicians would prefer exile to submission to the proletarian dictatorship, or that they would refuse to work for the new state power. In Russia the factory committees were almost at once obliged to deal with the problem of actual factory management, as the majority of employers with their staffs, and often even with their foreman, left the factories.

If the Russian working class had been as well educated, cultured, and technically qualified as the British, German, or French, it might have been able to grapple with the problem of production and management with the help of the few engineers who remained and were willing to work for the Soviet state. Moreover, such a working class would probably have been on terms with the clerical and technical staff allowing of co-operation; there is no such wide social gulf between operatives and the rest of the factory staff in advanced capitalist countries as there was in Tsarist Russia.

A further difficulty, which finally wrecked the attempt at workers' control, was the tendency of each factory committee to be concerned only with the interests of its own undertaking. They raised prices irrespective of the consumer's needs and irrespective of the prices charged by other undertakings. The workers began to consider themselves as the owners of the enterprise, and a condition closely approaching anarchy developed.

In many enterprises the workers had taken control even before the November Revolution. The attempts made by the Menshevik-led trade-unions to regain control of the workers in the factories were unsuccessful and were opposed by the Bolsheviks because they did not, as yet, have a majority in the trade-unions. When, at the Trade-Union Congress of January 1918, they had acquired a majority, they amalgamated the Central Association of Factory Committees with the Central Trade-Union organization.

At the Second Trade-Union Congress in 1919, Lenin was already declaring that "today it is insufficient for us to limit ourselves to proclaiming the dictatorship of the proletariat. It is inevitable to give a certain state character to the trade-unions, inevitable to merge them with the organs of state power, inevitable that the building of large-scale industry should pass completely into their hands."

In 1920 at the Third Congress of Trade-Unions, the Factory Committees were deprived of any share in factory management. The loss of privilege for the workers contained in the abolition of the Factory

Committees was supposed to be compensated for by increased unionization of the workers. They were, as so often in the future, given the shadow for the substance; trade-union membership instead of real workers' control through the Factory Committees.

In 1920 also, the Menshevik opposition was suppressed. This opposition may be called the democratic opposition, and consisted of those who maintained that the Revolution was a bourgeois-democratic one, not a socialist one, and that the trade-unions should protect and fight for the workers, not be subordinated to the state.

In 1917, at the All-Russian Conference of Trade-Unions, the Mensheviks had expressed their conception of the Revolution and of the function of the trade-unions as follows:

> The Revolution must make of Russia, politically and economically, a European country. Our backward labor movement must become a European one. It must acquire the same forms of organization as those in the highly developed capitalist countries of Europe. This applies to our political life as well as to the Trade-Union Movement.

The Bolsheviks, on the contrary, declared in 1920 that the trade-unions ought to become "organs subordinated to the socialist power."

In effect, all this meant that the workers themselves could not be trusted with the power; they must be "guided"—or coerced—by their organized vanguard, the Communist party. The Mensheviks and Social Revolutionaries having by this time been proscribed, all the high trade-union officials were Bolsheviks. Nevertheless, Lenin still thought that the workers needed protection against "their own" government, and envisaged the trade-unions as affording them that protection. Even *before* the introduction of the N.E.P. he had declared: "Our present government is such that the proletariat, organized to the last man, must protect itself against it. And we must use the workers' organizations for the protection of the workers against their government." *

This statement was hardly consistent with the policy of making the trade-unions "organs subordinated to the socialist power." But Lenin wanted to camouflage the complete subordination of the workers to the state. In place of the former Factory Committee, which had meant real workers' control of industrial enterprises, he instituted the Troika (triangle, or 3-horse carriage). The Troika consisted of the factory manager, the secretary of the communist cell, and the representative of the trade-union in the factory. It was supposed to run the enterprise.

* *Complete Works of Lenin,* Vol. 26, p. 67; Moscow, 1930.

Obviously, even if the trade-union representative had been freely elected and not a Party member, he would have had little power against the other two members of the Troika. But in any case, all three were usually Party members; and, if it happened that one of them was not, he was all the more powerless against the other two. For the non-Party man was "outside the law" and subject to arbitrary dismissal, arrest, or even execution, should he do anything so "counter-revolutionary" as to oppose the interests of the workers to those of the state, or voice the grievances of those he was supposed to represent against a Party decision. Thus, although in theory the "workers' representatives" in the Troika had the right to discuss hours and wages, in practice they dared not do so. Fear was reinforced by ambition: the way to a "cushy job" or social advancement was through applauding the decisions of the Party, not through representing the interests of the workers.

Wages and hours in the U.S.S.R. are fixed by the Commissariat of Labor, so the factory workers' representative had not even the nominal right to discuss the questions most vital to the workers. About all he could do was to suggest minor reforms such as that drinking water be made available in the factory, or baths installed at the mines. Even such amenities were, however, subject to the availability of funds over which he had no control.

There has, in fact, never since 1920 been any organized workers' control over factory managers; but, prior to the First Five Year Plan, the free market and the comparatively personal freedom of the workers acted as a check against abuses. Since 1929 the managers have been driven by "the Plan" to disregard even the State Labor Code and to ignore the actual hours and wages decreed by the Commissariat of Labor. "The Plan" comes before aught else, and the manager knows that if he fails to fulfill it he is "for it"; whereas, if he works his men harder, they dare not complain and have no redress.

The trade-unions, so long as Tomsky lived, made feeble efforts to protect the standards of the working class. *Trud,* the official organ of the Soviet trade-unions, used occasionally to expose the breaking of the Labor Code. In April 1934 it stated that instead of the official seven-hour day "overtime is practiced on a large scale, especially in the heavy industries. Cancellation of the prescribed holiday, every sixth day, has become a common occurrence." In 1934 a special investigation by the all-Ukrainian Committee of the Machinists' Union reported: "In the factories of the Machine Trust the employees usually work from 14 to 16 hours a day—without being paid overtime." * Similarly, it was reported that in the Dan Basin mines the night-shift worked 9 or 10 hours instead of the 6 prescribed by law. At one steel plant near Moscow the operatives had worked an average of 15 hours a day for three months.

Of course, the Communist argues that the workers had "volunteered" to work overtime without wages to speed industrialization. In fact, they had no choice. If a Party man got up—on orders from the center—to propose more work, speeding up, overtime, anyone who objected was at once brought to the attention of the O.G.P.U. and, if not liquidated, terrorized into keeping his mouth shut. Russia is the one country where the workers are expected not only to submit but to cheer when their wages are reduced or their hours increased.

Although the facts behind the façade are for the most part carefully hidden in the U.S.S.R., they are upon occasion revealed in the Press at the preliminary to a little blood-letting to relieve the pressure. When the workers' discontent, as reported to the Kremlin by the ever-present O.G.P.U., becomes so acute that there is danger of an outburst, a few Party and trade-union officials are sacrificed to appease the proletariat. The workers' grievances are aired for a few days or weeks in the Press; specific instances of abuses, "malpractices," etc., in various enterprises are published. The blame is then laid on individual factory managers, trade-union bureaucrats, or technicians; and these are dismissed, expelled from the Party, sometimes shot. Since it would be wasteful to sacrifice those Party members in whose complete subservience to the Stalinist machine there is the greatest confidence, it is usual to pick on those of whose "loyalty" there is some doubt. Often, therefore, the best men in an enterprise are chosen as the victims. Sometimes, however, popular discontents require victims of high rank, as for instance in 1937, when all the members of the secretariat of the Central Trade-Union Council were branded as "enemies of the people," and four of them arrested and charged with Trotskyist sabotage. Prior to this, in March, the Central Trade-Union Council had publicly deplored the flagrant violations of the rights of the trade-unions and said neglect of the needs and demands of the union members was the chief characteristic of the entire trade-union system in the U.S.S.R. *Trud* in April stated: "In all the unions, from the central boards to the craft committees, the undemocratic system is in use. General meetings are practically non-existent. For years there have been no elections to

* These quotations are taken from an article on "Organised Labour under the Soviets" by Manya Gordon. *Foreign Affairs*, April 1938.

the Central Unions." All this did not mean that anything was changed thereafter. The Soviet Government plays with the workers like a cat with a mouse, continually raising their hopes and continually dashing those hopes.

The abuses are, of course, caused not by individuals, but by the Soviet system of exploitation which exacts them in contravention of the paper laws and decrees of the Soviet Government. The factory administration, being told it must produce a certain quantity of goods according to the Plan, is forced to throw overboard all standards of working conditions. Each manager is between Scylla and Charybdis; he may be accused of sabotage if he does not fulfill the plan, and he may be accused of it if he does, if scapegoats are required. Since the state puts production first, the welfare of the workers last, it is safest to neglect the latter. Moreover, the trade-union officials or the engineers can be held responsible for the bad labor conditions. Non-Party men, even when administrative posts are open to them, dare not take them. For they are far more likely to be made scapegoats than Party men, and conditions of work make either breaking of the laws or non-fulfillment of the Plan unavoidable.

The Soviet Government attempts to disown responsibility for the disgraceful working conditions by placing responsibility for factory inspection, sanitation, insurance, and general welfare on the trade-unions, which are powerless to improve matters.

In March 1937 Stalin abolished the Troika. Although it had never been of the least use to the workers as a means of defense against excessive exploitation, it had hampered efficient management. Obviously, three men, all Party members and all ambitious, quarreled, and had at times different views as to the best way to make the operatives work harder.

By abolishing the Troika, Stalin was destroying the last feeble remnant of workers' rights, for it would upon rare occasions happen that the workers' representative was stronger—i.e., had more backing in the local Party Committee—than the factory manager. Moreover, so long as in theory the workers had the right to question the ukases of the manager, it was always conceivable that the pressure of working-class discontent would one day find means to express itself.

Since the abolition of the Troika, says the Soviet Press, the factory manager has been "relieved of endless worry and given freedom to do *what is necessary.*" Of course, Stalin always makes a display of giving the people something when he is in fact depriving them of even the little they have. So Zhdanov, the Leningrad Party boss, announced that the workers would be in a position to state their grievances more freely now that the trade-unions had no longer any part in the administration of the factory. When, however, some trade-union leaders were so foolish as to take this pronouncement seriously and began to discuss the terrible plight of the workers, they were at once arrested as counter-revolutionaries.

Examination of the "laws" of the Soviet Union is really a waste of time, for the secret police are always above all the laws, and literally any expressions of dissatisfaction are dubbed "counter-revolutionary" and the people punished accordingly. The only value of the laws, labor codes, and regulations consists in their duping of foreign tourists and "friends of the Soviet Union." They are like a fine silk dress covering the filth, the sores, and the deformities of a beggar. As the Abbé Custine remarked a century ago of Tsarist Russia, "After a few months' stay in Russia, you no longer believe in laws."

Trade-unions have, in fact, ceased to exist in Russia as completely as in Nazi Germany. The Nazis have been honest enough to admit it, and the Bolsheviks haven't. There is practically no difference between the German Labor Front and the Russian trade-unions. Membership is compulsory in both cases—proving their value to the government; and they possess neither the functions nor the authority of trade-unions in the Western sense of the word. Strikes are forbidden, and when intolerable misery causes them to break out, the strikers are shot down by the O.G.P.U. troops. The function of the trade-unions in Soviet Russia is that of slave drivers, and that of a government employment bureau. They also act as the collectors of the forced loans, which amount on an average to one month's wage a year deducted from each worker.

Kléber Legay, the French miners' delegate who visited the U.S.S.R. in 1936, was astounded to find armed guards everywhere in the Donetz coal fields, not only at the entrance to the mines, but also down below in the workings, in the offices, even in the eating houses. The explanation given him was that these soldiers were there to prevent any counter-revolutionary acts. How comes it, M. Legay remarks, that the miners themselves down in the pits should be suspected of being counter-revolutionaries when they are supposed to be the proud and happy owners of their means of production? If, he asks, the working-class unanimity which the Soviet Government boasts of is a reality, why give visitors the impression that the regime survives only because it has guns to sustain it?

He also notes the fact that these guards all have to be fed and supported by the workers, and that they are mostly young men; whereas he saw many old men of sixty working in the mines while the young soldiers stood by watching them.

This French miner was also horrified at the lack of provisions for safety in the mines. Everything, he says, is apparently done on the principle of producing as much as possible as cheaply as possible, so that even elementary precautions to save life are not taken. He gives in his book * a detailed account of the failure to ensure safe workings, and is appalled that thousands and thousands of miners, including the women who also work underground, should be exposed to the constant risk of death or mutilation for the sake of cheap production.

When accidents occur, the blame is placed on the engineers and technicians, as in the famous Schakti trial, which condemned eight of the accused to death. As M. Legay remarks, either the factory inspectors don't exist or don't do their job, or it would have been quite impossible for the "wreckers" to have deliberately prepared and caused explosions. Not only this, but the miners themselves would have been aware of any such plot. In other words, unless there were general assent, it would have been impossible to prepare an explosion in a mine by the accumulation of dust.

Accidents occur frequently because precautions against them would be expensive, and the state is more interested in paying armed guards to prevent strikes or acts of sabotage by the miners than in saving the miners' lives.

The veritable enslavement of the working class to the parasitic state began in 1930. In that year Stalin started to "rivet" the workers to their jobs. They were forbidden to leave the work they were engaged on without permission of the management. In January 1931 it was decreed that former railway workers were compelled to return to work on the railways, and ten years' imprisonment or the death penalty was prescribed for "lack of discipline" among the transport workers.

In February 1931 came the device subsequently copied by Hitler, the work certificate, containing details of the workers' social origins, history, training, type of employment, past sins of omission and commission, fines, reasons for dismissal.† The whole working population was docketed, and each individual's record written down, as in the case of convicts in other countries. Whereas the workers were forbidden to leave their jobs, however bad their conditions of work, the various trusts were given the right to transfer them at will from one

* *Un Mineur français chez les Russes.*
† In Germany they have labor books of the same kind.

town or province to another, regardless of their consent. This was all the more terrible in Russia than in Germany, where a similar, though less far-reaching, "mobility of labor" was later instituted; because in Russia the shortage of housing was such that being sent to a new town meant having no room to house oneself or one's family.

In spite of the decrees, the misery of the workers was so great that they continued to wander from place to place seeking more tolerable conditions of work, seeking a town or a district where they could buy sufficient food with their wages not to starve, or where a room might be available to house their families.

In April 1931 Stalin added rewards to punishments in the endeavor to keep the workers at their jobs and make them work harder. Henceforth preferential rations were decreed for the shock brigades and also priority in the allocation of rooms to live in and fuel to warm their "living space." Starvation everywhere made the amount of wages received a minor question; so, like slaves, the workers were rewarded with a little more to eat if they worked harder.

Next came a decree making the workers responsible for damages to material. The man or woman put to work on a defective machine had henceforth to pay out of his or her wages the decreased value of the finished product caused by neglected machinery or ignorance.

By the following year (November 1932) the worker was punished by dismissal if absent a single day from work. In the case of illness he must send a doctor's certificate showing that he had a temperature of at least 100°. Illnesses without temperatures were not admitted as an excuse for remaining away from work.

When in the same year the Co-operatives were placed under the direction of the factories, it meant that the dismissed worker immediately lost his bread card and also his wife's and children's bread ration. The workers were truly enslaved by this time. Anyone who incurred the factory manager's displeasure could be immediately thrown out of his job *and* his room if, as was frequently the case, the house in which he lived belonged to the factory; and at the same time be deprived of his right to buy bread for himself and his family. The astonishing thing was that so many men preferred vagabondage to this slavery. This applied in particular to the young single men. Those with families were restrained by the certainty of starvation for their children; nevertheless some went off and left their families, continually adding to the numbers of the homeless children in Russia, who were still officially supposed to be the orphans of the civil war period.

Stalin's remedy for evils due to the intolerable misery he had caused was, as ever, repression. In a final attempt to tie the half-starved workers to their jobs and the famine-stricken peasants to their farms, he resorted to an old Tsarist police measure, the obligatory interior passport; but in a more universal and rigorous form. The whole urban population, and all the peasants living near the large towns, had to secure a passport in which it was written down what were the social origins of the bearer, the members of his family, and his occupation. No one was henceforth allowed to move from the town in which he lived to another, or even leave his house for a single night, without permission of the police. This measure was designed to prevent migration of labor and to stop the starving peasants from flocking to the towns in search of work. Residence in Moscow became a much-prized privilege because of the better food provisioning of the capital. But all the important towns were a little better off than the small towns and villages in respect of food supplies; so that urban residence in general became a privilege.

A Byzantine immobility was imposed by law. Henceforth each worker and peasant was to be tied down to the job to which Providence had called him. The only historical parallel is the edicts issued by the decaying Roman Empire from Diocletian to Theodosius, whereby perpetual and hereditary membership of trade guilds was decreed for the industrial workers, and attachment to the soil for the cultivators. Productive labor had then, as in Russia under Stalin, become so onerous and so poorly rewarded that the state tried to enforce by decree that each man should follow his hereditary craft.

As early as November 1930, the Labor Exchanges were closed down and the unemployed told they were to go without question where they were sent and to whatever kind of job the state decreed. At the same time, unemployment relief was abolished, since in theory there was no more unemployment. In reality, unemployment never disappeared; but the state washed its hands of responsibility for it and took the line that if you were unemployed it was your own fault and you should starve.

Actually, as anyone living in Russia knows, there has always continued to be unemployment. Official proof of this fact was given in 1933, when, with the introduction of the passport system, tens or hundreds of thousands of persons "not performing work of national importance" were expelled from the towns.

Even the official Soviet statistics have revealed unemployment. The Soviet Union Year Book gives the following figures of total numbers of workers and employees in different years:

Year	Number of Workers and Employees in State Industry
1928	3,096
1932	6,481
1933	6,229
1934	6,531
1935	7,066
1936	7,675

In large-scale industry and construction, the decline in 1933 was over a million, against which there was a rise of 200,000 in the number of wage-earners on the land. Many urban workers had been forced back to the villages whence they originally came. The great capital investments in industry under the Five Year Plan had failed to relieve the population pressure in the villages, which is Russia's age-old problem.

The Soviet Government has "liquidated" not unemployment, but the unemployed. It starves them to death or rounds them up and sends them to forced labor in the concentration camps, where they die off in a few years.

I myself saw one of the round-ups of the "beggars" in Moscow (see Chapter IV). Fred Beale, the Gastonia striker who preferred to risk jail by returning to the United States to life as one of the privileged in U.S.S.R., has given in *Proletarian Journey* a heart-rending account of the hordes of starving workers in the Ukraine in 1932:

> At the Kharkov Tractor Plant there was not a day that I did not see large groups of people waiting outside of the gates looking for work.... Most of them were turned away, particularly those who came from collectives. I remember one old man, ragged and freezing, begging for a job. Being hungry, he was ready to do anything. He pestered the young official who did the hiring. "Go away, old man," said our young Communist bureaucrat. "Go to the field and die."
>
> As the old man silently and quiveringly turned away and walked down the ice-covered road, the young man's eyes followed him with contempt. "It's time we put these old people out of the way," he remarked.

* * * * *

The crowds of roving peasants were augmented by discharged workers from factories, workers who couldn't keep up with the Stalin pace, or who had grumbled, protested, or fallen into disfavor with their overseers. For a worker to get fired in Soviet Russia means death by starvation, unless he can learn the art of begging, or is fortunate enough to have some kind relative in the capitalist countries.... So the Tractor Plant and our foreign colony there was besieged by droves of begging and pleading people, seeking a few crumbs of bread, some potato peelings, or some fish bones. Not a day passed without groups of these disinherited workers and peasants, young and old, men and women, knocking at our doors. They would dig into the garbage boxes and fight like packs of wild dogs for food remains.

The Stalin clique positively hated these intruders. The hungry folk stood in the way of the bureaucrats anxious to make a good showing before the visiting delegations and tourists. Indeed, of what use was the propaganda put out in America, claiming that the Soviet worker was prosperous and always employed, if these hungry, shelterless, jobless "beggars" were permitted to expose the truth? The Soviet authorities, with the aid of the Communist Party members of the factory, who were eager to win favors from the high officials, would round up the starving people in the streets, collect them in great herds, and turn them over to the G.P.U. It was a weekly occurrence. Sometimes a raid would be improvised a few hours before the arrival of a foreign delegation. I confess that I even took part to some extent in these human dragnets.

In spite of all the Draconian legislation, the Russian workers have continued to struggle against their enslavement. That struggle cannot be carried on in the open. Outwardly the workers must continue to shout that "life has become joyous" and that their conditions of life are wonderful. They cannot organize or strike, for the O.G.P.U. is always at hand to carry away to the concentration camps all who murmur a complaint. But all the repression has failed to prevent many thousands of workers from leaving their jobs and seeking better wages in some other town or place. Most serious of all for the Soviet state has been their refusal to work harder, the unwillingness or the physical incapacity of the ill-fed, ill-housed, dragooned working class to produce more. The productivity of labor in the U.S.S.R. remains far below that of labor in capitalist Europe, and even further below that of American labor. The Russian standard of life remains an Asiatic, or colonial, standard; and the productivity of Russian labor cannot be increased until the workers are given sufficient nourishment, decent housing, and some hope of amelioration in living standards in general.

The introduction first of so-called socialist competition, and then in

1935 of Stakhanovism, has succeeded in producing pacemakers who earn 10 or even 20 times as much as the ordinary workers, but it has not succeeded in stepping up the general level of labor productivity to any considerable extent. When one reads Soviet boasts of record-breaking in the mines or industries by Stakhanovists, it must be borne in mind that these men or women usually have other workers under them to perform the subsidiary tasks, or to work under their direction. The Stakhanovists have come to perform the function of foremen, or gang leaders, and are hated by the ordinary workers whom they drive, and whose piece-rate wages are reduced when some new record has been set. There have even been murders of Stakhanovists by desperate workers who could not keep up the pace and feared dismissal.

In the period of the First Five Year Plan there was still enthusiasm, faith, and hope to spur a large number of the workers to a maximum effort. But the Plan not only failed to improve their condition; in the end they were worse off than at the beginning. When bread was derationed in 1934, its price was doubled and wages increased only by 10 per cent. Worst of all from the point of view of the feelings of the masses, was the ever greater differentiation in standards of life as between themselves and their rulers. A bitter saying began to be heard: "Yes, *they* have constructed socialism for themselves." The workers became more and more conscious of the fact that all their privations and toil and misery had gone, not to make a better world for themselves and their children, but to provide luxuries for their rulers.

As more and more "commercial" shops were opened, and things they could never afford to buy were displayed in the windows, bitterness increased. Earlier, when the meat, butter, eggs, chocolates, fruit, clothing, etc., had been supplied to the ruling group in "closed distributors," the masses were not fully aware of the great gulf between them and their rulers. Luxury then was not displayed, but hidden and unavowed. But as the years went by it became obvious to the dullest intelligence that the fruits of their labor were not for the working class, and never would be.

After the hellish years of semistarvation, 1934, 1935, and 1936 seemed better. There was enough bread, even if most workers and peasants rarely ate anything else. It became possible for some of them to buy sugar and herring, fats and vegetables, in small quantities. But by the end of 1936, with the ever-increasing military appropriations, the standard of life again began to deteriorate, and with it production figures fell. The old vicious circle began again: less food for the workers and therefore less production of goods to sell to the peasants to produce food. Moreover, the mad "record-breaking" of the Stakhanovists had caused machinery to deteriorate rapidly. Lathes and other machines were aged before their time, and new ones had to be imported from abroad. Butter and other necessities were again exported to pay for imports of machinery, as during the First Five Year Plan, and food queues again appeared in the streets.

In effect, the sacrifices imposed on the people from 1928-33 to pay for industrialization had been vain. For two or three years the imported machinery made it possible to produce a little more and to give the workers and peasants the minimum necessary to keep them above the starvation level. But the state's policy of encouraging record-breaking without regard to deterioration of capital annulled the brief gains. From 1936 onward, production in the basic industries fell. Worse still was the condition of the railways. The Press reported coal, steel, automobiles, and grain left waiting at the depots in huge quantities.

Undoubtedly the economic crisis which set in in 1937 was one reason for the purge. Discontent was so general that a scapegoat had to be found. Since the workers and the peasants loathed the Communist officials who dragooned them and who lived in comparative luxury, the execution or imprisonment of thousands of Party members was in one sense a human sacrifice to the outraged proletariat and peasants.

In March 1938 *Pravda* accused the "Trotskyist wreckers" of being responsible for the holding back of wages to the workers and manufactures to the peasants. "Today," it wrote on March 6, "everyone can see for themselves just who is responsible for the unsatisfactory functioning of the rural co-operatives, just who held back supplying the toilers with such goods as sugar, salt, *makhorka* [low-grade tobacco], which are available in surplus quantities in our country."

The workers were to understand that neither Stalin nor his system was responsible, but the "Trotskyists." It is more than doubtful whether the workers at this stage of their experience were convinced, but the tumbling of so many heads, the fall of so many of the mighty "boyars of the bureaucracy" may have assuaged their discontents a little. Human nature is such that when people are very miserable, it is a comfort to them to know that others are suffering even more. Hitler's persecution of the Jews offers the same kind of psychological comfort to the German people, or is at least intended to.

However, Stalin has played this game a little too often. The disorganization of the national economy was intensified by the mass arrests. Conditions went from bad to worse, and it was little consolation to the workers to know that if they were only serfs, those sent to the concentration camps during the purge were slaves. The difference between "free" labor and penal labor in the concentration camps is no longer very great.

In 1938 there were indications of widespread ca'canny, veritable strikes on the job, and even perhaps strikes of workers, who stayed away from the factories. In January 1939 it was publicly admitted that in 1938 the Plan had collapsed. Production at the end of that year had sunk to *below* the 1935 level. The very sharp fall during December in the production of coal, iron, steel, and rolled products is only to be explained by something in the nature of strikes.

Daily Production in Thousands of Tons

	Planned Figure	Official Figures of Actual Daily Production			
		Dec. 14	Dec. 15	Dec. 17	Dec. 19
Iron	45.6	37.6	34.5	28	26
Steel	56.1	44.5	41.0	34.8	32.6
Rolled Products	43.6	39.1	36.8	28.5	25.2
Coal	390	356	347.6	294.7	?

By January 1939 production had been pulled up to the early December figure, which was less than that for December 1935.

Car-loadings which had reached a daily total of 100,000 in the summer of 1938 dropped to 50,000 in mid-December, but part of the drop here may legitimately be claimed to have been due to snowstorms.

A hint of what had been happening is given in an article in *Pravda* (January 15, 1939), in which it thundered against "lax executives" who were "afraid to fire shirkers for fear of creating for themselves difficulties with labor supply." The possibility of strikes is, of course, not admitted in the workers' fatherland; so *Pravda* had to speak of shirkers when strikers was probably meant.

Although Stalin's unprecedented severity and terrorism enable him to deal with "labor troubles" in a manner which must be the envy of a harassed capitalist, even he cannot always prevent strikes of a kind. When life offers no hope, when in very truth you have "nothing to lose but your chains," you may let the O.G.P.U. do its worst. Death can sometimes be preferable to life as a starved and overdriven slave, even to the Russians so long inured to misery and oppression.

Again Stalin cannot afford to liquidate the workers as a class, as he liquidated the Kulaks. Their wholesale refusal to be bound to their jobs, whatever the conditions, forces the factory managers to be "lax" upon occasion if their whole labor force is not to be transferred to the O.G.P.U. concentration camps. Hence in 1939 the original regulation forbidding the re-employment of dismissed workers was modified to permit it after a six-months interval.

It is by now difficult for Stalin to think up any new decrees to bind down the working class. Their wages are so low and their housing so terribly bad, with the exception of the foremen and Stakhanovists, who act as slave drivers, that their standard of life cannot be further reduced without decreasing production. However, late in 1938, following the 50 per cent fall in production, Stalin thought of one last method of making the toilers toil harder and preventing their striking on the job. On December 29, 1939, immediately following an order to increase the productivity of labor by 25 per cent *and a cut in piece-rate wages of 14 per cent,* Stalin issued a decree which annulled Article 119 of the much-advertised Constitution. According to the latter, "The right to rest and leisure" of the toilers is insured by the institution of annual vacations with pay for workers and employees, and by the provision of sanatoria, rest homes, and clubs serving the needs of the toilers. The right to go to the sanatoria and rest homes has for many years been restricted to managers, foremen, Stakhanovists, and the very few ordinary workers who were adept at licking the boots of the factory bosses. But there remained the holiday period with pay, and there are some elementary social services for all, in particular free medical service when sick, maternity benefits, some medical care for the workers' children, and very small pensions for old workers. The new decree limits full "social security" to those who remain years at one job. The worker is henceforth only entitled to all the social services provided under law if he has remained at one and the same factory or institution *for more than six years.* If his labor book shows a record of from 3-6 years' work at one and the same place, he gets 80 per cent social security; if 2-3 years, 60 per cent; if less than 2 years, only 50 per cent.

Justifying, with cruel irony, this deprivation of full social services under the law for the majority of the "toilers," the organ of the Department of Justice stated: "All former theories of labor and labor laws in the U.S.S.R. have been permeated with capitalist counter-revolutionary spirit." *

Free and guaranteed social services, and the humanitarian sentiment which inspires them, are thus now officially designated as capitalist; and Lenin and the old Bolsheviks are told off for their bourgeois way

* *Socialist Appeal* (New York), Feb. 4, 1939.

of thinking because they decreed annual vacations, medical attention, and unemployment benefits for the proletariat. Under Stalin's "socialist" state, the workers must be deprived of any and every right they had won under the capitalist system.

The truly amazing aspect of this new decree is the virtual admission by Stalin, when he promulgated it, that he now considers the workers responsible for everything wrong with the state of Russia. He referred to the "disorganizers" among the workers, to the "individual, ignorant, backward, or unscrupulous people who cause industry, transport, and the whole national economy great damage." Since a few wicked workers could hardly damage the whole national economy, it must be the majority of the working class which is wrecking it. In 1930-32 the Kulaks and the non-Party specialists were the scapegoats; from 1936-38 it was the old Bolsheviks. The companions of Lenin having all been liquidated as Bucharinist-Trotskyist saboteurs, wreckers, and counter-revolutionaries, and as German-Japanese-British spies, there remains no one else but the workers to put the blame upon. So one cannot escape the conclusion that, by 1939 under "the dictatorship of the proletariat," the proletariat had become counter-revolutionary and was wrecking its own heritage!

There is a terrible negatively progressive force inherent in the use of terror and repression as a means of government. Want begets inefficiency, and inefficiency repression and terror, which in turn begets more want and greater inefficiency—and so leads to more repression and more terror. This, in ever-accelerating tempo, has been the history of the U.S.S.R. In 1939 Stalin attempted to break the vicious circle by directing the terror against neighboring peoples, hoping that national "glory" would reconcile the Russian people to their lot and make it possible to secure their consent, as well as their subjection, to his rule. If he cannot succeed in doing this, it will not perhaps much longer be possible to clamp down the lid on the seething discontent of the Russian workers and prevent the explosion which would wreck the experiment in "socialism."

The facts given in this chapter prove that the "social security" which is always cited by friends of the Soviet Union as compensation for the low wages earned by the Russian workers is only a myth. It is guaranteed in the Soviet Constitution; but this, like its other provisions, is mere eyewash for the foreigners. The Russian worker is unprotected either by the state or by a trade-union, and lives always on the brink of the abyss of unemployment, hunger, and homelessness. He can be dismissed by the manager without appeal, but he may not himself leave his job or go to a different town to seek work. He has no defense against wage reductions and no security in the miserable tenement room out of which he and his family can be turned into the street at three days' notice. His work, his food, his roof, his liberty, are subject to the caprices of his overseer. The Webbs' statement that the Soviet worker knows that his old age is provided for and that his children "will at all times have the essentials of health" is but a cruel and shameful mockery of his insecurity. At any moment his children may be turned into the streets to starve, and in old age he must exist on the charity of his relatives or die of starvation. Even before Stalin's latest decree reduced pensions for most old workers—for very few have worked consecutively without interruption at their jobs for six years—pensions were so tiny that old men went on working after sixty if they could keep up the pace. The pensions were calculated on the old uninflated ruble, and are now sufficient to buy at most a few loaves of bread a week.

Since 1929 the Soviet Government has carefully veiled the real condition of the working class by ceasing to publish cost of living figures or indices of prices. This has made it impossible for foreigners to have any conception as to the decline or rise in real wages. The Russian citizen, of course, knows quite well that in such and such years his standard of life decreased because the price of all foods rose sharply; but the foreign tourist, told that the workers' wages are double what they were five years ago, is suitably impressed.

The rise in the average *nominal* wage of all workers and employees is shown below:

Rubles per Year

1924-5	1925-6	1926-7	1928	1930	1931	1932	1933	1934	1935	1936	1937	1938
450	571	624	703	936	1127	1427	1566	1858	2269	2776	2772	3447

In May 1937 the average monthly wage for workers in factory industry was *Rs.* 231 as against about 50 rubles in 1926-27. As against this fourfold increase in the *average* wage, however, the worker was paying five times as much for black bread and eight times as much for potatoes, while meat cost him ten times more than in 1926, and sugar seven times as much. As regards clothing, all the "gigantic successes on the industrial front" meant to the Soviet worker was that he had to pay nine times more for a pair of boots than in the "bad old days" of 1926, and twenty-five times more for woolen cloth, and five times more for cotton cloth. Other prices had risen in proportion.

As was often impressed upon me while working on "capitalist" statistics at the Communist Academy, an "average" figure always conveys a false idea as to the actual earnings of the majority, and a Marxist must therefore never employ average figures as an index of labor conditions. In Soviet Russia the inclusion under the heading "workers and employees" of well-paid specialists and of Party officials paid enormous salaries, entirely invalidates the figure of 231 given as the average wage. The general level of earnings was well below 200 rubles. According to a report made to the "Party actives" in Moscow in 1935, the usual wage for qualified workers was around 200 rubles, and that for laborers 100 rubles.*

Nor do the above calculations take into account the great deterioration in quality of the manufactured goods, the prices of which had risen so steeply. The kind of shoes or boots the worker was able to buy in 1926 would last him for several years, but the kind he bought in 1937 had soles little better than cardboard.

The workers' standard of life did not improve after the First Five Year Plan. On the contrary, it deteriorated further in 1935, owing to derationing of bread and sugar and other foodstuffs. It then slightly improved in 1936, owing to small reductions in food prices other than bread. Since 1939 it has again deteriorated, owing to higher prices, reduced piece-rate wages, and the shortage of food in the shops.

In a country of very low living standards, such as Russia, the price of bread is all-important, since it is the staple diet of the great mass of the people. To the mass of Russian workers earning 100 to 200 rubles a month, the doubling of the price of bread which accompanied derationing was the heaviest blow yet struck at them by their government. Formerly the industrial workers had received a ration of 800 grams of bread a day. Most of them ate only the black (rye) bread, and it had only cost them 12½ kopeks a kilo in 1932 as against 85 kopeks in 1937. True that the price of bread had been increased more than once between 1932 and 1935; but the *doubling* of the price when it was derationed, counted as a "great triumph of socialism," was one of those backhanded blows to which the worker had by now grown accustomed. As I have remarked in another chapter, when in the

* The large earnings of the Stakhanovists also increase the "average" wage. Leon Sedov, writing in the Trotskyist *New International* and quoting from figures given in *Pravda* of Nov. 16, 1935, showed that an ordinary miner was then earning between 400 and 500 rubles a month, whereas a Stakhanovist got more than 1600 rubles. Workers driving a team underground received only 170 rubles if not Stakhanovists. Some workers in the mines were earning only 150 rubles or less. The Soviet Press does not hide these facts; the large earnings of the Stakhanovists are cited to encourage other workers to emulate them.

U.S.S.R. one read in the newspaper of some great socialist achievement, one's heart always sank, since such an announcement inevitably heralded some fresh burden to be imposed. It was of little use to tell the worker he could now buy as much bread as he liked when his miserable wages no longer sufficed to purchase the minimum needed to feed his hungry children.

I remember hearing two women in our courtyard discussing the matter one evening as I returned from work. "Now," said one of them, "we shan't be able to afford a *kasha* (hot mush of cereal) dinner any more."

Such was "socialist progress."

Barmine, the ex-Soviet diplomat,* tells in his book of a conversation he had with the porter of his apartment house, whom he found mending shoes at midnight in his tiny little room:

> "Why do you work so hard?" I asked him, knowing that his working day was not eight or ten hours long, but more or less endless.
>
> "Why? Because we are hungry. I have five mouths to feed and they pay me 120 rubles."
>
> "But a general increase of 10 per cent has been made in all wages to compensate for the increased price of bread since derationing. Surely that has made things all right for you?"
>
> "You think so? We are seven, counting my wife and the five kids. We need seven kilos of bread a day since bread is the only food we can afford to buy. The price of bread has been doubled and I have had my wages increased by only 8 rubles a month. Either I've got to work nights, or steal, or we shall all starve."

This worker, whose case was normal, had to pay 178 rubles a month for bread if his wife and children were not to starve. Taking it that his wife earned another 90 rubles, they had about 218 rubles income, out of which 178 went for bread, leaving an insufficient amount to pay for lodging, heat, light, and forced loans and dues, even if they never tasted meat, or herring, or margarine, or even potatoes.

The textile workers whose conditions I have described elsewhere were even worse off than this porter, for they couldn't earn extra money cobbling or performing other personal services for the well-paid bureaucrats of Moscow.

The complete abolition of rationing meant in sum that the higher-income groups could henceforth freely purchase meat, butter, eggs,

---

* *Vingt Ans au Service de l'U.R.S.S.*, Paris, 1939.

and other scarcity goods at "commercial prices" in any quantities they could afford. For the mass of the wage-earners, employees as well as workers, the change was one for the worse. Their real wages were lower, but they could now gaze through the shop windows at all manner of appetizing foodstuffs which they could not hope to buy.

Since the Soviet Government publishes no cost of living statistics the only way to calculate the improvement or deterioration of the condition of the Russian working class since the Revolution is to compare wages and the prices of the necessities of life before the World War and now. Taking the year 1937, when the Russian workers' real wages were higher than in the two previous years (and higher than in 1940), we get the following comparison:

Workers of average qualifications in constructional industry and of mechanics in large scale industry: Average monthly earnings:

1914*	(in rubles)	1937
43.68		232.0

RETAIL PRICES OF FOODSTUFFS IN 1914 AND 1937

	August 1914	1937
Black bread per kilo	0.06	0.85
White " "	0.12	1.70
Beef " "	0.54	9.60
Veal " "	0.63	10.60
Pork " "	0.59	11.00
Herring " "	0.15	6.00
Cheese " "	0.98	14.80
Butter " "	1.17	20.00
Eggs, 10	0.25	6.50
Milk per liter	0.14	1.70
Total	4.73	82.75

The above prices show that the cost of staple foods in 1937 was about 15 times higher than in 1914, as against only a little more than a fourfold increase in wages. Since the average wage figure for 1914 was calculated on those for workers only, while the 1937 figure includes also clerical workers, specialists, Party officials, and the highly paid shock workers, it is certain that the average wage of the majority of workers was below 232 rubles a month. Even at 232 rubles the decline in real wages has obviously been very great.

* Figures taken from appendix to John Reed's *Ten Days That Shook the World*.

Whereas in 1914 a worker of average qualification could purchase 90 kilograms of beef or 38 kilograms of butter with his monthly wage, he could buy only 24 kilograms of beef and 11.5 kilos of butter in 1937. Since 1939 he has been able to buy even less than these quantities, and often had to stand hours in line to obtain the tiny quantity he could afford.

Expressed in terms of black bread, the staple diet of the working class today even more definitely than before the Revolution, the average daily wage now buys 9 kilograms as against the 24 kilograms it bought in 1914.

When it comes to computing the real wages of the Russian workers with regard to the purchase of manufactured goods, the decline in his standard of life is even more strikingly revealed.

Most articles of clothing now cost twenty times more than before the Revolution.

Cost of Most Essential Manufactures (in Rubles)

	1914	1938
Calico per meter	0.15	3.50
Woolen dress goods per meter	2.80	125
Heavy woolen overcoating per meter	8.40	250
Men's shoes per pair	12	250
" " " " lowest quality	—	65
Rubber galoshes per pair	2.50	18.70
Men's suits, one	40	890

Soviet apologists argue that money wages alone cannot give a true picture, since the workers now enjoy the benefit of social services which did not exist in Tsarist times. It is true that the workers now get free medical attention of a sort; that there are crèches and kindergartens for a small proportion of the workers' children and schools for the great majority; that working women get leave with pay before and after childbirth; that the worker is entitled to a fortnight's holiday with pay; and that some other minor social services have been provided by the state for the workers and employees. These social services have been severely curtailed (see page 187 above) since 1939, but they never compensated for the steep fall in real wages. The foreign tourist who used to be so impressed with the crèches, hospitals, schools and rest houses, did not know that he was being shown places accessible only to the Party bureaucracy and to a few foremen and shock workers. The hospitals and schools shown to the tourists were usually those reserved for the highest Party officials; those for the ordinary workers were for the most part pretty terrible places, with poor food, and an underpaid and overworked staff. If one had a relative in hospital one took food to him regularly if one could possibly afford it.

The worker is certainly no better housed than before the Revolution; most of them live in conditions of overcrowding which could hardly be equaled anywhere in Europe. Rents have remained low for those who live in the old houses and apartments. In the new blocks of flats built by the housing co-operatives they are fairly high. It is, however, true that charges for rent, light, and gas have not increased nearly as much as the prices of food and manufactures.

In 1937, before social services were curtailed, 26 million persons were covered by social insurance, and for this purpose 5.5 billion was deducted from the total wage fund of 83.1 billion. The peasants do not enjoy the benefit of social insurance. Neither peasants nor workers are entitled to unemployment pay, and pensions for old workers are so very low that all who can do so continue to work.

Taken all in all, the Russian working class enjoys far smaller benefits under the Soviet Government's much boasted social insurance than the English, German, or French workers derive from the social services long existent in those countries.

I remember once in Moscow reading in the *Manchester Guardian* how a careful unemployed worker spent his unemployment pay. We calculated that to secure the diet possible for an unemployed family in England one required at least 1000 rubles in Moscow; that is to say, at least five times as much as workers of fair qualification were then earning in the U.S.S.R.

In 1938 real wages must have fallen somewhat below 1937, since in the latter year the ruble was further depreciated by an increase in the turnover tax on manufactured goods. In January 1940 the price of many kinds of food was increased 35 per cent, and in April 1940 the prices of butter, eggs, milk, meat, vegetables, etc., were increased between 25 per cent and 100 per cent according to whether the price had already been increased in January or not. Only bread is still sold at the old price.

I have already referred to the lowering of piece-rate wages in December 1939. A Press campaign was started in November and December 1939 to "strengthen labor discipline and increase the productivity of labor." In other words, the drive against the peasants begun in the spring of 1939 was accompanied by renewed pressure upon the working class to force it to work harder and to rivet each worker more firmly to his job. An article in *Pravda* on December 22, 1938, refers to such "flagrant violations of labor discipline" as: uncontrolled transfers from one factory to another, drunkenness, malingering, loafing, purposely turning out defective goods, absence from work without permission, chronic lateness, abuse of sick leave to obtain supplementary employment elsewhere, occupancy of factory living quarters by persons not entitled to them, and "other practices disorganizing to Soviet production."

All the crimes referred to in this article have for years been punishable, as we have seen earlier in this chapter. The significance of this latest attempt to stop them is the proof it affords that whatever the compulsion and savage penalties imposed, it has in practice been found impossible completely to enslave the Russian working class.

The factory manager who should dismiss the workers in his enterprise for being a few minutes late for work, for getting drunk, or occasionally missing a day's labor, would very soon find himself without any workers to carry out his production plan. Were the factory administrations to apply the labor laws in their full severity, soon the whole working population would be in the concentration camps of the O.G.P.U. or wandering in starving hordes along the roads. Most Russian workers have never been inured to the strict discipline of modern industrial life; few can, however hard they try, keep up the pace set by the Stakhanovists without breaking down or feeling the strain so intolerable that they risk dismissal in order to take a day's rest. There is a limit to the physical and psychological endurance of the ill-fed workers; times when all the terrors threatened by the O.G.P.U. cannot keep them working.

CHAPTER VIII

THE COST OF SOVIET INDUSTRIALIZATION

"It is only when the people submit blindly that a master can order tremendous sacrifices to produce very little." *

Thus spoke the Abbé Custine concerning one of Stalin's prototypes, the "Iron Tsar," Nicholas I, who made it a crime at common law to go on strike. In the Abbé's eyes the edifices erected by the Tsars represented "not the force of a great country, but the uselessly wasted sweat of a great people." But tourists from the "capitalist world" to Stalin's empire were less perceptive than the clerical visitor from France to the nineteenth-century empire of the Romanovs. They admired the gigantic edifices and were indifferent to the wasted sweat and the misery of the Russian people.

Communists and fellow travelers, many of whom at home had never seen the inside of a factory or a power station, journalists and authors, schoolteachers and "intellectuals" of all kinds, went on conducted tours of the Soviet Union and worshiped before the shrine of the machine. It used to remind me of the story I had been told years before by a Jewish-Russian emigrant to the United States. He came with other emigrants from a village in South Russia. Arrived in Philadelphia, he and his fellow villagers were astounded at the streetcars, the automobiles, and the factories. They had never in their lives seen these things before; they did not know that they existed in Europe, and therefore became firmly convinced that the United States was the most wonderful country in the world.

Many of the tourists to the Soviet Union were in like case. The factories and power stations in the U.S.S.R. were something they had never seen before at close quarters, and they felt sure it was "socialism" which had created them. Nor apparently were they aware that the crèches, maternity homes, kindergartens, and other social services so much boasted in the U.S.S.R. were far more widespread and available to a far larger proportion of the population in western Europe than in the U.S.S.R.

For them it was enough that new factories, power stations, etc. had been erected in Russia since the Revolution. They were not interested

* Quoted by Souvarine in his *Stalin, A Critical Survey of Bolshevism.*

in the social cost or in the utility of these concrete signs of Soviet industrialization.

Yet for the Russian people the much-admired "gigantic successes on the industrial front" meant only hardship, undernourishment, and overwork. These great edifices did not minister to their wants, and never would. The story of the peasant woman who saw a tractor for the first time, and exclaimed sadly and longingly, "What a lot of nails could have been made out of all that iron," illustrates the tragic farce of the Five Year Plans. The people required food, clothing, shoes, and houses to live in, and ordinary tools to make a living. They were given instead a stone, in the shape of a few great factories producing either goods for export to obtain money to import more machinery, or armaments to defend the Soviet state. Not to defend *them,* for they had literally "nothing to lose but their chains."

On May Day, 1932, I walked in the procession in Moscow side by side with an Austrian who had seen service with the Red Army in the civil wars as an aviator. Not yet having learned to hold my tongue on all occasions, I could not help remarking, as we passed the foundations of the Palace of Soviets, that it would have been better to have built flats for the workers first.

"Ah," he said, "don't you realize that this is an Asiatic people? In order to make them obey the government, palaces must be built to overawe them and to give them concrete proof of the power and glory of the government. This is far more important for social stability than giving the people decent houses to live in."

Admirers of the Soviet Union point to the statistics of industrial growth—so much more iron and steel produced, so many more industrial workers, so huge an investment in capital construction. The cost is never reckoned, and no comparison can be made between the social cost under "socialism" and capitalism. We do know, however, that the cost of the construction carried out under the First Five Year Plan was very much higher than had been reckoned. By the end of 1932, *Rs.* 120,100 million had been invested (since October 1928) instead of the 91,600 million planned. Yet the industrial construction and output both fell short of the plan. The increase in the note issue provided for in the Plan was *Rs.* 1,250 million; but the actual expansion was *Rs.* 6,400 million. The social cost was accordingly very much greater than the estimate. The population paid in decreased consumption for the government's gross underestimate of the real cost of its planned capital investment.

The tourists were incapable of judging whether the "Giants of the

Five Year Plan" functioned to their full capacity or not. But everyone in Russia who had anything to do with industry or trade knew that jerry-building, poor materials, incompetent or skimped work, hidden defects, made the factories and power stations erected at the cost of so much sweat and misery incapable of producing more than a fraction of what they had been planned to produce. The machines imported in exchange for the food and manufactures so sorely needed by the Russian people, or in exchange for the timber produced by the wretched prisoners of the O.G.P.U., deteriorated rapidly and soon became defective or unworkable. These defects and shortcomings were, in fact, often referred to in the Soviet Press. But they were always ascribed to the sabotage or the ignorance or the inefficiency of individuals, *never to the system which was in fact responsible*. Yet it was the system to force engineers and technicians, all the qualified experts, to work under Party bosses who knew nothing about the enterprises of which they were in charge, and could always put the blame on the non-Party specialists when things went wrong. These wretched men, the specialists, were in a hopeless position. They must obey orders even when they knew the orders would disastrously effect production. If they protested at being told to complete a job in six months which could not be properly done under a year, they were called saboteurs, wreckers, and counter-revolutionaries. So they got the job done and hoped the inevitable defects might not come to light till long afterwards. In any case, they could only live in the present; however well or badly they worked, the result was the same: the concentration camp awaited them in the short or the long run, so they tried to make the run as long as possible. The best way to put off the evil day was to scamp work and allow others to scamp it, close one's eyes to defects, say that everything was going splendidly, and flatter the Party boss who stood over you. Any specialist whose conscience drove him to the indiscretion of questioning or criticizing the orders of the ignorant Party chief was "for it." The Party was all-powerful, and there was no defense and no redress against it.

I knew one engineer, A, who had been in and out of prison three times. He was by then quite philosophical about it. He was highly qualified, and in between imprisonments he had a high salary and lived well. He was conditioned to injustice and had no hope for the future. His wife always had a suitcase ready packed for the moment when the O.G.P.U. should once again knock at the door and take him away. This man's position was better than that of many, for his qualifications were so special that he was pretty confident he would never be shot, however often he was made into a scapegoat.

The social cost of the "gigantic successes on the industrial front" cannot be exactly computed. For in 1930 the state Planning Commission was purged of the non-Party experts capable of computing it, and it was decreed that statistics must "play a practical part in the war of communism against capitalism"; that there must henceforth be only "class statistics." This was a roundabout way of saying that statistics henceforth should not be reliable, but should serve the needs of propaganda. Since that date, those statistics which could not be manipulated to prove the successes of "socialist construction" have quite simply not been issued at all. Such are the statistics dealing with prices, currency, housing, and cost of living. The least said about these matters the better for the reputation of the "workers' fatherland."

The Soviet Government has discovered all sorts of ingenious ways to delude the simple-minded tourist. When one visits a factory in Russia, it is usual, if one asks, to be given the *planned* figure, not the real one. In the course of my work at the Commissariat of Light Industry, I visited many textile factories. At the first of these, at Ivanovo-Vosnysenk, I was given a production figure by the manager which I could not reconcile with what I had learned in the weaving rooms from the workers themselves or with my experience at Promexport of what this factory had been able to send us for export. At last, after I had bothered and wearied the manager, he exclaimed, "Oh, I see now; you want the *factichiske* figures, not the *planove*. All right, here they are." The factual figures were about 35 per cent less than the planned ones. Since I was a foreigner, he had naturally given me the planned figures, not the real ones, as that was the usual thing to do with foreigners.

Successes are usually claimed on the basis of figures of "value," but the statistics of production as given in rubles are useless since prices are arbitrary. For instance, it may be stated that the total production of shoes in 1939 is to be 1,000 million rubles, as against 500 million in 1926. But no one knows, and no one can compute, just what the value of the ruble is going to be in 1939 or what it was in 1938 or 1926. Again, if retail trade turnover figures in a certain year are much higher than in the previous year, this does not necessarily mean that more goods became available for the consumers. There may have been less goods, but the state may have increased its profits on such sales 25 per cent or 50 per cent.

When Stalin, after the conclusion of the First Five Year Plan, computed its realization as 93.7 per cent, and said this meant that industrial production by the end of 1932 was three times the prewar figure, he implied that he was speaking of volume or quantity. In reality he was basing his calculation on arbitrary values translated into more or less fictitious rubles. No one knows therefore what was in fact accomplished. In those branches of industry for which volume or quantity figures were published, production fell short of the plan. This was notably the case with regard to iron, steel, and electricity. Coal, which made a better showing, was 14 per cent below the planned figure. (See table, page 206.) Since the factories could have fulfilled their production plans only if provided with the fuel and raw materials necessary, it is obvious that the failure in fuel, iron, and steel production involved the failure of other industries for which no figures other than value were ever published. Nevertheless it was claimed that the metal and machine-building industries had greatly exceeded their planned figures of production. Either this was a plain lie, or the plan never was a plan. An economy in which there was so little co-ordination between the parts that the *planned* production of iron and steel was vastly in excess of the planned production of the heavy industries, cannot be called a planned economy. Either there was no real plan or it failed.

It cannot, of course, be denied that the output of coal, iron, and steel had been very greatly increased by 1932; but these gains had been won at a social cost which no country not ruled over by a ruthless and all-powerful despotism could have contemplated. It is also doubtful whether the development of Russian heavy industry compensates, from the point of view of national strength, for the degradation of agriculture and the drastically reduced standard of living and morale of the working class which accompanied it.

The figures for 1932, poor as they are in comparison with the Plan and the enormous sacrifices the Plan had imposed on the people, do not reveal anything as to quality. Actually, bad workmanship ruined or decreased the utility of anything from a quarter to three-quarters or even more of the total production of many industries. In the textile industry, in which I was then working, it was "normal" for 80 per cent of the cloth to be defective. It was, of course, sold; but we had the greatest difficulty in securing a sufficient quantity of undamaged goods for export. (See Chapter IX.)

Stalin's remedy for what was the result of speeding up, undernourishment, and ignorance, was, as ever, drastic punishments. In 1933 he decreed five years' imprisonment for bad workmanship.

The result of neglecting the human factor was most clearly shown in the failure to increase the output per worker. In spite of piece wages, threats, and paltry rewards, the undernourished, badly housed, and overdriven Soviet worker could not be forced to work harder; it was physically impossible for him to do so. The output per worker was planned to increase 100 per cent, but the result showed that it can have increased little, if at all, since the number of wage-earners, planned to increase from 11.3 million to 15.8 million, actually increased to 22.8 million. In other words, 7 million more workers were needed than had been estimated as necessary to produce the *full* planned figures of production.

The cost of the "gigantic successes on the industrial front"—the actual investment in industrialization during the First Five Year Plan—came to 120 milliard instead of the 86 milliard planned.

The finances of the country were in such a chaotic state that the State Bank stopped publishing balance sheets. The Plan provided for an increase of *Rs.* 1,250 million in the note issue (which amounted to 1,774 million in October 1928) but by October 1932 it had already been expanded by 4,626 million. The people paid through inflation and a sharp rise in prices for the government's underestimate of the real cost of its planned investment, and for the terrific wastage entailed by the system.

The rise in prices in the four and a half years of the Plan gave the ruble only something like one-tenth of its previous value insofar as commercial prices were concerned. In view, however, of the rationing system and the "special distributors," the ruble had all sorts of values, depending on who was the recipient and who the purchaser.

It testifies to the qualifications, capacities, and honesty of the old Tsarist-educated "specialists" that the actual result of the Plan was practically identical with the figures originally prepared by the Gosplan experts, who in 1930 had been imprisoned or shot for "sabotage." Sabotage in the U.S.S.R. only too frequently means realism, clear-sightedness and specialized knowledge.

Although the results of the tremendous investment in industry were so meager, there was at least something to show for all the sacrifice. In agriculture there was no progress at all, but a terrible decline. Ten milliard rubles were invested in agriculture under the Plan, mainly in the form of tractors; yet the grain crop in 1932 was 26 per cent *below* the prewar level (69.9 million tons as against 94.1 million). The production of industrial crops (cotton, beets, etc.) had decreased 50 per cent. It was admitted that of the 147,000 tractors supplied to the farms, 137,000 were already in need of major repairs. As against the tractors, the livestock had been reduced in five years from 276 million to 160 million.

So disastrous and wasteful had the First Five Year Plan proved that even Stalin saw he must not try to repeat it. The ravages must be repaired, the wounds of society healed. The Russian people, that sorry and starved nag which Stalin had harnessed to the heavy machine of "socialist construction," must be allowed a little rest and a little nourishment if it were not to collapse altogether. No Plan at all was produced in 1933, and the Second Five Year Plan, when it came, provided for a more modest increase in production.

The famine continued and was even intensified through the terrible winter of 1932-33 and on into the spring. Then, as if Providence were taking pity on the most afflicted people on earth, the weather helped to produce the best harvest in years. It was still below the prewar level, and the figure of 89.9 million tons of grain took no account of rotted grain or losses in transit; nevertheless, the numbers who died of starvation decreased. In socialist Russia one accounted it as wonderful happiness if there was nearly enough bread for everyone.

Until 1935 cost-accounting was at a discount in the Soviet Union. Everything was being done by force; and, since the general scarcity of food and manufactures for all but the Party bureaucracy was so great that money had almost lost its function as a measure of value, the money cost of construction was regarded as of minor importance. It was assumed that so long as the construction plans were realized, nothing else mattered; and inflation was rapid and unchecked. As late as 1934 many new enterprises were being constructed at a cost 50-100 per cent higher than the estimates.

But if rationing were to be abolished and some stability given to the ruble, accounts had to be kept and considered of importance. Therefore, from 1935 on the Bolshevik leaders started to demand cost accounting in all enterprises, and to stress the importance of the "bookkeeper." The wretched accountants who had belonged to the lowest social strata were suddenly elevated to almost as high a rank as the engineers. However, the dearth of skilled accountants, the fact that they were almost always non-Party men, and their subordination to chiefs whose main concern was to make a good showing, rendered the keeping of accounts in Soviet enterprises the work of clever swindlers rather than of experts. Ordjonikidze, Commissar of Heavy Industry, might rail against the managers who "kicked out their bookkeepers because they conscientiously did their jobs"; but few would dare to go against the orders of the Party man on whom their living depended.

However, the keeping of accounts has at least done something to restrain the anarchy of Soviet economy, even if the accounts are often "cooked." Unfortunately, the Soviet Government, unwilling to let its own people or the outside world know how far performance falls short of the Plan, has published fewer and fewer statistics since 1935.

Soviet propagandists have sought to throw dust in the eyes of the world by their boasts as to the "size" of the new factories and power stations. The "planists" of the Western world have faithfully mimicked them. It came to be argued that if socialist construction in the U.S.S.R. had produced something larger than the capitalist world, then of necessity socialism was superior to capitalism. It was perhaps unconsciously felt that since the United States, the most advanced capitalist country, had the *tallest* buildings in the world, if Russia could produce the *biggest* industrial enterprises it would somehow have proved itself superior. This Asiatic conception of progress and grandeur was adopted by the Western admirers of the Soviet Union.

In a backward country such as Russia, only the enslavement of the people could make possible the rapid erection of gigantic power stations, canals, roads, and factories without credits from advanced countries. The Pyramids could not have been erected except by slave labor, and the same is true of the "giants of the Five Year Plan." Some "liberals" go so far as to excuse even slavery, such is their worship of the machine and of planning. But for the most part, the admirers of the Soviet Union maintain, in face of all the evidence to the contrary, that the industrialization of the Soviet Union has been carried on at the same time as an *improvement* in working-class conditions.

It is also true that the nearer a country's level is to zero, the more imposing can its progress be made to appear if reckoned in percentages. If in 1928 you have one rubber-goods factory and in 1929 you have two, you have progressed 100 per cent in one year. Russia had earlier periods of very rapid industrial progress in the past under her Tsars, precisely because she was so far behind the rest of Europe at the beginning of her modern history.

Souvarine, whose great book constitutes the classic history of the decline and fall of socialism in Russia, and whose wide historical knowledge, Gallic wit and eloquence remind one of Gibbon, has thus described the "achievements" of the Soviet Union:

> In fact the Plans, insofar as they have been fulfilled, have exacted the sacrifice of the contemporary generation, which was bled and op-

pressed in the name of a slender material progress, doubtful for future generations, and with very problematic perspectives for economic progress in the present.... The bureaucracy, under the pretext of enforcing the "socialist sector," in reality a new sort of state capitalism, was postponing the human conditions of socialism to the Greek Kalends.

Up to 1932 the Soviet Government could count upon the enthusiastic labor of a section of the workers. But since 1932 everyone has lost faith and nearly everyone is exhausted, dissatisfied, and anxious to secure a "cushy job" instead of working hard. Moreover, two factors militate against any possibility of repeating the effort of 1928-32. Too many engineers, technicians, administrators, specialists of all kinds, have been killed off or are now human wrecks in the concentration camps. The qualified personnel inherited from the Tsarist regime has been wilfully destroyed by Stalin, and the new "Soviet intelligentsia" has not the knowledge, experience, or devotion to its work of the old "bourgeois" specialists. In the second place, there is no longer any class left possessing tangible wealth which can be seized to pay for new imports of machinery. All the gold in private possession came into the hands of the state long ago either through Torgsin or extorted by the torturers of the O.G.P.U. Except for their privately owned livestock, there is no longer anything left of which the peasants can be expropriated. The standard of life of the workers cannot be reduced further. In a word, the Soviet Government must now rely on increased production to provide increased revenue to pay for machinery imports; and increased production is precisely what cannot be achieved under the system.

Since 1937 industrial production has been slipping backward. The purge of 1936-39 had the inevitable result of disorganizing the national economy. How could enterprises function according to any kind of plan whatsoever when managers, accountants, clerks were being arrested in thousands and herded off as prisoners to cut timber or work in the mines under the O.G.P.U. guards? Those who escaped arrest were too frightened and demoralized to work efficiently. The decline in production has been cumulative, since the less consumption goods were produced the less incentive the workers had to try and increase their earnings. There may also have been strikes at the end of 1938. (See Chapter VII.)

Above all, the Stakhanov system—the tremendous speeding up without regard to the depreciation of machinery—has had the unavoidable result of decreasing total production from year to year as more and more machinery became unworkable.

Soviet statistics have become more and more incomplete and obscure in order to hide the failures. The "control figures" in the basic industries appear to have been slashed again and again in 1938 and 1939 to make it seem that "the Plan" was being fulfilled 90 per cent when it was often only 50 per cent of the original planned figure.

"The Plan" has in fact almost ceased pretending to be a plan. For if, year by year and quarter by quarter, the Plan is altered to fit in with the failure to execute it, and production in one breach of industry no longer bears anything but a haphazard relation to production in an allied branch, there cannot be said to be a Plan at all. Each industry is producing just what it can regardless of Plans, or former capital investment, or theoretical capacity. For years past there has been a far more general anarchy in Soviet national economy than has ever been the case in capitalist economy, even at times of worst crisis.

In all the disillusionment brought by the Russo-German Pact and Stalin's war on Finland, the idea nevertheless persists that Russia is a "socialist state," still sanctified even if she has sinned. The belief of the die-hard Stalinists is based on the obsession with the socialist formula, "state ownership of the means of production and distribution," the belief that the condition of the working class has improved and is better than under capitalism, and on the tenacious myth that Russia's national economy is "planned," and that the U.S.S.R. therefore cannot suffer from economic crises or unemployment.

The fact that the condition of the working class is worse, not better, than before the Revolution has already been proved in Chapter VII. The planned nature of Soviet economy is as much of a pretense as the claim to have improved the condition of the masses. Not only do the planned figures of production bear little relation to the actual figures, but first "socialist competition" and then "Stakhanovism" have reduced the whole conception of planning to a farce. Obviously, if one branch of industry (or even certain factories within one branch of economy) overfulfills its plan, it will have procured a larger amount of raw materials than it was allowed under the plan at the expense of some other industry. If, on the other hand, another industry has failed to fulfill the plan, it will have precluded fulfillment of the plan by an industry dependent upon it for raw materials. Soviet "statisticians" endeavor to convince the world that the plan has been fulfilled by discounting failures on one "front" by successes on another. But in reality this cannot be done. To take the simplest instance, if the iron-ore production plan has been exceeded, and the coal production plan has failed, a lesser amount of steel is necessarily produced. Nor can the plan for consumers' goods production be said to have been fulfilled if the planned figure for perfumery production has been exceeded and that for textiles fallen far short.

The following table shows how far short of the plans actual production has been in industries for which figures have been published. It should be noted that the *control figures* were much higher than the *planned figures* given in the table. The so-called "control figures" are merely aspirations, not possibilities or actual potentialities. For instance, the control figures for coal and oil under the First Five Year Plan were 90 and 45 million tons respectively as against the 75 and 21.7 planned and the 64.7 and 22.3 actually produced in 1932.

	1932 Plan	Actual	Percentage of Planned Figure	1937 Plan	Actual	Percentage of Planned Figure
Coal (million tons)	75.0	64.7	86%	152.2	127.1	84%
Pig iron (million tons)	10.0	6.2	62%	16.0	14.5	91%
Steel ingots (million tons)	10.4	5.9	56%	20.1	17.8	89%
Oil (million tons)	21.7	22.3	103%	46.8	30.6	65%
Locomotives	1,641	828	52%	2,800	1,583	53%
Freight cars (2-axle)	12,600	20,152	184%	118,000	66,100	56%
Tractors	53,000	50,640	94%	195,000		
Automobiles	105,000	23,879	24%	230,000	200,000	100%
Cotton fabrics (million meters)	4,588	2,417	53%	5,100	3,450	68%
Leather footwear (million pairs)	80.0	84.7	106%	180	164	90%
Canned goods (million cans)	550	906	164%	2,000	874	44%
Matches (million cases)	12.2	5.6	47%	12.0		
Paper (1,000 tons)	900.0	479	53%	1,000	833	83%
Electricity capacity (million kw-hrs.)	22,000	13,540	62%	38,000	36,400	86%

It will be noted from the figures in the above table that the Second Five Year Plan came nearer to realization than the first, probably due not only to the fact that a comparatively modest increase in production had been planned, but also to the putting into operation of some new enterprises—in particular blast furnaces and rolling mills—erected during the period of the First Five Year Plan. It can also in part be ascribed to the better food position in 1936 and 1937.

As regards labor productivity, it is difficult to reconcile the claim made by the Soviet Government that it had increased 82 per cent in the heavy industries during the Second Five Year Plan, with a statement made in January 1938 by the Commissar of Heavy Industry that costs of production had increased. However, Soviet statistics have to perform varied and contradictory functions according to whether the world is being convinced of Soviet successes, or factory managers being spurred to drive their workers to a greater intensity of labor. Labor productivity must have increased in view of all the speeding up, but it would seem that what has been won on the swings has been lost on the roundabouts through the rapid depreciation of machinery and the neglect of repairs.

The Third Five Year Plan was not announced until 1939, and even then full details were not given as for the previous ones. It would appear that conditions are not such as to make it desirable for the government to publish figures which would either reveal the recent decline in production or make it appear that little increase was contemplated in the production figures. At the eighteenth Party Congress held in March 1939, only a bare outline of the plan was given, without detailed programs for the various industries. As before, only a small increase in consumers' goods is planned—38 per cent of the total production of industry by 1942 in *value,* as against 42 per cent in 1937. Since it is always the consumers'-goods industries which fall furthest short of the planned figures and since it is on these goods that profits instead of losses are made, there is no expectation of relieving the goods shortage, even should the current Plan be fulfilled. In fact, according to an article in *Industriya* on March 26, 1939, the planned output of shoes by 1942 is to be less than a pair and a half per head of the population, and that of cotton cloth only 27 meters as against 16 in 1937. The textile figures are least likely to be realized, since the cotton industry has all along fallen very far short of the plan.

Of the total investment in industry to be made by 1942 82 per cent is to go to the industries producing capital goods as compared with 83 per cent under the Second Five Year Plan. The maladjustment between the production of consumers' goods and capital goods is accordingly to be continued and, as before, this will prevent the stabilization of wages and prices. In other words, the ruble will continue to be inflated as in previous years.

Since 1937 the Soviet Government has shown itself to be more and more reluctant to publish statistics of production in volume or quantity. Production has so far lagged behind the plan in many branches of industry that the control figures have been slashed over and over again to hide the failures. This reduction of the planned figure to bring it closer to the actual production in itself vitiates the whole plan. For instance, the plans for the engineering industries are based on the plans for the coal, iron, steel, and other metal industries, and cannot be fulfilled if the basic industries lag far behind the plan. Slashing the control figures for coal, iron, and steel enables the Soviet Government to keep up appearances, but does not solve the problem of the engineering industry, nor that of the agrarian economy and the light industries dependent upon the supply of tractors, spare parts, and machinery.

In the absence of complete figures for 1938 and 1939 one can only piece together the information published in the various Soviet trade journals, or revealed in occasional articles in *Pravda* and *Izvestia*.

I have referred in Chapter VII to the Press campaign for the "tightening of labor discipline" which began in the fall of 1939, and which lifted a corner of the veil hiding the recent failures to fulfill the industrial plans. Anxiety was revealed in particular over the condition of coal, iron ore, and petroleum production. The fact that since September 1939 the Soviet Government has ceased, with few exceptions, to release statistics of industrial production in itself indicates serious failures. Output in value, which gives no indication of the real situation of Soviet industry, is now all that is usually referred to.

The failure to fulfill the plans for the last quarter of 1939 has, however, been admitted, as also the fact that the quantitative production of the basic industries was not higher than in 1938.

Industriya on November 17, 1939, stated that steel production has steadily lagged behind the planned figures, and in October was below the 1938 figure. This fact is ascribed to the short, irregular deliveries to the steel mills of iron ore, coke, and fluxes, and to the shortage of skilled labor. The same newspaper, on December 12, 1939, revealed that the production of coke in 1939 was only 16.6 million tons, which is less than the figure for 1937 or 1938.

Press comment indicates a serious fall in coal production, and very poor results in the production of aluminium, nickel, and other rare metals.

As regards oil, *Industriya* on December 12, 1939, and again on January 6, 1940, stated that the development of work in the oilfields had been highly unsatisfactory, and that the deep wells (which in the Baku district account for a large percentage of the total output) are so badly operated that 40 per cent of them are permanently inactive.

The organ of the machine-building industry in December disclosed the failure of the great Gorki automobile works to fulfill its plan, owing mainly to the very high proportion of defective products. The parlous condition of the tractor plants and of those producing spare parts has already been referred to in Chapter VI.

One could go on citing further items of information of this kind, but the declining production of Soviet industry is already fairly well known. One can characterize the state of Soviet industry in 1940 as one in which the normal deficiencies arising out of poor or moderate harvests, industrial inefficiency, capital deterioration, and a growing shortage of raw materials have been intensified by the strain of the Finnish war, and the need to maintain a large army in a state of preparedness for war.

If there had been no war, the rapid deterioration of the machinery imported during the period of the First Five Year Plan, combined with the liquidation or imprisonment of a large proportion of the technicians and skilled workers, would in any case have reduced the U.S.S.R. to a condition in which new imports of machinery and the assistance of foreign technicians, can alone halt the fall in production apparent since 1938.

The cost of financing the much-boasted industrialization of the U.S.S.R. has been borne in the main by the peasantry, but is in general financed by an enormous tax on food and a very large tax on the manufactured goods sold to the consumer. The taxation of the people's food has already been dealt with in Chapter VI, where a few details were also given of the amount of the turnover tax on manufactured goods in 1937.

The Soviet Government, as we have seen, collects from the peasantry, in one form or another, nearly a half of the produce of its labor on the collective farms, at a price which bears no relation at all to the cost of production. It sells this produce to the consumers at a profit of several hundred per cent. In this way it obtains, as the monopoly purchaser, not only the food to keep the urban workers alive, but also raw materials for industry, such as cotton, flax, wool, and hides, at similar arbitrary prices.

The state sells manufactured goods for mass consumption at a price which averages double what it costs it to produce them. Insofar as manufactured goods are concerned, the state exploits the consumer rather than the producer; but, since producers and consumers are in the main the same people, it is really immaterial whether we say that the workers' wages represent only a tiny fraction of the value (selling price) of the goods they produce, or whether we say that the state takes advantage of its monopoly position to force the workers to pay double the worth of the goods they consume.

The state's enormous profit on the goods it sells is taken in the form of a turnover tax—i.e., a sales tax rather than a trading profit. In other words, the state's profit is not collected at the factory as employer's profit, nor at the state shops as a trader's profit, but is collected in the form of a tax. In this way the loss on the goods produced in most of the enterprises producing capital goods is made up out of the profits on consumers' goods. Both the cost of industrialization and the losses due to the inefficiency of the greater part of heavy industry are paid for by the peasants as producers and consumers and by the workers and employees as consumers.

Put in Marxist terminology, the surplus value created by the labor of the peasants and workers is appropriated by the state, which uses it as the government decrees. Since the people have no voice in the government, Soviet economy is a perfect example of state capitalism.

The turnover tax constitutes the government's largest source of revenue. In 1939 it constituted 70 per cent of the total state budgetary revenue. Of this total, the tax on bread and other foods usually constitutes above two-thirds. The turnover tax on manufactured goods, although never nearly so high as on food, varies according to the nature of the goods. Usually it is highest on goods of mass consumption and lowest on luxury goods not purchased at all by the mass of the people. In general the tax is levied at a rate to preclude demand far outrunning supply of any particular article. But since there is always a shortage of the goods of mass consumption, long queues along the street leading to the shop doors have remained a permanent feature of Soviet life.

When the output of light industry falls far short of the plan, as frequently happens, or when the cost of construction of new enterprises is higher than the estimate, as almost always happens, the turnover tax is increased to ensure the necessary government revenue to meet obligations. For instance, the newspaper *Finansoya Gazetta* of January 10, 1940, gave the actual yield of the turnover tax in 1939 as 96.5 billion rubles as compared with 80.4 billion rubles in 1938. This increase of 16 billion rubles is the largest advance recorded over the past five years, and it coincided with an increased scarcity of consumers' goods. Since the scarcity of manufactured goods on sale in 1939 was more marked than in any year since 1935, it is obvious that the increased revenue from the turnover tax was due to price increases. (That such increases occurred in the case of most goods is witnessed to by the reports of foreigners.) Figures of total retail trade given in the Press for 1939 as compared with 1938 confirm this impression. *Pravda* on January 28, 1940, admitted that in many cities and especially in the rural districts retail distribution is very poorly organized and not infrequently essential articles are lacking.

In 1937, *before* the increase in the turnover tax in 1939 and the further steep increase in 1940, the plan provided for the following contribution by the turnover tax toward the total state revenue:

Turnover tax receipts	76.8 billion rubles
Direct taxation (including Kolkhoz income tax)	3.0 " "
Government loan subscriptions	4.5 " "
Savings bank deposits	1.0 " "

The actual receipts from the turnover tax came to 73.9 billion rubles in 1937, whereas the total value of retail trade was 125 billion. It is therefore clear that the state took a profit of more than 100 per cent on the cost value of the goods it sold. In addition one must take into consideration the profits made by the factories producing the manufactured goods sold, and those allowed to the distributing agencies.

How very small a quantity of manufactured goods is available for the Russian population can be calculated from the figures of the gross value of production. In 1935, when the total population of the U.S.S.R. was estimated to be 165 million, the gross value of consumers' goods turned out by the food industry, light manufacturing industry, and local industry (allowing for profits and depreciation) was 28 billion rubles of so-called 1926-27 purchasing power.

Even if the national income had been equally distributed, which of course is very far from being the case in the U.S.S.R., each citizen would have been able to purchase only 170 rubles' worth of goods. Actually, the ruling Party bureaucracy took a very large percentage of the manufactured goods available for consumption. Moreover, the shock workers (Stakhanovists), foremen, technicians, and specialists, all enjoying incomes several times larger than those of most workers, must have consumed the lion's share of manufactured goods. It is unlikely that the majority of the population had as much as 70 rubles a year to spend on clothing and shoes and other vital necessities. An examination of the prices of manufactured goods (see Chapter VII) indicates the miserable standard of life of the workers and peasants.

What socialism has come to mean for the Russion people is illustrated by a story told in Moscow in 1932. A Communist party propagandist goes to a village and gives the assembled peasants a glowing account of the Five Year Plan and the wonders of construction of socialism. After he has spoken one of the old peasants gets up and says: "Yes, comrade, it sounds wonderful, but look at our clothing—nothing but rags to wear and nothing to be bought in the village shop." The Communist answers him angrily and scornfully: "You making all that fuss about clothes! Why, in places like Africa and the South Seas people have no clothing at all." The peasant scratches his head and then says thoughtfully: "I suppose they've had socialism for a long time there."

The greatly reduced standard of life of the workers as well as of the peasants as compared with Tsarist times has been dealt with in other chapters. This is not admitted by Soviet apologists, who carefully refrain from comparing wages and prices now and before the Revolution, but try to convince their readers of the improvement in working-class conditions by citing money wages and keeping silent about prices. The argument is also put forward that the Russian workers are investing in the future, content to live poorly now in order that the country may be industrialized for the benefit of their children. It is, of course, absurd to suppose that the Russian people, workers, employers, or peasants, really desire to go on living on the barest level of subsistence for the benefit of future generations. Only force can compel them to do so, and if Soviet democracy were a reality, the Plans would provide for a rapid increase in the production of consumer goods. Such an increase would probably lead to a more rapid development of heavy industry as well as of light industry than has been accomplished by Stalin's forced depreciation of the general standard of life of the producers, and huge investments in heavy industry and construction. No people could work efficiently on the meager diet of the Russian worker, living as he does in crowded tenements and forced to spend much of his "leisure" standing in line to secure clothing and other necessities, or attending long, dreary meetings where the sorry farce of pretending that "life is joyous" has to be played out over and over again. The psychological strain of pretending that they are happy, and of always saying the opposite of what they think, and the constant fear of arrest, are not the least of the factors impairing the efficiency of the Russian workers.

As regards the peasants, it is clear that, if the Soviet state increased the quantity of consumers' goods and lowered their prices, the peasants could be induced to produce a very much greater quantity of food than they do at present; and this, more than anything else, would give an impetus to the development of the whole national economy. (This is an important fact to bear in mind in considering Russo-German relations; for if Germany supplies large quantities of even the cheapest and shoddiest manufactured goods for the Russian villages, the peasantry may be stimulated to work as they have never worked before.)

Lastly, if the Soviet Government were not forced by its own policy to maintain huge numbers of soldiers, militia, armed guards, and O.G.P.U. spies to keep the people in subjection, it would have far greater resources for industrializing the country. There is little doubt that the number of persons employed by the state to coerce and terrorize the working population is a good deal larger than the capitalist class in most other countries. If one also takes into account the huge bureaucracy, it is obvious that under Stalin's socialism the actual producers of the country's wealth have to maintain a larger number of persons performing no productive labor than is the case under the capitalist system.

The "friends of the Soviet Union," driven into a corner, will still fight on with the statement that unemployment has been abolished in the U.S.S.R. That it had not, really, been abolished when the claim was first made I have demonstrated in other chapters. But even if the Soviet Government's contention is accepted, the same can be said of Nazi Germany. If the state has the power to compel men to labor for the barest subsistence on the production of armaments and military fortification works; or if, as in Soviet Russia, it herds millions into concentration camps where they labor as slaves in building roads, canals, and railways, or in cutting timber and working in mines in the Arctic, unemployment can, of course, be liquidated.

Undeveloped countries under the capitalist system, such as the United States during most of the nineteenth century, and also Canada and Australia, did not suffer from unemployment. The enslaved negroes of Africa, forced to labor under European masters on the plantations, are never unemployed. If this is all the plan-mad "liberals" of western Europe and America care about, let them admire and welcome the Soviet and Nazi systems, or the methods of exploiting colored races adopted by all the imperialist powers.

Soviet apologists will sometimes explain and excuse the terrible exploitation of the Russian people by Stalin's government as the "inevitable" consequence of the backwardness of Russia. All the horrors are explained as due to the need to develop the productive forces of the country; once this has been done there will be prosperity for all. In the first place, the system prevents the development of Russia's productive forces; secondly, since planning in the U.S.S.R. is no more than a farce, nothing has been learned. There is no guarantee at all that future generations will enjoy the benefits of a "planned economy" of abundance. It is not at all certain that, were the U.S.S.R. ever in a position to produce enough of the necessities of life to ensure a good life for all, this could be done under the Soviet system any better than under the capitalist system. The new techniques for production for use instead of for profit have *not* been worked out in the U.S.S.R., although it is fervently believed by Western liberals and socialists that they have. All that the Soviet Government has done is to create the machinery for a scarcity economy.

As L. E. Hubbard points out in his carefully documented and objective account of Soviet "planning": *

> If an economic crisis be defined as an unpredicted disturbance in the orderly development of production and consumption, resulting either in a shortage of effective demand—that is, in the phenomena usually termed underproduction or overproduction—then the economic history of the Soviet Union, since planning superseded the relatively full market of N.E.P., has been a succession of crises, for at practically no period during that time has there not been a shortage of something. In 1932, for instance, a real shortage of food of all sorts, in other years shortages of boots, sewing thread, matches, etc. If planning is immune from some of the defects of capitalism, it seems to possess peculiar faults of its own.

In effect, up to 1935, when rationing was abolished, one could have defined the difference between the "anarchy of capitalist production and distribution" and the anarchy of Soviet planning as the difference between having no money to buy goods, and having money but being unable to buy goods with it. Inflation had insured that you had the "purchasing power," but industry had failed to produce goods for you to purchase. Since the abolition of rationing and the spurt up in prices

---

* *Soviet Trade and Distribution.*

in 1935, even this difference has become less marked. Since 1935 the shops have been stocked with goods too expensive for the majority of the population to buy. But queues still form in the streets to purchase trousers, shoes, textiles, and other necessities, of which, in spite of the very high prices, there are not nearly enough to meet the "effective demand."

Mr. Hubbard, writing in 1938, predicted that when the period of heavy capital construction—involving boom conditions under capitalism as under "socialism"—came to an end in the Soviet Union, and it was time to let the people "enjoy the results of their saving," there might be renewed unemployment in spite of the planning. Purchasing power would then have to keep pace with production, and this would require financial planning, which is more difficult than other planning. In other words, he foresees difficulties if and when the present scarcity economy gives place to an economy of relative abundance.

However, the rulers of the Soviet Union are not likely ever to let themselves be faced with this problem. If and when the productive capacity of the industries producing consumption goods increases, they are likely to take more for themselves and to increase the numbers of those employed in their personal service. Moreover, with the general depreciation and waste and inefficiency, the U.S.S.R. is unlikely to produce anything much beyond bare necessities for the mass of the population for several generations. What is constructed in one Five Year Plan has often gone to pieces by the time the next Plan is completed.

Stalin's actual problem is precisely the opposite of the one envisaged by Mr. Hubbard in the future. Economic crises and unemployment in the "capitalist world" are caused by a rapid decline in capital investment throwing large numbers of men out of work and leading to a fall in the effective demand for consumers' goods. In the U.S.S.R. there has been, ever since 1932, and increasingly so since 1936, a decline in the rate of new capital investment in industry. This decline has been caused by the stagnation of agriculture and the consequent failure of the state's revenue to increase, by the need to spend so much of that revenue on repairing or replacing machinery worn out before its time, and by the failure of the new factories and workshops to work up to the level of their planned capacity. Secondly, the tremendous investment in armaments production has meant the diversion of capital investment from "means of production" into "means of destruction" and has had its unavoidable economic consequences in "socialist" Russia as in the capitalist world. Armaments cannot produce goods of consumption, nor, once they are made, can they give employment to anyone but soldiers. Hence if the whole population is to be "employed," they must be utilized for the purpose for which they were intended: war.

In embarking on a course of imperialist expansion as Hitler's junior partner, Stalin may have aimed, among other things, at solving Russia's recurring unemployment problem, and at acquiring new capital by the expropriation of the capitalists in conquered lands. The problem of unemployment in Russia has existed for decades in the form of excess labor on the land, and the Soviet Government has failed to solve it on account of waste, muddle, and inefficiency in industry. The huge capital investments have not increased industry's productive capacity to anything like the extent that a similar investment would have done under another system; and forced collectivization of the peasantry hampers the modernization of agriculture.

In Chapter VII I have shown the simple means adopted by the Soviet Government to cure unemployment during the First Five Year Plan—viz., physical liquidation of the unemployed and the underemployed, or their conversion into convicts doing forced labor in the Arctic timber camps and constructing roads, railways, and canals. A "capitalist" government able and willing to herd all the millions of unemployed into slave gangs paid no wages and constructing public works or palaces for the ruling class in return for the barest subsistence, herded into barracks at night, and fed worse than pigs, would have little difficulty in solving the unemployment problem.

It is to be surmised that the crisis in Russia's national economy, which had been growing in intensity from 1936 to 1939, was the basic cause for the Russo-German Pact. In the first place, Stalin knew that the Red Army, if put to the test, would crumple up before the German Army, and that neither Soviet transport nor industry could supply the army for any length of time. Secondly, it was essential for the U.S.S.R. to import new machinery and enlist the aid of foreign technicians. But it was impossible to pay out cash or goods for this assistance, and Germany was the only country with whom barter credits could be arranged on a big scale. German economic and technical aid had become essential to the survival of the Stalinist regime.

Soviet aggression can in part be explained as due to the failure to increase the productivity of the country, and to the meager return from the large capital investments in industry over the past decade. Looking for new sources of capital accumulation, and hoping to reinvigorate the decaying Soviet state by the tonic of national aggrandizement and glory, the Soviet Government in 1939 secured temporary new sources of revenue through the expropriation of the property of conquered Poles and Finns.

Stalin's "socialist" government started by enslaving the Russian peasants and workers, and must now enslave other peoples in order to survive. It is so weak that the cost of its war of conquest in Finland has proved far higher than any material gains won, but in eastern Europe there may be easier prey which can be seized and devoured by the U.S.S.R. without war.

CHAPTER IX

THE NEW METHOD OF EXPLOITATION

LENIN, AS WE HAVE SEEN, recognized that, with the institution of the N.E.P., state capitalism, not socialism, would develop in Russia if the world revolution did not rescue the Bolsheviks.

Today, Soviet economy has become the most perfect example of state capitalism in existence, since the state exploits (takes profit from the labor of) all the people, and since the people have no share at all in the government, and no means of any kind to control it. In Marxist terminology, all the "surplus value" (i.e., the production of the worker over and above what he gets back in the form of wages) created by the labor of the people is taken by the state as profit, and the state uses this profit as the government decrees. The workers, like the peasants, have no say at all as regards the disposal of the wealth created by their labor. The Communist party, although not in theory the "owner" of the means of production, appropriates to itself or for its own purposes the profit derived from the labor of the rest of the population. One can call the system state capitalism with the Bolshevik party drawing the dividends.

If the trust magnates of the United States were able to acquire control of all land and productive capital, to abolish representative government, and draw their dividends not as individual owners but as a ruling and directing group, the result would be in essence the same economic and political system as that of the U.S.S.R. It would, of course, be a far more efficiently run state, and it is unlikely that large numbers of people would starve, as they do in Russia; but basically it would be the same type of state capitalism. The fact that the ruling group in the U.S.S.R. is composed of men who did not start life as capitalists makes no vital difference; it means that they are far more incompetent, but it does not mean that they are not exploiters. Collective exploitation is no more "moral" than individual exploitation.

It is an extraordinary proof of mankind's inability to see realities behind façades, and its incorrigible propensity to examine the label on the bottle instead of the contents, that so many of our "liberals" and "socialists" fail to realize the true nature of the Soviet state. They think that because there are no capitalists in the U.S.S.R. there cannot be any exploiting class, and that therefore of necessity Russia is a socialist state according to the original conception of the word socialism.

Let us admit with the Communists that the Soviet system is *not* capitalist. But let us refuse to follow their strange logic that because A is not equal to B it must be equal to C. There is in the Soviet Union a "new society," a society in which the method of exploitation is new. Instead of the worker and peasant being exploited by a capitalist or a landowner, he is exploited by the state. The state "appropriates" the produce of all men's labor beyond what is required to keep them alive at the lowest level of subsistence. (The only reservation which needs to be made here is that at times the state does not even allow them that much, and large numbers die of starvation, undernourishment, and disease.) This appropriated "surplus value" is used by those who own the state—Stalin and his satellites—to give themselves the best possible material conditions of existence, to maintain huge armies of functionaries and soldiers, and to finance industrial construction. The number of functionaries was reckoned by Stalin in 1933 to be eight million. Some of these millions—the engineers, technicians, accountants, qualified administrators, clerks and typists—are performing as "socially necessary" labor as the workers and peasants. But a majority of the eight million are more parasitic than the capitalist class. Their "social function" consists in "Party activity"—i.e., talking, praising Stalin in writings and speeches, making hypocritical speeches to "the masses," or in O.G.P.U. activity—spying on the productive workers and the specialists, and occasionally arresting them and subjecting them to mental, if not also to physical, tortures. Another "function" of the parasitic Party members is to occupy positions as commissars or as chairmen and directors of the state office organizations, or as directors or managers of factories, in which capacity they interfere with and ruin the work of the non-Party specialists. They further perform the "labor" of driving others to work. In Russia there is a stock joke about being "a responsible worker" as signifying the man who stands by and looks on while others labor.

Of course, if you are a mystic, you can say that, Stalin being the Supreme Father, or a kind of proletarian Mikado who in some mysterious way unites in himself the souls of all his people and leads them by divine inspiration, this is "true" democracy. You can believe that, in sacrificing both material well-being and liberty to Stalin, the people are sacrificing to themselves, since he is their god in their own image. This is Stalin's own conception of himself, as he testified at his sixtieth birthday: "Your congratulations and greetings I credit to the account of the great party of the working class, which gave me birth and raised me in its own image."

The semimystical and altogether nauseating outpourings in the Soviet Press in praise of Stalin assign to him such a universality; he is the fountain of all goodness and all strength and of all achievement of the whole Russian people; he is the divine *Vozd* ("leader"). He is the nation as a totality, the "image" of themselves set up by the working class. By praising him, the working class is supposed to adore itself. He is the "infallible," the "incomparable," "our sun" and "our soul." He is the proletariat's—or the Russian's—god "created in its own image."

The Soviet apologist who is not satisfied with the mystical explanation for the rightlessness of the workers and for their oppression by the state, will argue that since the profit obtained from the labor of worker and peasant is invested in capital construction for the future benefit of "all the toilers," the latter have nothing to complain of. This argument ignores several pertinent facts. In the first place, the profit is often wasted in new enterprises which are so badly run that they fail to pay the social cost of their construction before the machinery in them wears out. In the second place, much of the profit goes to supply a comparatively luxurious life for the army and the bureaucracy, instead of to raise the general standard of life. Thirdly, more and more of the national income has of recent years gone to support the armed forces which keep the workers and peasants in subjection, and to develop armament production to defend, not the people of Russia who in effect have "nothing to lose but their chains," but the power and wealth of the government.

Whereas those who are moved by the humanitarian and libertarian hopes formerly held out by Socialists have already turned their backs on Stalin's Russia, there remain a great number of people whose sole interest in socialism is in seeing an "orderly and planned" economy take the place of capitalist anarchy, and who accept paper plans instead of the evidence of their eyes when they visit the U.S.S.R. These people, among whom the most prominent are Sidney and Beatrice Webb, are not in the least interested in the emancipation of mankind. They think that "planning" justifies all, excuses all, and they desire to see everyone put to school and subjected to strict discipline for their own good.

People of this type of mind look upon the Russian people as so many rabbits in a laboratory, subjects for a "great social experiment" which is going on too far away to menace the comfortable security of "enlightened" Western intellectuals.

It was only when Stalin, in 1939, began to inflict on other peoples the treatment which he had hitherto only been able to inflict upon his own, that the admirers of the U.S.S.R. began to recoil. Yet, as Max Eastman has expressed it, the bombing of Finland was a polite and civilized gesture compared to Stalin's domestic policies.

The reality of Stalin's Russia is in fact so horrible that most people, even in this age of conditioning to horror, refuse to believe that such things can be. The truth is discussed as an atrocity story; and so anxious are men to believe in the existence of the socialist heaven that they accept the crudest communist propaganda as gospel truth. Those who have accepted Russian communism as a religious faith, and whose reasoning powers have become atrophied, will no doubt continue to worship their bloody idol and to glorify the human sacrifices made to it. But it is still possible that those whose adherence to Stalinism is due to ignorance of what the U.S.S.R. is really like, to despair concerning our own outworn social system, and to the generous impulses which impel men and women to struggle for a better social order, will realize in time that slavery is slavery, even if coated o'er with a thin cast of Marxist dogma.

The Webbs have probably done more harm to the liberal and progressive movement of western Europe than any Hitler or Mussolini. With the immense prestige of their long life of service in the British labor movement, and of their published works of careful historical research, they have led the procession of socialists and liberals into the abyss of totalitarianism. The conception of socialism as a juster, better social order, which was a beacon to those who desired human freedom, has become a blood-red light of warning. Socialism has been degraded to the level of the beasts, become synonymous with injustice, cruelty, oppression, and misery. Liberalism has been similarly corrupted, deprived of meaning. Anyone whose human sympathies and intelligence are not atrophied must exclaim: If Stalin's Russia is what these socialists and liberals want, give me reactionary capitalism!

The Webbs and the rest of the totalitarian liberals made the Soviet Union not only respectable, but admirable. With their Fabian mantle they hid the horrors, the starvation, the misery, the degradation of the human spirit and the barbarous method of government of the U.S.S.R. Not only this; their support emboldened Stalin to throw aside all restraint. If the Webbs could swallow the purges and the terror, the whole Western socialist and radical movement could be made to swallow it. Prior to the Russo-German Pact, Stalin was courting the democracies, and had it not been for the chorus of praise which went up from the Western "liberals," he would not have dared to execute thousands and condemn hundreds of thousands—perhaps millions —to the concentration camps without trial. By shutting their eyes and sealing their lips to the atrocities committed by the Stalin regime, these "liberals" not only made themselves accomplices of those crimes but destroyed the basis of all humane social endeavor.

No recent phenomena have been more sickening to the soul than the cold-blooded disregard of the lives of millions displayed by a multitude of plan-mad "liberals" in western Europe and the United States, their deliberate falsifications, their misleading of public opinion, and their transvaluation of all values. "Liberal" journals refused to publish condemnations of the Moscow trials, lied to their readers, put new meanings on old words. They redefined liberty to mean subordination; they justified executions, tortures, imprisonment of innocent men and women, even the shooting of children for theft, because it was done in the name of "planned economy." Sadism became a virtue if it was socialistically administered sadism. Compared with their attitude, the open and avowed Fascist seems almost decent and clean, for he is at least honest. Consciously or unconsciously, they subscribed in their writings to the Soviet newspapers' concept that "information does not consist in the dissemination of news, but in the education of the masses"; "information is an instrument in the class struggle; not a mirror to reflect events objectively." To lie was to protect the socialist fatherland; "to tell the truth was to be a reactionary or worse." *

The primary question is precisely the one which the Webbs completely ignored: Who owns the state? Their twaddle about the "vocation of Leadership"—a euphemism for the Communist party—proves only their ignorance of history and of psychology, and their willful blindness to the constraints which keep the Russian people subservient to the bureaucratic state.

---

* In the United States perhaps the most glaring example of this attitude of mind of so-called liberals was to be found in the *New Republic,* in particular in the writings of George Soule and Malcolm Cowley. The former's redefinition of liberty to mean "subordination to a common purpose" would be as acceptable to the Nazis as to the Stalinists. As Max Eastman has pointed out in his brilliant chapter on "The Motive-Patterns of Socialism," such liberal writers as these have prepared the ground for an American totalitarian tyranny. The *Nation* cut free of Stalinism sooner and more completely than the *New Republic,* but it refused publication of Max Eastman's letter on the Moscow treason trial in February, 1937.

Not only were the Webbs naïve,* they also make many statements which are positively untrue, as, for instance, when they state that "to this day the rulers of the U.S.S.R. receive only the equivalent of the earnings of the most highly skilled and zealous craftsmen."

The "party maximum" which in Lenin's day was a reality, had long ceased to be anything but the thinnest of pretenses in 1934 when the Webbs visited the U.S.S.R. All it meant was that the greater part of the income of the rulers was paid in kind.

Since 1935 the profits taken from the productive labor of the Russian people by the Bolshevik party are no longer hidden, and have also steadily increased in volume. But long before 1935 the style of living of the Party bureaucracy, as compared to that of the workers and specialists, revealed how large a dividend it was drawing from its investment in Stalin's counter-revolution.

Since the abolition of the closed distributors in 1935, the salaries of high officials have been anything from ten to thirty times as high as the wage of a worker of average qualifications. When I left the Soviet Union in the summer of 1936, chairmen of large enterprises were already receiving 2,000-3,000 rubles a month, and, although no one knew for certain the amounts being paid to Commissars and others holding the highest positions in the state, it was said they were receiving 7,000 or more.

The Soviet Government never publishes figures showing the salaries of the highest functionaries, nor does it reveal the distribution of the national income. Such statistics would make it too glaringly obvious to the outside world that Russia is as far from being a society of the equal as of the free.

Our friends the R's, who ranked as just-below-the-top Party bureaucrats, had a very large modern flat, a big *datcha,* and a private automobile all paid for by the Commissariat for which R worked. One of their two servants was also paid for by the Commissariat, and R received a handsome entertainment allowance over and above his salary. The R's were higher in the social scale than anyone else we knew, but their standard of life was far below that of others one heard of.

* To cite only one example of the tragi-comic naïveté of the Webbs: Of this socialist paradise where most of the workers live in crowded flats or tenements where one lavatory is often shared by thirty or forty people, and if there is a bathroom it is usually occupied by a whole family; and where most workers can never afford sufficient food for their families, they write with unconscious humor of the "daily shower" and of "the restriction of eating to something less than the demands of appetite" having "assumed the dignity of social obligations."

Alexandre Barmine, the Soviet diplomat who escaped being kidnaped by O.G.P.U. agents in Athens when his time came to be purged, thus describes the "happy life" of a Soviet aristocrat: *

> Let us pause for a moment to consider the life of an influential personage in the government. He lives in comfort in the Government House in Moscow, in an eight-roomed apartment, with two servants for a household with one child. For rest he has a Villa No. X of the Central Committee, with one, three or four servants; where he can, if he so desires, enjoy a private cinema show, where there are plenty of guest rooms for his friends and a sports room. All this at the expense of the state except for the small rent he pays for his town flat. He has one or two automobiles and chauffeurs at his disposal. He can satisfy any whim, even an expensive one, by merely ringing up on the telephone. His son grows up like a millionaire's son, served by six servants, provided with toys imported from abroad, looked after in illness by the best doctors. He knows that when one wants anything papa has only to telephone. Does our high official desire to enjoy the fresh air of the Caucasus or the Crimea? He will be just as well accommodated as at home, and will travel there with his whole family in a *wagon lit*, in a special carriage or on a special train, at the state's expense.

The luxurious life lived by the Soviet aristocracy, which the ordinary citizen glimpses only from afar, and which is in direct contravention of Lenin's injunction that the Party members should receive salaries no higher than a worker's wage, is one of the most striking features of Stalin's Russia. The restraint and comparative moderation which still prevailed in 1932 have been openly discarded since Stalin told his henchmen to "live joyously," seeking thus to ensure the loyalty of the Party. Since 1935 the expectation of life of a Party member has not been long. At any moment he may lose Stalin's favor, or be ruined by accusations leveled at him by men on the next rung of the ladder seeking to supplant him. But while the going lasts it is exceedingly good, and since the poorest worker is as liable to be arrested as the high and mighty Party boss, the latter may well consider it worth while to gather as many rosebuds as he can as quickly as possible. At least when he comes to face the firing squad in the cellars of the Lubianka Prison, or finds himself a laborer in a concentration camp,

---

* *Vingt Ans au Service de l'U.R.S.S.* Paris, 1939. This book, published also in England, but not in the United States, is one of the very best which has been written on the U.S.S.R.

he has the satisfaction denied to the workers and peasants of knowing that he has had a good time for a few years.

The real work of administration and construction was not done by the privileged Party men, but by the "specialists"—a term which in the U.S.S.R. designates engineers, technicians, accountants, scientists, professors, teachers, doctors, and men like my husband, who were specialists in foreign trade or banking, or had other qualifications essential to the carrying on of the enormous administrative tasks of the "socialist state." In this category must also be included the black-coated workers. All these people, from the highly qualified engineer earning a thousand or two rubles a month to the typists and clerks existing somehow on 100 to 150 rubles, are included under the general category of employees. During the period of rationing and closed distributors, the wretchedly paid clerks and even the shop assistants, being all classed as employees, were able to obtain less food than the workers in industry, whose bread ration was double theirs. With derationing, the standard of life of the lower-paid employees came to approximate that of the working class. A typist might earn a little more than a textile worker, but the better-paid clerks earned less than skilled mechanics.

It had been Lenin's and Trotsky's policy to use the educated non-Party elements and to afford them comparatively decent material conditions of existence, although discriminating against them and their children socially, and never allowing them to occupy positions of great responsibility. In the N.E.P. period, it had been true that the non-Party specialists, when highly qualified, drew higher salaries and enjoyed a greater degree of material prosperity than the Party officials. With the Party maximum first at 275 rubles and later at 300 rubles, and no special buying privileges for Party members, the engineers and other specialists drawing 500-700 rubles a month could live better than Party members. In those days the Party's proud boast that its members occupying the highest posts in the state lived on the same material level as the working class had some validity. It was even then not actually the case, since the high officials had better flats, the use of automobiles, special sanatoria and rest homes reserved for their exclusive use, and a number of other privileges. But it was true with regard to the general run of Party members, as I had seen for myself in 1927 and 1928.

Stalin put an end to the privileged position of the specialists with the liquidation of the N.E.P. and the inauguration of the First Five Year Plan. The "Party maximum" became a farce once Party officials could buy food and clothing for a fraction of what these things cost the unprivileged, while the specialists came to be treated as pariahs socially, and their salaries were drastically reduced through inflation. Moreover, it was they who were made the scapegoats for all the failures and privations caused by Stalin's agrarian and industrial policies. Stalin's utter stupidity in liquidating or demoralizing the qualified personnel who alone could have secured the successful carrying out of the Five Year Plans has been one of the tragedies of Russian history. With power stations, blast furnaces, and factories being built by the colossal sacrifices of the Russian people, it was essential to secure the willing and wholehearted collaboration of the engineers and technicians, statisticians, men with administrative experience, scientists. But Stalin has always imagined that compulsion and terror were the best way to secure efficient service. Instead of continuing Lenin's policy of conciliating the specialists and rewarding loyal service, he inaugurated a policy of arresting, shooting, or terrorizing all the non-Party specialists, while reducing their standard of life to that of the working class, or even below it. His suspicion and hatred for all intellectuals—which extends even to the intellectuals in the Communist party—seems to be almost pathological. Distrust and hatred of educated people and of science itself is one of Stalin's most marked characteristics and may date back to his failure to shine at school, and to the low estimate of his intellectual capacities held by Lenin and the brilliant crowd which surrounded him. Relegated by the Party in pre-Revolutionary days to the performance of humdrum organizational tasks or to the planning of acts of brigandage, Stalin has all his life hated intellectuals from the depth of his savage Caucasian soul.

In the years I worked at Promexport and in the Commissariat of Light Industry, I was continually amazed at the number of specialists who, in spite of every discrimination against them and the overwhelming difficulties of their work, continued loyally and conscientiously to carry out their duties. It was the non-Party specialists who had ensured the reconstruction of industry and transport after the breakdown of the Civil War period, and even now, when they went in constant fear of arrest, most of them continued to devote their brains and energies to their work. Their material rewards grew smaller and smaller, they worked twelve or fourteen hours a day to overcome the muddles created by their superiors, the Party bosses, and whenever there was a serious failure they were blamed for it and accused of being "wreckers."

The tragedy of these people was that in the very effort to work conscientiously and honestly they endangered their existence. Specialists who perceived that a "plan" could not be carried out without wrecking machinery or fatally depreciating it, were accused of sabotage, of being counter-revolutionaries preventing the "construction of socialism." Statisticians who made careful estimates based on an intelligent survey of materials available or production capacities were flung into concentration camps because they would not draw up plans which they knew could not be fulfilled. The Gosplan specialists who drew up the original Five Year Plan were shot for sabotage, yet in 1932 it was found that the actual achievements under the Plan came to just about the figures of increased production which they had estimated could be achieved. But the achievements had been won at a cost infinitely greater than would have been the case if the whole national economy had not been dislocated by the attempt to carry out fantastic plans bearing no relation to real possibilities.

I remember a young agronomist, a distant relative of my husband's, who came to visit us one evening in the fall of 1931. He was faced, he said sadly, with the choice of either going to prison that year for drawing up a plan for beet production which could be fulfilled, or of going to prison later for drawing up one which would satisfy the Party authorities, but could not possibly be fulfilled. In agriculture as in industry, Stalin demanded the drawing up of impossible plans which either could not be fulfilled, or which would cause terrible distress if carried out. Then he persecuted both those who said they were impossible and those who of necessity failed to carry them through.

The position of the non-Party specialists was particularly difficult in that they were everywhere working under the orders of a "Party man" who knew nothing and need learn little about the enterprise he controlled, since his retention of the post and of the privilege which went with it depended not on knowledge, conscientiousness, or administrative capacity, but upon his being politically reliable; in other words, upon his being a Stalin yes-man and a good slave driver. When things went wrong he could always lay the blame upon the non-Party specialists who worked under him, accusing the latter of being wreckers and counter-revolutionaries. Yet only too frequently he took no notice of the advice of the specialists. The only way in which the latter could save their lives and liberty was to render themselves indispensable to their Party bosses, either by helping them to cook accounts, put on false fronts, and in general make it appear that the enterprise was fulfilling the plan, or even overfulfilling it, when in reality production was defective, machinery deteriorating, and insufficient quantities of goods being produced. The best way to make a good showing and earn praise and rewards was to produce as large an amount as possible without paying any attention to quality.

The great art in Soviet Russia, as practiced in particular by clever and not too scrupulous specialists in the service of their Party masters, was *blat,* a word difficult to translate but meaning camouflage, favors done for favors received, the working out of personal combinations which make it possible to get around the obstacles created by the plan which is no plan. In every enterprise the *blatmeister* became more indispensable than the expert. It is he who can convince visiting Commissions and the O.G.P.U. that all is going according to plan, when in reality everything is in a mess. It is he who can obtain the materials necessary for fulfilling the plan, but unobtainable through "normal" channels. By providing the head of another enterprise with what he lacks, or by "connections" in high places, the *blatmeister* is able to secure materials to fulfill or overfulfill the plan. The plans having been drawn up without regard to real possibilities, and being continually disorganized by attempted "overfulfillment of the plan" by those seeking honors and advancement, there are never enough materials for the fulfillment of the plans of all the enterprises. So only those who do not rely on the official channels for securing supplies can hope to obtain enough materials to fulfill their plans.

Suppose, for instance, that I am the head of a rubber goods factory which badly needs some chemical or other to continue manufacturing overshoes. The supply of this chemical is limited, so that I am unlikely to be able to obtain a sufficient quantity of it to fulfill my plan if I rely upon an official application in the "normal" way. My *blatmeister,* however, finds out that one of the departmental chiefs of the Chemical Trust, Comrade G., wants some building materials to finish his new summer residence outside the city. Though I have no such materials at my disposal, the director of the Building Co-operative of the Rosa Luxemburg Machine Tool factory has. By furnishing the latter with a supply of galoshes for his factory shop, I obtain the building materials for Comrade G., and the latter in return supplies me with my chemical. Thus—not "according to the plan"—do Soviet industry and trade function after a fashion.

One of the best *blatmeisters* I ever met was a certain M at Promexport, who was a genius not only at working out "combinations" to secure delivery of our goods but also at presenting figures in such a way as to make it appear that the plan had been more than fulfilled. He was so useful to the chairman of the organization that the latter— an old Party member—managed to wangle him into the Party. This was no mean feat, for at that time the proverbial camel had about as much chance of passing through the needle's eye as most "intellectuals" of entering the Party. M was promoted to vice-chairman, but eventually got arrested when an R.K.I. investigation revealed Promexport's exaggeration of its achievements. The chairman, of course, abandoned him to his fate. But even the O.G.P.U. recognized his usefulness, and he was soon put in charge of a section of the construction work on the Volga-Moscow canal. Another *blatmeister* at our office was F, the head of the transport section, who was invaluable at securing railway wagons for our goods at the expense of other organizations. But he was too obviously cynical and too frequently drunk to join the Party, and eventually got himself arrested for trying to supply a hospital, which badly needed sheets, with some from our export stock. Both M and F were decent fellows, not informers but wanglers. It was conditions of work in the U.S.S.R. which drove them to turn their talents to *blatmeistering*.

A far more unpleasant type of *blatmeister* was a certain V, the titular head of one department at Promexport, who acted as general factotum and toady to Kalmanofsky, the chairman. He attended to the letting of the chairman's *datcha* ("country house") and other personal affairs, was always at his side, fetched and carried for him, flattered him, and made himself useful in innumerable ways. Quite useless at his office job, he was invaluable to the chairman for securing whatever he personally required and in general in attending to his private affairs. V had no dignity at all. The chairman often treated him like a dog, stormed at him and vented his temper on him. This chairman was not stupid; he was in fact an able and intelligent man, an educated Jew who could appreciate merit and liked men like my husband who stood their ground and were never subservient. Under the capitalist system Kalmanofsky might have been an able and even an honest executive. But the Soviet system drove him to reward his *blatmeisters,* and to sacrifice real efficiency and profit on foreign trade for the sake of making a good showing. He and M together were so clever at window-dressing that Promexport got a banner as the best export organization, and K received a decoration and a private motor car. In fact, according to my husband's experiences in other export offices, Promexport really was much better run than most, if not all.

My husband went back to work at Promexport in 1933, finding his position there as finance manager under Kalmanofsky preferable to the higher rank of vice-chairman of another organization. Being a vice-chairman, if you were non-Party, was a rare distinction; but

Arcadi found it an impossible one. Decisions concerning the work were arrived at in the Party nucleus, which he was not entitled to attend, and yet he was made responsible for the results. His chief at Lecterserio, although a friend of ours and a decent chap, was entirely unsuited to his job. He was voluble, excitable, full of vigor and the joy of life, a keen Party member of the sincere kind who had been an excellent officer in the Red Army during the Civil War, but had no administrative ability or business knowledge. Everything was thrown onto Arcadi's shoulders, and his being non-Party made him too vulnerable and aroused too much jealousy. He was glad to go back to work under Kalmanofsky, who, although neither so honest as B in either his personal dealings or the manner in which he ran his enterprise, was much cleverer and cannier and a safer person to be with. Or so it seemed to us at the time. I have heard that both of these chiefs of Arcadi's were liquidated later in the great purge—Kalmanofsky only after he had first thrown many of his subordinates to the lions. (See Chapter X.)

The most honest and conscientious specialists usually came off worst. Engineers who could not bear to see beautiful new machinery shattered by reckless speeding up, or rapidly deteriorating through neglect of cleaning and repairs, the carrying out of which would involve a slackening in the mad pace of production; accountants trained in "bourgeois methods" who could not bring themselves to cook accounts in the interest of the director or chairman; heads of export departments who endeavored to get a fair price abroad for goods sold, and accordingly managed to sell smaller quantities than those who had overfulfilled the plan by selling far below the world price—these were the kind of specialists who inevitably, sooner or later, found themselves accused of sabotage, wrecking, and counter-revolution, and disappeared into the concentration camps. Again, it was the flatterers, the sycophants, the men without dignity or pride, who got on well with the Party bosses by constant toadying, who secured promotions. The wonder was that so many of the old educated class, the men who had received their training under the Tsarist regime and whose "cultural" standards were "bourgeois," continued to work as well as they were permitted to, without hope of reward and without losing their dignity and integrity.

Of course conditions varied in different enterprises, some Party men being decent, honest, and anxious to do their jobs as well as possible. But such Communists rarely got to the top of the tree. The Communist who devoted his main energies to mastering his job, learning from his specialists and from experience, had no time to spend making up to the great, and thus secure promotion.

An Italian writer described Soviet society as a society based on calumny instead of competition. Calumny was another important method of securing promotion, especially among Party members from 1935 onward in the period of the great purge. If you could discredit, calumniate, and accuse your superior or your rivals, and get them expelled from the Party or arrested, you could secure a better job. Not only this, but often the surest way of protecting yourself from an accusation which would ruin your life or cause your death was to get in your accusation first. This applied with particular force to the so-called scientific institutions, like the Communist Academy—later christened the Academy of Sciences—where I worked my last three and a half years in Moscow. Here "research" work often consisted of a careful perusal of other people's writings to spot their "deviations" from the Party line and denounce them.

My claim to be a "textile specialist" rested on my book, *Lancashire and the Far East*. I did in fact know a good deal about market demands, prices, and costs of production from the studies I had made in the factories of Lancashire and Japan; I thought that in the job offered me at Promexport I should find something of the satisfaction my husband found in doing real work instead of talking and writing a lot of foolishness and lies. I was to find myself much mistaken.

Arcadi knew his people, and understood how to get really useful work done in spite of the many obstacles. He had tact and an uncanny understanding of men's minds which enabled him to make his Party boss think he had made a decision himself, when in reality he had adopted one of Arcadi's suggestions. Acardi, being without vanity or personal ambition, was content if he could get a job well carried out even if he got no credit for it. He was respected by the better type of Party men, who recognized his ability, his real qualifications and wide knowledge, and his integrity. He also had a dignity and a spirit which made it impossible for anyone to bully him, and I think his long residence abroad and his Western manner and behavior over-awed even his Party bosses at times. At any rate, Arcadi survived the purge of the non-Party specialists in 1930-32 and managed to get a good deal of satisfaction at times out of the work he performed.

I, however, was treated at Promexport like a valuable ornament. The chairman and vice-chairman liked being able to say that they had a "foreign specialist" in their enterprise, were extremely polite and even friendly, occasionally consulted me when they had men from other export organizations or commissariats in the office, took me to dinner with visiting foreign buyers, and for the rest did not care a rap what I did with my time. My immediate superior, the chief of the textile export department, was the afore-mentioned *blatmeister* M. A nice little man who had worked in England for some years and knew the language perfectly, he had little time to spare from *blatmeistering* to attend to his own department. The assistant manager was an ignoramus called Bessonoff, who knew nothing and did no work at all as far as anyone could see. But he had once been Lenin's chauffeur, and this entitled him to a cushy job for the rest of his life. The real responsibility fell on a poor man who had been the manager of a department store in Tsarist times. He was tall and stooped, with a drooping mustache, and prematurely aged. Kindhearted, extremely courteous to everyone, conscientious and hard-working, he yet had neither the knowledge nor capacity to run an export business of these dimensions. We were exporting cotton goods all over the world: to China, the Dutch East Indies, India, Persia, the Argentine, and some European markets. Persia was the largest market and the traditional one for Russian textiles. The Russian industry was adapted to this export trade, which had been carried on in Tsarist times, the taste of the Persians was known and catered to, and in any case the U.S.S.R. had a practical monopoly there.

But our other markets were far more difficult. Here we succeeded in selling only because we were ready to undercut everyone else. My job was supposed to be that of advising what kinds of cotton cloth should be exported to different countries, and at what prices they should be sold. Obviously the price question should have been the affair of the Russian trading organizations on the spot, but at that date few qualified men were allowed to work abroad. The men like my husband, of long experience in foreign trade and finance, were no longer allowed to work abroad. The employees of the Commissariat of Foreign Trade from 1930 on had to be Party men of proletarian origin, or old Bolsheviks without taint of heresy. Men of such qualifications rarely had any others. Nor could they usually speak any foreign language, and they often had not the faintest idea of how to trade. A Russian-speaking friend of mine at Arcos in London was asked by the Russian in charge of the department where he worked what a bill of exchange was and found it difficult to get the Russian to understand because he had not the most elementary notion of the functions of a bank. Eventually the foreign staffs, which had become so useless, were drastically reduced.

The export organizations, therefore, had to do most of their trading at long distance from Moscow. Foreign buyers were advised to come to Moscow to make their purchases, and we had fairly frequent visits from big merchant buyers in England and Germany. In consequence of the utter uselessness of our trading representatives abroad, we took to exporting through middlemen. Our sales to the Argentine were effected through the Manchester firm of Bakerjan, and those to the Dutch East Indies through a large London firm of merchant shippers. Mr. Bakerjan was an amiable Armenian who no doubt made a huge profit on the Soviet exports which he sold in competition with Lancashire goods, but who was very polite about it. For hours the vice-manager and I and Mr. Bakerjan would sit over the pattern books while he chose his stock. Often, however, what he chose could not be delivered and we had to pay fines. The real "live wire" of our department was a young non-Party technician, V, who knew the Russian cotton industry from A to Z. V would be able to say from memory not only which factory could produce which goods, but also which one was likely actually to be able to produce them under pressure. When Mr. Bakerjan, or the representative of the English firm which sold our textiles in the Dutch East Indies, pleaded for wider goods, or bleached goods, it was V who went off to visit the factories in Ivanovo-Vosnysenk and Tver to try and get them produced. V not only worked, but continually studied. He had all sorts of ideas for improving production, he made gallant efforts to secure export prices which would give us a little real profit, and he never pretended that he had succeeded in exporting the planned quantity of goods when he hadn't. Of course he ended up in prison. He was non-Party, he was of bourgeois origin, and he was well qualified and keen about his job. Few men of his type survive in the U.S.S.R. It was from him that I learned of the virtual extinction of the vast textile handweaving industry which had existed in Russia before the First Five Year Plan. The Soviet Government had liquidated this industry by treating the village and small town weavers as "capitalists."

At first I used to spend much of my time making elaborate calculations of the price at which our goods could be sold in competition with English and Japanese cloth of the same kind. If the Japanese sold prints of such and such yarn with so many threads per inch at so much, we could, I argued, sell ours by asking a price just a little lower. M let me do my pretty calculations in peace, but got really irritated if I wanted him to make use of them. What should he, or the chairman, care whether or not we secured a fraction of a penny more a yard on our goods? Neither they, nor Promexport, nor the Commissariat of Foreign Trade would get any credit for that. All that mattered was to fulfill the plan, and the plan demanded the export of so many hundreds of thousands of yards of cloth a month. Price was a secondary question, and if they stopped to bother too much about that they would fail to fulfill the plan. Moreover, it was easier to secure foreign currency by exporting a large quantity of goods at a very low price than to export a smaller quantity at a higher price. In any case, the ruble having a shifting and largely fictitious value, the factory cost of production and freight charge had little to do with the prices at which Soviet goods were sold abroad. If we obtained 20 or 25 per cent of the factory's production cost, we had done brilliantly. It was more usual in the case of textiles to get about 15 per cent of it. This percentage was called the *perecreta,* and, although it varied considerably for different types of goods, it gave some indication of the real value of the ruble. The *perecreta* was kept secret to avoid foreign accusations of dumping, and in order that gullible tourists might continue to tell the folks at home what high wages the Russian workers were earning. For, of course, the same cloth we sold abroad for a song was also sold in Soviet shops—when available at all for the internal market—at the full cost of production plus a big profit for the state.

I started on my work at Promexport full of enthusiasm. With V's assistance I visited factories in different parts of the country and found out what they were capable of producing. I "advised" my chiefs of the needs and tastes of foreign markets: widths, designs, quality, and so forth. I produced long reports concerning the possibilities of producing goods of the required width and quality at various factories, and made careful calculations concerning competitive prices at which Soviet cloth could be sold in different countries. My reports on my visits to the textile districts were received politely, sometimes even with enthusiasm. I was given a foreign specialist's food card, which was worth literally thousands of rubles. For in those days (1931-32), as I have related elsewhere, little besides bread and a small ration of sugar was obtainable on the ordinary citizen's food card, whereas those privileged to go to the foreign specialists' food distributor were able, like the Russian Communist party functionaries, to buy milk, butter, eggs, meat, and other supplies untasted by the majority of the population.

Although I was treated with honor and ensconced in a cushy job, my work was absolutely useless. The Promexport charwoman who received 90 rubles a month, lived with her children in a corridor, and existed on black bread, cabbage soup, and an occasional herring, was performing a more useful social function than I was. No notice was taken of my reports for the simple reason that my suggestions, if acted upon, would have made it appear that neither the textile factories nor the exporting organization was "fulfilling the plan." To give a concrete example: the factories working for export had in many cases looms wide enough to produce the 27-inch cloth required to make a pair of Chinese trousers, and China was one of our principal markets at that time. But to have produced the required width would have meant producing a lesser number of thousands of yards per quarter, than if they continued to manufacture the traditional Russian width of 24 inches. To produce a lesser number of yards would have meant "nonfulfillment of the plan"; and a lot of people would have got shot or sent to concentration camps. The export organization in its turn would have been able to export only a smaller yardage than before and would also have failed to fulfill its plan. So we continued to sell a narrow cloth at great loss, since naturally the Chinese would buy a cloth too narrow to be convenient only if it were offered at bargain prices. It was simpler and safer for us to denude the Soviet market of the cloth of which the Russian people were in desperate need than to export a smaller quantity of the right kind of cloth at a higher price. In general our concern was not to get a good price abroad, but to send over the frontier as many carloads as possible, and then boast of the tremendous increase in our exports. The textile and other departments of Promexport made so good a showing in those years that the chairman was given a decoration and presented with a private automobile. This was done at the cost of denuding the home market of vital necessities, and for a return in foreign currency which was pitifully small in comparison with the sacrifices made by the Russian population.

The cloth we sold was very defective because the workers were forced to work at top speed on machinery which was often old and almost always neglected as regards cleaning and repairs. They could earn a living only if they paid no attention to quality. They too had their "plan" to fulfill, or woe betide them. Losing one's job was no joke when it also entailed losing one's room and having one's family turned into the street. At one period the percentage of defective cloth, even in the good factories—which meant those working for exports—was as high as 80 per cent of their total production. It all had to be printed, since bleached or dyed cloth showed up the defects too clearly.

The bad quality of Soviet production was largely due, insofar as the textile industry was concerned, to the introduction of what was called the functional system—an imitation of American mass production methods which were entirely unsuited to the old looms and confined space of the Russian factories, and to the lack of skill of the average worker. When I was working at the Commissariat of Light Industry and tried to point out the disastrous results of setting a weaver to perform one function on 20 or 30 looms working at top speed, instead of all functions on two, as she had been accustomed to do, the Russian "specialist" who worked beside me told me I had better shut up, since several Russian engineers who had made the same kind of criticism had been arrested for sabotage. A year or two later the functional system was abolished, and those made to bear the responsibility for its adoption accused of wrecking. Thus are mistakes "rectified" in the Soviet Union after they have caused untold loss, and after those who originally pointed out the mistakes have been liquidated.

I had transferred to the newly created Commissariat of Light Industry in the early spring of 1932, hoping that, having failed at Promexport to find work to do which would enable me to earn, as well as to receive, my bread, I might find a useful function to perform if I got closer to the direction of industry itself. However, my work at the Commissariat proved to be more futile even than at Promexport, where I had at least done the useful job of putting into correct English the letters we sent abroad. At the Commissariat I did a lot of traveling around, and got an intimate close-up of the terrible condition of the Russian textile workers. I am, of course, not an engineer; and that was the kind of knowledge I now required. But even if I had been so qualified no one would have paid any attention to my recommendations. After a year's work as a "textile specialist" I was glad to accept an offer to work in the Institute of World Economy and Politics at the Communist Academy. Here I could at least cultivate my own garden, study and learn, read and write. After my experience of Soviet industry and trade I relished it.

Petrov's delicious satire, *The Little Golden Calf,* published about ten years ago when a little "dangerous thinking" was still permitted in the U.S.S.R., provided it took a humorous form, gives a picture of how work is done and how life is lived in the Soviet Union, which is a joy to all who have lived there. One story in it tells of an accountant in a Soviet office who, in order to escape one of the periodic "cleansings of the apparatus" and to get a little peace, manages to convince people that he is mad and to get himself sent to a lunatic asylum. Eventually his deception is discovered, and he is sent back to work at his old job. The other clerks and accountants cluster round him to hear of his experiences and he tells them: "It was simply wonderful; of course it was a bedlam there too, but at least in that bedlam they did not think that they were constructing socialism."

One could not work long at a Soviet Institution without realizing that it was all a bedlam; but, if one were wise, one did at Rome what the Romans do; one continued to pretend that one was constructing socialism even if one knew very well that one was only helping to create chaos, and playing a part in a gigantic hoax which might have been funny were it not so tragic. The German specialists were the ones who found it most difficult to adapt themselves to the bedlam. One of the characters in *The Little Golden Calf* is a German specialist brought to the Urals, who waits week after week, and month after month, to start work. The director of the trust who is supposed to tell him where to start working is never visible. Either there is a notice on his door saying, "Just gone out for a few minutes" or another notice saying, "Very busy, cannot be disturbed." At all other times he is away traveling on a *komanderofka*. The German gets more and more exasperated and angry. The Russians simply can't understand him. "Why," they say, "the man is drawing a huge salary and has nothing to do; why on earth isn't he satisfied?"

Such conditions as those I found in the textile industry were, of course, not peculiar to it. The same causes led to the same results in other industries. Defective workmanship and inefficiency were inevitable, since every man's job, and frequently life and liberty, depended upon his fulfilling a plan which had been drawn up without reference to capacity, at the command of the dictator Stalin.

Soviet industry and transport, which had recovered from the destruction and neglect of the Civil War period and had been functioning fairly smoothly since 1924, have never recovered from the mass arrest and imprisonment of experts in every field in the purge of 1930-32. Most of these experts had worked loyally for the Soviet power since 1920, although not pretending to be Communists. The manner in which they had devoted their brains and energies to ensuring the functioning of industry, transport, and the educational system had proved that men will do the job they are interested in even if the material rewards are small and their position in society unhonored. It had also proved that the Revolution had not destroyed the patriotism or the ideals of social service of the Russian professional classes.

The Five Year Plans could not be realized, except on paper, owing mainly to the liquidation or demoralization of the only people who could ensure the proper functioning of the national economy. Each year the muddle and waste became worse, and more and more of the honest and well-qualified Russians were liquidated or in fear and despair gave up trying to bring order out of chaos. By the time the Soviet Government started relaxing class distinctions (which it did by decree in 1933), and also modifying the terror against the non-Party specialists, it was too late to undo the damage done.

The more arrests were made the worse became the conditions of life of the mass of the people. Food became scarcer, clothing and shoes, galoshes and other necessities almost unobtainable, housing deteriorated.

The O.G.P.U., grown to be a monstrous *imperium in imperio,* by sweeping countless victims into its prison camps, began to exercise a dominant role in the economic life of Russia. "Kulaks"—a term which covered all the peasants who resisted collectivization—engineers, scientists, university professors, "counter-revolutionary workers," Trotskyists—all came into the power of the O.G.P.U., against whose sentences there was no appeal, and which had its own factories and farms as well as being in charge of the timber camps, canal construction, road and railway building, and other "public works." The Soviet system came to depend more and more on prison labor in order to be able to function at all. Those not themselves in the prison camps were driven by fear of being sent there to accept speeding up, regimentation, the deprivation of the last vestiges of trade-union rights, forced contributions to state loans. They had to work like slaves in factory, mine, workshop, and offices, in spite of the weariness engendered by lack of food, constant physical and mental strain and the hopelessness of their lives.

Terror and compulsion engendered terror and compulsion, so that what had started as a purge became a system. "Socialist" economy came to require ever more prisoners in order to function. In the period between the first and second of the great purges the O.G.P.U. was reduced to arresting homosexuals and all accused of ever having been homosexuals, in order to obtain sufficient labor for its Arctic timber camps, where mortality was so terribly high that few survived a five-year sentence, and those condemned to ten years were counted as dead by their families.

The number of the O.G.P.U.'s victims before the second and greater purge, which began in 1936, was, however, comparatively small, perhaps one or two million* as against 5-7 million in 1937 and 1938. Moreover, the earlier victims died off rapidly, and at the outset there does not appear to have been any great desire to profit from their labors; the intention was rather the death of the "Kulaks," "wreckers," and other "counter-revolutionary elements." At least this is the only conclusion to be drawn from the manner in which the prisoners in the timber camps were treated before the reform of May 1930, when it was apparently decided to keep the prisoners alive and working rather than to murder them.

It is worth quoting at some length from the account given by Professor Tchernavin, who escaped to Finland from Solovetsky Island in 1932, together with his wife and his ten-year-old son who had been allowed to visit him. The heroic story of that daring escape has been related by Madame Tchernavin, whose book † is a sincere, honest, and unornamented account both of the life of the intellectuals in the U.S.S.R., and of the gallant and seemingly impossible feat of walking with a child across Karelia to the Finnish border without a compass.

I know both Madame Tchernavin and the Professor, who is now working at the Natural Science Museum in London, and they are as honest and trustworthy people as could be found. Prior to his arrest, he was Professor of Ichthyology in the Agronomic Institute of Leningrad. His book, *I Speak for the Silent,* is restrained, cautious, and entirely free from self-pity or exaggeration. What he relates from personal experience is only what was whispered all over Russia when I lived there. Accounts of the tortures inflicted by the O.G.P.U. and the brutality of the concentration camp guards passed from mouth to mouth in Russia, and constituted one of the weapons of terror for keeping the whole population in fear and subjection. No stories that have come out of Nazi Germany are more terrible, and whereas Hit-

---

* Some idea of the number can be obtained from the fact that in the White Sea-Baltic, during the construction of the canal between these two seas, there were in 1932 not less than a quarter of a million prisoners, of whom 28 per cent (70,000) were partially amnestied in August 1933. At the Solovetsky Island camp, in the summer of 1931, according to the account of Professor Tchernavin, there were 14 sections and in each section there were usually 20,000 prisoners, which makes a total of 280,000. If one assumes that there were an average of 100,000 prisoners in each of the known camps in the U.S.S.R. in 1932, there would have been a total of 1,300,000. However, the number of camps was then, and is now, an O.G.P.U. secret. Professor Tchernavin states that a prisoner who escaped in 1932 reports two new camps created since Professor Tchernavin's time, one for the double tracking of the Baikal Amur railway with 450,000 prisoners, and another at Dimitrov near Moscow with 250,000. See further (pp. 256-7) for various estimates of the number of persons imprisoned during the past decade.

† *Escape from the Soviets.* New York, 1935.

ler's victims are counted in thousands, or tens of thousands, Stalin's are counted in millions.

When the great purge of 1936-38 carried off my husband, I knew to what he was condemned, as everyone in Russia knew what awaited their loved ones when the O.G.P.U. got hold of them.

Below I quote from the account given by Professor Tchernavin in the *Slavonic Review* of January, 1934. Since it appeared in England, many of the admirers of the Soviet Union who at that time simply refused to read authentic accounts of this nature, have had their opinion changed by the Russo-German Pact and the Finnish war. But the Finnish war was a war like others, whereas the cruelties inflicted by the Soviet Government on millions of Russians for years past, have no parallel in modern times. Dachau appears almost a model prison compared to the Russian concentration camps; yet before 1939 the so-called liberals and progressives of the United States, England, and France, had nothing but praise for the Soviet Union, and condemned torture, imprisonment without trial, and systematic brutality only when they occurred in Nazi Germany. It is because of the little attention paid in the past to the accounts of the rare few of Stalin's victims who have escaped from the hell of the Russian concentration camps, that I reproduce below some lengthy extracts from Professor Tchernavin's narrative:*

> The great mass of prisoners are exiled under Article 58 of the Criminal Code, namely, for what is called, "Counter-Revolution," a conception which is interpreted extremely widely in the U.S.S.R. The enormous majority of those deported under this article do not even know what they are accused of; many do not even know either their sentence or the term of their exile.
>
> . . . .
>
> Criminals, that is prisoners who have committed a real crime, are no more than 10 per cent. in the camp; among them are professional robbers, confirmed thieves and also embezzlers and swindlers. These are usually exiled by sentence of a court.
>
> All actual criminals are in a privileged position and, as opposed to the "Counter-Revolutionaries," are called the "socially near." They play a very important part in the camp, as we shall see.
>
> . . . .

* Quoted from "Life in Concentration Camps in the U.S.S.R.," by permission of Professor Tchernavin personally given to the author.

The Concentration Camp of Solovetsk

The words "special destination" used in connection with the Solovetsk camp meant simply the destruction of those who were sent there. The officials of the camp made no secret of this with the prisoners and told them so the first day after their arrival, but even without any telling all would have become quickly convinced of this.

In May, 1930, Ogpu decided to change the regime in the camps, as their reputation for cruelty had passed over the frontier; at that time the name was also changed, and instead of the words "special destination" was submitted "camps of labor and correction."

. . . .

Conditions of Life in Solovetsk to May, 1930

I was brought to the camp on the 2nd May, 1931, that is a year after its reform. Most of the prisoners, however, were persons who had experienced the regime of "special destination," and their simple and terrible narratives confirmed the dreadful picture of the past. Apart from that, the camp officials and especially the warders had not yet had time to change their character. Their remarks and shouts and even the very language that they used, with special words, were a lively evidence of the period of extermination of prisoners. News of that time very rarely reached the press. The most detailed account of it is given in the notes of an Ogpu official, Kisilev, who escaped abroad and published them under the title of *The Camps of Death*. According to him the number of prisoners at that time amounted to 660,000.

. . . . . .

The chief work was the preparation of timber for export and the laying of chaussées through Karelia, from the White Sea to the Finnish frontiers. These roads—the Kem-Ukhta and the Loukhi-Kesteng tracks, passing through quite unpopulated districts, have a strategic significance and are directed against Finland. In the neighbourhood of these roads, the trees were cleared away and enormous areas were drained. Apparently places d'armes and aerodromes were being got ready in case of war with Finland.

These works were carried out in quite intolerable conditions. Clothing and footwear were not served out to the prisoners. Their quarters were unimaginably close and dirty and were not heated. Often for those who were working in the forest no quarters were provided, and they camped in huts made of branches. The food was disgusting and quite insufficient. The work was assigned on such a basis that only the strongest and most experienced would be able to complete it, and that only with the greatest exertions and in not less than fourteen to sixteen hours. On such a reckoning every prisoner was given a daily "task"; whoever did not complete it had no right to return to the barracks for the night and got no food. Frozen and hungry, he could not perform his task next day.

A Regime of Extermination

Then punitive measures were taken, as if he were slacking maliciously. In the winter they "put him out in the cold," that is, stripped him naked and put him on the stump of a tree. As in this latitude the winter temperature is seldom higher than 10 degrees C., the stripped man soon loses consciousness and dies: or else his arms and legs are frozen, after which he dies of gangrene. In the summer they "put him to the mosquitoes," that is, they stripped him naked and tied him to a tree. In the northern forests there is such a mass of mosquitoes that they bite to death even beasts covered with as thick a skin as cattle; of course a man could not endure this and died. Besides this, they beat them terribly at their work, and many were put in the punishment cell where they died of cold and starvation. Thus the Ogpu quickly got rid of prisoners who could not stand the heavy work. Even the best workers were not free from blows and insults. As a rule, all were beaten even without any reason. They were beaten for the slightest protest, for any grievance; in a word, everyone was beaten who did not satisfy their warders or whose clothes were wanted by them. There was a special way of doing this:—the warder would order the prisoner to bring him something out of the wood and as soon as he was fifty yards away, would shoot him in the back. Then a document would be drawn up saying that the prisoner was shot "in an attempt to escape." The prisoner could not disobey and refuse to go in to the forest, as they would kill him for disobedience.

Prisoners often ended their lives with suicide. Self-mutilation was equally widely practised. The prisoner, knowing that the task was beyond his strength and that this was equivalent to torture and death from blows and punishment, resolved to sham an accident and with his axe cut off his fingers or his hand at the wrist. For such people there was a special name, "self-cutters." They were treated with particular cruelty: after a terrible beating, they were compelled to stand in front of the line of prisoners on parade and to hold in the remaining hand the fingers they had cut off and to cry out: "I am a shirker." The language of Solovetsk has a special term for this, *filon*. If the "self-cutter" did not die from the blows or the loss of blood or gangrene, he was sent to an "invalid gang," that is to one of the special posts in the camp where were gathered together the lame, tuberculous, scurvied, impotent and aged. All these were sent "to the bend" (*na zagib*), meaning to death, which was bound to follow on such conditions of existence, instead of any officially pronounced sentence of shooting. The chief invalid gang was on a beautiful island on the Gulf of Onega, the Kond Island. ... Thither in autumn they took as many as 5,000 crippled prisoners; and in spring, when the navigation opened, the chief of this gang reported their end to the Head of the camps.

The position of young women was everywhere miserable: Ogpu men of all ranks compelled them to live with them. Those that resisted were set to specially heavy work and subjected to terrible humiliation, insults and blows. Those that surrendered went from hand to hand and generally fell sick of venereal diseases, which are widespread among the Ogpu staff.

Besides this, the destruction of the prisoners was not a little assisted by spotted typhus of which were continual epidemics, as all the prisoners were covered with fleas. The sick were taken to one of the islands, where they died without any attention.

In spite of this terrible regime it was extremely rare that the prisoners protested, as everyone there well knew that the result would be wholesale slaughter, whatever the form of protest. Thus ended the strike of the Georgians at Solovetsk in 1928 and other similar demonstrations.

Escapes were also rare and in most cases unsuccessful, as the absence of any supplies of food, the bad clothing and the enormous distance to the frontier made them almost impossible. Of course, all who were caught trying to escape, after terrible blows and tortures were shot. For the "Kaery" (Counter-Revolutionaries) this is in full force to the present day.

All the cruelties mentioned above are inflicted on the prisoners by the overseers and warders consisting of criminal prisoners, under the general inspection of the Chekists. Shooting, then and now, is carried out only by the higher officials of Ogpu, among whom there are many who like this work. These prisoners, therefore, are faced with this dilemma: either to be flogged or to flog others and at this price buy themselves a better lot. To join the warders gives a man a life with plenty to eat and drink, but to keep one's post one had to show one's zeal and ardour.

· · · · · · ·

A New Policy

The second period began about May, 1930. By an order from Ogpu from Moscow the policy in the concentration camp was radically changed. A commission was sent out to investigate the camp regime, which, of course, was very well known before. The Commission announced that this regime had been established "without orders." About fifty overseers or warders taken from among the criminal prisoners who had made a particular reputation for cruelty were shot and some of the staff received appointments elsewhere.

The question of what led to the change of regime and how permanent the change, was of lively interest to the prisoners. The general reason, it seemed, was the enormous influx of prisoners in 1930, as a result of the execution of compulsory collectivisation and failures which had appeared in the Five Year Plan. Instead of tens of thousands there were now sent hundreds of thousands. If tens of thousands could be kept on some island of the White Sea and in the depths of the Karelian forests, this proved impossible for hundreds of thousands. The work of Ogpu in the camps was inevitably bound to become well known, and in consequence care had to be taken to preserve at least some little decency in appearances, especially because undesirable reports had already penetrated abroad in 1929 and 1930. Much harm had been done by accounts which appeared in the foreign press and especially the evidence given on oath by the student Malyshev, who had escaped from the Solovetsk camp. The campaign which broke out against forced labour in the timber trade, which was the principal work of the camp, deprived Ogpu of its chief advantage, currency.

To counter these "campaigns of the capitalists," the Soviet Counter-Agitation produced a crudely falsified film called "Solovki," and also some clamorous articles in the Soviet newspapers and periodicals; but the interest shown abroad in the camps was too strong and too continuous, and the policy of extermination of prisoners was impossible.

Commercial Basis of the Camps

Apart from this, the policy of extermination was commercially disadvantageous to Ogpu. With the colossal growth in the number of prisoners there were opened wide perspectives of utilising them. With the reform of 1930, the concentration camps, whether at Solovetsk or elsewhere, were turned into parts of a most colossal enterprise of slave labour run by Ogpu. They were ordered externally to take the aspect of corrective institutions. The introduction was prescribed of special newspapers, broadcasts, and library organisation.

Under the cover of this motto Ogpu reorganized its "business side" on a colossal scale, drawing vast profits from the camps as commercial enterprises. It will be enough to acquaint oneself with the present structure of the camp to convince oneself of its real objects.

In structure and functions the camp exactly corresponds to the Soviet state commercial enterprises. To start with, it is divided into "sections" aiming at profit by production and trade. The administration of a "section" consists of the following "parts": producing, trading, and accountancy. At the head of each "section" is a director with two assistants. All this is an exact copy of any Soviet productive enterprise. The work of production is different in various sections and camps, but their commercial character is identical.

* * * * * * *

The Journey to the Camp

Prisoners are taken to the concentration camps from all the U.S.S.R. prisons which are scattered over the vast territory of former Russia. They are conveyed in goods trucks or special police vans with bars inside and bars on the windows and doors. The trucks are meant to contain twenty-eight persons, but actually as many as sixty of the convicts are shut up in them. They are packed so tight that they are never able to lie down at all, but have to crouch down. It is equally impossible to stand up and walk about in the truck. An armed guard of special Ogpu troops accompanies them. The special trains provided are very slow. The *étape* on which I was conducted from Petersburg to Kem, a distance of about 500 miles, took nearly six whole days, and it may be noted the great majority of the prisoners have to travel over a far longer stretch than I had. Convicts appeared at the Solovetsk camp who had come even from the Far East, a distance of as much as 6,000 miles away which had taken 6 to 7 months. The death rate was enormously high in the case of such long expeditions.

We were not fed at all during the six days of the journey. On our departure we each had a dry ration given us consisting of a piece of black bread, weighing about a couple of pounds (one kilogram) and two salted herrings. But the chief hardship of the journey was neither the crowding nor hunger, but the intolerable thirst we suffered from, which was still further accentuated by the dreadful stuffiness in the trucks. We were given hardly anything to drink during the whole of the journey. One reason for this may be that prisoners' trains do not stop at any stations (for fear of their being seen by any foreigners) but are shunted on to sidings where there is no water. During the whole of our six days we were given water only three times; immediately after leaving Petersburg and twice on the journey. It was brought to us in pails. Those who had mugs got rather more than those who had not—the latter received theirs in the hollow of their hands, only two or three mouthfuls in fact. There were not many who had mugs, because vessels of all kinds were forbidden in the prisons.

* * * * * * *

We reached the distributing centre towards dusk. Although we were exhausted by the journey and tortured by hunger and thirst, we were kept the whole night through in military formation. Our numbers were checked, the roll was called, our documents were examined, and after all this we were searched and sorted out. We could hardly stand, and yet we were given neither food nor drink. The first to be sorted out were those who had previously worked in the Cheka or the Ogpu, and had been exiled for bribery, murder, unauthorised shooting of prisoners and other serious crimes. They were immediately given a privileged position; separate quarters were provided for them and they were fed much better than the rest. To them were allotted the administrative posts of the camp, especially those in the "Information and Inquiry" and the "Culture and Education" departments. Ex-Red Army soldiers, who had also been convicted for criminal offences, strode on to parade next morning in their military uniform, carrying rifles in their hands and were appointed to be our "guard."

The Quarantine Company Accommodation

This sorting was over by about 4 A.M., and then we were marched off to the "quarantine company." Although this is within the bounds of the camp and is surrounded by barbed wire, it has round it an extra wire fence. The building which houses the quarantine section is a long wooden hut-like structure with small windows, most of which have been broken and the gaps covered over with filthy rags. The interior is divided off by two wooden partitions into four rooms called "platoons," a term in keeping with the military organisation of the camp and the division of the prisoners into "companies." The chinks in the partitions were, in places, large enough for a hand to be inserted. The chinks in the outer walls of the hut were smaller but it was possible to look out through them, and when a blizzard raged the snow piled up on the plank beds we slept on. A platoon room was rather more than thirty yards long by five wide, and so resembled a long corridor. A double row of plank beds were laid along both sides of this corridor, and on them the prisoners sleep huddled together. Each sleeper is entitled to a width of just over eighteen inches—a space which he has to make do for all his possessions as well as his own body. He has also to consume on his plank the miserable food doled out, for the building contains nothing else but these bunks. The floor is put together with thin laths which bend beneath the foot, and both the walls and the roof (there is no ceiling) are covered with a layer of dirt and smoke. The hut is heated—but only when the cold is intense—by a miserable little sheet-iron stove, which has a round iron pipe roughly let into an opening cut through on the roof.

As 250 prisoners go to a "platoon," the whole hut contains 1,000 men. The quarantine hut, like all the others, is bug-infested, and life in it is a terrible trial to the prisoners. It is impossible to keep the bugs down, because the walls are of planks or of wood, and the bunks, being roughly hewn, encourage the vermin to breed in the chinks and holes in their thousands. A convict has no means whatever of getting hold of them. As neither bedding nor mattresses is ever provided in the camp, he has to sleep on the bare boards and use his clothes for his pillow and covering.

"Education" and Roll Calls

Every morning and evening, and sometimes during the day also, the prisoners are lined up and checked over. Before the roll is called, they have to stand in rows like soldiers for one to two hours on end, and when hailed by the officer in charge of the roll with, "hey, you lousy fellow" or "hail there, you riffraff," they are obliged to answer in proper military fashion.

When I was in the quarantine company, our chief was an ill-educated fellow who had been a burglar in civil life. He was our "education instructor." The "Education" consisted in haranguing us two or three times daily, before the roll was called. It was impossible to understand what he said, and he himself did not know the meaning of many of the words he used, but to make up for any deficiencies he larded his speechifying with numerous indecencies. The usual gist of what he said was to the effect that we were "a lazy, lousy crew" whom he, our chief and instructor, would teach to lead a hardworking and honourable life, and make us "literate and politically educated." He explained to us that until 1930 the camps had been meant to exterminate the prisoners, but now that they were "re-educating" us.

If we could have been outside the camp, the whole thing might have appeared laughable: a semi-literate burglar as the teacher and educator of professors and scholars whose names were known throughout the length and breadth of Russia, of engineers and other professional men, and of peasants whose life had been spent in honest toil. But it was no laughing matter for us, who realised only too well that we were delivered up body and soul to the clutches of him and his like.

Food Rations

We had to listen to our educator's speech before we were given—next day!—our food ration. This was brought to us in dirty wooden tubs which were dumped down on the floor. According to "regulations" we were supplied in the morning with thin, very thin, "gruel" and boiling water. At midday we had our dinner, which was soup, or rather water in which a bit of dried fish or else salt horse or camel flesh had been boiled. But even this wretched mess of often rotten meat and fish did not always reach our mouths because it was eaten up by the lesser officials and the guards, while we had to put up with water which had fermented cabbage leaves of the previous year swimming about in it. At four o'clock a second helping of boiling water was given out. In addition, those in the quarantine company were supposed to receive one pound (400 grams) of bread, but in fact only three-quarters of a pound (300 grams) was issued.

Both food and water were issued in very limited quantities—about a glassful of liquid for each. No vessels for food were given us, and, literally dying of thirst as we were, after the journey and after a day of torture in the camp without food and drink, we now had nothing to eat the stuff out of. Fortunate were those who succeeded in picking preserve tins from the refuse dumps. The others got their skilly in the hem of their shirts and presented their clasped palms for their hot water.

When it is remembered that the convicts who came to the distributing centre were exhausted by prison life and the fatigues of their long trek, it is not to be wondered at that the starvation regime on Popov Island made the death rate enormous. The hospitals were always crowded out. It is true that we were no longer killed off by floggings nor by being shot down, as our predecessors of 1930 had been, but hunger, cold, dirt, vermin did their work as effectively as ever.

"Disinfection" and "Medical Examination"

The "quarantine" itself consisted in our being strictly isolated and marched off on the first day to the "baths." The water there was absolutely cold except for two small tubs of tepid water which each of us was given. We were obliged to undress in the cold passages, and then our head-hair was cut with No. 0 clippers and our body-hair shaved with blunt razors. After this operation, which was carried out by criminal prisoners, our bodies became covered with scabs and cuts, and many of us suffered from skin rash. We lost all resemblance to human beings. After the "disinfection" our clothes were returned to us, but what had been fur and feather before was now rags and tatters. It is not hard to imagine the scarecrows we were turned into.

After leaving the quarantine, we presented ourselves for medical examination, which was carried out by those of us who were doctors, and always under the strict supervision of Ogpu soldiers. The doctors were previously instructed what percentage of prisoners they might return as suitable for physical labour and what percentage as totally unfit. As they were themselves prisoners, they did not dare to break the Ogpu orders and were often obliged to return as "fit" persons who were thoroughly ill. During my time there were three health categories: (I) those fit for hard physical labour; (II) those fit for light physical labour; and (III) those unfit for physical labour. The last group included doddering old men and persons who were seriously ill, hardly able to put one foot before another. These were set to work in the offices or given jobs as night watchmen. To this class belonged those who could not walk without assistance or who were bedridden to the end of their days. I. G. Formanov, for example, who was seventy years old and had been a professor of the Agricultural Institute at Moscow was put into the third class. He had been condemned to ten years' exile for the affair of the 48,* and was brought to the camp on a stretcher after his legs had become paralysed in prison.

But these categories were not adhered to firmly. Thus, when the Ogpu needed extra workers, as it did in 1931 for the diggings of the White Sea-Baltic Canal, the convicts of the second and third groups were re-examined, and all those who had arms and legs at all were transferred to the first group, i.e., were entered as fit for hard physical labour.

. . . .

Conditions at Kem

A special application for my services was made in June, 1931, by the Fish Industry department of the camp. Until then I had been employed in loading balans (a special kind of bean), in spite of my having been put into the second category. I was sent to Kem, which is the centre of the Solovetsk camp. It is a tiny provincial town or, more properly, a seaside village.

As a specialist I was put into the "cleanest" company where only responsible workers were, but except for the type of prisoner it was in no way different from the others, nor was our system of life any different.

Reveille was at 7 a.m.; the squad overseer passed down the corridor shouting: "Get-up." The prisoners rise and run off to wash. The wash basin and the latrine are in the same place, and while ten men are satisfying the needs of nature (each with his queue round him) five others, with their queues too, are washing. One thousand men have to wash in half-an-hour. The dirt and stink of the place is beyond imagination. The floor is so disgusting that one shudders to walk on it. Neither soap nor towels are provided. Just a splash of water over our hands and face and we all run off across the yard to queue up at the kitchen window for our "gruel." No one cares whether it rains or snows—we stand in the open for our food. On getting the ladle-full of millet boiled in water, most

* i.e. The execution in 1930 of 48 specialists accused of "wrecking" the Five Year Plan.

249

of the prisoners gulp their portion down where they stand, without bothering to go back to their bunks in the hut. After that they have to get the documents authorising them to go "outside the wire" and start work in the town. The "work-book" has to be obtained from the officials on duty, and in it must be entered the hour and minute of reporting for work. After that, the convict must go into the office and ask for his pass to go "outside the wire." Once he has his pass he must hurry up and "line up," hand the pass over for the sentry to check as he passes through the camp gates, and then go under convoy into the town. He is now one of a gang that is marched along the streets, which are plastered with thick, clinging dirt. In the town all the prisoners are gradually distributed among the various institutions, where their names are entered in a book as they turn up for work.

The day's job goes on without interruption and without food until 5 o'clock; and then, if the work is not specially urgent, the convicts hang around in gangs until the convoy forms them into a general column and leads them back "behind the wire." Only after they have been checked up and their documents handed in are they free to go for their dinner. This is often so repellent as to be uneatable even by a hungry prisoner, and he goes off to his hut to consume there the remains of his daily ration of bread, if he had not already eaten it the same morning. Those engaged in production work are given just over a pound (500 grams) of bread a day, and those on hard physical labour nearly two pounds (8000 grams).

At 7 p.m. documents have to be obtained again and the prisoners again go under convoy to their work, which continues till eleven. Not till midnight do they get back to the hut for their "supper"— a ladle of boiled millet and hot water—and so to bed, which means lying on the eighteen-inch bare bunk. Even if sleep can be obtained in the dreadful fug and stink, where the prisoners are packed so tight that they are obliged to lie on their sides and, as soon as they are on the planks, are covered all over with bugs, their "rest" period comes only to a total of six hours, out of the twenty-four; all the rest of the time they are on their feet—working or marching to the town or standing in queues. In addition all are checked over every night. This wakes the convict up; the overseers are never quick about getting the counting done and are always afraid someone may have escaped.

All this does not of course kill the prisoners off, but it is easy to imagine how such a regime wears them down. Those who do not receive food-parcels from their homes infallibly fall ill of scurvy, or break out in boils, and many others contract consumption and heart disease.

The Means Used to Make the Prisoners Work

Since the spring of 1930 prisoners are no longer beaten or tortured or killed for not carrying out their allotted tasks. But Ogpu realises thoroughly well that forced labour does not yield good results and that special measures are necessary to induce a prisoner to put all his energies into his work. The means are of two kinds; compulsory and encouraging. The reduction of the bread ration from 800 to 300 grams—an amount insufficient to sustain life for prisoners on heavy physical work—belongs to the former category. Systematic refusal to work is punished by detention in a cell for periods up to thirty days, the prisoner being led out daily to his work. He may also be given solitary confinement and a charge of "incorrigibility" may be brought against him. "Incorrigibles" are shot, not out of hand as they used to be in 1930, but only after sentence has been passed by the court of the Information and Inquiry Department. The main threat used against the specialist is that of being transferred to do "general labour" as a navvy, and, in addition, being formally charged with "wrecking" or "sabotage," a crime which entails either an increase in the period of confinement of as much as three, four or five years, or, usually, death by shooting.

The measures of encouragement are as follows: Convicts who carry out their tasks are paid by Ogpu at special rates. The reward they receive is officially called "prize" money, but the prisoners call it "press" money. Labourers may get 3-4 roubles a month and specialists with high qualifications 25-30. The sum received may be spent once a month in the camp store on such "prize" products as two or three packets of shag (each packet containing nearly 2 oz., 50 grams), 7 oz. (200 grams) of melted lard and the same amount of dirty treacle sweets.

There are other kinds of allurements which are far more effective and make the prisoner work and strain his strength to the utmost. The first of these is permission for an interview. If a prisoner carries out his work unexceptionably for six months he may, at the discretion of the authorities, be allowed to see some close relative, usually one only. The interview may take place "in public conditions," that is, in the camp headquarters, and last for two hours on each of one to five days. In the case of a "personal" interview, which is the reward for specially exemplary and good work, a prisoner is set free to see his family in the "free quarters" which are rented for the purpose of interviews from the local inhabitants and are, naturally, under the supervision of the guard. On these occasions all documents are taken away from the prisoner's family, and it is not uncommon for all the members of the family to be subjected to a night search. The prisoner is not exempted from his daily work, but he is at least free to live with his own folk from midnight to 7 a.m. The dream of a meeting like this, which may be granted for a period of one to seven days and in exceptional cases for ten or even fourteen, keeps him alive for a whole year, and on the memory of it he lives till the next meeting. No imagination is needed to realise how hard a man tries and works when he knows there is a chance of living together with his nearest and dearest, even if it is only for a few days.

Another and less powerful means is the promise of a reduction of the sentence. Every prisoner, however hopeless his position, lives on the dream of being one day free, and Ogpu counts on this to extract from him the last ounce of his strength. In August, 1931, an Ogpu order "on the reckoning of the days of labour" was solemnly read out in all the camps. For those prisoners who had performed their duties in an exemplary manner three months were to be counted as four; in other words a sentence of four years could be converted into one of three. Prisoners who "voluntarily" agree to work beyond the appointed periods, declaring themselves "shock workers" and enrolling in the special brigades of "enthusiasts of the Five Year Plan" or "reforged workers," could count each two months as three. Those sentenced to three years thus had their spell reduced to two.

Ogpu announced to the world that the construction of the White Sea and Baltic canal, the biggest work which has recently been undertaken, was a marvel, and yet, after the convicts had put the whole of their vigour into an enterprise beyond their physical powers, it was announced on 1st January, 1933, that the "reckoning of the days of labour" was discontinued. This meant that those who had received a bonus of six to nine months saw their sentence prolonged again.

A new enticement was the promise of an amnesty. In the summer of 1933 the "amnesty," which applied only to the 70,000 convicts of the White Sea-Baltic camp, was solemnly announced in all the Soviet newspapers. In reality it was not an amnesty at all, but only the re-establishment, as a special act of grace, of the "reckoning of the days of labour" (which had been granted and afterwards repealed) for the 70,000; but for the vast majority of prisoners the "reckoning" was not restored. (I heard of this amnesty from a prisoner who has just escaped into Finland from one of the camps.)

Ogpu a Business Concern

I am of opinion that this side of Ogpu's activity has not been appraised at its proper value. Ogpu is not only an organ of political detection, but also a concern with colossal economic resources behind it. With a slave army of more than a million convicts, consisting of first-class labouring material—peasants inured to hard work—and the finest specialists and technicians in all branches of knowledge, Ogpu is able to carry out works, the importance of which reaches beyond the boundaries of the U.S.S.R. The timber-felling operations of Ogpu in Karelia have undoubtedly had an influence on the world timber-market. The cutting of the White Sea and Baltic canal by forced convict labour and the construction of motor highways right up to the borders of Finland constitute an immediate threat to the liberties of that civilized and democratic State. The building of the Moscow-Volga canal, which has been begun by the prisoners of Dmitrov camp, and the construction of a number of new railways by those confined in the camps of Syzran and Kungur have facilitated the export and sale of oil, grain and fish at the cheapest rates.

The incredible fact that the Soviet Government ruined its own industry in 1930, just in the full swing of the Five Year Plan, when by the organization of wreckers' trials and the deportation of hundreds of thousands of peasants, the very best workers were torn from their roots, really meant that they were transferred to the slave gangs of the Ogpu which became the main industrial undertaking of the U.S.S.R. This special role assumed by Ogpu and its business concerns—the concentration camps—also affects the conditions under which the convicts live and makes their plight still more hopeless. Their labour is one of the foundations on which rests the whole regime of the U.S.S.R., and Ogpu cannot stop hunting for such game; for if it did, it would undermine the very basis of the Soviet State.

Siliga,* a Jugo-Slav Communist who is one of the very few others besides Professor Tchernavin to have escaped from a Soviet concentration camp, and whose experience is more recent, computes the number of prisoners in 1932 to have been about five million. He refers to the statement of a fallen O.G.P.U. official that the number of arrests during the First Five Year Plan, according to police statistics, was 37 million. Siliga says that this figure is obviously exaggerated and must include the names of persons arrested several times. He himself considers 10 million a probable figure. Krivitsky † puts the number of arrested in the single year 1937 at half a million, while Souvarine ‡ refers to a communiqué in the emigré *Courrier Socialiste* estimating at 7 million the number of prisoners in the concentration camps alone. Souvarine says that after a careful examination of all the evidence

* *Au Pays du Grand Mensonge.* Paris, 1937.
† *In Stalin's Secret Service.* New York, 1938.
‡ *Stalin.* New York, 1939.

available he comes to the conclusion that between 1930 and October 1937 15 million persons were condemned to penal labor in the O.G.P.U. concentration camps. In 1938 and 1939 at least a million more must have been added to this total as the great purge continued on its course. Many—probably the majority—of the condemned during the past decade are of course already dead.

It is obviously impossible for us to compute with any degree of exactitude just how many millions have suffered, and are suffering today, in the Soviet concentration camps, where, according to Siliga, whom I met in Paris in 1938, men are "beaten like dogs and made to work like slaves." If there is ever another revolution in Russia the secret archives of the O.G.P.U. may disclose the actual figures. One thing is certain. The size and scope of the "public works" run by the O.G.P.U. require several million slaves, and fresh victims have continually to be found to keep this vital sector of "socialist" economy functioning. To retain its labor force the O.G.P.U. practices a cruel joke upon the prisoners who have lived through their term of purgatory. When the White Sea-Baltic Canal had been completed the O.G.P.U. discovered that a majority of the liberated "had become so fond of working collectively on the canal," that it shipped them off to another great construction project: the Moscow-Volga Canal.

Of recent years the proportion of Party members and workers among the condemned has risen higher, in contrast to the earlier period when peasants and non-Party specialists formed the chief source of forced labor. The campaign for "labor discipline" in the factories has entailed mass arrests of workers, in particular of the unskilled, who were most inclined to go from factory to factory seeking more tolerable conditions of work; but also of the class-conscious older workers who could not accept Stalin's counter-revolution without murmuring.

When Krivitsky on his return from abroad expressed his astonishment at finding a very large O.G.P.U. force at the summer resort of Mitsche, the head of the force replied simply: "Don't you know that there is a locomotive factory in the district employing several thousand workers?" And a young woman present at the dinner at which this remark was made, said: "Of course, nowadays it is the workers who are grumbling more than anyone else."

Krivitsky, Souvarine, Barmine, Max Eastman, and others have told in detail the story of the great purge of 1936-39, which followed the murder of Kirov at the end of 1935. After reading their books there is no longer any mystery about the confessions. There seem to have been various causes and various kinds of victims. But in the main it seems clear that, Stalin's policy having brought the U.S.S.R. near to ruin, a majority of the Central Committee of the Party as well as of the rank and file members had determined to depose him. If they had truly plotted they would probably have succeeded, but they appear to have made the mistake of thinking that when the great majority were against him they could get rid of him legally by an overwhelming vote against him. Knowing what was in the wind, Stalin decided to strike first; and by arresting, executing, or imprisoning his opponents in batches prevented the formation of a united front against him in the Politbureau, the Central Committee, and the Army.

Beyond this compelling reason for what was in effect Stalin's liquidation of the original Communist party * was the need to find new scapegoats to appease the anger and disillusionment of the workers. The Kulaks having already all been liquidated, and the non-Party specialists having already been purged, a new devil had to be found responsible for the miseries of the people. The new devil was found to be the "Trotskyist-Bucharinist-Fascist vermin," the agents of the Nazis and of the Mikado, alleged to be hiding in their thousands in every branch of the Soviet economy and to be occupying the highest positions in the state. There is little doubt that the falling of so many important heads gave satisfaction to the workers, who had come to hate the Party bureaucrats with a bitter hatred.

The new purge gathered momentum in 1936, and reached its climax though not its end with the shooting of Tukashevsky and the other leading Soviet generals in 1937. In this purge the Revolution started to devour its own children, or rather one can see it as counter-revolution from within, in which Stalin set out to liquidate all the remaining Socialists in the Soviet Union. Now it was more dangerous to be an old Party member than to be non-Party. All who had played a leading part in the October Revolution were suspect, and most of them were shot or imprisoned. The *Politkatajan* (the association of those who had done hard labor under the Tsar for political offenses) was dissolved,

---

* Professor Florinsky, in his *Toward an Understanding of the U.S.S.R.*, shows that the purge involved the expulsion of nearly half a million Party members, and that this means about 25 per cent of the total membership. It also involved the expulsion of about half the Party candidates. This calculation is based upon the official figure of new admissions to the Party in the two years 1937 and 1938—admission to the Party having been closed from 1933 to November 1936—and of the decline in the total number of Party members between 1934 and March 1939. Florinsky also reminds his readers that Stalin himself has said that expulsion from the Party is comparable to execution by the firing squad for army men. Florinsky gives figures showing that an overwhelming majority of the delegates to the Eighteenth Party Congress in March 1939 were men under forty who were boys or youths at the time of the Revolution.

and almost every family which lived in this association's giant block of flats suffered the loss of at least one member. The Society of Old Bolsheviks was suppressed, and there began the systematic arrest, execution, or imprisonment of the Bolshevik Old Guard. By 1938 Stalin had liquidated most of the members of the Politbureau (highest organ of the Communist Party), and of the Central Committee of the Party, the Council of People's Commissars, and the Executive Committee of the Soviets. The great purge also eliminated from the scene all the eighty members of the Council of War, the chief leaders and deputy leaders of the O.G.P.U., the members of the Commission who drew up the new Soviet Constitution, the heads of the federated republics (Russian minorities), and the Russian heads of the Comintern, together with thousands of Germans, Poles, and other foreign Communists who had taken "refuge" in the U.S.S.R.

It seemed that, having created a society where want, misery, social injustice, and terror reigned supreme, a society which was the very antithesis of the society of plenty and social equality which had been the aim of Lenin and the Bolsheviks in 1917, Stalin set out to destroy all those who still retained any vestiges of the Marxist faith. The names of the executed and imprisoned which appeared in the Press meant little to the foreign reader; but to the Russians they were the names of those who had led the Revolution in 1917, or who for years had occupied the highest positions in the state. The unjust perished with the just, the corrupt and oppressive officials with the best and most honest, Stalin's oldest friends together with his old enemies who had recanted of their Trotskyist or Bucharinist heresies but had never been forgiven. With the great, fell countless minor victims whose names never appeared in the Press and who disappeared without trace or trial.

An exact computation of the numbers executed and imprisoned from 1936-1938 is impossible; most of them never got a mention in the Russian Press. But there is plenty of evidence to show that, whereas Hitler's victims in the German concentration camps were to be counted in mere tens of thousands, Stalin's are to be counted in millions.

By 1936 Stalin had proceeded so far along the path from Party dictatorship to Red Tsar, had gone so far in transforming the U.S.S.R into a National Socialist state, and was so determined to make the crudest patriotism and worship of the "Leader" take the place of the international socialist ideal, that it was the revolutionaries of yesterday who constituted the greatest danger to his power. He now needed only men without principles or revolutionary pasts who could be made to obey him by privileges and threats, and would unquestionably accept the new cult of fatherland and Leader.

In 1937 his fears led him to weaken the basis of his own power: the Soviet Army, Navy, Air Force, and the O.G.P.U. were attacked. The Red Army was purged of all its best generals and of two-thirds of its officers.

Mussolini, at least, understood what Stalin was doing when he wrote in the *Popolo d'Italia* early in 1938:

> Stalin does not resort to castor oil to punish Communist leaders who are so stupid or criminal as still to believe in Communism. Stalin is unable to understand the subtle irony involved in the laxative system of castor oil. He makes a clean sweep by means of systems which were born in the steppes of Genghis Khan.... Stalin renders a commendable service to Fascism, by cutting down thousands of revolutionists as Fascist spies.

The first purge had dealt a fatal blow to Soviet economy; the second purge shattered Soviet morale. So long as Party members had felt safe provided they toed the "Party line," so long as young workers could enter the Party via the Consomols (Young Communist League) without descending to be spies and informers hated by their fellows, and so long as the Red Army was immune from purges, materially privileged, and not subject to excessive political interference, there was a solid framework to hold up Stalin's government. But since 1936-37 no one has felt safe, and the Red Army officers have been subjected to a system of control by Political Commissars who have the right to cancel the officers' orders and issue their own instead. Just as the expert in industry and transport is subject to the Party manager, so also was the military expert subject to the Political Commissar. In May 1940, obviously as the result of the consequences of this system in the Finnish war, the military officers were again put in full command of the army.

The contradiction in Stalin's policy is that, while endeavoring to substitute national patriotism and loyalty to himself for socialist ideals, he has undermined the strength of the national army, and continually frightens into opposition even those ready to toady to the great. The more men he executes and imprisons on suspicion of plotting against him, the more people desire to see him overthrown.

Stalin, as usual, attempted later to disclaim responsibility for the "excesses" of the purge which he had ordered. Early in 1939 Soviet sympathizers abroad were led to believe by Walter Duranty, Louis Fischer, and other Soviet mouthpieces that Stalin himself was angry at the frame-ups and shootings and mass imprisonments and that he had wanted the terror restricted only to those whom it was essential to destroy as proved enemies of the state. But most people in Russia must realize from experience that the object of the purge was to destroy among Party members the very idea of resistance to Stalin's despotism. Only when all feared for themselves, their friends, and their families, could Stalin feel safe from a revival of communism in Russia. According to the Trotskyists Stalin years ago revealed to his closest friends his great sociological and historical discovery: that all regimes in the past fell only because of the irresolution and vacillation of the ruling class. According to this Stalinist doctrine any ruling class if ruthless enough in its struggle against its enemies can cope with all dangers.* This theory would explain Stalin's partiality for Hitler. According to Krivitsky it was after Hitler's party purge of June 1934 that Stalin began to admire him and try to ally the U.S.S.R. to Nazi Germany.

Stalin could terrorize men by his utter ruthlessness, he could even force them to do work of a sort without hope of reward beyond a mere subsistence for their families; he could speed up the workers and lay heavy tribute on the peasants. But two things he could not do: he could not knout machines into submission, and he could not make his soldiers willing to fight and die for him. Hard-driven and neglected machinery, rails and trucks worn out by too heavy loads, lorries shaken to bits on bad roads, driven by men whose sole concern was to get through their allotted tasks and save their jobs—all these could not be forced to continue working by threats of starvation or imprisonment. Men might bow down before Stalin, but machinery he could only break.

In every enterprise broken machinery and flagging production could be camouflaged for a time. In a society where everyone was constrained by fear to cover up deficiencies and mistakes instead of setting them right, pretense, cheating, and camouflage became a fine art, and to lay the blame on someone else became the first lesson of the young Soviet worker. Everyone conspired to hide the defects in his own work and to denounce others lest he himself be denounced. When total breakdown threatened an enterprise, the O.G.P.U. would shoot or imprison a few expiatory victims and the game of camouflage would begin again under new management.

Stalin's Empire of Façades may survive—for the spirit of the Russian

---

* *Socialist Appeal.* 30.6. 39.

people is too broken by their long sufferings for the spirit of rebellion to burn strongly—if Stalin can keep Russia out of war. But his very weakness may lead him into war, or into defeat without war by Germany. Fearful of everyone, knowing the bitter hatred which the Russian people feel toward him, distrustful even of the O.G.P.U. and the army on which his power depends, alone in the Kremlin without friends and without anyone who dares to tell him the truth, drunk with his own power and yet fearful of the shadows, it was natural that Stalin should have sought to conciliate and ally himself with the most dangerous of his external foes. Having linked his fortunes to Hitler's, he follows the German star. Speaking no foreign language, knowing little of conditions in the outside world, and having purged the Comintern and the Commissariat of Foreign Affairs of those who might have had the knowledge and the courage to present him with realistic reports, it is difficult to see how Stalin's foreign policy today can be intelligent or well-informed enough for him to avoid becoming Hitler's vassal.

CHAPTER X

ARREST

AT LONG LAST we obtained our flat, in January 1936. Paid for years before in *valuta* and in rubles, long since due to us by the length of our stage of membership in the Co-operative, but awaited in vain for so many years that we had almost given up hope of getting it, suddenly it was ours. Not without a struggle, not without another threatened "strike" by Arcadi, who said he would leave Promexport if the chairman would not help him to secure his rights, but finally ours. We had to move in the middle of the night because a struggle was going on as to who owned our old rooms at Ordinka. Both the Commissariat of Foreign Trade and the Commissariat's Co-operative into whose block of flats we were moving, claimed possession, and if we didn't let in the people to whom the Co-operative had allocated the rooms, they would not give us the key of the new flat. So we did a lightning move at 1 A.M., sending Emma on first with my sleeping son in her arms to take possession and sit on the floor with him till we arrived with the furniture, after letting in the new occupants of our old rooms.

The flat had three rooms, a kitchen, and bathroom, but alas, no bath. After nearly two years with a bath and no hot-water heater we now had a hot-water heater and no bath. Such is life, but we were too happy at getting the flat to complain.

We sold Arcadi's bicycle and typewriter brought originally from Japan, to buy furniture. We reveled in our possession of a flat all our own. No longer had we to share a bath and lavatory, no longer tumble over another family in the kitchen. We ate and slept in a different room. We had real privacy at last.

We should have known that misfortune awaits the fortunate. I remember saying to Arcadi after we moved in that, having at last got a home of our own in Moscow, we should perhaps now soon be leaving the U.S.S.R. For all my life I had been giving up homes as soon as I was comfortably settled in one. When I was eleven we had given up our London home to go abroad on account of my father's consumption. In 1914 the war had deprived us of our Surrey country home. In 1928 I had abandoned the little flat in London which my mother and I had lived in since my father died and which I had only a short while before leaving England had the means to make comfortable. I had left Japan just after we had started living in a little house of which we alone were the tenants. Now, after five and a half years of waiting, we had our own flat in Moscow. It would surely be our fate to move again soon.

For the first time in all those years we could unpack our bags and trunks and have ample space for everything. For the first time Jon had a large floor space to play in.

I finished *Japan's Feet of Clay* early in March, but it took me three weeks of wangling to secure the paper on which to have it typed. Ordinary Russian paper was gray, soggy stuff, a little like blotting paper. It was recognized that it would be a disgrace to have my manuscript presented to an English publisher on such paper. But I could not secure a supply of something better until Varga had himself spoken to a Vice-Commissar at the Commissariat of Light Industry. That three week's delay prevented my being away in England when they took Arcadi.

On March 10 we had a housewarming party to celebrate Jon's second birthday. But without Jane and Michael, parties were rather dull and lifeless. Our old friend from Japanese days, "Mentich," was visiting Moscow from the South, where he worked; and to him I opened my heart freely, knowing he was as loyal and devoted a friend as one could possess. A Party member who had fought gallantly in the Civil War, he took no pleasure in the material privileges he received, longed for the good old days when a revolutionary's life was honest and dangerous, and was trying to get himself sent on an Arctic expedition. He was a true Russian, huge, blonde and blue-eyed, ponderous as a bear and with a laugh which warmed one's spirit. He was arrested a month or so after Arcadi, and I have always hoped that they got sent to the same concentration camp, for in the postcard I received later from Arcadi from Archangel he said he had found an old friend among the prisoners with him.

On the night of April 10-11, Arcadi wakened me saying, "We have visitors." I sprang out of bed to see a soldier in the passage. Two O.G.P.U. officers in uniform were in our sitting room, together with the janitor of the block of flats. The O.G.P.U. officers told us we must not speak to each other, and started on a methodical search of the whole flat. We had hundreds of books, and they went through every one of them, shaking out their leaves, scanning their titles. They went through all my papers as well as Arcadi's, but they couldn't read English, and, strangely enough, they accepted Arcadi's word for the contents of my manuscript and other papers. We sat silent and tense. The slight up-and-down movement of Arcadi's right foot crossed over his left was all that betrayed his feelings. As the hours passed and the search went on, I said to myself over and over again, "They will find nothing and then they will go. They will find nothing and then they will go." Thus defensively did I reason, although I knew only too well that the innocent were just as likely to be arrested as the guilty.

When Arcadi went to the toilet, the soldier went with him, presumably to see that he should destroy no papers. Emma awakened, indignant and nervous, but as ever unafraid, and protested when the noise the officers made searching in cupboards and drawers in the bedroom threatened to wake Jon up. Arcadi told her to keep quiet.

When his eyes and mine met, we gave each other a smile and a look of confidence and calm. One must keep calm. Is it a dream? Has the end come? Is this now happening to us which has happened to so many others? Will the nightmare pass, or is this the end of our life and our love?

Slowly the dawn came, but the search went on. The O.G.P.U. officers were polite, silent, methodical. They selected a few books to take away, including a volume of Marx and one of Keynes. They took all my letters from Arcadi, preserved through the years. They took my address book. These, some office papers Arcadi had been working on at home, and the books they packed in a bag. At seven o'clock Jon wakened, and we gave him breakfast. At eight o'clock they told Arcadi they were taking him away to be examined, but the search was not yet completed. I made him coffee. My mind now was filled with only one purpose: to strengthen him for the ordeal before him. I knew he was innocent, but I also knew of the terrible, long, exhausting examinations to which the O.G.P.U. subjects its victims. Arcadi had been up all night, and might be confused, too tired to think clearly. By this time they allowed us to talk a little. Jon was around the place, and him they could not silence. I might have asked Arcadi what I should do when he was gone; what I should do if he were imprisoned. But I still felt sure he would come home in a few days or a few weeks. I wanted only to give him strength and confidence. I asked him no questions. I let him rest half-sitting, half-lying on the couch with his head sunk down and his face very pale. I packed a small suitcase with brush and comb, soap, toothbrush, and a change of linen.

At about nine o'clock they took him away. We kissed for the last time. At the door I said, "What can I do; shall I go to R?"

He shrugged his shoulders. "No one can help," he said.

No words of love passed between us; they were not needed. Reserved to the last and calm to the last, he gave me a gentle smile and was gone. I never saw him again. He passed out of my life on that lovely April morning, in his English flannel jacket, his black head hatless, a slight figure between the two khaki-clad O.G.P.U. officers.

Emma was in tears. I sent her out with Jon. I walked from room to room trying to think what I could do, to whom I could go, where I could discover what Arcadi was accused of. Finally I found myself vomiting. Fleetingly I remembered learning in a psychology class that the stomach, not the heart, is the seat of the emotions.

"It must be a mistake," I reasoned to myself. Queer things were going on at Promexport. The manager and assistant manager of a department had been arrested a few days before. That last evening Arcadi had told me about it, but he had not suggested that he himself was in danger. In order to maintain Promexport's position as the leading export organization, Kalmanofsky, the chairman, had continued to sell certain goods abroad which should, according to the new policy inaugurated in 1935, have been retained for use in Russian industry. This had just been found out by the "Workers' and Peasants' Inspection" authorities; and Kalmanofsky had placed the blame upon the manager of the department in question, although this man had only carried out Kalmanofsky's orders and, being non-Party, would have lost his job had he refused to do so. As finance manager of Promexport, Arcadi signed all contracts; and, although he was in no way responsible for the kind of goods exported, it would have been a more or less "normal" procedure to rope him in for examination. This was, I believe, from what I learned later, what actually occasioned his arrest. But once you are in the hands of the O.G.P.U., they don't let you go easily. If they find nothing against you on one count, they hunt around for some other charge. The concentration camps are always hungry for men, always in need of more labor. Almost every citizen has at some time or another said something, or been reported to have said something, critical of the regime, or of the Party line, or it can be established that he has been friendly with some other accused or condemned person.

That first morning I went to the O.G.P.U. office in Petrovka, where the officers had told me I could get information as to the reason for the arrest. It was the free day and it was closed. Next day I went again and waited in a queue with others, only to be told that no information could be given me yet. I went each day, and was always given the same answer. I went to the Commissariat of Foreign Trade. No one could or would help me. But R, always kind, told me not to worry, said of course Arcadi was innocent and would be home again soon. Others shunned me. Friends were afraid to speak to me. When someone is arrested in the U.S.S.R., it is as if the plague had struck his family. All are afraid of any contact, afraid to be seen talking to the stricken family. I was comparatively lucky. Several friends stuck by me. The R's told me to come to their flat, in the same block as ours, whenever I felt like it. They had lived for years in the United States and had not lost all their decency and courage.

At the Institute many shunned me, but I was not dismissed. Varga was kind to me and tried to get information as to why my husband had been taken.

One man at the Institute whom I had known years before in London tried to console me by showing me mine was the lot of all. He said, "I don't suppose there is a family in Moscow which has not lost one member in the past years either through arrest or through typhus."

I went to the Anikeevs, and he said to me: "You know Arcadi *would* always joke about everything, and that is very dangerous."

I went to Kalmanofsky, the Chairman of Promexport, in his home. He faced me in a dark room lit by a small lamp on his writing table. He was nervous and ill at ease. His fine Jewish eyes showed panic. I could see he was already afraid for himself, and that no help could come from him. Perhaps it was he who had falsely accused Arcadi to save himself.

I went to Z, our ex-O.G.P.U. friend. He promised to make inquiries. Two days later he told me I had nothing to fear, Arcadi was being held for questioning in connection with the case of the other men arrested and, since he could not be held responsible merely because he also had signed the fatal contract as finance manager, I had nothing to fear. He advised me to go to England with my book; and by the time I came back he was sure Arcadi would be free.

I then made my decision. I had got my visa to go to England and return, having applied for it through the Institute before Arcadi's arrest. I had even managed to secure permission to exchange rubles for £30 for my trip to England to see *Japan's Feet of Clay* through the press. I could take Jon out of the country into safety and return. All through that long week of anxiety, of traipsing from place to place and person to person, I had feared for Jon. He was not a British subject because he had been born in Moscow. I knew how the O.G.P.U. took hostages, how they frightened men into false confessions by threatening reprisals on their children. I must get Jon out of the country while I could. Arcadi would want me to save him whatever happened.

So I left one evening ten days after Arcadi's arrest. Before leaving I gave in a letter for him, saying I was going but would return; I shall never know whether or not the O.G.P.U. let him have it.

After we had passed the Russian frontier into Poland, the sick feeling I had had for days began to pass over. My heart sang, "Jon is safe; Jon is safe." Looking after him on that three-day journey without a sleeper took all my energy and thought. He was excited and restless. In the first days after Arcadi's arrest he had hunted for his father all over the flat in cupboards and even under the beds. At Berlin, where we waited three hours, we had a bath, and I gave Jon the first banana he had ever tasted. Arrived in London at my mother's flat, I wept for the first time. I think I determined then that somehow or other I would keep Jon in England. He must not grow up in that terrible atmosphere of cant and lying and cruelty and militarism. I had got him safe in England, and he must stay there.

My delay, first in getting paper and then in waiting after Arcadi's arrest, had made it too late for Faber's to publish my book that season. It would have to wait till September. Their reader, G. F. Hudson, Fellow of All Souls at Oxford, who was unknown to me then but who in future years became one of my best friends, sent in a very favorable report. Mr. Faber, who had had sufficient confidence in me to contract for the book and pay me an advance on royalties a year before, encouraged me to hope the book would be a success. I began to think that if Arcadi were imprisoned and I could make a reputation in England it might help me to get him out.

Vera telegraphed that they were taking away our flat, and I must come at once. Leaving Jon at a small nursery school in Sussex, for my mother was too old to look after him alone, I hurried back to Moscow.

Emma had saved the flat by barricading herself in for three days. She had bolted the door and refused to open it. Armed with a letter from Varga, I went to the house management and raised hell. They had intended to put in a friend of the House Committee's chairman. Once I showed them that I was no cowed wife of an O.G.P.U. victim, but a foreigner still employed at the Academy of Sciences, they abased themselves with profuse apologies.

The flat was saved for the time being, but the news about Arcadi was very foreboding. Vera had ascertained that he was now accused of a *political* offense. What offense they would not tell her, but everyone knew that a political charge was far graver than a mere charge of having done wrong in business.

There began for me the saddest, gloomiest, most trying and anxious period of my life. Day after day I went to the Public Prosecutor's office and stood in queues waiting my turn to speak to an official there. According to the Constitution, the State Prosecutor has "supervision of the exact observance of the laws," and "no one may be subject to arrest except upon the decision of a court or with the sanction of the Prosecutor." So in theory the Prosecutor is supposed to know why a man or woman is arrested, and one is supposed to be able to obtain information at his office as to the charge. One would imagine that the Prosecutor should sign the warrants of arrests executed by the O.G.P.U. Actually, when Arcadi was arrested, no warrant or any kind of paper was shown to us. Perhaps the Prosecutor does sign a batch of blank slips for the O.G.P.U. to fill in, but such a formality, if it does take place, is meaningless. After, as before, the promulgation of the New Constitution, the power of life and death was left in the hands of the O.G.P.U., which continued to arrest anyone it pleased. The only difference the "inviolability of the person" clause in the Constitution made was that citizens now had to try and ascertain at the Public Prosecutor's office why an arrest had been made, and to send in appeals through him instead of direct to the O.G.P.U.

Each time I finally got to an official at the Prosecutor's, I was told to come back in four days or in a week's time. When I came back, and had again spent hours standing in line, I was told that the case was now in the hands of another official. When I got to the other official the process was repeated.

After five weeks of this I finally managed, through the help of R, to get to one of the Assistant Prosecutors, called, as far as I remember, Levine. He spoke German, and our conversation was brief:

"Ihr mann hat in ausland gearbeitet?"

"Ja."

"In Japan."

"Ja."

"Nun, er hat dort was gesagt dass er sollte nicht sagen."

That was all. Arcadi was in prison because of some remark he had made six or seven years before in Japan.

Perhaps Anikeev was right. Perhaps it was one of his jokes which had been reported and filed away in his dossier, which had got him into trouble.

I started to appeal. I wrote appeals to the Prosecutor, to Yezhov, then Assistant Commissar of the Commissariat of the Interior (O.G.P.U.), finally to Stalin himself.

I never received even an acknowledgment of any of them.

Meanwhile I was going twice weekly to the O.G.P.U. to fill in a form asking to be permitted to visit my husband. Nothing ever came of this either. Arcadi had been transferred in May from the Lubianka to the Butirky Prison. This meant either that his examination was completed or that the Lubianka was so full that he had been transferred while awaiting further examination. We could not know which of these alternatives it meant. If he were already condemned one must go to the prison every three days to see if his name was yet written up on the list of those being sent away to a concentration camp. The O.G.P.U. does not even inform the arrested man's family when he has been condemned and is to be sent away. They must watch the lists. It might be days or months before the arrested person was removed to a distant prison or concentration camp, and one had no means of knowing whether he or she had already been sentenced or not.

Vera had a friend who knew a woman whose husband was a sort of trusty among the condemned political prisoners in the Butirky Prison, and who was allowed a visit from his wife once in twelve days. Through this woman we found out that Arcadi was not among those already condemned, so was evidently still in solitary confinement, or with others still under examination. No one in the queues at the prison and at the Prosecutor's expected an arrested relative to be given a trial. It was taken for granted that all would be condemned without trial in secret, or, if a miracle occurred, released similarly without trial. The articles in the New Constitution guaranteeing trial in open court "with participation of the people's associate judges (Articles 103 and 111) were a dead letter from the beginning, for they contained a rider: "with the exception of cases specially provided for by law," or "except in special cases." These articles were only intended to delude foreign "friends of the Soviet Union," like Mr. D. N. Pritt, K.C., M.P., and others equally gullible, who failed to appreciate the significance of the addition of the words "except in special cases." No citizen of the U.S.S.R. took the New Constitution for anything more than was intended, a thin façade to cover the naked police regime, a cruel mockery of the millions condemned without trial.

Every eight days one could take food and every sixteen days a change of linen to the prisoners. To do this one went early in the morning with a sack or pillowcase and stood in line after filling in a form stating exactly what was in the sack. If anything forbidden, like cigarettes, was included, everything might be rejected.

The first time I went, a friend of Vera's, an old Social Revolutionary from Siberia, went with me to help. For the form had to be carefully filled in, and I might make a mistake over some of the Russian words. Vera's friend was a Socialist of the old kind. For hours that morning she helped poor, illiterate women in the queue who could not fill in their own forms and feared their pitiful supplies of black bread and onion might be rejected unless they could sign their names on the form. Many of the women with their breadwinners arrested and children to support were obviously half-starved themselves, but they brought bread for their husbands. The case of most of the people waiting with us was so much more terrible than mine that I began to be almost ashamed of my grief. I had food and Jon had food. I could support him and, being English, I was not likely to be arrested myself. But these wretched women faced starvation for themselves and their children. There was no poor relief, no workhouse. Their neighbors and relatives were too poor to help or too afraid to help. Even if their children were old enough to leave alone, it was almost impossible for women whose husbands had been arrested to get work.

The proportion of working-class people standing in line seemed to be very high. There were different days for different letters of the alphabet. As far as I remember our day included all those whose names began with A, B, C, and D. At this one prison it took hours before one's turn came to hand in one's sack to the O.G.P.U. official and it was therefore obvious that the prisons were full of "politicals."

Strangely enough, there seemed more good will and friendliness among these people than in other queues—a comradeship of the damned. These people had little left to fear or hope for. The worst had befallen them already.

The great consolation one got by giving in food at the prison was the proof this afforded that one's husband or brother, father or wife, still lived. For in the later afternoon one was given a receipt signed by the prisoner himself, and on the days for giving in clean clothing one received back the soiled linen. When I got Arcadi's underwear back for the first time since his arrest I nearly broke down. It was five weeks since they had taken him away, and this was the first occasion we had had to supply him with a clean vest, shirt, pants, and socks. The stuff we got back was filthy, sweat-stained, black with grime. Somehow this brought home to me more vividly than anything else what he must be suffering. The prisons were terribly crowded, and I pictured him in the heat and dirt of a crowded cell. There would certainly be bugs, he would be sleeping on a plank bed, and the room would be airless. He who was so fastidiously clean had had to wear the same clothing for weeks.

Yet I comforted myself in remembering his philosophic spirit, and his gift for understanding men and never losing his self-control. He would know from the foreign chocolates and soap I had sent him that I had been to England and come back and was still at liberty. That should give him good heart to endure. He might guess that I had left Jon safely in England. In any case, he knew I could provide for our son, and that I could fight for myself. The O.G.P.U. would not be able to force him to a false confession through threats against us.

It was a perfect summer in Moscow. One lovely day succeeded another. At first I would sit on the balcony in the evenings looking down and hoping against hope that Arcadi might come walking along. One day in the street I met Berkinghof's wife. He had been taken off the train to prison on his arrival from Mongolia, where he had been the Trade Representative. She and their young son had been brought to Moscow by a false telegram purporting to come from him. They had lived well for years, but practically everything they possessed was in Mongolia. Varya was haggard and white, fearing most for the future of their small son, whom they adored. She was trying to get a job, but was refused employment everywhere.

One heard of one arrest after another among friends and acquaintances. The scythe was sweeping higher. Important people began to be taken. Everyone I knew began to look afraid. It was clearly hopeless now to try and get anyone to help; all were afraid for themselves.

The radios in the street blared out, "Life is happy, life is joyous," and Varya and I smiled bitterly as we said good-by in Tverskaya Street.

Vera did all she could about Arcadi, showing the same bold spirit as in her youth. But she was as helpless as I. She bravely assured me that no innocent man would be allowed to suffer; and, since Arcadi was of course innocent, he would eventually be released. Poor Vera was clinging still to her belief in the Communist party. A year later, in April 1937, she was arrested herself when nearly all who belonged to the proud category of those who had done hard labor as politicals in Tsarist prisons were purged by Stalin. The revolutionaries of the past were all suspect to the tyrant.

Finally, late in July, I received a cable from my publishers in London that I must come at once to see my book through the press. It was impossible to tell how long Arcadi's examination would last. It might be months more or only weeks. I had begun to think that the best way I could help was to become well enough known in England to exert pressure in Moscow. Standing in line at the Public Prosecutor's and sending in appeals was clearly absolutely useless. Moreover, my son had to be provided for in England. I must make some money. I had plenty of rubles, since the thousands we had received from the sale of the typewriter were only partially expended, but none of this could be exchanged for *valuta*.

I decided to fly to England and come back after my book was published. This time, however, I could not secure a return visa. They gave me an exit visa, but told me to get my return visa in London because my British passport was about to expire. This was a valid reason, but I could not be sure that it was the real one. However, I had no choice. I must go to England and could only hope it was true that a visa to return to the U.S.S.R. would be given me in London. All this time the treatment I myself had received encouraged the hope that they were not going to imprison Arcadi indefinitely. True that I was English, but other foreigners had upon occasion been arrested and examined. Surely if they were trying to frame Arcadi they would do something to implicate me as well. I had the terrible feeling all along that perhaps he was suffering for my sins. I had never *done* anything against the Soviet Government, but I had *thought* a lot against it; and I had not always been cautious enough in speaking to English friends when on holiday in England. Occasionally I had revealed a little of the truth as to conditions in the U.S.S.R. to intimate friends; Arcadi, on the other hand, had not only never spoken dangerous thoughts, but had in fact accepted the U.S.S.R. and had been convinced that no change for the better was possible through a change of government. He had worked extremely hard, giving all his knowledge, energy, and devotion to his job, feeling that this was the only way for conditions to be improved. Being a Jew and a Russian, he was far more of a fatalist than I; far more resigned and philosophical concerning ills that could not in his view be cured, but could be ameliorated if everyone tried to do his own job as well as possible. Indignation and anger were in his view "unnecessary" and futile.

I left everything I possessed behind in Moscow: books, clothes, linen, furniture, and of course money. The money I left with Vera, telling her to continue paying the 200 rubles a month we always allowed to Anna Abramovna and Arcadi's son Vitia. Anna Abramovna had had a job for some years past, and Vitia was now in his teens.

To keep the flat safe and occupied, I had already installed in it a man and his wife whom I knew to be decent people who would vacate it if and when Arcadi was set free. They were glad to take Emma on as their servant. In the second room I placed Vera's son and his wife and child, leaving Emma the smallest room as hers by right, whether employed by the other inmates or not.

The last night I did not go to bed at all. After packing up everything we possessed, I sat down to write a long letter to Arcadi in case he should come home or be sent away before my return—or in case I never got back. I assured him that whatever happened, even if I did not see him for years, I would continue to love him. That life without him was unbearable and unthinkable and that, if he were condemned, I would return and try to be near him, leaving Jon in England. I left the letter with friends, but Arcadi was never allowed to receive it.

I left by air at 4 A.M. Emma came with me to see me off but was not allowed to come to the airport. She wept and clung to me, saying good-by forever. I assured her I should come back; she was certain that I would not. She was right and I was wrong. I myself had a fear she might be right as I said good-by to Moscow, where I had known such great joy and such grief. Lovely Moscow in the early morning sun with the blue sky over the Kremlin. One of the loveliest cities in the world, and the grave of communist hopes and of the communist ideal. Nine years before, almost to a day, I had stood in the Red Square for the first time, my heart full of enthusiasm and faith. Now I was flying away to the west leaving the dearest person in my life inside the prison house which the U.S.S.R. had become. Tears blinded my eyes as the plane rose in the air.

I never got back to the U.S.S.R. I tried again and again in 1936 and 1937 to get a visa, but was each time put off by Maisky. He told me to be patient and to wait, until at last I realized that it was hopeless. Perhaps he feared that I should be arrested too if I went back, and in that event he would have a lot of trouble with the British Foreign Office. Or perhaps he had been forbidden to give me a visa.

Late in August 1936 Arcadi was condemned to five years' imprisonment. Vera telephoned from Moscow to London to tell me. If I had been in Moscow I could have seen him once for a few minutes before he was sent off to an Arctic concentration camp. Vera saw him behind bars separating them by several feet.

From Archangel he sent me a postcard assuring me of his love and telling me to be cheerful.

Early in 1937 I received a second postcard, this time from Ust Usya in the far north of Siberia, where there was a mining concentration camp. In May 1937 I received a third and last postcard telling me he was well and that he had now been given office work. This implied that previously he had been doing physical labor in the mines. I have never had another word from him to this day. Perhaps the first year of hard labor had ruined his health, for his heart was already strained and enlarged from overwork when we lived together. Whether he was shot or whether he died from hardship, ill treatment, cold, or lack of food, I shall never know. It is possible even that he still lives, broken in health, and deprived of all hope of release. Perhaps of all my many letters and postcards to him not one was ever delivered; and, feeling that I had abandoned him, he ceased to write. This is the bitterest thought of all, but I do not believe he would doubt my love and my loyalty. His three postcards were full of confidence in my affection and in his own. In the last one he had said that one year of our five years' separation had already passed, and he lived for the day when we should be together again.

It is possible that he still lives. But it is impossible that we should ever meet again, since I can never return to the U.S.S.R. and he can never leave it.

Emma continued to write to me and to send parcels of food to Arcadi until the late summer of 1937. Then I ceased to hear from her for four months. Finally, in December of 1937, I received a letter from her saying she had been four months in the "Krankenhaus" (obviously meaning prison) and had been very frightened, but that now she was out and had at once sent Arcadi a food parcel. She also sent me a new address for him. After that I never heard from Emma again. Perhaps she was arrested again; perhaps her letters were stopped. She had proved the most loyal and fearless of my friends. Only she had dared to go on writing to me after Vera was arrested. She had been my last link, my last source of information about Arcadi. Our flat had been confiscated, and those I had installed there thrown out. My money left with Vera had been taken by the O.G.P.U. Emma had my clothes and my books. I had told her to try and keep my books safe, but to sell my clothes and linen to buy food for Arcadi. Emma once silenced, I was as cut off from Arcadi as if he were in another world.

In the summer of 1938, while I was in China, Litvinov told Lord Chilston, the British Ambassador, that Arcadi Berdichevsky was still alive. But he gave no proof, and it was obviously to the Soviet Government's advantage to keep my mouth shut by an assurance that my husband was still alive. So long as I had hope, I would keep silent and not tell the truth about Russia, which I, having lived there so long as an ordinary citizen, know so much better than most foreigners.

I did not ask the help of the British Foreign Office until 1938, because I feared to harm Arcadi by doing so. When I did go to the Foreign Office the official there did all he could to help me. I made appeals from England to Moscow, and an appeal also went signed by Professor Laski, Bertrand Russell, Kingsley Martin (Editor of the *New Statesman*), and C. M. Lloyd, with covering letters supporting the appeal from Bernard Shaw, and Beatrice and Sidney Webb. Both Shaw and the Webbs had known my father, but it was Bertrand Russell who made them support the appeal. Professor Laski sent off the appeal himself and many reminders afterwards. But we never got any reply.

It would be wearisome to tell of all the appeals and all the people whose aid I enlisted. It was all futile. The Soviet Government, assured of the enthusiastic support of so many "liberals," disregarded my case. I was probably foolish not to have made a public scandal out of the matter. I should have utilized the prestige given me by the success of *Japan's Feet of Clay* (published in several foreign languages as well as in England and America) to raise a dust in the press. Arcadi's case was so clear a proof of the fact that men are condemned without trial in the U.S.S.R.—not only without a trial but without any real charge against them. Vera had ascertained from the O.G.P.U. that Arcadi had been condemned for "having been friendly or acquainted with a Trotskyist." That was all. I gathered from Vera's letter that the "Trotskyist" may have been Berkinghof. Arcadi's "friendship or acquaintance" with him consisted only in his having worked under him and in my having known him years before in London. It seems obvious that the whole thing was a frivolous, trumped-up charge made when nothing else could be found against him. He had had the strength to resist all their attempts to force him into a false "confession." So he got no trial and disappeared in silence, like so many thousands of others.

The shadow of the O.G.P.U. stayed over me too long. I lacked the courage to proclaim to the world what had happened and risk his death. Now I think I might have saved his life by being bolder, for until the signing of the Russo-German Pact the Soviet Government was trying to appear as a "democratic" government. It would have dismayed some at least of the "friends of the Soviet Union" to learn that the Soviet Government is even more cruel than the Nazi Government. For the latter does at least allow some communication between its prisoners and their relatives, and does inform the latter when a man dies or is shot.

It has taken me years to become free again in mind and spirit. Whatever the consequences, I wish I had had the courage to proclaim the truth about Russia sooner. I have not the conceit to imagine that my voice could have affected public opinion any more than those other few voices which of recent years have told the truth about Soviet tyranny. But I wish I had been earlier among the goodly company which tried to save the world from the consequences of a false belief in the goodness and strength of the U.S.S.R. That belief has played a large part in bringing about the present European war, in which millions are being killed and mutilated. Against the tragedy of the Second World War, my own personal tragedy is insignificant indeed. That in itself has helped me to make the decision to speak out boldly about the U.S.S.R., whatever the consequences to my husband if he still lives.

PART III

CHAPTER XI

NAZI GERMANY AND SOVIET RUSSIA

THE FAILURE of the West, at least until 1939, to see the similarity between the economic and political organization of the Nazi and Soviet states was largely due to the erroneous idea that *ownership* is more important than *control*. Actually it is the other way round, whether we are considering a capitalist corporation "owned" by many shareholders but controlled by few, or a modern totalitarian state. It makes no practical difference to those who monopolize the political power in Russia and Germany whether in theory the factories and mines, railways, power stations, and banks are owned by capitalists or by the whole people. The vital point is that the government—i.e., the Nazi or Bolshevik party headed by its leader—has the force to compel the use of the productive capital as it directs and to appropriate as large a share of the profits as it thinks fit. The fact that in Russia those who direct the business enterprises are officials paid a salary by the state, whereas in Germany they are still called the owners or corporation directors and live on their profits or private salaries, makes no practical difference except in the matter of efficiency.

In modern large-scale industry it is usually the head employees of a corporation, those whom Americans call executives, who run the show. The stockholders who "own" the capital and "employ" the executives are often powerless. In Russia the Communist party appoints the executives, while the "ownership" is vested in the state. This communal ownership is meaningless, so long as the people have no means of controlling the government. In Germany ownership of land and productive capital remains in the hands of the "capitalist class," but absolute control is vested in the state. The German capitalists are almost as powerless as the Russian people, since in both countries political power is monopolized by the ruling party. (Since in Germany money power still exists, although subordinated to the political power, there is a little more freedom and independence for certain elements in the population than in Russia.) In both countries the state is in fact owned by the ruling party, which administers it free from popular control of any kind either in the economic sphere or in the political, and utilizes the resources and man power of the country for its own ends regardless of public opinion. In both countries the producers of all kinds are exploited by the ruling party, the bureaucracy, without having any say in internal or foreign policy.

Germany has the great advantage over Russia that the executive class and the technicians have not been liquidated. With the exception of the Jews and the minority of "Aryans" who have gone into exile, they are working with a greater or lesser degree of willingness in the interests of the Nazi state. As Hitler himself has expressed it, he has compelled the possessing classes to contribute by their ability toward the building up of the new order; since he could not afford to allow Germany to vegetate for years, as Russia had done, in famine and misery.* The far higher level of education, technical knowledge, and general culture in Germany would in any case have given Germany a great advantage over Russia; but Stalin has deliberately increased the disparity. His hatred and fear of all intellectuals has caused him year after year to execute, imprison, harass, and demoralize the small number of qualified men available in Russia. Today there are few "specialists" left from Tsarist times, which means there are very few men who have been properly trained and taught and are capable of being efficient administrators or technicians. Not only this, but the best, most intelligent, and qualified Party men have of recent years been "purged"; and the young "Soviet intelligentsia" has received an education in which politics, or rather loyalty to Stalin, was more important than knowledge or passing examinations.

It is obvious that Hitler, unlike Stalin, is not afraid of clever and talented men; that he has sufficient confidence in himself and in his hold over his countrymen to select the ablest men to occupy the highest positions in the state. Were it not so, the German war machine could not function so perfectly, nor Germany be able to surprise her foes by lightning strokes of supreme audacity.

Rauschning's books afford an intimate close-up of Hitler, which suggests that his intelligence and sagacity, when not drowned in a sea of mysticism and megalomania, are far greater than Stalin's. He appears as a man who grasps, as Stalin is quite incapable of doing, what must be the basis of a great state, what are in fact the real bases of power. He knows how to make men serve his purpose while thinking they are serving their own, while Stalin has no other conception than rule by the knout. According to Rauschning, Hitler possesses in supreme degree the gift of simplication; the power of seeing reality behind pre-

* *The Voice of Destruction,* by Rauschning.

tenses, of disentangling what is fundamental from what is mere embroidery, and of explaining himself clearly to simple men. It is this gift which enables him to realize that a revolution in the form of property is less important than the monopoly of political power. Questioned by Rauschning as to whether it was intended to attempt a synthesis between economic liberalism and a socialist economy, and as to whether private economic interests should be eliminated, Hitler gave a reply which shows his complete awareness that *control,* not ownership, is the basic question; and also his understanding of the need to allow scope for human instincts instead of seeking to crush and distort them. He says:

> The instinct to possess cannot be eliminated.... The problem is how to adjust and satisfy these natural instincts. The proper limits to private profit and private enterprise must be drawn through the state and general public according to their vital needs.... The needs of the state varying according to time and circumstance are the sole determining factor.... Therefore I may change or repudiate under changed conditions tomorrow what I consider correct today.... Only fools believe in a cut-and-dried method of changing the social and economic order.

. . . .

> There will be no license, no free space, in which the individual belongs to himself: This is socialism—not such trifles as the private possession of the means of production. Of what importance is that if I range men firmly within a discipline they cannot escape? Let them own their lands or factories as much as they please. The decisive factor is that the state, through the Party, is supreme over them, regardless whether they are owners or workers. Once directors and employees alike have been subjected to a universal discipline, there will be a new order for which all expressions used hitherto will be quite inadequate.... *Why need we trouble to socialize banks and factories? We socialize human beings.*

It would seem that Hitler was guided by those whom Rauschning describes as the intelligent realists who found that certain machinery was being created in what he calls the class organizations of the country's economy, by means of which a considerable influence could be exerted on industrial undertakings. He writes:

> This "structure of graded classes" was the most suitable instrument for the control of economy. It would not do, these people maintained, to allow the national economy to become one great body, self-determining according to its own needs. In that case, it would

even more than heretofore absorb and put itself in the place of the state. If that was the meaning of the corporative state, then national socialism could have nothing to do with it. *No, not the organization, but the control of economy;* the subordination of economy to the guidance of the National Socialist Party: this was the aim of these people, who recognized no specific economic laws, but held that the national economy could without harm be made subject to rules independent of its own terms of reference. To these people the "structure of graded classes" was a means of gaining control. The only organization they were interested in was that of an instrument of control over economy.

The manner in which the Nazi state circumscribes the German businessman in every one of his activities has reduced "private ownership of the means of production and distribution" to a legal fiction, and converted the capitalists into administrative officials of the Nazi state. The owner, or director, of a factory or other enterprise must pay his workers as much, or as little, as the government decrees. He can neither dismiss workers nor take on new ones without a government permit. The state controls the prices at which he buys and sells, and the amount of raw material he may purchase. The distribution of dividends and the rate of interest paid on investments are limited by the state to a maximum of 6 per cent, or in rare cases 8 per cent. Profits must be invested according to government instructions, and shareholders may be forced to make capital investments which are unprofitable but regarded as a national requirement. On the other hand, government subsidies ensure the development of unprofitable industries and government orders ensure markets for goods which would otherwise be unsalable, or salable only at a loss. Every capitalist and corporation executive is forced to belong to group organizations through which production and distribution are controlled both horizontally and vertically. These group organizations act as the go-betweens of private enterprise and the state. They distribute raw materials among their members, fix prices, etc. They have "leaders" who are appointed by the state and are, of course, Party men. The function of the Estates is somewhat similar to that of the Trusts in Russia, which also control all the enterprises in one branch of industry. The grouping and control of industrial enterprises in Nazi Germany has been facilitated, and the transition to a state-controlled economy rendered less noticeable by the prevalence of cartels in pre-Nazi Germany and by the close connection between the trusts and banks and the state which has always characterized German capitalism. As Marx had foreseen, the concentration of capital, or of capital control, renders the transition to socialism easy and natural. The state has only to take over, or to subject to its control, the monopolies previously in private hands. Since small-scale independent enterprises would be impossible to control effectively, the Nazi state has forced them all into what are in effect state-controlled cartels.

The German "capitalist" has not won security under the new regime. On the contrary, he fears always that he may lose his capital by being forced to use it, not where he conceives it will secure him a substantial profit, but in whatever enterprise the government decides it shall be invested. If he leaves his money in the bank, because he may not invest it as he pleases and is fearful of losing it, the tax controller may confiscate it. Or the Nazi party may inform him that he is to be "honored" as the founder of a new enterprise for the production without profit of an *Ersatz* product. Even if allowed to use his profits for extension of his own plant, the German factory "owner" or shareholders can only secure the new machinery if they have a government permit. Whichever way he turns, the German "capitalist" finds the government waiting for him, to make sure that his "property" or capital is utilized in the "national interest."

In this situation the German "possessing classes" living on rent, profit, and interest, would obviously much prefer to abandon their status as capitalists, and become state officials earning a sure and definite salary. What have they to fear from the establishment of "socialism"? State ownership of the means of production, provided they continued to be employed as the administrative personnel, would relieve them of their anxieties and give them a security they have long since lost. But the Nazi state refuses to become the owner of the industrial enterprises, shops, and banks, preferring to leave the owners to cope with the difficulties of production and labor management.

Markets with price movements dependent on the business cycle have been supplanted by markets dependent on state policy, but the markets continue in existence. Private enterprises do not buy and sell as agents of the state who risk nothing by faulty calculations; they have to act on private calculation and risk loss as under a "free" capitalist economy. To quote one of the best books written on the Nazi state:

> The system is a strange mixture of state interference and planning combined with private management—an economic system which is neither competitive capitalism nor the planned economy of state socialism nor state capitalism. It is so bewildering in its complexity

that the capitalist no longer knows whether he is a capitalist or whether he has become a mere agent of the State.*

While realizing, as socialists have long since realized, that "money is nothing and production everything," the Nazi leaders have not, like the Communists, failed to recognize the need to retain money as a standard of measurement and value. Acutely aware that inflation, with all the frightening memories this brings to the minds of the German middle classes, would be fatal to them politically, the Nazis have avoided it by keeping the amount of money *in circulation* down to the limit of the quantity of consumption goods available. Instead of destroying the old financial system, they have adapted it to their own ends, and converted it into an instrument for the absolute control of investment and consumption. Instead of shooting Dr. Schacht, they utilized him as their wizard of finance; and, although Hitler discarded him eventually, he retained him until the system of state financial control had been perfected. "Financial discipline" was Schacht's slogan, and under his tutelage the Nazi Government long avoided what he called any overstepping of the "boundaries set by the effects of credit expansion on the national economy." In Soviet Russia there was so little real planning that the amount of money paid out for capital construction and wages bore no relation to the volume of goods available for purchase by those who received the money. Hence the colossal inflation of the past decade in Soviet Russia. The Nazis, appreciating equally with the Communists that "money is nothing; production everything," nevertheless knew that money as a standard of measurement must retain its function even in a socialist, or a controlled, economy. As Hitler stated in 1937:

> The problem of our living standard is a production problem, a problem of work, the organization of labor and the distribution of its results.
> We have given to the German currency that unique and only real coverage which is at the same time the indispensable condition of its stability, the stability of its purchasing power, namely, goods on the market. With every purchase we made we had to have the additional volume of products. This simple but true Nationalist Socialistic economy and currency policy has permitted us to increase our production to capacity and at the same time maintain the purchasing power of our reichsmark.†

* *The Vampire Economy. Doing Business under Fascism,* by Guenter Reimann, New York, 1939.
† Quoted in Alfred M. Bingham's *Man's Estate.*

Banking in Nazi Germany is completely state controlled, but here as in industry the expert has been left to manage the practical details. State control of the banks has enabled the Nazi Government to secure credits up to the limits set by the need to prevent inflation. State obligations can be forced on the banks as on industry. So absolute is the state control of financial institutions that the Nazi Government has seen no advantage in *owning* the banks. It has, in fact, raised extra revenue by selling back to individuals the government-owned shares of private banks and corporations inherited from the Weimar Republic. As one writer has observed, "Now that the control over the banks is complete and final, the Government is no longer interested in holding their shares." Such sales of shares by the government amounts to the same thing as the sale of state bonds; it is equivalent to the transfer of the savings of individuals to the government.

With regard to banking, as with regard to everything else, the Nazi Government has been concerned with the substance of control rather than with the shadow of ownership.

While Nazi Germany has lost nothing politically by allowing the old possessing and executive classes to continue to function as the business executives of the state-controlled industrial enterprises, it has gained a great deal through the retention of the services of those who are qualified to run great enterprises and to secure the efficient working of factories, workshops, mines, and the financial system. Many of the advantages of a socialist planned economy have been gained, without the inevitable losses incurred by a sanguinary revolution, a frontal attack on private property, and a bureaucratic administration. Whereas in Russia the new executive class is ill-trained or untrained and too ignorant to ensure the proper functioning of the state-owned enterprises, in Germany the business executives are for the most part men who know their jobs. More important still is the advantage gained by Germany through retention of the profit motive. The German "owner" or executive is in reality as much a servant of the state as the Russian bureaucrat, but his living depends on his running his enterprise efficiently enough to secure a profit. The Russian directors and managers, on the other hand, receive salaries which do not depend upon the manner in which they carry out their work. The amounts received and the retention of their positions depend mainly upon their loyalty to Stalin—or upon his henchmen's estimate of it—and upon their ability to court and flatter those in the highest positions. Taking care always to say the right thing is the best way to earn a good living, not mastering the details of the industrial enterprise or office you are in charge of.

This is not to say that corruption, patronage, and politics do not also play an important role in Germany. There also only Party members may occupy key positions in the government, and the favor and patronage of Party officials are of vital importance to the capitalist "owners" of industrial and other enterprises. But in Germany the fact that industry and trade have not been socialized relieves the Nazis of the necessity of running the enterprises themselves. If the results they demand are achieved, they can afford to leave the owners or executives to direct the enterprises—and to bear the responsibilities and the odium of exploiting the workers. Although the bribing of Party officials by businessmen may have become so much a matter of routine as to be considered part of the overhead expenses of a business concern, it does not necessarily entail complete subservience to the Nazi officials in every detail of the administrative work. To survive, the German capitalists must maintain "good relations" with the officials at the Ministries which allocate raw materials, issue permits for new construction or for engaging new workers, give subsidies for export, and so forth; but they must also compete against other capitalists on the market and are thus keyed up to maximum efficiency in their administration of their enterprises. The qualified men who, either as owners or as executives of shareholders, run the industrial enterprises, may be irked and annoyed, even exasperated, by the Party bureaucrats who control them, watch them, and at times interfere with them; but they are not, like the specialists in Russia, continually being arrested or shot for "sabotage," "counter-revolution," and "wrecking." Their talents and knowledge have not been lost to the nation; they continue to run its economic life instead of being sent to cut timber or to dig canals or break stones in concentration camps on the theory that that is the way to construct socialism.

Communists will retort that this is because Nazi Germany is a "capitalist" state, and therefore the "capitalists" naturally support the Nazi Government and don't require liquidating. However, to maintain that National Socialist Germany is a capitalist state and Stalin's Russia a socialist one, is to ignore the absolute control by the Nazi Government of all "means of production and distribution," and the similar status of workers and peasants in the two countries. The "will of the Party" and its leader is the supreme law in both countries; in neither have the people, whether workers or capitalists or ex-capitalists, got any political rights, any means of controlling the Party, which is synonymous with the government. In neither country have the workers either the right or the possibility of organizing to protect their own interests. No German industrialist or banker, however important, can get control of the executive power; and even his power to bribe officials is limited by the strict control of his expenditure exercised by the government, and by the fact that the highest Nazi leaders are too well provided for materially to need to take bribes. No German capitalist can act in any way contrary to the will of the Party, which, as in Russia, is armed with every weapon of coercion by its ownership of the state, and which also disposes of revenue very much larger than the total income of the capitalist class. In both countries there is a huge bureaucratic apparatus, but it is far smaller in Germany both absolutely and proportionately to the size of the population. In both countries there is a large secret police force, but here again the O.G.P.U. greatly exceeds the Gestapo in size, if only because of the need for a vast apparatus to coerce the Russian peasants and guard the millions in the prisons and concentration camps.

Both the U.S.S.R. and Nazi Germany may be termed state capitalist, but in one the old capitalist and professional classes have been liquidated, while in the other they survive to serve the interests of the Party.

Communists abroad still cherish the illusion that, whereas in Germany the condition of the working class has been greatly worsened since Hitler came to power, in the U.S.S.R. the material and political position of the workers has enormously improved under the Soviet Government. The facts given in the preceding chapters completely disprove this contention; there is no doubt that most of the Russian workers have even less to eat, are worse clad, and probably worse housed than under the Tsar. In Nazi Germany the skilled workers may be a good deal worse off, but the mass of the unskilled are probably no worse off and in some ways may have gained by the Nazi revolution. The millions of unemployed who were starving when Hitler came to power have certainly gained a security they never had before, even if it is security on very low real wages and at the sacrifice of liberty and the right to organize in trade-unions.

Of course it is true that such security of employment as the German workers and middle classes have enjoyed of recent years has been at the cost of losing their lives later in Poland, Flanders, or France. But young men at least prefer even the hazards of war, with its excitement, its appeal to the spirit of adventure, and its imagined glories, to the boredom and the slow process of degeneration, physical and mental, which prolonged unemployment entails. "Rushing down a steep place into the sea" was no doubt more exhilarating for the Gadarene swine than slow starvation in their sties would have been. The failure to recognize the appeal which war has for young men who have neither pleasures, nor distractions, nor hopes of a satisfactory life, has been one of the fundamental mistakes made by the comfortable classes in the democratic countries. Whatever the material gains and losses of the German workers, they, like the Russian, are now in servitude to the all-powerful state. The method of controlling them in Germany has been closely copied from Stalin's Russia. There are the same state trade-unions (called Soviet trade-unions in Russia and a Labor Front in Germany), the same labor books, the same state-decreed rates of wages, the same necessity to go to work wherever the state orders; in a word, the same regimentation or militarization of labor.

The German employer, now called the "factory leader," is even expected to perform the same function as the Russian factory manager, in teaching Party doctrine to the workers. Those "factory leaders" who don't spend enough time doing National Socialist propaganda among their workers, or whose workers fail to pay up their dues to the Labor Front or to respond to appeals for contributions to the Winter Help, or to show sufficient enthusiasm when asked to make sacrifices or perform "voluntary" services asked for by the Party, fail to receive a share of state subsidies and state orders and are sometimes removed—i.e., expropriated. Stories are even told of German employers contributing sums from their own pockets rather than have their most efficient workmen come under suspicion of the authorities.

In Germany as in Russia labor has been speeded up, but German intelligence and the higher standard of life of the German workers, have prevented this process being carried to the same point of exhaustion leading to a fatal decline in quality, as has happened in Russia.

Hitler has further copied Stalin by some sugar-coating of the pill of servitude. To match the much-boasted Russian social services, holidays with pay, and so forth, the Nazis instituted the "Strength through Joy" activities, the trips to the seaside, the workers' sports organizations. Since Germany has long had other social services in a far more generous and universal form than the U.S.S.R. has today, there was less opportunity in Germany for ballyhoo about state care for mothers and children, free medical services, sports grounds, playgrounds, and so forth.

One's difficulty in appraising what, if any, benefits the German workers have derived from the National Socialist regime to compensate for their loss of political, trade-union, and juridical rights, is the dearth of unprejudiced reports about Germany.* The number of foreigners who have shut their eyes to all the evils in the Soviet Union is legion, and the number of those who shut their eyes to any good features of the Nazi regime is correspondingly great. In the case of Russia visitors have been blinded by their hopes; in the case of Germany they have been blinded by their hate.

Many militant and "class-conscious" workers have suffered severely under the Nazis. Social Democrats and Communists have been shot or languish in the jails and concentration camps. Keen trade-unionists hate the regime for having deprived them of political freedom and the right to organize and to go on strike in defense of their interests. But it is doubtful whether even in Germany, where the working class was probably more politically conscious and more soaked in socialist doctrine than the working class of any other country, the majority of the workers actively desire to overthrow the regime which has given them security of employment and socially a higher status than under a "free" capitalist economy. Few have any illusions about the Soviet system, and especially since the Comintern sponsored Popular Fronts against fascism, which degenerated into national fronts against Germany, they must recognize that the international socialist ideal is dead. The German worker is as much of a patriot as the French or the English; and he, to only a slightly lesser degree than the German middle classes, has felt Germany to be encircled by a hostile world which, while proclaiming liberal and free trade ideals, has shut the door on German exports, and denied Germany its living space.

A brief consideration of the position of the farmers and peasants in Germany, as compared to that of the Russian peasants, shows great similarities, but also such vital differences of degree in the exercise of the state power in the control of agriculture as to constitute a difference in principle. In both countries the agrarian producers are forced to sell their products to the state at artificially low prices, and in both countries the state has assumed the role of monopolist middleman with regard to the purchase of grain, fodder, and industrial crops. In Germany this function is performed by the Reich Nutrition Estate, which also strictly controls the sale and the prices of most other foodstuffs. But in Germany the state does not make a profit even comparable to the profit taken by the Soviet Government on the sale of

---

* Otto D. Tolischus, whose reports in the *New York Times* have been both objective and informative, will perhaps remedy this deficiency in his forthcoming book.

food. The fact that the German farmers' net income has risen under the Nazi Government indicates that they have gained, not lost, by the virtual elimination of the free market and the middleman. The fact that the price paid by consumers for food has not risen substantially proves that the increased income of the farmers has not been derived from the lowering of the standard of life of the urban workers. It is, of course, true that the quality of the manufactured goods the farmers buy has deteriorated, and also true that it is the large landowners who have benefited most by the increased prices paid to the agrarian producers. Nevertheless it is unlikely that the peasants and tenant farmers are worse off than before the Nazi revolution. The German Government did not, at least until the present war, force the farmers and peasants to give up the food they needed for their own consumption. Nor has there been anything like the same wide disparity as in Russia between the purchase price of grain and the selling price of bread. Instead of taking advantage of its monopoly position, or of its absolute control of prices, to raise the price of bread and other foodstuffs to the urban workers, as the Soviet Government has done, the Nazi Government has secured a more equitable distribution of the limited supply of foodstuffs by keeping retail prices low and instituting rationing of scarcity foods such as fats. Whereas in Russia the ruling bureaucracy secures fats, meat, and other "luxuries" in fairly large quantities while the workers go without, in Germany all classes get the same ration; and it is the "capitalists" whose food consumption has been curtailed. A proviso must here be made with regard to the high Party bureaucrats who apparently, as in Russia, have means to procure more food and to live better than the mass of the population.

The German farmers and peasants may grumble at the price controls and desire the return of a free market; they may complain at the poor quality of the manufactured goods they buy and think themselves exploited by the towns; but they have probably suffered less and gained more under the National Socialist regime than other classes of the population. Moreover, they have never been threatened by mass starvation nor had their incentive to produce completely destroyed by forced collectivization, forced sales, and failure of the towns to provide manufactured goods of prime necessity. In the case of the agricultural producers, as in the case of industry, the retention of private-property forms and the greater reward obtained by harder labor and efficiency have prevented the decline of productivity. Nazi Germany comes nearer to feeding itself than the old Germany, whereas Soviet Russia produces less food per head of the population than in Tsarist times. The Nazi Government has never shown a tendency to treat the peasantry as a colonial area for excessive exploitation and to create an unnaturally wide gap between the level of industrial and agricultural prices. On the contrary, the Nazis have, if anything, favored the peasantry above other classes, seeing in them the reservoir of good soldiers and the "purest Aryan" element in the German population.

Although the fact that it has not abolished the capitalist class has prevented the Nazi Government from winning the admiration of foreign socialists and totalitarian liberals, it derives a very important internal political advantage from the retention of the machinery of the profit system. In Russia the ruthlessly exploited workers know that it is the Soviet Government, owning the enterprises in which they work, which is responsible for their low wages, for the lack of food and manufactures and housing, and for the intensive speeding up. In Germany, however, although a minority of the workers may realize that their "factory leader" is as helpless as they are themselves, the majority may be expected to lay at least a portion of the blame for their working conditions on the factory "owner."

This advantage may be largely an illusory one in view of the intelligence and political knowledge of the German workingman, but it cannot be denied that retention of the private-profit system enables the Nazi Government to restrict consumption and collect taxation more indirectly and therefore more smoothly than the Soviet Government. The Nazi Government has found "unearned income" from dividends, rent, and bank deposits too useful a means of keeping down consumption and channeling off a large proportion of the national income as savings for capital investment and nonproductive public expenditure, to abolish it. The capitalists instead of the state get the opprobrium of being exploiters, but the state takes all the profit of the exploitation beyond a minimum left to the capitalist to conserve for his personal needs. The "capitalist class" has to act not only as "work agents" but also as tax collectors.

Retention of the old economic structure but the institution of a new type of management has enabled the Nazi Government to divert an enormous proportion of the national income to the production of armaments, the development of *Ersatz* production, and in general to the production of capital goods at the expense of goods of consumption, without producing the inflationary symptoms which a similar diversion of the national income to capital investment and armaments production has produced in the Soviet Union. The purchasing power in the hands of consumers in Nazi Germany has been kept down in proportion to the diminished supply of consumer goods. Until the present war there was no comparable decline in the value of money and real wages to that which occurred in the Soviet Union in the past decade. There has been a decline in quality of consumers' goods but not on anything like the Russian scale, while the cost of living rose little if at all above the 1929 level as compared with its ten- or twenty-fold rise in Russia. All in all, it may be said that without any hullabaloo about socialist planning, the Nazi Government has been far more successful than the Soviet Government, not only in utilizing all the resources and labor of the country, but also in avoiding inflation while correctly estimating and fully controlling the entire production of the country.

The burden of the huge government expenditure and of the immense armaments program has of course, in Germany as in Russia, been borne by the producers; but in Germany it has been largely financed by forcing the so-called capitalists to "lend" money to the state and to pay heavy taxes. Many of the "loans" pay no interest and, although in theory the bondholders are supposed to be entitled to repayment at some indefinite future date, in fact the capitalist class has been subject to a huge capital levy. All this probably means that the mass of the population do not conceive of the Nazi Government as their exploiter, but rather as a government which has been responsible for a more equitable distribution of the national income. It has even been suggested by observers who have resided in Nazi Germany that the regime has come to rely for its mass support mainly upon the proletariat. If this is an exaggeration, it seems at least probable that the workers, peasants, and middle classes are more satisfied with the Nazi Government than the capitalists, and perhaps a greater proportion of these classes are, or were, enthusiastic for Hitler.

It should not be forgotten that it was the German middle and lower middle classes who suffered most from the inflation which followed Germany's defeat in the first World War, and also that the professional class and the small businessman suffered almost as greatly as the workers in the economic crisis which began in 1929. Under the Weimar Republic it was the middle classes who suffered most from the fact that Germany was a country with a highly developed and trustified heavy industry without an empire affording her secure foreign markets, and shut out by rising tariff walls from the greater part of the world. The great trusts, having no foreign trade monopolies, squeezed their profits out of the narrow home market, and in so doing crushed the middle classes down to almost a proletarian level.

If Germany can acquire an empire, not only will there be a field for employment and advancement for the youth of the middle classes, but there will be so much larger and securer a market for German industry both at home and within the new empire that the small industrialist and trader hopes to be able to breathe again. Hence the receptiveness of the German middle classes to Nazi propaganda, and its support of German aggression. Patriotism and the desire to avenge the humiliation of defeat in 1918, megalomania, and delusions of grandeur all play their part; but self-interest, real or imaginary, is equally potent, or perhaps of primary importance.

The German victories in the present war, and the extraordinarily high morale of the German soldiers, prove that the same people who in the twenties were Social Democrats believing in an international ideal, can turn to a ferocious nationalism when that ideal is dead together with the world conditions—free trade and free movement of capital—which gave them birth.

As regards the German capitalists, they no doubt feel that half a loaf is better than no bread, and fear both that the overthrow of the Nazi Government would lead to anarchy and that the defeat of the Third Reich in war would be the end of the German national state. They also, even if thoroughly disillusioned concerning Nazi rule, see no alternative. They and the conservative agrarians wished to avoid war against France and England, but now that the war is on they must support Hitler to the end. The idea that the German conservatives and army leaders would revolt against Hitler with a French army ready to march into Germany, and with victory still a possibility, was always fantastic although it was the fond hope of many English statesmen. On the other hand, the German capitalists hope that if Germany wins an empire there may be some loosening of the restraints imposed upon private enterprise by the present military-socialist regime. They have by now become so dependent on the state that they dare not risk the overthrow of the government from within or from without. All they can strive for, and hope for, is the predominance of the Right wing of the Nazi party against its extremist and reckless Left wing, and a greater share of political power to the army, in which conservative influences are comparatively strong.

In spite of the dissimilarities as well as the similarities of the Nazi and Soviet states, it is obvious that the German state is already in such absolute control of all land and productive capital that "going Bolshevik" today would entail little change in the existing social and economic order. It would mean merely the addition of a theoretical state ownership for the practical state ownership already in existence. Already the exigencies of the present war are fast wiping out even the pretense of private capitalist ownership. Hence the futility of imagining that Hitler and the Nazis could be overthrown by a "Bolshevik" revolution. It is also impossible to conceive of a return in Germany to a free capitalist system and parliamentary democracy; but it is possible to hope for a revival of democracy in a new form, enabling the people to control their government and to administer the state-controlled or owned land and capital in their own interest instead of in that of the Nazi party.

It is one of the ironies of history that the Nazis, who came to power as the bitter enemies of Socialists and Communists, and with few or no preconceived economic theories, have transformed the German social and economic system into something more closely approximating a socialist economy than that of the U.S.S.R., ruled for two decades by a party determined to establish socialism. In neither country has the new form of economy produced prosperity or freedom or social justice. But in Germany today there is probably a greater social and material equality than in Russia, while from the point of view of planning and abolishing the "anarchy of capitalist production," abolishing economic crises and unemployment, and utilizing resources and productive capacity to the full, there is no doubt at all that Nazi Germany is more "socialist" than Soviet Russia.

It might be argued that, whereas the Nazi party prevents the new German system from functioning as a planned socialist economy meeting the needs of the population, because it desires to obtain the means to wage aggressive war and to increase the territory of the German Reich, the Soviet Government prevents the development of the capitalist method of production and distribution which, in a large backward country possessing enormous natural resources, could ensure many years of progress and prosperity. Germany was ripe for socialism when the Nazi party came to power, and by now has her national economy organized on semisocialist lines; but the new system is prevented by the Nazis from producing for use in order to produce for conquest. Russia was ripe only for capitalism when the Bolsheviks seized power and, with her large peasant population and slightly developed industries, totally unsuited for socialism. Since Lenin died the Bolshevik Government has, however, prevented the development of Russia's productive forces along the semicapitalist lines which could have secured far greater efficiency, less waste, and increase of prosperity. It has instead foisted upon the Russian people a bastard economy which produces neither for use, as a socialist economy should, nor for profit, as a capitalist economy does. Instead it "wastes the blood and sweat of a great people" upon the erection of giant edifices of doubtful utility, in providing for the needs of a gigantic bureaucracy, and in producing armaments for defending a people whose conditions of existence are so miserable and whose hate and mistrust of their government is so profound that they have nothing to live for and nothing worth dying for.

The Soviet Government spends its main energies diverting the natural flow of economic forces into new channels where the sandy soil swallows up all the life-giving waters. Thus the Russian people are kept at an Asiatic level of subsistence by the cruel repression of all "bourgeois" tendencies toward greater well-being through individual effort. Private enterprise is forbidden to improve the people's standard of life, while "socialism" imposed by force on an unwilling people of low cultural level cannot do so. The social cost of coercing the peasants and workers is so great that the benefit from such industrial progress as has occurred is lost. As the productive forces of socialized industry and agriculture have been augmented by huge capital investments, the means to enforce state ownership and to compel the workers and peasants to toil for the state have proportionately increased. The ever-increasing cost of maintaining an administrative and coercive apparatus gigantic enough to force the Russian people to work for the state wipes out all the gains "on the industrial front" and all the benefits which should be derived from the elimination of private rent, interest and profit. Each step forward in the development of modern large-scale industry has been accompanied by two steps backward in the productivity of labor on the farms and in industry as a whole; while the decline in the material well-being of the population and in its morale has proceeded retrogressively at an even more rapid tempo. A house built upon sand, however vast, cannot endure; nor can a state founded upon hunger and despair and supported by terror alone.

Although, like Stalin, Hitler has rejected the humanitarian content, the democratic spirit, and the internationalism of Marxism, he understands Marxist economic theory and political science much better than Stalin has ever done. This is apparent from his insistence that the statesman must go along with the historical driving forces, not against them; and that the statesman cannot create, only stimulate, natural growth. Hitler might even subscribe to Marx's thesis that "law can never be higher than the economic structure and the cultural level conditioned by it."

That Hitler appreciates his debt to Marx is obvious from the following quotation from the *Voice of Destruction*:

> I am not only the conqueror but also the executor of Marxism—of that part of it which is essential and justified, stripped of its Jewish-Talmudic dogma.... I have learned a great deal from Marxism.... I don't mean their tiresome social doctrine or the materialistic interpretation of history, or their absurd marginal utility theories and so on. But I have learned from their methods. The difference between them and myself is that I have really put into practice what these peddlers and pen-pushers have timidly begun. The whole of National Socialism is based upon it. Look at the workers' sports clubs, the industrial cells, the mass demonstrations, the propaganda leaflets written specially for the comprehension of the masses. All these new methods of political struggle are essentially Marxist in origin. All I had to do was to take over these methods and adapt them to our purpose. I had only to develop logically what Social Democracy repeatedly failed in because of its attempt to realize its evolution within the framework of democracy. National Socialism is what Marxism might have been if it could have broken its absurd and artificial ties with a democratic order.

When Rauschning says in reply that surely what he describes is the same thing as Bolshevism in Russia, Hitler exclaims:

> Not at all! You are making the usual mistake. What remains is a revolutionary creative will that needs no ideological crutches, but grows into a ruthless instrument of might invincible in both the nation and the world. A doctrine of redemption based on science thus becomes a genuine revolutionary movement possessing all the requisites of power.

The fact that Hitler prefers his own mystical race theories, his visions of the "destiny" of the German people, and his half-digested Nietzschean theories about master men and slaves to any "doctrine of redemption," need not blind us to the fact that historically speaking he has performed for Marxian socialism in Germany the same "service" as Lenin performed in Russia. Lenin, unlike Hitler, was essentially a humanitarian and an internationalist; but his disregard of the democratic content of Marxism and his transformation of the Russian Communist party into an instrument of personal power for his successor constituted a rejection of those "ties with a democratic order" to which Hitler attributes the failure of Social Democracy. One might go further and say that the Nazis have adapted the essentials of Marxist theory to the conditions of postwar Germany, as the Russian Communists adapted them to the conditions of Russia in 1920. Both are *national* parties with a *national* ideal; but the U.S.S.R., having inherited a vast empire from the Tsars, has no need to conquer the lands of other nations to obtain the necessary resources for an autarchic planned or socialist economy, while Germany must conquer other nations before she can establish "socialism in one country."

The need to key up the whole population for the mighty effort to conquer England and France and thus form a European empire forced the Nazis to subordinate everything else to military efficiency. They could not afford to experiment at their leisure with economic theories, nor to risk dislocation and famine. They had to rule by consent of the majority of the German people if the latter were to fight willingly and enthusiastically. Hence they had to compromise as between the interests of all classes and endeavor to reconcile class antagonisms in the national interest. Also, they had to be fairly honest with the German people, however greatly they deceived other nations. For instance, Goering proclaimed to the world that the German people must do without butter in order to get guns; but Stalin pretended that the Russian workers had butter, although most of them have almost forgotten the taste of it.

The Russian Communist party is still hampered by the democratic origins of its Marxist theory, by what Hitler calls its tiresome social doctrine, and its doctrine of redemption. The rulers of Russia have continually to twist the meanings of words and to cloak their real aims in an effort to retain the allegiance of the youth nurtured in Marxist and Leninist theory, which, although presented to them in expurgated editions complete with commentaries which change the meaning, nevertheless retains the elements of a dynamic faith, which, taken seriously, would destroy the Stalinist bureaucracy. The Catholic Church in the Middle Ages was unable completely to crush the spirit of Christianity, and the Protestants who went back to the Bible as the source of their religious faith repudiated and for a time looked as if they would destroy the authoritarian Church of Rome. The Communist party hierarchy is always in danger of a similar revolt. The Nazi party's influence is founded on weak and nebulous theories and on strong nationalist emotions and faith in the Leader. They are not forever constrained to twist their theory to fit the facts; the two are more or less in harmony. Their aim is the maintenance and extension of their own power and that of the German state (the two are practically synonymous), and this they have all along proclaimed.

Insofar as the young and idealistic Nazis are inspired by a faith wider than the belief in Germany's destiny, it is a faith in their mission to destroy the pluto-democracies, and set up a new world order to end European anarchy and recurring war. The rulers of Russia, even more than the Nazi leaders, are concerned primarily with the maintenance of their own power and privileges; but they must pretend that they are acting in the interests of the workers of all countries and that they desire the emancipation of mankind. According to Hitler, the rulers must be free of all moral or theoretical prejudices and become omnipotent by being able to control the ideas and sway the emotions of the masses. The Bolsheviks, he observed to Rauschning, are only now, by devious routes and after having sent packing the whole body of Marxist doctrine, coming round to the same point of view.

In contrasting his method of government to Stalin's, Hitler told Rauschning that terror, although necessary to the retention of absolute power, must not be used indiscriminately, for "too much frightfulness does harm since it produces apathy." Apathy, he went on, is a defensive form of rejection behind which the masses can hide until they break out in sudden unexpected actions and reactions.

Stalin may be satisfied with the sullen apathy or stupefied servility his terror has spread throughout the Russian population, but Hitler with his plans of conquest cannot afford to rule by terror alone. He must have a people imbued with enthusiasm and hope, not a people sunk in despair, if he is to fulfill his ambition to conquer Europe. The might and frightfulness of the Nazi regime is directed mainly against other nations, that of the Soviet Government against its own citizens. Hitler would never have dared to set out on a colossal war to dominate all Europe had his people been sunk in the same hopeless apathy as the terrorized subjects of Stalin. Men must have an ideal, however debased or false, to die for; and Stalin has deprived most Russians of both ideals and hopes. André Gide found the breaking of the human spirit the most terrible feature of the U.S.S.R. Nowhere else in the world, he wrote, is the human spirit more bowed down (*"plus courbé"*). The Nazis have broken the spirit of many of those who opposed them by their ruthlessness and cruelty, but it is clear that they have not broken the spirit of the whole German people as Stalin has broken that of the Russians, and as would have been the case in Germany if Hitler had tried, like Stalin, to rule by terror alone. The difference between Stalin's Russia and Hitler's Germany, as a Jewish friend of mine once expressed it, is that in Russia everyone cringes, while in Germany everyone boasts.

The above is not to be construed as an apologia for Hitler, or as showing a failure to appreciate the horrors of the Nazi regime. Those horrors have been described in countless books, and whereas everyone knows the bad side of Hitler's Germany, few are aware of how favorably it compares with Stalin's Russia. My approach to Nazi Germany has naturally been from the East, not from the West, whence most writers have viewed it. Seen from Stalin's Russia, Nazi Germany appears rather less horrible than as observed from the democratic states of western Europe and America. I cannot, of course, claim any inside knowledge of Germany. My descriptions and my judgments in this chapter are based on the reports of others and upon the facts which are plain to the outside world, or have been proved by the present war. Moreover, even the worst descriptions of Hitler's Germany written by those who have left it do not compare in extent and depth of horror with what I saw and heard with my own eyes and ears in the U.S.S.R. The very fact that so many Germans and German Jews have been allowed to leave the country and tell the world about it, instead of being shot or immured for life in concentration camps, proves the *comparative* mildness of the Nazi regime. Another of the main reasons why most Westerners view Nazi Germany with so much greater loathing than Soviet Russia is the greater honesty and courage of the Nazis. Whereas every act of Stalin's betrays the doctrine to which he pays lip service, and the hypocrisy of the Soviet Government is almost unparalleled in history, the Nazis have proclaimed to the world what they were doing. They have denied our humanitarian and liberal values, whereas the Stalinists have pretended to be observing them more fully than we do ourselves. The disillusioned admirer of the U.S.S.R. who still wraps himself in the tattered remnants of his lost illusions, maintains that, since the aim of the Soviet Government as stated is good, whereas the aim of National Socialism as shouted from the housetops is horrible, there must be more virtue in the U.S.S.R. and more hope for the future of mankind in Soviet Russia than in Nazi Germany. Personally it seems to me that a diabolical system is more dangerous and harmful when it decks itself in the fine trappings of mankind's best aspirations and hopes than when it openly proclaims itself as the soul-destroying monster which it is. Few of the best elements among the youth of the Western world are attracted by the Nazi doctrine of race domination and force. But many give their allegiance to Stalin in the belief that the U.S.S.R. is the model of a more humane as well as a more rational society. The devil has always known that he was more likely to tempt mankind if he assumed the guise of a beautiful woman than if he appeared complete with tail and horns.

Not only this, but German National Socialism, in spite of its horrible features, appears a little more likely to bear the seed of a better ordered world than Stalin's bastard socialism, which is nothing but a mockery of the hopes of all who have striven for the emancipation of mankind.

The Nazis have proved that a state-controlled economy functions less wastefully and can ensure the full utilization of resources and man power, the abolition of unemployment, and perhaps also a more equal division of the national income than a "free" capitalist economy which dooms men to starve in the midst of plenty, and to walk the streets looking for work while factories stand idle and raw materials are wasted. The fact that this new system—call it state capitalism or socialism as you please—has been perverted to serve the ambition of a man and a party, and converted into the most terrible apparatus of ruthless aggression the world has yet seen, does not alter the fact that the Germans have proved the superior efficiency of a socialist, or semi-socialist, economy. The Russian experiment, on the other hand, had seemed to prove that socialism is unworkable.

Nor have the German people, I believe, yet had all the humanity driven out of them, and their minds completely perverted or atrophied by the constant practice of hypocrisy and the redefinition of words to make them mean their opposite, as is the case with those who follow the Communists. Given economic opportunity and peace, the Germans may yet get rid of the brutal element now uppermost among the Nazis, and develop the progressive features of National Socialism: its Socialism as distinct from its rampant Nationalism. I recognize that it is also possible that Nazi rule over Germany might instead eventually degenerate into as terrible and weakening a despotism as Stalin's over Russia, but there would appear to be more likelihood in Germany of the eventual democratization of the system.

Wherever the arm of Stalin's government extends, it blights all hope of progress and prosperity. The desire for the opportunity to do productive and creative work is blasted by the frost of repression or stifled by the corrupt bureaucratic apparatus. Whenever a revival in some form or other of private enterprise and initiative has brought a slight improvement in the condition of the Russian workers and peasants, the Soviet Government has hastened to stamp it out. Constrained by a theory which has become as stultifying as a rigid religious dogma intolerantly upheld, the Soviet Government keeps the Russian people at a medieval level of subsistence. Universal want and misery and a deadly apathy are the outstanding characteristics of the U.S.S.R., whose natural resources are equaled only by the United States. There is a good deal of truth in Malcolm Muggeridge's verdict concerning the Nazis and Bolsheviks. The former, he says, is a barbarism which may, and probably will, make war on civilization; but the Bolshevik government makes war on life itself. So long as a social system allows for the development of productive forces, and so for greater prosperity, there is hope that a people will revert to, or recreate, a set of moral, cultural, and social values, which means a civilization. But when men have to live the life of half-starved, poorly clad brutes as in the U.S.S.R. because the system does not allow of prosperity, there can be no new civilization.

It also seems to me that it is far worse, far more destructive of the creative and social instincts of mankind, to commit or applaud crimes committed in the name of an ideal betrayed, than to commit them openly and unashamedly. The German people is not as calloused in its soul as the Russian is, because it has not been forced for years to pretend that black is white; it has only been told by its government that black, not white, is the best of colors. Those who do not accept this view, even those who accept it, are not made color-blind. To kill and murder and persecute for the sake of national grandeur or personal aggrandizement is horrible enough, but it has been done by other nations at other times and they have recovered their sanity and their humanity afterwards. To kill and murder and persecute and persuade yourself that this is done for the sake of humanity, destroys the inner core of man's integrity and deprives us of all hope for the future. In men whose minds have thus been perverted, there is no spark of humanity or sanity left to rekindle, no possibility of revolt or reaction against evil, inhumanity, and barbarism.

For all his cruelty, ruthlessness, and mysticism, and in spite of the sickness of his soul, Hitler is a product of the western European civilization which he rejects; whereas Stalin remains a Caucasian bandit. Hitler is subtle and imaginative and diabolically clever, and believes in his own twisted and perverted ideals. Stalin is cunning, brave, and has great force of will; but he has no intellect, little imagination, and no ideals whatsoever. Stalin can destroy, but he cannot build. Whereas Hitler, according to Rauschning, could neither sleep nor eat after murdering Roehm and his other old comrades on June 30, 1934, Stalin has killed off without a qualm the whole generation of the Bolsheviks who led the 1917 Revolution. Stalin seems to kill as an animal kills, without hesitation and without suffering any pangs of conscience afterward. His is the mentality of the primitive mountaineer who carries on a vendetta for generations without fear or remorse. Rauschning describes Hitler as having been a nervous wreck after *his* purge of the Party; yet what are a thousand Nazis shot in 1934* in comparison with the hundreds of thousands of Communist Party Members killed in Stalin's bloodthirsty heresy hunts?

Instead of vilifying those he had murdered, as Stalin does, Hitler said of them: "They wanted everything for the best, but in their own stubborn way. Therefore they were doomed to err, and succumbed to the verdict under which all those must fall who do not learn to obey." True, he did not say this in public; but at least he did not accuse either Roehm or von Schleicher and von Bredow of being foreign spies.

Stalin may be said to have the amorality of the brute, but many sensitive intellectuals in the Bolshevik party who for years carried out Stalin's will, and in the end even "died for the movement" in dishonor, suffered from the same sickness of the soul as Hitler. That sickness arises from the denial of one's humanity through belief in a sacred dogma, and in a "divine" purpose or destiny. The leading Bolsheviks who made false confessions before they faced the firing squads of the O.G.P.U. sacrificed themselves for "the movement" or "the Party," as Hitler had sacrificed Roehm and the others whom he claimed had had to be sacrificed "for the greatness of the movement."

The mystical belief in the inevitable triumph of socialism and in "the Party" as the sacred instrument of a divine historical purpose, was probably more potent than the mental tortures inflicted upon them by the O.G.P.U. in causing the old Bolsheviks to confess to crimes they had never committed. By declaring themselves traitors they hoped, not to escape death, but to "die for the movement" by preserving the unity of the Party and thus warding off the imminent revolt of the Russian masses which might destroy all hope of socialism in Russia. The mystical belief in a national destiny which makes the idealistically minded youth in the Nazi party—as distinct from the brutal or power-seeking careerists—ready to inflict terrible sufferings on innocent people of other races or nationalities, is paralleled by the

* The June 1934 purge of the Nazi party was the occasion when Hitler by playing the Right off against the Left and the Left off against the Right, secured absolute power for himself and the Nazi party. He sacrificed the S.A. extremists led by Roehm (who wanted to expropriate the conservative capitalists and landowners) to appease the Conservatives, but at the same time he terrified the Conservatives (the Nationalist Party) by also murdering von Schleicher and von Bredow. Thus he ensured his complete control of the Nazi party, and the servility of the Conservatives.

sincere Communist's faith in his Party as the sacred instrument for establishing the rule, not of his nation, but of his "class." The Marxist belief that society is inevitably tending by its own economic momentum toward the socialist millennium, can impel humane men to justify the conscienceless and cruel deeds of the Soviet Government, as a similar belief in the "divine destiny" of one's nation can compel decent men to inflict the horrors of war on other nations. Sensitive men like Bucharin could stifle their scruples by saying, "We must be ruthless because the sword of history is in our hands." In the coarser minds of brutal men—and this in Russia today means in the minds of the majority of surviving Russian Party members—this theory begat complete amorality. The sensitive idealistic fanatics are so certain of their own rightness that they convince themselves that all means are justified: lying, cheating, massacre, and murder. The cynics and the brutes take advantage of this convenient theory to further their own advancement.

The manner in which the O.G.P.U. obtained "confessions" from the most devoted and stubborn Bolsheviks whom no threats to themselves or their families, nor bribes, nor long solitary confinement had been able to break, as told by W. C. Krivitsky, the ex-O.G.P.U. agent, illustrates what can happen to the minds and purpose of men who believe that personal integrity must be sacrificed to a cause. It is made clear that they were finally persuaded to make false confessions of crimes they had never committed by persuading them that the Party in spite of Stalin was still the Party of the proletariat, still the chosen historical instrument for the emancipation of the toilers; and that it was their duty as Bolsheviks to lie for the sake of the Party, as well as die for it in the Lubianka Prison. Krivitsky shows that in ninety hours of continuous argument with Mrachkovsky there was never any attempt on the part of the O.G.P.U. examiner to prove the prisoner's guilt. The conversation opens with the O.G.P.U. examiner, Sloutsky, trying to convince the prisoner Mrachkovsky, that he, Sloutsky, is also an old Bolshevik who also had fought and been wounded in the Civil War. If Mrachkovsky could once be convinced that Sloutsky had not "degenerated into a police hound" and had "still some soul in him," then perhaps Mrachkovsky could be persuaded to sacrifice both his life and his honor for the sake of "the Revolution." Then Sloutsky begins to talk about the internal and international situation of the Soviet Government, of the perils from within and without, and of the need to save the Party at all costs as the only savior of the Revolution. Sloutsky goes on to tell Mrachkovsky that he knows quite well that he is not a counter-revolutionary, but tries to convince him that some others had actually plotted with foreign powers to overthrow the Soviet Government.

There followed days and nights of argument which brought Mrachkovsky to the realization that nobody else but Stalin could guide the Bolshevik Party. Mrachkovsky was a firm believer in the one-party system of government, and he had to admit that there was no Bolshevik group strong enough to reform the party machine from within, or to overthrow Stalin's leadership. True, there was deep discontent in the country, but to deal with it outside of the Bolshevik ranks would mean the end of the proletarian dictatorship to which Mrachkovsky was loyal.

Both the prosecuting examiner and his prisoner agreed that all Bolsheviks must submit their will and their ideals to the will and ideals of the Party. They agreed that one had to remain within the Party even unto death, or dishonor, or death with dishonor, if it became necessary for the sake of consolidating the Soviet power. It was for the Party to show the confessors consideration for their act of self-sacrifice if it chose.

"I brought him to the point where he began to weep," Sloutsky reported to me. "I wept with him when we arrived at the conclusion that all was lost, that there was nothing left in the way of hope or faith, that the only thing to do was to make a desperate effort to forestall a futile struggle on the part of the discontented masses. For this the Government must have public 'confessions' by the opposition leaders."

Finally, still cursing Stalin, but persuaded he must sacrifice himself for the Party, Mrachkovsky agreed to sign the "confession" demanded of him as his last and crowning sacrifice to the Revolution to which he had given his life. His state of mind, after being argued with for three days and nights without sleep, may be compared to that of a fervent Catholic before the Counter-Reformation who, although still believing that Antichrist sat on the throne of Saint Peter, had been persuaded that to overthrow the Pope would involve the overthrow of the throne of God.

Max Eastman, in his fine and illuminating book, *Stalin's Russia,* has shown the close connection between Stalin's frame-ups and the false confession of the old Bolsheviks with Leninist theory. He writes:

> The mystery of the Moscow confessions is insoluble to those who do not realize what can happen to idealists who renounce the old moral code of truthfulness, and adopt a principled belief in public lying. Although camouflaged in Russia by the intellectual verbiage

of the Hegelian-Marxian dialectic, this is really the same renunciation of intelligence for animal will, of reason for blind instinct, of civilized enlightenment for barbarian "dynamism" that we see in Germany....

One has only to compare Hitler's repeated injunctions to his followers to "trust in your instinct"; Goering's statement, "I have no conscience. My conscience is Adolf Hitler"; and Hitler's scornful remark to Rauschning, "Is an easy conscience more precious to you than the rise of a new Germany?"

Eastman continues:

> Anybody who understands that can understand the Moscow confessions. And he can understand why the prodigious lies told in those confessions have prospered among the devotees of Stalinism throughout the world. The question of their truth, in knife-edged form, was never raised. They were judged by the will only, the will to solidarity and power. Their function was the destruction of "Trotskyism," which is now nothing but a name for any rift, or threat of a rift, in that totalitarian will. Compared with this supreme function, the question of their correspondence with fact is subordinate altogether. To slur the question is a matter of gang loyalty.

As Eastman also insists, an understanding of this mental and social process, and its rejection by all who call themselves liberals and progressives, is essential to the survival of civilization. "Those who swallowed the lies told in these trials, or agreed to assist with silence or suspended judgment in their propagation, are to be guarded against as political totalitarians."

The strange "sickness of the soul" which led so many American and western European intellectuals to glorify the crimes of Stalin and the Communist party committed in the name of a class, while at the same time condemning and loathing the crimes of Hitler and the Nazi party committed in the name of country or race, is a sickness fatal to the survival of civilized values; and if it spreads it must lead us all back to barbarism and a new Dark Age.

Stalin not only forces men to sacrifice themselves for the movement he has betrayed, but also to dishonor themselves before he kills them. He takes delight in slaking a desire for *personal* vengeance on all who have ever opposed him, criticized him, or aroused his envy and hatred by their superior intelligence and ability. Stalin once told Kamenev and Derjinsky that his idea of the greatest pleasure life can give is to "plan an artistic revenge upon an enemy, carry it out to perfection, and then go home and go peacefully to bed."

Hitler is more impersonal than this, and shares with Lenin, although in lesser degree, the nobility of devotion to an impersonal ideal. But Lenin was at heart a liberal intellectual and had a cold, clear intellect and an almost superhuman self-control, whereas Hitler is an apostle of violence and a man of violent and ungovernable passions subject to hysterical outbursts of rage. By upbringing and temperament Lenin was an aristocrat as well as a man of brilliant intellect, fitted as few men have been to persuade men to aim at an international and sublime ideal. He never knew the feelings of social and educational inferiority which have shaped Hitler's character, warped his mind, and fitted him to lead a people suffering from a similar sense of national frustration, humiliation, and envy. Lenin's aim was the emancipation of the proletariat and "therewith of all mankind"; while Hitler's aim is the universal hegemony of the German nation. One aim may be noble and the other ignoble, but both are "ideals." Under Stalin the communist aim has come to approximate closely to that of the German National Socialists. From the beginning there was a basic similarity between Lenin's conception of the Bolshevik party as the will and the intellect of the proletariat, and Hitler's conception of the Nazi party as the "representative of the general good" of the German people. Communists see in the Party the vanguard of the class-conscious proletariat, and justify its monopoly of political power because it is supposed to represent the real interests of the proletariat. Hitler says: "In place of the masses—the voting herd periodically intoxicated by words—there is now a people's community, developed from the masses, the incorporated nation awakened to self-consciousness: our Party." It is perhaps on account of this basic resemblance that there is an even closer similarity between the "philosophy" of the Nazis and latter-day Communists than between the social, economic, and political systems which they have established in their respective countries. The Communists hold any and every action justified if committed in the name of the proletariat with the proposed aim of ensuring the victory of the "socialist" revolution. The Nazis proclaim an equal amorality in the name of race and for the fulfillment of Germany's "destiny" to dominate the world. The greater or lesser degree of sincerity of Nazis and Bolsheviks does not greatly affect this comparison. The leaders of both parties are no doubt concerned mainly with the maintenance of their own power, but it must be conceded that whereas Hitler, like Lenin, himself believes in the mission he proclaims for himself and the Nazi party, Stalin cares for nothing except his personal ascendancy.

To accomplish their aims, both alike seek to destroy the bases of individual integrity and civilized behavior. The Bolsheviks say that there is only class justice, while Hitler says that justice is a means of ruling. Hitler is here as good a Marxist as the Communists. Hitler says that "there is no such thing as truth in the moral or in the scientific sense," and that there is Nordic science and a National Socialist science opposed to liberal-Jewish science. The Communists, for their part, insist that there is bourgeois science and Marxist science, and no such thing as pure science.* While Nazi Germany has expelled many of her best scientists because they were Jews, the U.S.S.R. has shot or imprisoned hers for their "servility to foreign science" or because they clung to non-Marxist biological, astronomical, medical, mathematical, or physical scientific theories.

Hitler tells his followers to distrust intelligence and the conscience, and to place their trust in instinct while proclaiming the will of the Nazi party as the law. The Communists similarly insist that intelligence, humanitarian feeling, conscience, and personal integrity must be sacrificed to the will of the Party, and decry any predilection for truth or for civilized standards of behavior as at best "rotten liberalism" or "petty bourgeois prejudice" and at worst counter-revolution, wrecking, or sabotage.

Hitler says that he is freeing men from the restraints of a chimera called conscience and morality, while the Communists say they are freeing men from bourgeois prejudices, that there is no morality except class morality, and that personal integrity and honesty are crimes against one's class. In the words of the Soviet apologists and admirers, Beatrice and Sidney Webb, "whatever contributes to the building up of the classless society is good; whatever impedes it is bad."

In Germany men are persecuted for their race, while in Russia they are persecuted for their social origins. In both countries the crimes of the fathers are visited upon the children, but in Russia the principle of tribal or communal guilt has been carried to further lengths. According to the Soviet criminal code, the traitor's whole family is severely punished even if they know nothing of his intentions and are entirely innocent—even when the culprit's "treason" consists only of

* Of recent years there has been a further intellectual and moral degeneration of Stalinist communism. It has no longer been sufficient for scientists and historians to say there is no pure science or objective history. They are now required to say that there is *false* bourgeois science and history and *true* Communist or "proletarian" science, history, etc.

his having wished to leave Russia and to have "escaped over the frontier." Hitler has learned more from Stalin than Stalin from Hitler, but in general has not carried his imitations of Communist methods to the same lengths as they have. Hitler's purges and massacres and persecutions have been *comparatively* mild. The number of victims tortured in the German concentration camps is not so very large compared with the millions shot and imprisoned or doing forced labor in Russia. Jews, socialists, nonconformists of all kinds have been allowed to leave Germany in thousands, but in Russia all who refused to worship at the shrines of the new gods have been liquidated; and no citizens, even those technically free, are allowed to travel abroad, much less leave the country. The German, if he dislikes the Nazi regime, can (or could before the war) leave the country. True, a capitalist cannot take his capital with him; but he is allowed to take some personal possessions. In Russia, on the other hand, it has been the assumption of the Soviet Government since 1930 that every specialist and many peasants and workers would rush to leave the country, with nothing besides the clothes on their backs, if not prevented by Draconian laws and penalties. No one is allowed a passport to leave the country, and "escaping across the frontier" is counted as treason for which savage reprisals are taken against the family of the "traitor." The Soviet law provides a penalty of five to ten years' imprisonment for the wife, children, mother, father, brothers, and sisters of any such "traitor" if these relatives knew of his intention, and of five years' exile to a remote part of Siberia with loss of citizenship to those who did not know of their relative's intention to escape.

Early in March 1940, during the war on Finland, it was decreed that any soldiers who surrendered to the enemy, whatever the circumstances, should be regarded as traitors. This means that the soldiers of the Red Army are now forced to fight for fear of the reprisals which will be inflicted on their wives and children. Stalin copied this device from Japan, who uses it to ensure the "loyalty" of her Manchurian Chinese soldiers. Hitler has not needed any such system of hostages to force German soldiers to die in battle.

The Soviet Government's suspicion that many of its citizens would escape from the socialist paradise if they could is probably justified. Perhaps Stalin has been wiser than Hitler in this respect. Whereas thousands of Jews and a goodly number of liberals have been allowed to leave Germany, and even former victims of the Gestapo have succeeded in getting out of the country to tell the tale of their sufferings to a horrified world, Stalin has shot or interred in concentration camps all whom he suspected of disliking the regime, and has prevented even the "free" citizen from leaving the country for a short visit abroad. Consequently, whereas the horrors of Nazi Germany are known to the whole world, very few people know anything about the suffering and oppression of the Russians under Stalin.

The Nazis have burned the books they disapprove of; Stalin has had them expurgated, revised, or rewritten to change their meanings. Both have abolished pure science, free criticism, philosophy, objective history, intellectual liberty, and freedom of the mind and spirit.

Only in regard to the substitution of a chauvinistic patriotism for the international ideal, has Stalin copied Hitler. I well remember the shock with which, in Moscow in 1934, we read in *Pravda* for the first time the statement, "Patriotism is the supreme law of life." From that time onward the "achievements" of the Soviet Union were hailed in the Press as accomplished for the glory of the Soviet or Socialist Fatherland. Soon even the words Soviet and Socialist were dropped and "the Fatherland" pure and simple took the place of the old internationalist slogans.

However, Stalin has been greatly hampered in this respect by the Marxist theories, which are still supposed to constitute the Bible of the Communist. The Nazis came to power as the most aggressively patriotic party in Germany, but the Communist party came to power as *international* Socialists, whose slogan was, "The workers have no fatherland." For the Communists in other countries the new Soviet patriotism was explained as signifying that in defending the U.S.S.R., workers the world over were defending the "socialist fatherland" which in the future would emancipate the toilers of all countries. But this twisting of Marxist theory into national patriotism was hard to put across in the West, and was successful only so long as Russia's national interest appeared to be the same as the *national* interest of France, England, and the United States, not the same as the class interest of French, British, and American workers.

It is clear that Stalin's attempts to imitate Hitler by substituting a national religion for an international ideal and to make his people worship him as god have failed to produce in Russia that readiness to die for leader and country which the Second World War has proved to exist in Germany. Perhaps the very ignorance, semi-illiteracy, and lack of culture of the Russian people have prevented Stalin being able to fool many of them for any considerable time.

Hitler has copied Stalin in his method of securing the personal loyalty of his adherents by planned corruption. In 1933 he gave his henchmen free rein to "get something out of it," allowing them to extort blood money from the bourgeoisie, as Stalin has allowed his lackeys to enrich themselves at the expense of the workers. The material advantages of the Nazi party members are less blatant than those of the Russian Communists, but they exist. Stalin, as I have already suggested, has no other social support than that of his Party followers and must bind them to him by allowing them to live far more luxurious lives than the old Russian bourgeoisie under the Tsar. Hitler, too, must allow material gains to his followers; but he does not rely on them alone to maintain him in power, so that their incomes in money or kind are proportionately less high as compared with the average German's income, than those of the Russian Party bureaucrats as compared with the half-starved, ragged peasants in their hovels and the undernourished workers in their tenements.

In the above brief comparison of the Nazi and Soviet regimes the most striking difference is not the theoretical distinction between state ownership and state control of land, capital, and human beings, but the far greater efficiency of the Nazi regime and its less absolute reliance on terror to maintain its power. In part this can be ascribed to the superiority of German culture, and to the greater harmony between Nazi theory and practice, declared aims and actual aims. It seems clear that the younger Nazi party is not yet so demoralized as the Russian Communist party, and contains a far larger proportion of able and intelligent and also of sincere members. It appears to be loyal to Hitler and to follow his lead willingly, as the Russian Communist party followed Lenin—not by compulsion, but on account of belief in his superior wisdom or political sagacity. Hitler has therefore been able to trust the Nazi party, and to retain that inter-party democracy which existed in Lenin's day, which Trotsky sought to retain but which Stalin destroyed.

Hitler maintains that all who join the Party—i.e., accept its duties and are worthy to join it—have a right to be heard, and conceives it as his duty to convince a majority of the members of the correctness of his views, or to change them. But Stalin purges and shoots and imprisons while changing the "party line" at his convenience without explanation or justification. There is also the important difference that in Russia membership in the Party is the *only* way to secure decent conditions of existence, but in Germany where want and poverty are not so general everyone does not desire to belong to the Party. Consequently, the Nazi party is alive and alert and full of initiative, as the Bolshevik party was in Lenin's day, whereas the Bolshevik party is a corpse, a lifeless organism drained of its lifeblood by the purges of recent years.

But there is another, and perhaps more potent, reason for Hitler's being able to govern somewhat more by consent of the governed than Stalin. Although the power of both dictators depends upon a monolithic party and the secret police, Hitler, unlike Stalin, does not depend entirely on the support of his Party and that Party's control of the secret police. He also has the support of considerable sections of the German people. He is probably supported by a majority of the old propertied and professional classes, for whom his rule is a lesser evil as compared with either Bolshevik anarchy or the impotence of a disarmed, powerless, and class-war-ridden Germany. Not only has the potency of the sentiment of national inferiority and of the desire for national aggrandizement proved far greater in holding Germany united under the Nazis than the largely imaginary fear of attack by the "encircling capitalist world," and the lost hope for a better social order have proved in the U.S.S.R. The preservation of the old private-property forms in Germany has secured the allegiance of the former capitalist and professional classes in spite of the severe repressions and burdens they suffer under the Nazi regime. A substantial section of the working class, disillusioned with regard to both social democracy and communism, has, it would seem, accepted the Nazi regime as affording the certainty of employment and the possibility of easier conditions of life should Germany succeed in acquiring an empire comparable to that of England and France.

Hitler therefore has been able to maintain power so far largely by balancing the capitalist and middle classes against the working class, and the army and the conservatives against the Nazi extremists. Since the old property relations have not been completely destroyed, the whole German population has not been reduced to an equal servitude. Although all are in fact completely subject to the state power, they have their varying and conflicting class interests. As Engels had perceived, there are historical periods when the warring classes are so nearly balanced that the state power acquires a certain independence in relation to both. Hence a balancing role is possible for Hitler's government. This enables him to rule as much by maneuvering as by terror, and gives greater strength to Germany than the Soviet system has given to Russia. Stalin can retain power only by sheer terror, by playing off individuals against one another and by giving unduly large material rewards to those who are loyal to him. There are no longer any "warring classes" to be played off against each other, since peasants, workers, and specialists are all alike slaves of the state. Whereas Hitler has the social support of a large number, if not of an actual majority, of the capitalists and professional classes, and perhaps even the support also of a majority of the farmers and industrial workers—as between whose interests he arbitrates—Stalin has no social support beyond that of the privileged bureaucracy which is itself in constant fear of death or the concentration camp. Hence the greater strength, resilience, and stability of the Nazi regime, its ability to rule by consent of a substantial proportion of the population, and its ability to concentrate its military force against other nations.

The vast size of Russia, its remoteness, and the illusions born of its discarded past as a workers' state, have all enabled Stalin's regime to continue in existence despite the appalling waste and muddle for which it is responsible, and in spite of the discontent of the huge majority of the Russian people. Stalin has sought to avoid war not only because Russia is vast and contains such great natural resources, but also because he needs most of his military strength to keep the peoples of the U.S.S.R. in subjection. Russia does not need to wage war to acquire the territorial basis of an autarchic state, and also could not wage war on a big scale. Nazi Germany could not have survived a year if the system there were as inefficient and repressive as the Russian; much less could she threaten to dominate all Europe. No "cut and dried theories" could be experimented with in Germany; her rulers have had to be guided by common sense in their reordering of the economic life of the nation. In this respect Hitler resembles Lenin, who, although he believed in a whole body of theory, never let it stand in the way of his genius as a practical statesman. Hitler differs from Lenin in that he does not evolve or adapt a theory to suit his practice, but denies reason and tells men to trust to their instincts and emotions.

In waging war against the world, Germany has the tremendous advantage of having developed a socialist method of production and distribution, a method which has substituted for production for profit, production for military power, the utilization of the labor of almost every adult man and woman, and the elimination of waste. It is the tragedy of our century that the socialist order of society has come nearer to realization in Nazi Germany than anywhere else in the world, but that social control of the means of production and distribution is being used, not to ensure production for peaceful use and plenty for all, but to ensure military supremacy.

Whether or not a semisocialist economy planned for war could be changed into a semisocialist economy planned to increase the material well-being of the people if Germany had a territory as large and as rich in raw materials as Russia, remains to be seen. It is always possible that the mad visions and horrible theories about master races of Hitler and the Nazis will be sloughed off in time; that with the death of the frustrated and embittered generation which grew up after the first World War, and the acquisition of the material basis for prosperity, the German Third Reich may become as peaceful and cultured as the older British and French imperialisms. This may be a vain delusion, but as I write it would seem to be the only hope for Europe.

CHAPTER XII

MAKING THE WORLD SAFE FOR STALIN

HISTORIANS OF THE future will no doubt discuss what might have been the history of Europe, perhaps indeed what might have been the history of the world, had not a false belief in both the internal and the foreign policies of the Soviet Government driven the western European Powers into a war which is likely to destroy the civilization we know.

Not only the "liberal" admirers of the Soviet Union, but a majority of the people and statesmen of France, England, and the United States had been convinced by the beginning of 1939 of two false propositions assiduously propagated by the Comintern and its manifold false fronts. First, it was generally believed that fascism and communism were not twins but opposites, and that therefore the U.S.S.R. could be relied upon to make an alliance with the democratic powers against Germany as soon as England and France sought for such an alliance. Secondly, it was believed that the Nazi regime was so detested by the German people, and was so tyrannical and so oppressive of the German workers that it would collapse as soon as the democracies opposed it with armed force. There was a general belief that France and England need only have the courage and the unity to "stand up to Hitler" to ensure the almost bloodless victory of the democracies. This belief was held most widely in the United States, and was not shared by Chamberlain and the other "appeasers"; but circumstances proved too strong for the latter to continue on their course.

Not only were both Russian strength and the virtues of the Soviet system enormously exaggerated, but Stalin's foreign policy was tragically misunderstood. It was imagined that he was playing from strength, when in reality he was playing from weakness. Litvinov's fine speeches at Geneva were thought to be genuine; it was believed that the Soviet Union was panting to fight the Nazi menace and anxious only to secure the democracies as allies *pour écraser l'infâme*. The few voices raised in warning went unheeded,* even such damning

---

* According to the authors of the *American White Paper*, the U. S. Ambassador to France, William C. Bullitt, warned his government early in 1939 of the coming Russo-German Pact, but his report was not believed.

proof as Krivitsky's of the fact that Stalin had for years been doing his utmost to secure an alliance with Hitler.

The natural hatred of German liberals, socialists, and Jewish refugees for the Nazi regime, which led them to exaggerate all its defects and hide all its strength and to picture the whole German people as ready to revolt at the first drums of war, was not discounted. Their view of Nazi Germany was accepted as substantially true, and the Comintern and its fellow travelers spread far and wide an illusion that the German people were so discontented that France and England could easily defeat the Third Reich.

Stalin played his hand cleverly. The Popular Front, perhaps the most gigantic hoax in history, achieved amazing success. In France, England, the United States, and a score of smaller countries, liberals, labor men, socialists, the "progressives" of all kinds who prior to 1934 had been dubbed Social Fascists worse than outright Fascists by the Comintern, forgot the past and jumped on the Soviet bandwagon shouting for a holy war against fascism. The din was so terrific, the forces converted to a policy of saving democracy from fascism by aid of communism were so strong, that finally even conservatives in England and France came around to the idea of an alliance with the U.S.S.R. and a war to stop German expansion. Those who had once thought of Nazi Germany as the bulwark against communism were as blind as those who conceived of Stalin's Russia as the "worker's fatherland," the champion of collective security, the shining angel of peace among the wicked capitalist powers. Both alike had become convinced by 1939 that Stalinism was the bulwark against Hitlerism.

Chamberlain and his group were forced to abandon the policy of appeasement by pressure from the Left at home, and by their own growing doubts concerning Germany's intentions. The United States also played its part by exerting moral pressure on England to wage war on Germany next time the latter erupted. The anger, indignation, and contempt of the American people, as voiced by their Press and their politicians, at the Munich settlement, were inflamed, if not actually instigated, by the Communists and their fellow travelers, just as similar feelings were fanned in England and France. Read such liberal American journals as the *New Republic* and the *Nation* in the fall of 1938 for the clearest expression of Comintern propaganda at the time; propaganda concerned to make the American people believe that Chamberlain had sacrificed Czechoslovakia out of fear of communism and love for fascism.

If the influence of the Comintern had been confined to such journals as these and to the Left intellectual circles they represent, the damage would not have been great. But the Comintern line was reflected in almost the whole American Press* and in the great English liberal and labor daily newspapers, influenced not only by the false prophets, the facile journalists, or blind idealists, from the Webbs and Louis Fischer to Vincent Sheean, Dorothy Thompson, and Heywood Broun, but by the great majority of columnists and commentators. All these "liberals" played down Soviet atrocities, purges, executions, and liquidations; and played up Germany's. They represented the world as divided up into satanic aggressor powers and virtuous democratic powers, with Stalin's Russia endeavoring, as the purest of the pure, to awaken France and England to their duty to crush Nazi Germany.

Years hence we may know whether Chamberlain's and Daladier's so-called appeasement policy was in fact due to the need for time to prepare for war, or to sincere hatred of war and to a belief that the only way to secure peace and a solution of the chronic economic crisis in Europe was to allow Germany to form an empire in eastern Europe to match the British and French African and Asiatic empires. It is not to be ignored that ever since the end of the first World War there had been a tendency in Britain—most clearly expressed by the powerful Beaverbrook press—to avoid European entanglements and concentrate on empire development and trade.

That fear of communism or fear of the Soviet Union played little or no part in determining British and French policy must by now be obvious. Fear of the Comintern and its anticapitalist, anti-imperialist propaganda died down in Britain when Trotsky was exiled by Stalin and the Comintern defeated by Chiang Kai-shek in 1927. British conservatives in 1938 were doubtful of the value of an alliance with the Soviet state, but they were not afraid of communist influence at home, or even in the Empire; for such influence over the workers had long since vanished and the Popular Front line had enormously weakened the influence over the colonial peoples once exercised by Moscow. Although France had a pact with Soviet Russia, informed Frenchmen were doubtful of its value; for French military men had a poor opinion of the Red Army even before Russia invaded Finland in 1939. But, as a high official in the French Ministry of Foreign Affairs informed me in the early summer of 1938, the alliance with Russia was necessary to prevent a Russo-German alliance.

---

* The best example of this is the repetition in countless journals in the United States of the "Cliveden Set" story invented by Claude Coburn (alias Frank Pitcairn), the well-known English Communist who edited *The Week*.

American pressure on Britain to "stand up to the dictators" or forever lose the good will and support of the American people played its part in inducing Britain to give a guarantee to Poland in 1939. It was felt in England that if the British Government was mistaken in its view that Germany would "go East" if not interfered with, and should instead, or afterwards, attack Britain and France, the American people would by then have turned their back on England. Since American approval and support is a consideration of very great, if not decisive, importance to the two great European democracies, the American desire that England and France should fight Germany cannot be ignored as one of the causes of the present war.

At the same time, the pressure of the British Opposition, first exercised over Spain, feebly pressed concerning China, but roused to frenzy after Hitler occupied Bohemia, at last had its effect. In March 1939 Chamberlain abandoned the policy of letting Germany form an empire in eastern Europe and guaranteed the frontiers of Poland and Rumania against German aggression. From that moment war was certain.

Stalin had accomplished his purpose. England once committed to fight against Germany if the latter attacked Poland, the U.S.S.R. could now at last secure the alliance with Nazi Germany which Stalin had been trying to arrange for years past. This would seem to be the explanation of Russian policy and is borne out not only by the evidence of Krivitsky but by close observers of the U.S.S.R. who are not blinded by the ideological fog.

In March 1938 I myself prophesied the coming Russo-German alliance in an article which I tried to get published anonymously in the London *Spectator,* but which the editor refused on the ground that such an idea was fantastic. My argument was based on the fact that at the last of the demonstration trials Britain had been restored to the position of villain-in-chief which she had occupied before Hitler came to power. This in itself indicated a reorientation in Soviet foreign policy, and the same impression had been created by a statement made by Stalin two weeks before the trial, to the effect that the final victory of socialism is possible only on an international scale. This statement could not be taken as an admission that Trotsky had been right all along; but, taken in conjunction with the terms of indictment at the trial, it foreshadowed an attempt to make friends with Germany. If this were so, the obvious new line for communist propaganda to take would be abandonment of the Popular Front of all democrats and democratic countries with the Communists against Nazi Germany, and a return to the pre-Hitler line of opposition to Labor and Liberal parties and anti-imperialism, with the idea of world revolution thrown in to attract the revolutionary socialists.

This was in fact the new line adopted after the signing of the Russo-German Pact a year and a half later, and it has greatly assisted Hitler.

The concrete warning given by Krivitsky in the articles published in the *Saturday Evening Post* in the spring of 1939 was ignored or discredited, equally with the warning given a year earlier to all who knew their Russia and the past history of the Comintern. Krivitsky, who had been the chief of the Soviet Military Intelligence Service in Europe but had at last broken with Stalin when ordered to murder an old friend and ex-O.G.P.U. agent, gave abundant proof of the fact that Stalin had for years been trying, by secret negotiations in Berlin, to get an alliance with Hitler, and that all his overtures to the democratic Powers, and his action in Spain, were but moves to attain this end. Demaree Bess, former correspondent of the *Christian Science Monitor* in Moscow and one of the few newspaper correspondents who of recent years has sent objective reports, uncolored by emotion, wish-fulfillment, or prejudice, had, also in the *Saturday Evening Post*, warned of a coming Russo-German Pact.*

Hitler's final decision to accept the Russian offer which he had so long rejected was probably due to England's decision to revive the Triple Entente (an alliance of France, Russia, and England), and to the Far Eastern situation. The influence of the Far East in European politics is usually ignored, but there can be no doubt that Japan's failure to subjugate China, and the signs of an Anglo-Japanese rapprochement in the early summer of 1939 played important roles in changing Hitler's policy. He had concluded his "Anti-Comintern Pact" with Japan with the idea that Japan, after a quick conquest of China, would be ready and willing to attack Russia, or, should Germany be involved in war with the western Powers, to immobilize Russia. But the war on China had showed up Japan's weakness and political stupidity in that she could neither conquer nor hold her conquests. At the same time the negotiations with Britain over Tientsin, and Japan's refusal to conclude a military alliance with Germany for fear of offending the United States and thus losing her war supplies, had offered additional proof to Hitler that Japan was no use to him as an ally.

* A few books, notably Peter F. Drucker's *The End of Economic Man*, also warned of a Russo-German alliance, but little or no notice was taken of them by the general public.

Japan and China therefore can be said to have played their unconscious part in radically changing the policy of Nazi Germany.

From world revolution, to champion of democracy against fascism, to collaboration with Nazi Germany and imperialist expansion—thus briefly can one define the three sharp changes in Soviet policy, and in the "party line" since 1917.

The first line was honest, hopeless, destructive, but sincere. Under Lenin's leadership the international ideal was never lost sight of, and Russia's national interest was subordinated to the final aim of world revolution to establish a socialist order. This policy failed completely, since nowhere did the promised proletarian revolution make headway.

The second line was dishonest, hypocritical, cowardly, and eminently successful. Russia's national interest became the paramount consideration of the Bolsheviks, and Comintern propaganda was directed toward one sole aim: the safety of Russia to be secured by embroiling the capitalist world in war, and in particular by luring or persuading England and France to fight Germany. At the Eighth Congress of the Comintern, held in August 1935, little or nothing was heard of the need to struggle against capitalism or imperialism. The delegates were told that henceforth the primary duty of every Communist was to help by all possible means to strengthen the U.S.S.R. and arouse popular hostility against Nazi Germany.

The old sectarian line of proclaiming the Labor and Social Democratic parties to be "Socialist Fascists" and worse than outright Fascists, was abandoned for a policy of seeking to assure the world that the U.S.S.R. had the interests of the British and French empires at heart, and that the idea that Moscow desired world revolution was, in Stalin's own words, a tragi-comic misunderstanding.*

Hoping to reconcile Labor and Liberal opinion in France, Britain, and the U.S.A., Stalin promulgated his paper democratic Constitution in 1936, while the Comintern, soft-pedaling on the theme of the dictatorship of the proletariat, called for defense of bourgeois democracy and a United Front against fascism. (It should be noted that for a considerable period after Hitler came to power the Russian Press was careful not to offend him, believing that the Nazis would be primarily anti-French and that the former close and friendly relations between Germany and Russia could be maintained. It was not the wiping out of the German Communist party and the destruction of all working-class organizations in Germany, nor the persecution of Communists, Socialists, liberals, and Jews which turned the Comintern into an anti-

* In his famous interview with Roy Howard.

Fascist propaganda office, but the fact that the Nazi Government openly threatened *Russia*.)

This change to the Popular Front line was not successful for several years, since, although it attracted large numbers of intellectuals into the Communist parties of Britain and the U.S.A., it failed to conciliate the British trade-unions or the British Labour party, which had a profound and well-founded distrust of the Communists. Nor did the purges in Russia entirely convince conservatives that Stalin had liquidated communism and become respectable. Moreover, the extreme form they took, in particular the shooting of the best Russian generals, raised doubts as to the strength of the Russian army.

In France, however, owing to the ever-present and greatly intensified fear of Germany, the Popular Front policy proved very fruitful. In the United States, where there was no strong labor or socialist movement to stem the tide, and where so many of the workers were unorganized and politically immature, the new "party line" also had a great success. This success in America, and the eventual success which the Communists won even in England, were gained mainly through the work of the many false fronts established by the Comintern. Leagues for peace and democracy, for intellectual freedom, and whatnot were able to make thousands of liberals, socialists, and pacifists swallow the party line without having any idea of what they were doing.

The Soviet Government clearly never had any intention of fighting Germany itself any more than it had the intention of introducing a democratic form of government in Russia. Both the championship of collective security and the sham Constitution were hoaxes designed to lure the "peace-loving powers" and the liberals and socialists and pacifists of all shades, into support of a war against the fascist aggressors. As soon as the British guarantee to Poland and Rumania in the spring of 1939 had made war practically certain and England was offering an alliance to Russia, Stalin withdrew and joined hands with Hitler.

There remains hardly any doubt that this is what Stalin had wanted all along, and that his democratic masquerade had been played out solely with a view to persuading Hitler to agree to an alliance with him. Hitler had refused to listen to Stalin's overtures so long as there was any hope of England's keeping out of Europe and allowing Germany to expand eastward. But once Britain offered an alliance to Russia, Germany was naturally constrained to accept Stalin's offer.

With the signing of the Russo-German Pact, Soviet policy made its third *volte face*. The fact that this third phase of Soviet policy is accompanied by a revival of long-dead slogans from the Comintern's international phase should not confuse us. The present vociferous denunciations of "imperialist war" are radically different from Lenin and Trotsky's slogans two decades ago. Then the Soviet Government and the Comintern were genuinely internationalist, making no distinction between the "warring imperialisms" and calling upon the workers in all countries to turn upon their capitalists and turn the imperialist war into a civil war. After September 1939 the fulminations of the Kremlin were directed almost exclusively against the democracies, the Allies were called the aggressor, the blockade of Germany a violation of international law; and Molotov publicly declared that a war on Hitlerism or any ideology had no justification. Since the Comintern had to keep up appearances, the workers everywhere were called upon to oppose the war; but the Kremlin knows that it is only in the democracies that defeatist propaganda can make any headway; any Communist in Germany who took the Comintern Manifesto seriously would be liquidated at once. As Hitler himself has said, the democracies cannot defend themselves against propaganda, for in order to do so they would have to become authoritarian themselves, whereas dictatorships are protected against the weapon of propaganda.

Hitler, of course, reckoned on this when he allied himself to Stalin, knowing that the Comintern could do him no injury but that its propaganda would be of immense value to him against the Allies. We do not yet know how important a part the Communists played in bringing about the defeat of France, but Hitler must owe them a great debt not only for having themselves been defeatists or Fifth Columnists, but also for having frightened many members of the French bourgeoisie into being appeasers and even traitors.

This third phase of Soviet foreign policy can be said to be designed exclusively in Stalin's own interest, not in the interest of Russia. The Kremlin's world policy has by now come full circle, from internationalism to nationalism to Stalinism. It was the failure of the West to perceive this fact which blinded it to the implications and the reality of the Russo-German Pact. Arguments have been put forth ever since August 1939 to show that Russia could not *really* wish Germany to win the war, since this could not be in *Russia's* interest. But Russia's interest is not by any means the same thing as Stalin's interest—is in fact the opposite of the dictator's interest. Russia's national interest would best have been served by peace at home and abroad, a democratic government at home and good relations with France and England, affording the possibility of loans for industrial development. But this would have necessitated the fall of Stalin's dictatorial regime; a change from government by ignorant gangsters for their own profit to government by the ablest and most patriotic men in Russia.

Stalin may well have felt before May 1940 that Hitler's fall would be disastrous to him. A revolution against the Nazis in Germany might not only have diverted Germany's aggression eastward but might also have inspired the cowed masses of Russia to rise up against their own tyrant.

Whereas the second phase of Soviet policy was eminently successful, it seems probable that its latest phase will be disastrous. In the Finnish war the Soviet Government revealed its weakness, if not to the whole world, at least to Germany. Hitler now knows that the U.S.S.R. is ripe for plucking; that if he defeats the Allies, he can enter Russia and convert it into a German colony, or at least into a German dominion, at his leisure.

The Red Army did manage at long last, with an advantage of 40 to 1 in man power, to defeat Finland. But this was not before Finland had demonstrated the weakness of Russia's military machine. Moreover, the effort of winning a partial victory in Finland appears to have disorganized the Russian transport system and to have gravely accentuated an already very unfavorable economic situation. This is indicated by the sharp rise in food prices and the references in the Press to the lateness of the spring sowing, the shortage of tractor drivers, and the need to train women to take the place of men tractor drivers, and to the lowering of wages and drastic increases in production norms in the factories in December 1939.

The Finnish war was probably an accident, Stalin having been confident that this little nation would not dare to fight him. Once involved in the war, he had to win some kind of a victory if he were to retain power at home. It would have been disastrous for him if the Russian people had come to realize that the Soviet colossus, whose foot had been planted so firmly on their necks, had not the strength to wield the weapons created by their unceasing labor. When one lived in the Soviet Union, in spite of one's disillusionment and one's perception of the chaos which reigned in industry and agriculture, one had an idea that the army was something apart—the one efficient Soviet organization. The best of everything went to the army, and the lack of necessities for the civilian population was frequently excused as being due to the need to supply the "defenders of the fatherland." Belief in the strength of the Red Army is, or was, perhaps the one surviving illusion among the Russian people, and belief in the strength of the armed forces at the disposal of the government is a potent deterrent against all thoughts of rebellion.

Once face had been saved in Finland, Stalin abandoned his original project of converting the whole of Finland into a Russian colony administered by Russia's puppet government at Terijoki. Peace was concluded as quickly as possible, and the U.S.S.R. retired into its shell determined to keep out of war at least until she had recuperated from the great effort of defeating the "Finnish White Guards." Fearful of a sharp fall in the 1940 harvest and terrified of an Allied attack on the open oil tanks at Baku, the Soviet Government in the spring of 1940 began anew to proclaim its neutrality, and to give hints to the Allies that she would welcome a renewal of friendly relations. The terrific assault by the Germans in western Europe intensified Soviet fears. The Kremlin had counted upon a long war from which both sides would emerge exhausted. To ensure such an outcome it was necessary to encourage Germany by promising supplies of food, fodder, and war materials, by diplomatic support, and above all by giving her the aid of the Comintern's vast propaganda machinery all over the world.

It may be presumed that Stalin never imagined Germany was capable of breaking the Maginot Line and bringing the war on the Continent to a speedy conclusion. At the height of the battle in Belgium and northern France in May 1940 the Soviet Government therefore began once more to court the Allies and to make it appear that she might enter the war on their side. This move was obviously designed to ensure a continuation of the war should Germany's defeat of France cause England to make a peace leaving Germany the master of Europe and placing Russia at her mercy.

Should this war end in a negotiated peace which would give Germany the control of eastern Europe, we might at last know peace in our time and even in our children's time. All the available evidence goes to prove that Hitler wants a continental empire, and would almost certainly devote the power and organizing ability of the German nation to the development of Russian resources if unhindered by England and France. German control of Russia, not as a colony, but as what one American journalist has described as a dominion, would occupy German energies for a long while to come. So long indeed that the present frustrated, embittered, and perverted postwar Nazi generation would die out before the task had been completed. As regards the Russian people, they would gain, not lose, by being ruled under German tutelage instead of by the incompetent and savage Kremlin clique. Russian national consciousness is weak, and the old middle and upper classes, whose patriotism was alive, have most of them been liquidated. All Stalin's efforts to create patriotism in Russia have been frustrated not only by the backwardness of the country but by the liquidation of the middle classes, and by the social system. The peasants and a majority of workers have been so disillusioned, have been driven down to such semibrute material conditions of existence, that any regime which gave them enough to eat, rooms to live in, and clothes to their backs would be an improvement. Shocking as this may sound to the "Friends of the Soviet Union," German hegemony would be a boon to the Russian masses, if only because German National Socialism ensures the full development and utilization of resources, and Stalin's National Socialism does not. If you have to be a slave of the state, it is better to belong to a state which feeds you and clothes you than to one which starves you. Moreover, once the economy of scarcity had been developed by German organizational genius and technical knowledge, into an economy of abundance both in Germany and Russia, freedom might at last be won by the Russian as well as the German people.

Of course, should German arms be completely victorious, but Germany be faced by a hostile United States excluding her trade from the New World, she could not be content with dominion over eastern Europe and the U.S.S.R. But if Germany were no longer blockaded or boycotted the more moderate wing of the Nazi party, in alliance with the army leaders and the conservatives, might get the upper hand. Central and eastern Europe run by men like Schacht would not afford worse conditions of life to the people of the small nations of eastern Europe than did the Polish dictatorship, or than do the Hungarian feudal landowners, the corrupt Rumanian tyranny, or the Serbian oligarchy. The Germans might, indeed probably would, raise the standard of life of the millions who inhabit eastern Europe. Nazi excesses, brutalities, and megalomania might become a thing of the past, as have the excesses and cruelties which marked British and French colonial conquests up to less than a century ago.

Of course, a free federation of Europe would be infinitely more desirable, but the chance of that was lost in the years following the first World War. The choice now before us is no longer, since the defeat of France, one between such a free federation created after an Allied victory in which the forces of reason, humanity, and liberalism have survived the terrible horrors of modern war, and a Nazi domination of Europe. The choice before us is in all probability one between

Nazi domination of the greater part of Europe and the chaos and misery of revolution and a Stalinist victory.

No one not blinded by simple catchwords, or a naïve belief in the superior natural virtue of the Anglo-Saxon and French peoples, or by a supernatural belief that good must conquer evil, can now believe that a British victory gained with American aid can be won short of a cost in men, in starvation and disease and destruction over most of Europe, which would nullify the gain.

With France defeated and almost the whole continent of Europe under Nazi or Fascist domination, a successful British—or Anglo-American—blockade of Germany means the starvation of the French, Belgian, Dutch, Norwegian and other lately Allied peoples, not the starvation of Germany. A starving Europe means an anarchic, revolutionary Europe where Bolshevism may be victorious. The Communists of today aim at the establishment of their life-destroying "socialism" through war and chaos. They do not care how many millions die in battle or through famine in the process. Already in May 1940 Kalinin, titular head of the Soviet Government, called upon the workers of the world to prepare for the day of revolution which is coming. As the war spreads and brings misery to more and more people, communist propaganda is likely to be more and more successful. Europe may become something like what H. G. Wells pictured in his *Shape of Things to Come,* with millions dead and dying and the rest reduced to the life of brutes, like the Russian countryside in 1931-33.

In the ghastly destruction of modern war, if long continued, all civilized standards, all ethical values, all remnants of international law for the preservation of civilian life, will perish *on both sides*. A new Dark Age will have descended on Europe even more horrible than that which followed the break-up of the Roman Empire and the barbarian invasions. In those distant days the Mongol Huns followed the Teutons and were infinitely more savage and destructive. Today Stalin's Tartar-Slavs stand behind the Teutons and threaten the world with a despotism infinitely more terrible. A war to the finish between England and Germany might be followed by the domination of the U.S.S.R. over an exhausted and ruined Europe. It is worth recalling that Marx wrote in 1867 that if the continent of Europe persisted in capitalist excesses, the submission of man to the machine, the armaments race, the piling up of public debts, etc., then "the rejuvenation of Europe by means of the knout and by a compulsory infusion of

Kalmuk blood predicted so gravely by the half-Russian and wholly Muscovite Herzen... would end by becoming inevitable."

These words may be more prophetic than Marx's dreams of the emancipation of the human race by the proletariat.

I shall no doubt be accused of being prejudiced by my personal experiences in Russia, or called emotional and far-fetched in my view of what may be the alternative to Hitler. But those who shut their eyes to the horrible realities of Stalin's Russia as depicted by the abler pens of other authors who cannot be accused of being prejudiced by the loss of their loved ones or of their ideals, and who refuse to see that Stalinism is even more of a threat than Hitlerism to all the values they hold dear, are no less prejudiced, and I fear will be proved more blinded by their emotions and prejudices.

Emotions, prejudices, and blind faith in Soviet Russia did more to precipitate this war than any profit-seeking or "imperialist interests" in England, France, and the United States. Those who thought of themselves as liberals, progressives, and socialists, are more responsible than the conservatives and "reactionaries" for the destruction of our liberal individualistic civilization over a large part of Europe. In their blindness to the horrors of Stalin's Russia and their hatred of Nazi tyranny, they did their utmost to drive England and France into a war for which they were unprepared, and which in any case they could not hope to win except by the sacrifice of the values to preserve which they fought. Would it not have served the interests of liberals and democrats better to have let Germany establish her dominion over eastern Europe than to have clamored for a war which has destroyed France?

Liberals, socialists, even a substantial proportion of the "capitalist Press" in the United States, continue to repeat the fiction that Britain and France brought disaster upon themselves by their refusal to line up with Russia against Germany until it was too late. All the evidence points to the conclusion that there was never any possibility of such an alliance. Stalin, admiring and fearing Nazi Germany, which he knew possessed all the terrible advantages and few of the disadvantages of his own regime, was determined never to fight her. As soon as there was a prospect of war against Germany, he redoubled his efforts to ally himself with Hitler instead of with France and England. Championing collective security at Geneva and lambasting the British and French conservatives for their appeasement policy was one thing; joining up with them to fight Germany was a very different matter. Not only did Stalin know that after his drastic purges the Red Army was in no condition to fight a first-class enemy, but his whole outlook and method of government naturally inclined him to prefer Nazi Germany to the Western democracies, and to feel confident that totalitarian Germany would prove strong enough not to be defeated by the Allies except in a war so prolonged and destructive as to prepare the way for the complete breakdown of "capitalist" civilization in Europe.

The proof of this lies in his refusal to cement a military alliance with England and France, by putting up conditions which these powers could not agree to without destroying their own case as the defenders of the liberties of Europe—subjugation of the Baltic states and probably also the acquisition of the part of Poland which Russia obtained from Germany.

The old Comintern and fellow-traveler argument that the U.S.S.R. turned to an alliance with Germany in despair at the refusal of the democracies to halt German aggression simply does not hold water. Stalin's alliance with Hitler came about precisely at the moment when the democracies had decided to fight whenever Germany next attacked a small nation.

Chamberlain's cabinet may or may not have been aware of the secret negotiations going on in Berlin at the same time as the open ones in Moscow, where first a diplomatic and then a military mission had been sent by Britain and France; or they may have felt too certain that the Nazis would continue to refuse to ally themselves with the Communists. In any case, the pressure of the Opposition in England and of American public opinion must have prevented the British Government from saving both the peace of Europe and the interests of Britain and France. If the democracies, even at that late hour, had come to terms with Germany instead of futilely seeking an alliance with Russia, Germany might have confined her aggression to eastern Europe. For all the evidence available suggests that Hitler endeavored until the last moment to avoid an alliance with Stalin in the hope of securing a continuation of the British isolationist policy from the affairs of eastern Europe.

The Comintern had, however, been only too successful in its duping of public opinion in the West. It had succeeded in convincing the West that Communism and Naziism were irreconcilably opposed, that the one was an angel of light—or at least harmless and comparatively civilized—and the other a devil; and that Hitler was bluffing and that he would never dare to risk the arbitrament of war against the western Powers. It had also succeeded in convincing even conservatives who had few illusions and less love for the U.S.S.R. that Nazi Germany would not be satisfied with a continental empire but would inevitably, when once she had digested eastern Europe, turn upon France and England. This fear, combined with pressure from the Opposition at home and the influence exerted over British policy by the United States, sufficed to make Chamberlain's government abandon the policy of appeasement and enter upon the fatal policy of seeking an alliance with one totalitarian tyranny against another, only to find them both joining hands against the "pluto-democracies."

Stalin's Popular Front policy could not, of course, have been so eminently successful in helping to bring on the Second World War had it not been for the fact that capitalist democracy had for long been functioning too unsatisfactorily to satisfy large numbers of people in western Europe and the United States. Economic crises, unemployment, the decay of faith in the capitalist system, made many people wish to believe that the U.S.S.R. had proved that a new social system—socialism—is possible, workable, efficient, and productive of well-being, peace, and even liberty "of a new kind." If so many people had not believed the communist myth about Russia, they would have been allergic to communist propaganda for a holy war by Britain and France the real object of which was to make the world safe for Stalin.

Similarly, had it not been for the decay of faith in the capitalist system and the questioning or denial of its values in Germany, Italy, and elsewhere, there would be no fascist and Nazi dictatorships waging successful aggressive war on the present tremendous scale. Nor would there have been in France such bitter internal dissension, such chronic internal crisis and class war as to cause her military defeat.

But perception of the underlying causes of this war, economic and social and "ideological," does not absolve the intellectuals of the Western world from a large share of responsibility for the holocaust. Had they been better informed, more rational, and less emotional we might perhaps have been able to exert a little more control over our destinies. We should at least have known our own weakness and the strength of our enemies. However, the war seems to be proving the truth of the Nazi philosophy that men are not governed by reason but by emotion and instinct. At the time of writing, American liberals, isolationists, and pacifists by the thousand are repudiating their own theories and past convictions, overwhelmed by the emotional reaction to the defeat of France, the horrors of the war, and the fear of Germany. Stukas are more potent than rational convictions.

The view I have expressed above concerning the events which led to the war is contrary to that of most of the great array of American reporters, columnists, commentators, and authors of best sellers. Indeed, it is one of the astonishing phenomena of our age that the Gunthers,* Sheeans, Dorothy Thompsons, Lippmanns, *et hoc genus omne,* can continue to wield the influence they do over American public opinion after having so often been proved entirely wrong in their analysis of the world situation, and of British and French and Russian policies; and in particular in their verdicts upon the strength of Russia and the weakness and vulnerability of Nazi Germany. A fanatical hatred of Hitler, ignorance of economics and of historical forces, combined, in the case of writers like Dorothy Thompson, with uncontrolled emotional judgments, helped to delude the American people concerning the likelihood of a German victory should the French and British governments give way to the clamor for war against fascism. Hatred, emotion, and prejudice can never produce wisdom, any more than a blind, uncritical love such as inspired the plan-mad "liberal" fellow travelers up to the outbreak of the war.

In England and France these delusions were less widespread than in America, for in Europe irresponsible popular journalists wield less influence. Nevertheless, in England and France also the Comintern had succeeded in more subtle ways in influencing not merely journalists but also politicians of both the Right and the Left.

Hatred and the desire for revenge have never been, and cannot be, the basis for wise judgments. It was natural, indeed inevitable, that the Jews, being human, desired revenge upon their oppressors. The fact that such revenge could only be wreaked on the Nazis at the cost of infinite misery and wholesale death among the Jews who remained in Germany and Austria and Bohemia, was forgotten. A war on Germany would inevitably bring yet greater persecution, starvation, and death upon the Jews who had not been able to escape abroad. The Allied blockade designed to starve Germany out would inevitably first starve the Jews, since their Aryan oppressors would naturally feed their own women and children and let the Jews die of famine once there was not enough food to go round.

The tragedy of all war, and in particular of modern war, is that the innocent suffer more than the guilty. Desiring revenge upon the

* Perhaps it is not fair to place John Gunther in this company; but in respect to Russia his writings so closely reflected the views of Walter Duranty of the *New York Times* that he too played his part in spreading the Great Soviet Illusion. However, a journalist who takes the whole world as his field of knowledge cannot but be something of a chameleon.

Nazi Government to be accomplished by war meant condemning millions of innocent people to death on both sides, with no certainty at all of inflicting any suffering upon the Nazi rulers themselves.

For all my hatred of the Stalinist regime in Russia, I know a war upon the Russian people would accomplish no good and avenge no wrongs. The Russians themselves are suffering in greater degree than I ever did from the tyranny of their own government. Of what use would it be to fight *them?* I hope to see the collapse of the Stalin government within my lifetime, but this is more likely to come from within than from without—or it may come by the decomposition of the Kremlin clique after its acceptance of German aid and German tutelage.

Of course, the violent Hitler-haters will retort that Russia menaces no foreign nations. Even this has now ceased to be true, but in any case why should one confine one's sympathies to the Czechs, Poles, Dutch, Belgians, and other nations whom the Nazis have just begun to oppress in the same manner, but somewhat less ruthlessly than Stalin oppresses the hundred-odd races of the Russian Soviet Empire?

It might have been thought that the Russo-German Pact would have rudely awakened the Western world from its dreams about the peace-loving "socialist fatherland." It did cause a violent rush of disillusioned fellow travelers away from the communist fold. But subsequent events have proved that the effect of the poison of Stalinist propaganda could not quickly be thrown out of the liberal system. Men cannot readily atune their minds to a complete reversal of long-cherished political conceptions, least of all when their country or their ideals are in danger, and wish-fulfillment colors their thinking even more than in normal times. Hence it took a long time for the English and also the Americans to realize that the Russo-German Pact was more than a temporary and brittle accord between two irreconcilable antagonists. From September until early in 1940 conservatives and labor men and liberals, clinging to the old idea of the Soviet Union as a bulwark against Hitlerism, maintained that Russia's gains were Germany's losses, and thought that Hitler, having let the Bolshevik djinn out of the bottle, could not put him back again. Consequently almost the whole of the British Press watched the U.S.S.R.'s advance into Poland and the establishment of her dominion over Latvia, Estonia, and Lithuania without misgivings. The Left justified her as the liberator of oppressed peasants and workers, or excused her bullying of the Baltic states as necessary to her security; while the Right proclaimed that we could sleep easy in our beds because Stalin and the Red Army would take care of the Nazis in eastern Europe. The fashionable view in Britain was that expressed by Bernard Shaw, who assured the readers of the *New Statesman and Nation* that "Stalin has taken Hitler by the scruff of the neck." Winston Churchill, who might have been expected to know better, said in his broadcast on "The First Month of the War" that, although he regretted that the Russian armies were not "standing on their present lines as the friends and allies of Poland," he welcomed their entry into Poland and realized it was necessary "for the safety of Russia against the Nazi menace." Like the *Daily Worker,* the *New Statesman,* the *News Chronicle,* and even the majority of the conservative newspapers, Churchill was sure that Stalin's acts of aggression were aimed against Germany, and assured his listeners that "an Eastern front has been created which Nazi Germany does not dare assail." The same view was expressed in the United States, not only in journals like the *New Republic* and the *Nation,* but in the great daily papers.

The mistake made, not only by Churchill but by almost everyone in both Britain and the United States, was to identify Russia's national interest with Stalin's interest. It was argued that it could not possibly be to Russia's national interest to help Germany to a victory which would make her the master of Europe. It was thought that the key to an understanding of Soviet policy was Russia's national interest; and hence Churchill, Halifax, and apparently even Chamberlain, were confident that "the community of interests which exists between England, France, and Russia" must cause the U.S.S.R. to keep Germany out of eastern Europe. They were further blinded as to the true nature of the pact between Hitler and Stalin by their belief in the strength and power of the U.S.S.R. and its military machine. Communist propaganda over the years and gigantic military parades in Moscow before diplomats and newspapermen had done their work. Even those who disliked the U.S.S.R. were certain that it had a powerful army and air force well supplied and equipped.

Stalin is not the first ruler in history to have sacrificed his country's interest to his own, and no ruler has greater need to conciliate his most dangerous foreign foes in order to cope with those among his own people who would deprive him of his power. Stalin two years ago purged the Red Army not only of its best generals but also of more than half of its officer corps. To maintain himself in power he has executed or sent to concentration camps not only the founders of the Soviet state and the leaders of the Bolshevik Revolution, but also the engineers, the technicians, the administrators, the "specialists" of all kinds who alone could ensure the efficient working of Soviet industry and transport. All those suspected of questioning ukases of the Leader, all those who would not be his yes-men and blindly carry out his orders, however ruinous to the country, have been liquidated. Having thus strengthened his own position but irreparably weakened Russia, it was natural that Stalin should come to terms with the strongest and most aggressive of his external enemies. And having made his pact with Hitler it is also natural that, Hitler being the stronger, it is Stalin who follows and Hitler who leads. If the alternative to becoming Hitler's vassal and allowing Russia to be converted into a German dominion, is involvement in the main European war, Stalin will not hesitate to submit to Hitler; for a real war would destroy him as it destroyed the Tsars.

It required the hammer blows of the Soviet invasion of Finland to open the eyes of the British to the realities of the situation. Only then did they dimly begin to realize that a war to do away with Hitler would avail them little if Stalin took his place. But even at this juncture many voices were raised warning against any such action being taken in aid of Finland as might draw closer the bonds uniting Stalin and Hitler. The full consequences of Russia's weakness, as displayed in the Finnish war, were not drawn in Britain. Although the more realistic and hard-headed French discussed the advantages of action against Russia at Murmansk and in the Black Sea as a method of shortening the war against Germany, the British did not favor it. Some bombing raids on Baku, where oil is stored in open tanks, would have been a far more effective way of cutting off German war supplies than the ill-fated Norwegian expedition; but the Labor Opposition in England would obviously never have countenanced an attack on the U.S.S.R.

Until the Finnish war there was almost a ban on anti-Soviet articles in the British Press. The desire of the Left to cling to the tattered remnants of its faith in Stalin and the "socialist fatherland" was reinforced on the Right by the belief among conservatives that if Britain and France did not tread warily they might bring in the "mighty" Russian army on the German side, whereas if they were very polite to Stalin and condoned Russian aggression they might yet succeed in detaching Stalin from Hitler's embrace.

From Left to Right, British politicians and journalists made subtle distinctions between the nature of German and Russian aggression. Whereas the Nazis were just plain wicked, the Bolsheviks were merely fortifying themselves against a German attack in the future, or nobly rescuing Poles, Jews, and Balts from Nazi domination. So far as one who did not arrive in the United States until the end of 1939 can judge, American journals until December followed the British lead in excusing, or even finding comfort in, Stalin's acts of aggression. By April 1940 Winston Churchill was again holding out the hand of friendship to Russia, saying in a broadcast that Britain's affair was not with her. The liberal *New Statesman* went further, arguing that if only England and France had encouraged the U.S.S.R. to take what she considered the "minimum necessary to security" they might have secured her as an ally.

If the U.S.S.R. had been powerful, as was once supposed, the effect of the Allied attitude toward her might have enabled Stalin to acquire that hegemony over Europe which the French and British sought to deny to Hitler by force of arms. Had the Soviet colossus not had feet of clay, the European war might well have become one to make the world safe for Stalin. A Russia treated as a neutral by the Allies and courted by Germany, able to profit from the war to extend her boundaries but committed to neither side, might have become the arbiter of Europe or able, as the faithful Communists abroad still dream, to extend the Union of Soviet Socialist Republics over the whole Continent. But such an outcome as this was only conceivable on the assumption that the U.S.S.R. was a mighty, contented country with a functioning socialist economy to serve as a model for all mankind. Such a Soviet Union never existed except in the imagination of naïve American, British, and other foreign Communists, shortsighted tourists, and dupes of communist propaganda, and Jews and other Nazi victims, who were mentally and psychologically constrained to think the U.S.S.R. a paradise because its enemy, Nazi Germany, was a hell. The real U.S.S.R. has all along been a land of bitter poverty, social injustice, muddle, waste, and cruelty.

It is likely to have been the Soviet Union's weakness which led Stalin onto the perilous path of aggression in a desperate attempt to maintain his power at home. The Russian people, who long since abandoned hope of the dawn of the day of socialist plenty and justice, terrified by the purges and the ever-present fear of the concentration camp, ill-fed, ill-clothed, and ill-housed, were to be heartened by the tonic of national glory. Stalin's power, founded upon force and terror, was to be firmly rooted in the hearts of his people by the extension of Russia's boundaries to their old Tsarist limits by a series of bloodless conquests and by a revival of Pan-Slav dreams of Balkan hegemony. Those who still dreamed the forbidden "Trotskyist" dream of international socialism were to be conciliated—or converted into Stalinists—by the forcible extension of the boundaries of the Soviet "socialist" state. What the Comintern had failed to do, the Red Army would accomplish. That unity of the workers of the world to which the Stalinists still pay lip service was to be achieved by the subjection of workers, capitalists, and peasants alike to the dictator of the Kremlin.

The tyrant to whom none dares speak the truth, and who has for long been accustomed to think that if he is ruthless enough no one will stand up to him, can hardly have imagined that Finland would dare to resist his enormous army. The astute Ribbentrop may have opened dazzling prospects of national glory to Stalin, sitting uneasy in the Kremlin, fearful always that however vigilant his spies and informers, the anger and despair of his people may yet unseat him.

Stalin's conceptions of socialism are as far removed from Lenin's and Marx's as his Red Imperialism is from their hopes of world revolution. But if Europe is reduced by the war to the same miserable condition as Russia, his policy may be more successful than theirs.

The ghost of international socialism, established through the revolutionary action of the united workers of the world, haunts only the tombs and the concentration camps where Lenin's companions and followers lie dead, or suffer a living death. But if the idea of an international socialist society established through the overthrow of capitalism from within lives on only among the small band of Trotskyists, the Stalinist conception of a Soviet empire established over the ruins of Europe may prove to have some dynamic force. Can Stalin substitute for the torn banner of world revolution a new standard on which the old eagle of the Romanovs is painted red? Can the personal interests of Stalin be reconciled with a revolutionary policy which might at any moment involve Russia in a real war, and which would almost certainly sweep him from power even if it did not lead to the collapse of the U.S.S.R.? Will Stalin, in deadly fear of a victorious Germany, try to revive the specter of world revolution to destroy the Nazis; or has he already resigned himself to becoming Hitler's puppet? The moves of the dictator in the Kremlin are hard to predict but Russia's weakness precludes the possibility of any strong resistance to Germany.

One who has lived in the U.S.S.R. finds it hard to believe that the Soviet Government is capable of maintaining a military expedition on a large scale for any length of time, or that the Soviet transport system is equal to the task of transporting supplies for a long campaign without depriving the cities of food supplies. At the best of times such supplies are barely adequate; war must soon bring famine to the industrial workers. It is even doubtful whether German military experts, technicians, and efficiency experts could bring order into the hopeless confusion of Soviet economy for several years.

It is unlikely that the German Government has ever had the same illusions as the British and the French concerning the strength of Russia under Stalin's rule, else they would never have encouraged her to extend her dominion over the Baltic countries. But the Nazis may not have realized that Russia was so weak that even Finland could resist her. It may be true, as the Swedish Press suggested, that the Nazis were at that time playing a gigantic poker game to force the Allies to make peace by the prospect of the U.S.S.R. dominating the whole of northern Europe.

If the policy of the Allies were as realistic as Hitler's, less colored by out-of-date political conceptions, and less unconsciously influenced by communist propaganda, they would long since have realized both that Stalin's Russia would be of little or no use to them as an ally, should the Soviet Government offer to reverse its policy, and that even less faith is to be placed in Stalin's word than in Hitler's.

Hitler, no doubt, is confident that he will have no difficulty in forcing Stalin to disgorge his conquests, if and when Germany defeats England. In the meantime Hitler may well consider that Soviet aggression in eastern Europe and the Balkans serves a useful purpose. The small states there fear Soviet Russian domination more than they fear the Nazis, so that the Russian menace drives them to seek German protection. It must obviously be to Germany's advantage to establish her dominion over eastern Europe as the savior from Bolshevism instead of as a conqueror.

However, the ironies of history are incalculable. Should Stalin, in panic fear of Germany, or on account of the desperate need of food in Russia,* send the Red Army too far outside the borders of Russia, the Soviet Union may yet unwittingly save the British Empire. For should Germany and Italy deem it necessary—if only in order to save the food, oil, and other resources of the Balkans for themselves—to turn their arms on Russia while England is still unconquered, they might offer a peace to England enabling the latter to save herself and the Empire. Anyone who desires the preservation of England, and of what England stands for, must hope that she would grasp any such chance to make peace, and not court her own destruction by prolong-

* The fact that Bessarabia was expecting a bumper harvest was, no doubt, one reason why the Soviet Government seized this territory in June 1940.

ing the war with Germany in the false hope that an alliance with the Soviet Union could enable her to defeat Germany.

Even if it could, of what use would it be to save Europe from Hitlerism only to see it fall a prey to Stalinism?

Whether western Europe, and perhaps also America, follow the Russian or the German road, or are able to preserve civil liberty and a democratic form of government while adapting their economic and social order to the conditions of our age, is likely to depend upon whether or not peace is soon made with Germany. Should England succeed in blockading the Nazi-dominated continent of Europe and there create famine on such a scale as to produce violent revolution, it is to be feared that Stalinism will be established over the ruins of European civilization.

England now sees Hitler's Germany as the main "enemy of humanity." But Stalin's more barbarous Muscovite despotism may be the alternative to Hitlerism on the continent of Europe. The U.S.S.R. is too weak to conquer Europe but may yet inherit dominion over it as the result of a war to the bitter end between England and Germany.

At the other side of the world another Asiatic despotism, Japan, also awaits joyfully the ruin of Europe hoping to fulfill *her* world ambitions.

Should the war not soon be concluded the historian of the future may wonder why it was not more obvious to those of our generation that compromise with some evils would have been better than the creation of even greater evils by a long and destructive war in which European civilization was destroyed.

CHAPTER XIII

CAN NATIONAL SOCIALISM BE TAMED?

THE SECOND WORLD WAR may prove to be the nemesis of nationalism, swollen into such megalomaniac forms in Germany and Italy and Japan as to destroy the civilization which gave it birth. Or it may lay the foundations of a wider and more creative continental civilization based on a more rational social order. We who are living in this explosive and destructive age cannot know whether we are going to succumb to barbarism or whether we are on the threshold of a higher form of civilization.

When the feudal order broke up in Europe, the "Corsican ogre" played the same role as the "Nazi beast" today, and there were many who felt that civilization was being destroyed. Napoleon was defeated, but the national state and the capitalist social order, both affording for a long time the opportunity for great material and moral progress, conquered. The present war has already forced England to place both capital and labor under the absolute control of the state, thus establishing the foundations of a national socialist order. True that this is conceived of as an emergency measure "for the duration," but it will obviously be impossible to revert to a free capitalist order when the war comes to an end. For one thing, the Labour party will be determined to retain the new order and will be too powerful to be disregarded. The British "dictator" is, however, not an irresponsible "Leader" but a government of all parties appointed by the elected representatives of the people in Parliament, who retain the right to depose the dictatorial government and appoint another.

The fact that this English form of national socialism has been established by consent of all classes and parties, and that labor is participating equally with capital, may also help to ensure the survival of democratic rights and civil liberties. But should England find herself in a truly desperate situation economically as well as militarily, political liberty is likely to disappear as completely as in Germany.

It is just possible that we shall learn to accomplish in a free way the same miracles of organization as the Nazis have accomplished by tyranny, and to set up an economy for peace as scientific, planned, and unwasteful of labor and resources and intelligence as the German National Socialist war economy. It is possible, but it will be the hardest task mankind has yet been faced with, and it exacts a fearless examination of the virtues as well as the defects of the "Hitlerism" we detest, and of the fundamental causes for the present Armageddon.

Nationalism, while creating political democracy, also created total war. Since Napoleon, peoples have fought against peoples, not dynasties against dynasties. Mercenary armies have been replaced by conscript armies, and in the first World War it came to be realized that the men and women who make the guns and shells are as vital a part of the nation's fighting strength as the soldiers. Nazi Germany, wanting to make a national effort so intense and all-embracing as to overcome the material advantages of her opponents, has carried the process to its apotheosis by instituting a military socialist system under which the whole population and all national resources could not only be mobilized for war, but regimented for it during years of preparation. Hence her greatly superior striking force and the need for the democracies to imitate her methods and her system in order to withstand her.

For success in totalitarian war it is also essential that the population should be confident in its strength, in its leaders, and in its "destiny," and be sure of victory, or at least think victory probable. To ensure such social cohesion, a government may rely upon the spontaneous confidence engendered by past victories, upon natural national conceit or national ignorance, or it may only be able to ensure unanimity of purpose by terror, and by misinforming its subjects and creating artificial barriers to keep out knowledge of the facts and of enemy propaganda. The democracies rely, or have relied so far, upon the former free method of waging war. Germany and Russia rely upon the second method.

There is, however, a difference between enforcing by tyrannical means and misinformation a uniformity of belief which is already widespread because it results from past experience, and enforcing conformity to beliefs which are so patently false that no one holds them to be true. The Nazi Government does the former, the Soviet Government the latter. Not even the Gestapo could force the German people to put the effort they have done into winning the war unless they were at least partially convinced that their national existence was at stake, nor can the courage and initiative displayed by German airmen and soldiers be inspired by terror. Had one-tenth of the national enthusiasm, confidence, and efficiency displayed by the Germans in this war been displayed by the Russians in "constructing socialism," the U.S.S.R.

would today be a prosperous country without any further need for the O.G.P.U. to enforce the orders of the government and dragoon the workers like unwilling conscripts in the "battle for socialism."

German National Socialism is today in its explosive stage; at the stage when the creed which raised the Nazis to power is believed in by a sufficient number of the German people to produce a very high degree of social cohesion, and an excellent morale in warfare. Germany is at the pre-1931 stage of communism in Russia.

The fanatical nationalist creed of the Nazis can perhaps best be compared with that of the Arab nation under the Prophet Mohammed. It is unlikely to be fervently believed after the present tremendous war effort has been made, even if that effort is successful. If Germany should in the end be defeated, belief in the creed will be destroyed; but there is no other creed to take its place to ensure social cohesion. So that what is likely to ensue is anarchy, or the seizure of power by a desperate minority supported by the U.S.S.R. It is almost certainly the fear of this which has kept the most intelligent and least fanatic Germans loyal to the government in spite of their fears and their hatred of totalitarian tyranny. Thus the strength of the Nazis rests upon their success in propagating their creed among the masses, and upon the fear of their opponents in Germany of what might follow the overthrow of the Nazi Government.

Up to the closing year of the First Five Year Plan there was a similar faith and confidence among the Russian workers. Although the official creed was never shared by the peasants, the workers did for a time believe that they were constructing socialism, just as the sincerest Nazi members and their adherents believe they are going to construct a new and better European order under German hegemony. The Russian Communist party, however, destroyed belief among the masses in its own creed by its stupidities, its senseless cruelties, and its blatant self-seeking. Since 1932 the Russian workers have understood that socialism was being created only for their masters, and ceased for the most part to believe that a better life awaited them in the future if they sacrificed themselves in the present. Disillusionment, apathy, or smoldering rebellion among the Russian workers has since 1932 impelled the Soviet Government to rely on ever more fiercely repressive measures to secure obedience, on penalties instead of enthusiasm to ensure "labor discipline" and hard work.

The Nazis still believe in their own creed, but the Bolsheviks have ceased to believe in theirs. The Nazis have changed the "party line" only once, when they allied themselves with Communist Russia; and the change was not fundamental, since their basic aim remained the same: the aggrandizement of Germany. The Russian Communists, however, have changed their line so often that even the leaders are skeptical about their aim, and the masses are completely apathetic. There used to be a joke in Moscow about two Party members who were being considered for the same post. The higher Party authorities knew that one sincerely believed in the correctness of the official Party line at the time, whereas the other was, they felt, a cynical unbeliever. They chose the second without hesitation because he could be counted on to change quickly and remain "loyal" to Stalin when next the Party line changed.

I stress here the different stages of development and the great sincerity of the Nazi movement, because the greater strength of the Nazi creed is likely to subordinate the communist creed to itself, rather than vice versa. The communist creed is already dead or transformed into a national socialist creed, except among the small band of Trotskyists whom history has passed by. World revolution today means National Socialist revolution, German or Russian; and the survival of civilization is likely to be decided according to whether or not the former can be tamed and humanized and adapted to peaceful instead of violent change.

I never believed that England could destroy Nazi Germany in war without herself being destroyed, either physically or morally. But should the Nazi Government fail to reward the German people for their sacrifices and to conciliate the conquered by starting to organize for peace instead of for war, no doubt there would be the same breakdown of morale in Germany as in Russia. That in its turn would put an end to the Nazi empire; for if the Germans no longer support it, the small subject nations—who are not backward and ignorant Russians, Tartars, Turkmenians, and Caucasians, but either highly civilized or comparatively civilized peoples—would win their liberty. Whether or not Germany can hold her conquests will depend upon whether the Nazi leaders are intelligent enough to consolidate their gains by discarding the theory of racial superiority and abandoning the glorification of force and violence once these theories have served their purpose of girding the German people for the conquest of Europe. If the Nazis prove too stupid, or too drunk with power and the lust of conquest to stop, the inevitable reaction at home against the continued sacrifices demanded of the German people and the strength of the armed resistance and determination against them abroad will bring them to disaster.

Again it has yet to be seen whether the Nazi leaders will prove as corrupt and self-seeking as the Stalinist bureaucracy; whether or not the profits of conquest and of a semisocialist economy will be utilized in the main to raise the standard of life of the German people and of the conquered peoples, or to provide a luxurious life for the ruling bureaucracy.

These are political and psychological factors. From the purely economic point of view, the German national economy is clearly more easily able to switch from producing for war to producing for peace than is a competitive capitalist economy. The Nazi Government can, if it wishes, command investment for the production of houses, clothing, tractors, and machinery for the production of other consumption goods, instead of fortifications, guns, bombers, and shells. A productive apparatus working for profit and uncontrolled by the government finds it difficult to turn from the production of swords to that of plowshares, so that a deep economic crisis and mass unemployment always follow on even a victorious war. Germany can, if her rulers desire it, reconstruct Europe and rebuild its devastated cities more rapidly and with less financial difficulty than the capitalist states. Whether or not the Nazis will desire to do so, or will prefer to continue utilizing the machinery and labor power at their disposal to produce more armaments for further conquest is the question upon which the future of civilization in Europe will depend. There is, however, some comfort to be found in the reflection that, whereas a free economy producing for profit must continually seek new markets to maintain the rate of profit, state capitalism or national socialism can, if those who control the state desire it, concentrate in the main upon its own markets and need not continually endeavor to widen the area of its economic domination, once it has secured a continental empire and abundant raw-material resources.

It is usual to say that the Nazis will never be satisfied, and to picture the Germans as a peculiar people, more aggressive and power-loving and chauvinist than the British and French and other "peace-loving powers." This argument takes no account of past history or of the fundamental causes of German aggression. In the past Britain and France were just as aggressive, else they could never have acquired their great colonial empires. The scramble for colonies went on merrily all through the nineteenth century and came to an end only when most of Asia and Africa had been divided up. By the opening years of the twentieth century England and France had not only bitten off about as much as they could chew, but realized that further colonial conquest must lead to war between the imperialist powers. Hence the Open Door policy proclaimed for China by the United States at Britain's instigation. Moreover, the ease and security which colonial exploitation had produced in England and France conduced to a pacific temper and a desire to sit down and enjoy life. Why should we assume that the Germans would react any differently to the possession of a great empire? The argument that they are peculiarly aggressive by nature simply does not hold water. Until the Napoleonic wars the Germans had little national consciousness and were regarded as hopelessly peaceful people by the more "virile" French. French aggression from Louis XIV to Napoleon finally galvanized the Germans into abandoning their old pleasant unnationalist and pacific ways. They formed themselves into a nation under Prussian leadership, but by that time most of the "uncivilized" races and peoples had already been conquered by Britain, France, Holland, Belgium, and the United States. Since there were no more colored peoples to conquer, the Germans were driven, first in 1914-18, to attempt a redivision of Asia and Africa through the defeat of France and England, and then from 1933 onward to try to form a European empire.

However spurious Hitler's self-appointed mission to recast the world may sound to us, it obviously has an appeal for idealistic youthful Germans no less potent than the communist appeal for an international socialist order. Many young Germans no doubt fervently believe that it is Germany's "divine mission" under Hitler to unite Europe and create a new aristocracy of valor to rule it, as the Teutonic aristocracy ruled the nations of Europe in the Middle Ages. Hitler sees the concept of race superseding the concept of the nation, which is, one must admit, an equally artificial division, but one for which men have long sacrificed their own lives and those of others, as the Germans are now doing in the name of a racial ideal. According to Rauschning, Hitler has said:

> France carried her great Revolution beyond her borders with the conception of the nation. With the conception of race, National Socialism will carry its revolution abroad and recast the world. Just as the conception of the nation was a revolutionary change from the purely dynastic feudal states, and just as it introduced a biological conception, that of the people, so our own revolution is a further step, or rather the final step, in the rejection of the historic order and the recognition of purely biological values.... The process of dissolution and reordering will run its course in every nation, no matter how old and firmly knit its social system may be. The active

section in the nations, the militantly Nordic section, will rise again and become the ruling element over these shopkeepers and pacifists, these puritans and speculators and busybodies.*

He goes on to say that only the "tough and manly" element will endure in the terrible times coming, and that eventually a pact will be made with the "new men" in England, France, and America, when the latter "fall into line" with the vast process of the reordering of the world and voluntarily play their part in it. "There will not then," he concludes, "be much left of the clichés of nationalism, and precious little among us Germans." Rauschning also suggests that to the Nazi leaders the concept of race is a useful fiction upon which to build a German imperial system in Europe, not an actual belief.

Horrible as the Nazi racial theory sounds to us, it is in fact only an extension of firmly rooted prejudices of our own. It was the implicit belief in western Europe and in the United States that the white race is superior to the colored, and has a divine right to rule over the latter, which formed the moral justification first for Negro slavery, and later for the conquests which created the British and French empires. Even today it is the implicit belief that the conquest of colored peoples is altogether different, morally and politically, from the conquest of "white" peoples, which makes Germany's offense seem so much more heinous than anyone else's, and which gives rise to the widespread belief that the Germans are peculiarly militaristic, aggressive, and wicked. This belief also explains why Italy's conquest of Abyssinia was never held to have put her "outside the pale of civilized nations" like Germany; and why Americans who recoil in horror at Nazi Germany feel few qualms of conscience although they know that the United States supplied Japan with most of the metal and oil she used for three years to spread death and destruction and famine over China. Not only the British and French, but also the Americans regard the Far Eastern war as in an entirely different category from acts of aggression in Europe.

The wholesale bombing of Chinese civilians by the Japanese, the cold-blooded massacre of prisoners and male civilians at Nanking and elsewhere aroused a good deal of indignation in the United States, but the profits of American junk merchants, oil interests, and others supplying Japan were not interfered with. By 1939 little attention was being paid to China's sufferings, and few were as impressed at the sufferings of China's fifty million refugees, dying daily in their thou-

* *Voice of Destruction.*

sands, as at the sufferings of the victims of German aggression. Newspaper correspondents in northern France and Belgium reported in all innocence what they termed "the greatest migratory movement of a people in the history of the world," although the *total* population of France is little greater than the number of refugees in China.

There is an underlying conception of the Chinese as "just natives." Japan's aggression is thought of as in the nature of colonial conquest little if at all different from past British conquests in Asia and Africa and as little to be condemned, provided *British* and *American* interests are respected. True that the Americans were more sympathetic to China and more indignant toward Japan than the British, but they have given no more help to China than Britain did, and all along have given far more help to Japan than the British Empire. After the European war began, some 80 per cent of Japan's imports of war materials were obtained from the United States, most of whose citizens consider themselves to be champions of peace, and who recoil in horror at similar acts of aggression committed in Europe from which, as distinct from Japan's, America derives no profit.*

Although the British Empire has mellowed with the years and the natives are now treated better than a generation ago, today there is still forced labor in Africa, imprisonment without trial in India, and in general a denial of democratic rights and civil liberties in the whole colonial empire. France, while conceding a greater degree of social equality with her colonial subjects, exploits them somewhat more drastically than the British and is less inhibited by humanitarian scruples from putting down all disaffection and incipient rebellion by a "whiff of grapeshot." Although the natives would probably be worse off under Germany, since old conquerors are gentler than new ones, the treatment of subject peoples by all the imperialist Powers makes their professions of virtue, nonaggressiveness, respect for the rights of other peoples, and so forth, sound the height of hypocrisy in German and Italian ears, and tinges their professions with falsity for anyone not blinded by racial prejudice.

* Columnists like Walter Lippmann, and journals like the *New Republic*, which were most anxious that Britain and France should fight the Nazi aggressors, always opposed an embargo on American war supplies to Japan. Yet, since Japan was vitally dependent on American supplies of scrap iron, oil, steel, machinery, etc., while Germany was an industrial and military giant, it was obvious that, whereas the United States might have stopped Japanese aggression with little or no danger of war, England and France were certain to be involved in a possibly disastrous war by trying to stop Germany's establishing her dominion over Europe east of the Rhine.

The idea that standards and principles of civilized behavior and "nonaggression" do not apply to "the natives," i.e., the colored races, constituted the ideological justification for our past aggressions against weak and "backward" peoples, and the present-day denial of equality and liberty to the colonial peoples of the British, French, and other empires. This applies also to the United States; for, although the consequences have up to now been less serious, the treatment of the Negro, at least in the southern states, is on a par with the Nazi treatment of the Jews. For the colonization of Europe which Hitler plans, an "ideology" was required of the same type as the "white man's burden" under which Europeans, and in particular the English, have justified the conquest and subjection of colored peoples. By persuading ourselves that people of another race are less human than ourselves, we have justified actions committed against them which we condemn when meted out to other Europeans, or whites anywhere. Similarly, in order to justify the German colonization of Europe, the Nazis have invented the myth of "Aryan" superiority over Jews and non-Teutonic Europeans.

Our double standard in dealing with white and colored or half-colored peoples has already been referred to in an earlier chapter as the canker at the heart of our civilization, which started to lead us back to barbarism in 1914. During the past decade the fatal consequences of regarding aggression against Asiatics or Africans as on a different plane from aggression against Europeans, or people of European origin, has been even more clearly revealed. First Japan in Manchuria and then Italy in Abyssinia destroyed the very basis of collective security.

In *Days of Our Years,* after giving a terrible indictment of the ruthless exploitation of the African which we have liked to call the white man's civilizing mission,* Van Paassen quotes Haile Selassie as saying, "If Mussolini were permitted to attack Ethiopia with impunity a precedent would be set up which would destroy the moral basis of international relationships and pave the way for a series of bloody wars." "Divine justice," said the Abyssinian Emperor, "will settle its accounts to the last penny some day."

One may not believe in divine justice, but one can see that there is such a thing as cause and effect in human history; and that, just as

---

* He describes the natives working under the lash on the plantations, driven by European taskmasters under the system of forced labor, euphemistically called the contract system, which prevails in many parts of Africa under French and British rule, as well as under that of the other "colonizing powers."

the conquest and enslavement of the Mediterranean world put an end to the liberty of the Roman people, so today the enslavement of Africa and Asia is leading to the enslavement of Europe.

One must concede to the Marxists, and in particular to Lenin, the truth of their thesis that the imperialist struggle for the possession of, or defense of, colonies for monopoly exploitation, cheap unprotected labor, and super-profits, was the cause of the first World War. The Great Powers had formerly attacked peoples armed with the most primitive means of defense, deprived them of their liberty, taken away their land or forced them to work their own resources for our benefit—all in the name of a higher culture. In the World War we denied our civilized values in the effort of Europeans to massacre Europeans. At Versailles we sought to enslave Germany economically. In the years that followed we taught the Germans that only by force could they hope to win markets, raw materials, an opportunity to be as prosperous as ourselves. The oppressed when they rise, as was long ago perceived by Euripides, become more terrible than their former oppressors. Methods tried out upon the Negro, and to a lesser extent upon Asiatics, by British, French, Belgians, and others, government by terror and repression, are now being used against the weaker peoples of Europe by Germany.

The militarism of a vanquished nation seeking at all costs to "try the game again" must necessarily be more uncompromising and ruthless than what one might term Britain's naval imperialism. For the fact that the British Empire has been won and held mainly by the Navy has enabled Britain to own the largest empire in the world while retaining a pacifist temper at home. This in large part accounts for what appears British hypocrisy in German and Italian eyes, and for our quite sincere horror at the unashamed militarism of the fascist Powers. The Germans proclaim that might is right and we are shocked; but we have ourselves acted on the same assumption until quite recently. The Zulus, the Indians, the Moors, and many other peoples stood to us, in a military sense, in about the same relation as the little nations of Europe stood to Germany; and we had no more scruples in conquering them in the past. The same can be said of Americans in their past relations with Indians, and with Spaniards in South America in the days when American governments considered it the "Manifest Destiny" of the United States to seize rich lands from weak peoples, and Americans justified conquest by the strong as the law of nature.

Whoever wins the terrible war now in progress, Europe can know no peace so long as we blind ourselves to the fundamental causes of war in the twentieth century and take refuge in the childish conception of the world as peopled by "good" people and "bad" people, good princes and bad ones. First, all was going to be well if we got rid of the Kaiser. Now many people would be happy to put the Kaiser back if Hitler could be got rid of.

The tragedy of the past twenty years has been that knowledge of the fundamental economic problems which cause economic crises, militant nationalism, and war, began to spread too late and among too few people. By the time we were ready to offer concessions to Germany sufficient to raise her people out of the despair into which the world economic crisis had plunged them, they were already following the Nazi party, which promised to make Germany strong enough to seize what the world would not give her peacefully. The economic nationalism forced upon the German people had given birth to an exaggerated and destructive political nationalism.

It is now fashionable to decry the economic causes for Germany's emergence as the most terrible of aggressors. The fact that the desire for power and glory is inextricably entwined with the need for markets and raw materials, and that the Nazi leaders glorify conquest for its own sake, does not prove that economic causes for German aggression do not exist and are not those which enabled Hitler to win the support of the German people.

The bourgeois ideals of the nineteenth century, free trade, free emigration, and the free movement of capital, have perished along with the international socialist ideal to which they gave birth. The first World War started the drive towards autarchy; the world economic crisis accelerated the process. Nations which had starved or gone short of essential commodities during the war because they had relied on importing food and manufactures, naturally desired to make sure this would not happen again. Each little country erected tariff walls to protect its agriculture and its nascent industries and strove feverishly to export as much as possible while reducing imports to a minimum. When the world economic crisis began in 1929, the fall in the value of their agricultural exports drove the weaker nations of Europe which had no closed colonial markets near to bankruptcy. Unable to pay their debts, they dropped out of the international monetary system and started to trade by barter. Germany took the lead in organizing and profiting from this new system of trade—trade among the debtors who could no longer get credits from the United States, Britain, and France because they could not pay their debts and because the gold standard had broken down almost everywhere. Managed currencies, quotas, blocked credits, and barter trade led to the establishment of virtual state monopolies of foreign trade in one country after another. This new method of trading enabled the fascist Powers to defy the financial power of England, France, and the United States, which the Germans termed "international Jewish finance."

The partial breakdown of the international monetary system in the great depression and the contracting world market gave a strong impetus to planned economy and concentration on home production and home resources. Autarchy in all countries to a greater or lesser degree seemed the only way out of economic crisis, unemployment, and starvation. Even Britain, at the Ottawa Conference in 1931, abandoned free trade in her empire and endeavored to concentrate her trade more and more in empire markets by tariffs and imperial preference. This, plus the Smoot-Hawley tariff in the United States, dealt a deathblow to economic and political liberalism in most parts of the world. Economic nationalism produced an exaggerated form of political nationalism in the "have-not" countries which felt themselves being strangled by the contraction of the world market.

The weaker and smaller nations could do nothing. But Germany and Italy, whose nationalism was already intense and whose military spirit inspired them to break the bonds to which others had perforce to submit, bent the whole of their national energies to preparing for a war for the redivision of the world. To suit their aims they invented theories about racial superiority, "young nations," proletarian nations against the pluto-democracies, and about the superiority of the values of warriors and of the fighting spirit over the values of traders, money lenders, and bankers embodied in Western capitalist civilization. In a word, they went back to the values of the European aristocracy in the Middle Ages, but shorn of their Christian coating.

Stalin had invented autarchy, which he called "socialism in one country." Hitler in this respect is his pupil. Socialism in one country equals national socialism, and this equals autarchy, since obviously production and distribution cannot be planned if you are dependent on the vagaries of the world market or the favor of other nations for either manufactures or essential raw materials; nor if the markets in which you must sell your goods to obtain the exchange for the money to buy those materials are closed against you.

The Soviet Government, having inherited from the Tsars a vast empire covering one-sixth of the earth's surface and abundantly endowed with natural resources, could become almost self-subsistent without conquering new territory. Germany, having a comparatively small territory and an insufficiency of raw materials for her huge industry, had to seek a wider *Lebensraum* in order to make her brand of national socialism workable and capable of producing sufficient food and manufactures to give the German people as high a standard of life as the English or the Americans. This, basically, is the cause of German aggressiveness as compared with the "pacifism" of the U.S.S.R., and also the reason why the Nazi party holds power by consent of large numbers of Germans. They may hate the tyranny and cruelty, persecution and racial laws of the Nazi Government, but there seemed no other way out. As a German liberal in the United States once remarked to me, "It's horrible, but it works." Under the Weimar Republic the Germans felt the walls closing in upon them as markets vanished and unemployment mounted. Congresses and conferences on "peaceful changes," the "raw material and market problem," etc., produced only talk; and meanwhile Germany saw the black cloud of starvation coming. The Nazis were horrible, but they lifted the cloud.

The impetus toward autarchy in Russia was given both by the aim of creating a socialist economy and by the intervention of the Allied Powers following on the Bolshevik Revolution, and the fear of another attack by "the capitalist world." This fear was genuine in the beginning and impelled the Soviet Government to concentrate on industrial development and in particular on defensive armaments. The counter-revolution carried out by Stalin after he had got rid of Trotsky removed any fear of the Comintern's activities in England and France and made any attack on Russia more than unlikely. However, the pretense that there was such a danger was of great use to the Stalinist clique in maintaining its power. Then from 1933 onward there was a real danger of attack by Germany and Japan which gave some justification to the diversion of the national economy to the production of armaments.

In Germany memories of the starvation produced by the Allied blockade, not only during the World War but for many months afterward, were revived and intensified by the widespread suffering caused by the world economic crisis which by 1932 had halved the quantity of German imports, created an army of 6 million unemployed, reduced industrial production to 60 per cent of the 1929 level, and bankrupted the democratic Republic.

The Nazi aim of creating an autarchic system which would prevent a repetition of the terrible experiences of the last war and put an end to the great depression, naturally appealed to the mass of the German people, who, following revived hopes of peace and prosperity from 1925 to 1929, had been plunged into despair from 1930 onward. The rising tariff barriers all over the world, in particular in the British Empire and America—France had always tried to monopolize the trade of her colonies by high customs duties—and the world-wide drift toward autarchy, forced Germany to try once more to acquire her own empire to give her the same secure markets and raw-material resources as Britain, France, and the United States already possessed.

The fact that Hitler and the Nazis are inspired by megalomaniac dreams of world conquest and the thirst for power and revenge should not be allowed to obscure the economic compulsions which laid the basis for Nazi ambitions. Without those original economic compulsions the Nazis could not have won power nor held it, nor been able to lead an army into battle of such a caliber as to smash through the defenses of France and England.

It may be argued that Britain and France were prepared in 1938 to let Germany acquire the economic domination of all eastern Europe, but that this ample *Lebensraum* did not satisfy Hitler, who lusted for military conquest and the complete subjugation of other nations, and refused to confine himself to a peaceful economic hegemony. This is not to be denied, but unfortunately movements which acquire power through economic compulsions acquire their own momentum. The force generated in Germany to compel the victors of Versailles to allow her to absorb Austria, take the Sudetenland, and monopolize the markets of eastern Europe was so great that it pushed Germany much further than was necessary to solve her economic problems. Nevertheless that force may expend itself sooner than we think.

In one sense it is true that Nazi Germany did constitute a "bulwark against communism." For National Socialist Germany completed the process begun by Stalin of subordinating the world-wide struggle of classes to national interests. Lenin had learned through the experience of the first World War that the workers, or at least those of the highly industrialized countries, and their Social Democratic or Labor leaders everywhere, are patriots first and class-conscious proletarians second or not at all. He therefore determined to force them to be class-conscious international socialists by a Communist party dictatorship. His successor, Stalin, reversed the process, completely abandoning the attempt to "unite the workers of the world" against the capitalists of the world, and setting out to convert the Soviet state into a National Socialist state. But he is hampered by the traditions of his party and the backwardness of the Russian people, among whom national consciousness is a feeble growth.

Having learned his lesson from both Lenin and Stalin, Hitler secured power by going along with the strongest forces of the twentieth century: economic and political nationalism. Hitler from the beginning subordinated the class struggle in Germany to the *national* struggle to dominate other nations, and by compromising as between the various class interests he acquired tremendous power.

Clearly the "workers of the world," faced with recurring economic crises, unemployment, and the lowering of wage standards through the competition for markets, could either unite to overthrow their capitalist masters *or* unite with the capitalists of their own country, willingly or unwillingly, to defend or to secure markets, raw materials, and colonial populations to work for the profit of the conquerors. The British workers had long followed the second path. The German workers, once the most socialist and internationally minded of all workers, having had their beliefs shattered by the experience of the two postwar decades, have now been persuaded or constrained to follow the same path as the British workers. They now follow the imperial road instead of the international socialist road.

The British Labour party has views about improving the conditions of the colonial workers and peasants, and talks of giving freedom to India; but there is no question in the minds of the majority of the British working class as to the rightness of fighting to defend the Empire. They get little direct profit from the Empire, but taxation of the profits of those who do provides social services, unemployment pay, etc., while the huge renter class in England provides employment for large numbers of persons in the luxury trades and in personal service. The English middle classes in their turn secure employment for their sons all over the Empire, and for themselves in banks, merchant houses, and all the other establishments in "the City."

A great deal of nonsense has been talked and a great deal of lying has been done concerning the colonial question. British and French imperialists, while insisting that the colonies produce no profits, refuse to give up a single one of them, and profited from their defeat of Germany in 1918 to take over hers. Figures are given out by such respectable institutes of research as the Royal Institute of International Affairs in London, and by the League of Nations, to show how small a percentage of world trade is accounted for by colonies, and how small a part of the world's vital raw materials are in colonial territory. These figures are not correct; for they leave out India, Algeria, and other colonial areas not legally termed colonies. The fact that India is promised her freedom at some indefinite date and that Algeria is technically a part of France inside the same tariff wall, does not alter the fact that these countries are not self-governing and that their native populations have neither the political nor juridical rights which would enable them to defend their economic interests and raise their standard of life.

In any case, the real profit derived from colonies is not to be computed in figures of trade. Income depends more on the rate of profit and security of investment than on the amount of sales. Colonies are desired because acquisition of the key economic positions—railways, trading centers, public utilities, etc.—and the exploitation of poorly paid native labor yield super-profits. It is obviously advantageous to be able to acquire plantations and mines and other natural wealth without having to buy them, or by securing them at a very low price. In other words, robbery of other people's property, so long as the other people cannot resist you, is a quicker and easier way of getting rich than working. This is obvious to everyone when Germany rapes a small country and takes possession of its wealth and factories, land and mines. But the same kind of robbery carried on on a huge scale in the past by the present-day democracies is usually forgotten.

The following quotation from Alfred Bingham's *United States of Europe* expresses clearly and concisely the real value of colonies and shows the futility of thinking that even a return to the "open door" policy of the past would satisfy the "have-not" Powers if they were only reasonable:

> Those who argue the "open door" as the answer to the "have-not" claim to colonies ignore all these other considerations.... They have missed the point made by Marx, that colonies are desired for purposes of exploitation. If the Malayan tin mines were not owned by British capitalists, thanks to the British fleet, but belonged to the Malayans themselves, under the protection of a strong Malayan national state, then British and Germans would come to the tin market on an equal footing, and each would have to give good value for what they got.... But because the Malay States are under British "protection," the tin mines are predominantly British-owned, and the British can exploit the Malayans and their tin—that is, they can get something for nothing. They need not pay the Malayans for the tin, for they own it already; they need only pay such miserable wages as the Malayans can subsist on while extracting it, and they can levy tribute on all the rest of the world. It is not merely a question of being able to pay in their own money; it is a question of not having to pay at all.

I have dealt at some length here with the question of imperialism because free enterprise and the natural flow of capital to where the highest rates of profit can be secured has led us to monopoly, first national and then international, and so to imperialist conquest and recurring wars. Capitalist imperialism is now confronted with the collectivist imperialism of Germany, backed by Italy and perhaps Russia. Their armed clash, causing the death and mutilation of millions of men, has not been caused by any personal devil called Hitler, but by historical developments and economic compulsions. These economic compulsions are exploited by unscrupulous men and aggravated by the lust for power and glory; but they are fundamental, and only a fairer division of the earth's resources among the peoples of the world, and an economic system which produces for use instead of for profit, can give us peace.

Imperialism since the nineties of the nineteenth century, when the scramble for Africa came to an end, has sought to expand by peaceful means instead of war, by financial power instead of by military power. Financial imperialism requires huge capital resources, and a peaceful world maintained largely by British control of the seas and respect for international law. Today, however, it is not enough to have made investments in backward countries to receive your interest; unless you are prepared to go and collect it by force the debt may be, and often is, repudiated. Moreover, in India and other colonial areas industrialization and the growth of a native middle class prevent the imperialist Power from any longer completely controlling the economic life of the colonial country. Since we have become too civilized to employ naked power except in territories we already possess—and even in these the British hesitate to crush rebellion by force—foreign investment has long been declining. The return has become too uncertain. Hence unemployment at home, capital unemployed in the banks, and the trend toward concentration on the home market, which continually raises the height of tariff walls and reinforces the autarchic tendencies of the modern world.

Investment at home in well-developed countries produces only a small rate of profit often not worth the risk. Hence the continuing depression and the tragic spectacle of millions of unemployed men and women in a country like America, which has abundant resources and industrial equipment and people needing goods which the system cannot produce because their production would yield no profit. Such a situation, if long prolonged in a country too poor to feed its people when the industrial machinery is slowing down, inevitably produces some form of controlled economy: state capitalism, Hitlerism, or Stalinism.

Russia and Germany, having abandoned the capitalist system for rigidly state-owned or -controlled economies, practice a new form of imperialism which one can term collectivist imperialism. It is more systematic, uncompromising, and destructive of liberty at home and abroad than the old liberal imperialism seeking markets and raw materials for private exploitation.

Although the state was often behind the great capitalist interests seeking to "penetrate" into backward countries, the use of the state's armed forces to secure private capitalist profit had practically ceased in England, France, and the United States. A better-informed public opinion, the spread of civilized standards of conduct, and a limited extension of such standards even to colored races, political democracy at home, which enabled public opinion to check any governmental inclination to use the state power in defense of private interests abroad —all these factors had tamed capitalist imperialism and stopped the march of conquest. Also, as already stated, there were few backward parts of the world not already controlled by national or imperial governments; and, since further imperialist expansion must entail war between the Great Powers, it could not but be unprofitable. But this very fact rendered the position of the highly industrialized nations without colonies more difficult. The growing concentration of Britain, France, and England upon their own markets made it more and more impossible for Germany, the strongest and industrially most advanced of the "have-nots," to export manufactures in return for the essential raw materials with which her territory was so meagerly supplied. Consequently, the "have-nots" considered even war preferable to stagnation and decay if war could be made to yield new *Lebensraum*.

The free-trader who sees the evils of our time as due to economic nationalism is justified in his beliefs; but, since the historic and economic trend is away from free trade—in the democracies as well as under the dictators—it is futile to yearn for a vanished world. Somehow political nationalism must be discredited or tamed, but economic nationalism may contain the germ of a world order which is more likely to germinate than the international socialist order many of us once dreamed of. Such an order will require continental-sized economic areas either under one dominant country or as a federation of many free nations. If Britain could both defeat Germany and retain her sanity after the terrible effort made to win the war, a European Federation of free nations might conceivably be set up. But it never will be if we continue to think of nations as "good" and "bad" and to shut our eyes to the fundamental causes of twentieth-century crises and wars.

Whatever the outcome of the present war, we shall have found that there is much to be learned from the National Socialist system—if the social cohesion and economic planning that system ensures could be preserved by belief in peaceful construction instead of by a fanatical nationalist faith.

It has long been a truism that people of all classes will make sacrifices for the general good in war which they refuse to make for the general good in peaceful times. Men sacrifice their lives more readily than their profits, and Hitler and Mussolini have glorified war precisely because it inspires men to sacrifice of self for the community.

It must be admitted that it is doubtful whether all classes can be made to sacrifice themselves for the community, except in war or under compulsion. However, the new economic and social system, by making possible a compromise between the interests of the warring classes, could be directed to increasing mankind's material well-being and towards checking his destructive and stimulating his creative impulses if the democracy instead of a Party dictatorship held power.

In other words, can communal control of land and capital and their use in the interest of the whole community be established as a further extension of political democracy—or is dictatorial "socialism" the only alternative to our outworn social and economic system which dooms men to starve in the midst of plenty? Can we establish a planned economy, compromising between the interests of classes, and administered by the people for the people, instead of a Nazi or Communist slave state? Is socialism or state capitalism compatible with liberty? Some of the best minds in the United States are thinking along these lines, attempting to work out a compromise between capitalism and socialism, between a free and a controlled economy, between "democratic" government controlled or influenced by vested interests, and a true democracy.*

Those of us who were already disillusioned with the U.S.S.R. by 1932 looked upon the New Deal as perhaps the beginning of an attempt to create a state which would utilize its resources and man power for the benefit of the community, and preserve its democratic form of government while curbing and eventually controlling the irre-

* Among others: Alfred Bingham, John Chamberlain, Stuart Chase, Jerome Frank.

sponsible monopolists who have strangled the capitalist system and made it unworkable.*

Those hopes are somewhat faded but not quite dead. Ignorance of the real causes of the European war and the temptation to go crusading in Europe threaten to cause the American people to abandon their own problem of curbing their economic monopolists, and to miss their unique opportunity to create a liberal semi-autarchic and planned system of production and distribution in what is perhaps the one country in the world where it is geographically and politically feasible to do so without first conquering other nations.

If nowhere in the world there can be created a social system which allows men to work and to utilize the resources of the earth for their own benefit, we are bound to succumb sooner or later to some form of soul-destroying tyranny which will enslave us all, as the German and Russian people have been enslaved. In a chaotic world where men cannot get employment, and are plunged suddenly into misery through no fault of their own but through the obscure workings of an economic and financial system they cannot understand or control, they will accept servitude if it promises life. Like savages who are fearful of the thunder and think that drought and flood are caused by supernatural beings, men whose lives are ruined by mysterious economic forces they cannot understand will worship horrible bloody idols in hope of security.

Diseases cannot be cured by telling the sick that they are wicked, and wars caused by economic compulsions which have maddened aggressor peoples cannot be cured by counter-aggression.

England, if she persists in trying to fight Germany alone, will be driven to a like ruthlessness. For England cannot win, cannot perhaps even save herself, unless she disregards international law, humanitarian considerations, and pity for the innocent victims of war in France, the Low Countries, Scandinavia, and elsewhere being starved by the blockade. Already she has been forced to imitate the Nazi method of mobilizing economic resources for war by adopting state control of every economic activity, curtailing profits or establishing state ownership of land and capital, regimenting her people—in a word, establishing her own form of national socialism or state capitalism. Whether or not the English will be able to preserve civil liberty, democratic government, and a measure of the freedom they are fighting to defend must depend on how long the war lasts and how much destruction and privation it entails.

* Michael and Clark Foreman, mentioned in Chapter III of this book, attempted to embody some such idea as these in *The New Internationalism*, published in 1934.

More than a century ago Napoleon was defeated, but the equalitarian ideals of the French Revolution and the seeds of nationalism which he had spread over Europe triumphed. The capitalist economic and social system supplanted the feudal over all western Europe, and the ideal of national and individual liberty eventually divided Europe into a patchwork of national states.

It may be that the capitalist system and "bourgeois democracy," for which the destruction of feudal privilege by the armies of France and the creation of new productive forces by the Industrial Revolution both prepared the way, are now inevitably doomed to give place to some form of "national socialism." Free trade and private enterprise, mortally stricken in the last war, are being liquidated in this one. Small nations cannot endure, and great self-sufficient territorial empires must take the place of many small states in this epoch of closed empires and choked channels of trade. It is more than doubtful whether unity will be achieved by federation; it is far more likely to come by conquest.

Peace may at last come to Europe, not through the efforts of benevolent pacifists but through the extinction of liberty, as it came under the Romans. If the war goes on a long time it will not matter so very much which side wins; national socialism and totalitarian tyranny will in any case have triumphed. The men who inspired and led the French Revolution imagined that the destruction of feudal privilege would enable mankind to establish a just and happy society. Instead they got capitalism. Socialists may be similarly deluded in thinking that the overthrow of capitalism will lead to a society of the free and equal, and pacifists in thinking that peace will ever be established except by the might of the conqueror. National socialism may prove itself economically and militarily superior to our present social system, as so many admirers of the U.S.S.R. contend; but it may also inevitably entail a greater or lesser degree of tyranny and terror, the loss of both individual and national liberty except for the ruling nations or the ruling Party.

"Socialism" may be coming in a form unrecognizable and hated by both the revolutionaries and the reformers who for decades have worked for it and dreamed of it as the ideal society which was to abolish injustice and poverty. "Socialism" may mean tyranny, terror, the concentration camp, and the firing squad, secret police and the regimentation of the mind and spirit, whether it comes through "the dictatorship of the proletariat" or the dictatorship of a "national socialist" party.

Marx's, Engel's, and Lenin's great ideal of a new society of the free and equal may turn out to be a society of slaves, as has happened in the U.S.S.R. The hated Nazis may establish an order which is more socialist than "communist" Russia, but it will not in the least resemble the society which socialists wanted. As William Morris wrote long ago:

> Men fight and lose the battle, and the thing they fought for comes about in spite of their defeat. And when it comes about it turns out not to be what they meant, and other men have to fight for what they meant under another name.

Should Britain, provided only that she can save herself and the greater part of her Empire, not persist in the attempt to prevent Germany establishing her hegemony over Europe east of the Rhine, it is possible to hope that the moderately socialist aspirations of the Labour party will be realized. Those aspirations were expressed in a pamphlet entitled *Labour's Home Policy,* issued just after the establishment of the Churchill Cabinet. Labor's participation in that cabinet and the price paid to it in the form of abolition of war profits and the complete state control of capital, may enable the Labour party and trade-unions to realize the aim expressed as "a chance to recover the dynamic of democracy by a method based on socialism."

"During the present struggle," says the pamphlet, "the form of the new order will be emerging from the old." It goes on to outline the semisocialist program which the Labour party expects to be able to put into operation under the emergency powers given to the British Government to control capital, profits, and labor. Key industries and services are to be publicly owned and banks subject to public control; the direction of investment is to be state-controlled; individual ability is to be directed to the service of the community; "the function of the trade-unions in the national life" is to receive fuller recognition.

All this sounds rather like German National Socialism, but with the all-important difference that state capitalism in Britain, being established by the will of the majority of the people, is expected to be democratic. As the pamphlet expresses it, so long as the will of the people is nationally respected as the only valid source of power, the historic forms of parliamentary democracy will provide a highroad along which the nation can pass peaceably from an acquisitive to a socialist society.

Although these bright hopes may become dimmed in the "blood and sweat" of the war, it is possible that the subordination of vested private interests to the state which is now taking place in Britain in order to meet the Nazi menace may be diverted to purposes of democratic welfare after the war. The power which the war is giving, not to a party headed by a leader, but to the organized democratic forces, coupled with the weakening of the reactionary or obstructive capitalist interests through the curtailment of their profits and their power, and the lead now being taken by the boldest elements in the old ruling class, *may* lead to the establishment of a democratic form of national socialism in England. The concessions which will have to be made to India and to other subject peoples of the British Empire to ensure their loyal support in the war, may similarly lead to the establishment of a real British Commonwealth of Nations.

The feudal tradition of public service as the price of privilege and of an ordered as opposed to a competitive society, never completely destroyed in England under the capitalist system, should facilitate the transition to state socialism. The best elements in the ruling and possessing classes will probably serve the British "national socialist" state as devotedly as they have served the imperial capitalist state, and as their ancestors served the feudal monarchy. In this respect England would appear to have a great advantage over France where the possessing classes and the politicians were more corrupt, and where capital was less inclined to compromise with labor in order to save the country.

Totalitarian war, although it requires the complete regimentation of labor and capital, an end to private enterprise and trade-union rights, and the suspension of civil liberties, also requires faith on the part of the majority of the population that it is fighting for its national existence and for a just cause. That faith can alone ensure a good morale both in the armed forces and on the home front. Britain, although she is an imperialist power which holds other races in subjection, is today fighting for her national existence. This requires what the Chinese call mobilization of the people. Hence the democratic nature of Britain's new totalitarian system established by Act of Parliament in May 1940. So long as the large majority of the British people are anxious and determined to fight Germany to the bitter end democracy can survive, and probably will survive in England, in spite of the imitation of Nazi methods of control and organization of the national economy. But should the war prove so destructive of life and property that a substantial minority of the British people want to stop fighting but the government insists on continuing the war, Britain is almost certain to adopt the same tyrannical methods of government as Nazi Germany.

While there is hope for the creation of a new and perhaps better social order in Britain without the permanent loss of civil liberty and political democracy, this hope may be extinguished should the war cause such misery, starvation, destruction, and fear that the British virtues of restraint, political toleration, and willingness to compromise are destroyed.

On the other side of the picture it would seem possible that the war may lead to a certain moderation of Nazi tyranny at home. The morale of the German armies and workers will perhaps have to be maintained by concession of a little freedom to the German people. Obviously the effort required to wage this war cannot be sustained by the sinister activities of the Gestapo alone. Unless the German people support the government wholeheartedly and are ready to bear wounds and privation and death in the belief that they are fighting for a better world and better conditions of existence, Germany's effort cannot succeed over a long period. It is even conceivable that the needs of war may cause the German Government to relax its pressure on the Jews because it needs their talents and abilities. Although Germany started the war and is the aggressor, every German knows that it is the aim of Britain to starve the civilian population of Germany into submission by the blockade. The majority must also be convinced that defeat means the end of their existence as a nation. But should the German people become convinced that Hitler is leading them into unnecessary wars to satisfy an insatiable lust for conquest, German morale would weaken and Nazi Germany would lose its terrible strength.

It may sound the height of optimism to suggest it, but it appears just possible that the present war, while producing a planned national economy in Britain with the preservation of a large measure of liberty and political democracy, may modify the German National Socialist regime to allow of the revival of a little liberty. Or at least that it will give the upper hand over the gangster Nazi elements to the army leaders, whose traditions and values are less unlike our own. The army, not the Gestapo, is likely to dominate Germany more and more, and the soldiers of all ranks—that is to say, the German people—will have more chance to assert their will against the Nazi party.

It is just possible that the extremes will meet and that there will be an approximation from opposite poles of the Nazi and British economic and political systems—a synthesis of capitalism and socialism into a new social order preserving at least some of the values of the old order.

After all, it is worth remembering that the capitalist order superseded the feudal in greater or lesser degrees of "absoluteness" in the different countries of the world, and came in some as the result of wars of liberation and in others as the result of wars of aggression. Also there was a Counter-Reformation as well as a Reformation at the end of the Middle Ages, and in the end these two movements were very similar.

However, any such hope is obviously a vain one should the war go on too long and both sides be too frightened and suffer too much to preserve their reason. It may also be a vain hope should Germany be able to conquer England. But if neither side can *win* the war and neither side loses it completely, there would seem to be some hope that the coming of the servile state will be avoided or prove to be only a short and temporary phase of the history of the world.

Because I am English, and because I value the peculiar political and social virtues which long centuries of national security and prosperity have developed among the English people, I hope we shall not refuse any opportunity for a negotiated peace offered to us, even if this entails German hegemony over the continent of Europe. We cannot now "save" Europe except by destroying Europe and making our late allies hate us as much or more than the Germans. But we can save the British Empire, rejuvenate it and establish a juster social order for white and colored peoples alike within our own domain. I can see no way of preserving the liberal, compromising, tolerant, and good-natured side of the English way of life except by relinquishing our interest in Europe before we have been driven to imitate the Nazis or the Communists. The war has already forced us to reorganize our economic system and take the first steps along the road toward national socialism. This may prove to be an immense economic and social gain—provided a long and desperate contest with Germany does not drive us to imitate the vices as well as the virtues of German National Socialism. The old order is passing away, but whether or not we retain its best features—liberalism, humanitarianism, tolerance, and respect for law and for individual rights and human dignity—must depend upon how much we suffer and how violently we hate. Our human nature is the same as that of the Germans and Russians, and if we come to suffer as they have done either materially or in national humiliation we are unlikely to retain the virtues of civilized men and women.

Conversely, I have sufficient faith in human nature to believe that a Germany freed of her national inferiority complex, and with ample opportunity for economic development and for the exercise of the talents and organizing ability of her people in peaceful pursuits, will in time discard the twisted and barbaric precepts of the Nazis which they have accepted during the struggle for supremacy over the old imperialisms. If they are not discarded a German domination over Europe will not endure, while if they are discarded future generations may come to view the unification of most of Europe under German hegemony in the same light as they view Rome's conquest of the ancient civilizations of the Mediterranean world—as having put an end to war and civil strife and ensured a long era of prosperity and peace.

Should the New World aid an uncompromising England to carry on the war and attempt to starve Europe into submission, or cut off Europe entirely from contact and trade with the Western hemisphere, there will be little hope that National Socialism can be tamed. Just as the hostility and hatred of the capitalist states drove Russia after the Bolshevik Revolution to establish a despotic and inhuman system of government keeping the Russian people in abject subjection, so the hostility of the rest of the world to a Nazi Europe will encourage the growth of the worst and most cruel features of National Socialism. War conditions and a war psychosis will continue, the starving conquered peoples will be ruled by naked brutal force, and the productive forces which might be used to develop the conditions for government by consent and a prosperity which would annul the memory of past brutalities will as now be utilized for conquest and the repression of the conquered. The greater part of Europe may then come to resemble Stalin's Russia. Alternatively we shall cause the whole of Europe to detest us as its peoples suffer the horrors of starvation and disease caused by our blockade.

Unfortunately the pacifists who were most convinced, until the war began in earnest in the spring of 1940, that you cannot cast out Satan by Satan, now believe that total war can exorcise totalitarianism, and that by converting the free world into the image of the Nazi world freedom will be preserved. They are probably making as fundamental and tragic a mistake as those liberals and pacifists who supported the Soviet Union and its policies until August 1939.

The Communists hoped that the war would go on until Germany and England had destroyed each other's power and produced a revolutionary situation in Europe. Then they thought they could establish their own hegemony. It is because I am convinced that the Russian brand of national socialism is more terrible than the German and offers no other prospect than a return to barbarism; and because it seems to me that England cannot now win the war and preserve either liberty or civilized values, that I hope for a negotiated peace before we all fall a prey to Stalinism.

The entry of the United States into the war, by ensuring its long continuance, might cause the fusion of Hitlerism and Stalinism into one mighty movement of destruction, whether such a fusion came as the result of a close Russo-German alliance or as the consequence of starvation, disease, and revolution in Europe. All history teaches us that in times of gravest national danger, when the highest qualities of zeal, courage, self-sacrifice, and endurance are required to save a people, the more radical elements take the lead. This was the case after the French Revolution, when the young republic was fighting for its life and the Jacobins took control. It was to a lesser degree true in Prussia over a century ago when, in order to resist Napoleon's aggression, serfdom was abolished and the most radical elements among the Junkers took the lead. It will no doubt be so in Germany if she is ever threatened by defeat. It is this which makes possible an all-in alliance between the Nazis and Soviet Russia as the result of a long war.

So long as Germany is strong and confident of victory, the more conservative elements in the Nazi party are likely to maintain, and perhaps even to increase, their strength. But Comintern propaganda, in the United States as well as in Britain, is too useful to Hitler for it to appear likely that he would attack the U.S.S.R. while engaged in a life and death struggle with the British Empire.

Anyone who has felt in his nerves, and seen with his eyes, the long-drawn-out misery of the Russian people, the death of hope among the masses and the brutishness of their existence, the callous hypocrisy of the rulers and the cowed submission of the ruled, must hope that England and Germany will not carry on their war of mutual destruction to the point at which Europe will be made safe for Stalinism.

If Germany can be halted upon its mad course of conquest, but not destroyed, and the genius of the German people allowed to play the leading role in the reconstruction and unification of Europe, National Socialism may be humanized and democratized. But if Stalin establishes his black dominion over Europe, we shall be prevented from repairing the ravages of war, the productive forces will be blighted and choked as they have been in the U.S.S.R., and Europe may come to resemble those ancient lands along the Tigris and Euphrates where Mongol conquest put an end to the oldest of civilizations and reduced a population of millions to a few hundred thousands.

Index

INDEX

Abramovna, Anna, 17, 107, 270
Absolute monarchy, 130
Abyssinia, 341, 343
Academy of Science, 231, 265
Africa, 4, 132, 133, 145, 212, 213, 314, 342-4, 351
Agrarian: overpopulation, 150, 163; system, 147 et seq.
Agriculture, 45, 54, 147-71, 293; collectivization of, 147-71; see also Peasants; Commissar of, 164-5; investment in, 165, 201-2; mechanization of, 157; stagnation of, 57, 215
Agricultural production, 43, 47, 153, 155-7, 168
Algeria, 349
America, 5, 33
American(s), 22, 99, 314 et seq.; Communist party, 94; Press, 314 et seq.; White Paper, 312
Amtorg, 59
Anglo-Japanese, 316
Anikeev, 27, 95, 264, 266
Anti-Comintern Pact, 316
Anti-Semitism, 102
Appeasement, 312 et seq.
Archangel, 85, 261
Arcos, 16, 17, 19, 232
Arctic, 51, 213, 216, 271
Argentine, 232, 233
Armaments, 51, 57, 215, 216, 289, 347
Armenian, 79, 233
Army leaders, German, 291, 358
Asia (Asiatic), 4, 52, 79, 132, 133, 145, 183, 192, 203, 293, 314, 342-4; despotism, 140; system, 131
Assyrians, 52
Athens, 224
Australia, 45
Australian Communists, 114
Austria, 348
Autarchy, 346-8
Aveling, 4

Baku, 330
Balkans, 333

Baltic states, 325, 331
Baracchis, 114
Barmine, Alexandre, 191, 224, 254
Beale, Fred, 182-3
Bedniaki, 53, 99, 104
Beggars, 110, 183
Belgium, 341
Berdichevsky: Arcadi, 16, 17, 20, 59-62, 72, 82-5, 97, 228-30, 260-74; Vera, 62-6, 70-2, 265-73
Berkinghof, 87, 269, 273
Bernal, 99
Bess, Demaree, 316
Bessarabia, 333
Beveridge, Sir William, 75
Bingham, Alfred M., 282, 350, 353
Birth house, 113
Black Sea, 111, 330
Blat (Blatmeister), 228-9
Borkenau, Franz, 39
Borodin, 21
Brailsford, 10
Bread: cards, 50; derationing of, 117, 170; prices, 168-70, 190-1, 288; tax, 168-71
Bredow, von, 300
British: Empire, 134, 333, 342-4, 348, 357; Foreign Office, 273; working class, 38, 307
Broun, Heywood, 314
Bucharin, 15, 21, 45, 46, 49, 50, 255-6, 301
Bugs, 109-10
Bund, 16, 62
Bureaucracy, 44, 88, 90, 163, 191, 204, 213, 219-20, 288, 295, 308
Burns, John, 4
Butirky Prison, 267
Byzantine Empire, 69, 79, 181

Camps of Death, 241
Canada, 45, 213
Canterbury, Dean of, 5
Capital goods, 208 et seq.
Capitalist class, 47, 49; position of in Nazi Germany, 277-86, 289, 291-2
Cartels (in Germany), 280

365

Catholic(s), 5, 14, 123, 139, 295, 302
Caucasus (-asian), 51, 79, 96
Chamberlain, John, 353
Chamberlain, Neville, 312-5
Chartist, 4
Chase, Stuart, 353
Cheka, 40
Chiang Kai-shek, 46
Children, homeless, 92, 110-1, 180. *See also* Education
Chilston, Lord, 272
China, 21, 22, 46, 59, 87, 119, 131, 232, 235, 315-6, 341-2; Japan's war on, 341-2
Chinese, 92, 235, 341-2; Communists, 22; refugees, 341; revolution, 119
Chita, 21
Christian (-ity), 132, 135, 295
Christian Science Monitor, 316
Churchill, Winston, 12, 37, 329, 331
Civil war, 40, 42, 49, 56, 140, 226, 230, 237, 261, 301
Class war, 52
Classless society, 6, 129
Cliveden set, 314
Closed distributors, 68-9, 79, 85, 95, 201
Coal, production of, 186, 200, 206, 208
Coburn, Claude, 314
Cole, G. D. H., 57
Collective farms, *see* Kolkhoz
Collectivization, 15, 21, 48-57, 70, 71, 216, 288. *See also* Peasants *and* Agriculture
Colonies (colonial), exploitation and conquest, 171, 288, 322, 343 *et seq.*, 349-51
Commercial shops, 101-2, 184, 192
Comintern, 20, 21, 22-3, 29, 32, 45, 46, 80, 105, 118, 119, 120, 256, 259, 287, 312-4, 316-9, 325-6; work at, 73, 94
Commune, Paris, 37
Communist Academy, 94, 121, 190, 231, 234
Communist party: British, 13, 28, 30, 69, 94; German, 120-1; Russian, Stalin's liquidation of, 255-8
Concentration camps: German, 121, 240, 256, 285, 297, 306; Russian, 166, 186, 195, 213, 216, 238-54, 263, 267, 271, 272, 285, 297, 310; numbers in, 239, 253-4, 256
Congo, 125
Conservatives, German, 291, 300, 358
Comsomols, 55, 63, 75, 257
Constituent Assembly, 39

Constitution, New, 187, 188, 200, 206, 208, 317
Consultazia for mothers, 114
Consumers' goods, 207-8, 210, 213-5, 282
Control figures, 205-6
Cook, A. J., 13
Co-operatives, housing, 76, 79, 80, 194, 260
Corruption, 284, 308
Cossack, 51, 52
Cotton industry: Lancashire, 19, 28, 29, 231; U.S.S.R., *see* Textiles
Cotton goods, Russian export of, 232-5
Cost accounting, 202
Cost of living, 189-93, 290
Counter-Reformation, 302, 361
Counter-revolution, 33, 87, 90, 142, 230, 240, 243
Cowley, Malcolm, 222
Crimea, 86, 87, 111
Cromwell, 138, 142
Custine, Abbé, 177, 196
Czechoslovakia, 313, 315, 327

Daladier, 314
Datcha, 115-7
Dairen, 22
Dawes Plan, 46
Death penalty: for children, 156; for theft, 92, 156
Decembrists, 21
Dell, Robert, 134
Democracies, Western, 315, 325 *et seq.*
Democracy and socialism, 128 *et seq.*
Derjinsky, 303
Dictatorship: Bolshevik party, 135-8, 142-6; of the proletariat, 126-7, 142-6, 172, 188
Divorce, 105-8
Diocletian, Emperor, 181
Don Basin, 176, 178
Drucker, Peter F., 316
Duranty, Walter, 57, 257, 327
Dutch East Indies, 232, 233

Eastman, Max, 5, 83, 143, 221-2, 254, 302-3
Education, Soviet, 92-3
Egypt, 131
Electricity, 141
Employees, 225. *See also* Specialists
Engels, Friedrich, 4, 37, 38, 126, 127-31, 142-5, 309, 356
England, 5, 84, 94, 96, 99, 240, 261, 269,

307, 312 *et seq.*, 335 *et seq.*
English upper classes, 7
Equality of opportunity, 91-2
Estonia, 328
Euripides, 5, 26, 27, 90
Europe: Eastern, 322, 324, 340, 348; Western, 297, 312, 341
European Federation, 353

Fabian(s), 4
Factory committees, 172-5
Family relationships, 106 *et seq.*
Famine, 43, 56, 83, 86, 103, 148, 155, 170, 181, 202, 278
Far East, 20, 23, 29, 62, 72, 118, 162, 316, 341
Farmers, German, 287-8
Fascism (Fascist), 12, 30, 222, 255, 257, 313
Fellow travelers, 99, 325, 327
Fiji, 31, 115
Finnish war, 205, 209, 218, 221, 237-9, 314, 320-1, 330
Fischer, Louis, 257, 314
Five Year Plans, 51, 58, 70, 71, 103, 148, 165, 168, 169, 182, 184-5, 190, 197-9, 201 *et seq.*, 215-6, 225, 226 *et seq.*, 238 *et seq.*, 253; table of actual results, 206
Florinsky, 254
Food: cards, 79; shortage of, 50, 56, 71, 85, 166-7
Foreign Affairs, Commissariat of, 21, 59, 60, 95, 118, 232, 233, 260, 264
Foreman, Clark, 99-100, 354
Foxe, Ralph, 100
France, 240, 257, 285, 291, 307, 312 *et seq.*, 335 *et seq.*
France, Anatole, 117
Frank, Jerome, 353
French, 7, 8; Empire, 341; Revolution, 3
Free trade, 287, 345 *et seq.*, 352
Friends of the Soviet Union, 70, 178, 213, 267, 273, 322

General Strike, 11-3
Georgians, 141, 242
German(s), 7, 8, 22, 46, 98, 120-1, 134, *see also* Nazi; army, 216, 336 *et seq.*; Communists, 78, 105, 256, 317; Revolution, 43, 46, 140; technical aid to U.S.S.R., 216
Germany, 35, 36, 39, 45, 46, 102, 105, 133, 213. *See also* Nazi

Gestapo, 285, 306, 336, 358
Gide, André, 296
Gladkov, 43
Gordon, Manya, 176
Gorki, 135
Gosplan, 227
Gracchi, 4
Greek(s), 24; city states, 132; history, legends, 3, 4, 19, 31
Gunther, John, 327

Halifax, Lord, 329
Hamburg, 31, 59
Handicrafts, 48, 153
Harvests, 44, 55, 155-7, 202
Heavy Industry, Commissar of, 207
Herzen, 324
Hitler, 31, 83, 98, 105, 130, 133-4, 179, 185, 216, 258, 259, 278-9, 282, 285-6, 290-1, 293-7, 299-300, 303-11, 312-21, 325, 327-30, 332-4, 340, 345-6, 354
Hitlerism, 324, 328
Hoelz, Max, 104-5
Holland, 340
Homosexuals, 100, 238
Hoover, Dr. Calvin B., 53
Hospitals, 81-2, 113
Hubbard, L. E., 150-2, 214-5
Hudson, G. F., 265
Hungary, 322

Imperialism, 19, 38, 132-3, 310, 319 *et seq.*, 340-4, 346, 349-52; collectivist, 352
Independent Labour party, 10, 16
India, 232, 342, 349
Indian, 133, 344, 351
Industrial feudalism, 145
Industrialization, 16, 44, 46, 48, 49, 50, 56, 103, 136, 196-216, 293
Industrial production, 44, 186 *et seq.*, 196 *et seq.*
Inflation, 201-3, 214, 282
Inquisition, 5, 125
Insnab, 68, 86, 97, 101, 117
Institute of World Economics and Politics, 94, 117-22, 236, 264
Intervention, Allied, 42, 347
Intourist, 14, 57, 96
Iron, production of, 92, 186, 200, 206, 208
Izvestia, 120, 167, 208
Italy, 333, 335, 341
Italian, 103, 231
Ivanavo Vosnysensk, 85, 92, 199, 233
I.W.W., 100

Japan, 19, 20, 21, 23, 27, 70, 118, 122, 231, 261, 266, 306, 316, 341-2, 347
Japanese, 62, 72, 233
Japan's Feet of Clay, 112, 115, 121, 261, 264, 273
Jews (Jewish), 52, 54, 56, 102-3, 133, 185, 196, 270, 278, 294, 296, 297, 305, 306, 313, 327, 331, 343, 346
Justice, Commissariat of, 106

Kalinin, 49, 323
Kalmanofsky, 116, 229-30, 263, 264
Kamenev, 39, 303
Karelia, 237 *et seq.*
Keynes, J. M., 262
Kharkov Tractor Plant, 182
Khinchuk, 69, 70
Kiev, 57
Kipman, 71, 72
Kolkhoz ("collective farms"), 54, 56, 80, 98, 148 *et seq.*, 209, 211; Charter of 1935, 149 *et seq.*, 159, 166
Kremlovsky, 68, 102
Krilenko, N. V., 106-7
Krivitsky, W. C., 252-3, 257, 301-2, 315-6
Kronstadt sailors, 43, 139-40
Kulak(s), 47, 48-50, 65, 78, 87, 161, 166; liquidation of, 50-7, 97-9, 133-4, 161, 186, 238, 255

Labor books: Germany, 286; U.S.S.R., *see* Work Certificate
Labor: Code, 175; Exchanges, 181; Front, 286; productivity, 183-5, 207
Labour party, British, 3, 9, 11, 14, 40, 220, 317-8, 335, 349, 356-7
Labour Opposition (Britain), 316, 327-8, 330
Laski, Professor, 273
Latvia, 329
Left opposition, 15, 45, 47
Legay, Kléber, 178-9
Lenin, 3, 6, 11, 15, 21, 28-9, 33-40, 42-6, 49, 64, 83, 126-9, 131, 135-44, 148, 172-3, 188, 217, 225-6, 232, 256, 292, 302-4, 308, 310, 319, 332, 348, 349, 356; view of state, 129 *et seq.*
Leningrad, 31, 49, 139, 177
Lenin School, 67
Light industry, 208, 210, 212; Commissariat of, 94, 199, 226, 236-7, 261
Lippmann, Walter, 327, 342
Lithuania, 329
Litvinov, 272, 312

Lloyd, C. M., 19, 75, 84, 273
London School of Economics, 19, 57, 66, 75, 84, 99
London University, 8, 57; Labour party, 10, 70
Lubianka Prison, 224, 267, 301
Lux Hotel, 67
Luxemburg, Rosa, 142
Lyons, Eugene, 57

Machine Tractor Stations, 151, 156, 159, 164-5
Madyar, 119
Maisky, Soviet ambassador, 13, 14, 27, 271
Malay States, 350
Manchester Guardian, 23, 51, 57, 194
Manchuria, 21, 22, 306
Manufactures, retail prices, 193
Markets: free, 46, 288; and price movements, Germany, 281-2, 284; reconstitution of, 43
Martin, Kingsley, 273
Marriage, registered and common law, 100, 105-8
Marx, 4, 28, 37, 38, 64, 69, 126-31, 136-7, 142-3, 145, 173, 262, 281, 293, 323, 324, 332, 350, 356
Marx-Engels Institute, 64, 67, 70, 100, 119, 131
Marxism (Marxist theory, dogma), 4, 9, 11, 21, 28, 29, 35, 38, 63, 83, 119, 129, 137, 220, 293, 295-6, 307
Marxist(s), 33, 39, 129-30, 190, 210, 300, 305, 344
Marxist Dialectics, 302
Materialist interpretation of history, 137
Medical services, 92
Melnitskaya, 119
Mennonites, 98
Mensheviks, 35, 37, 39, 40, 45, 141, 173-4
Metal and machine building industries, 200, 206, 209
Middlemen, 47, 48
Mikado, the, 219, 255
Mikoyan, 102
Military communism, *see* War
Militia, 104-5, 110
Mithradates, 79
Mines (miners), 176, 178-9, 204, 272
Mohammed, 39
Molotov, 149, 152, 319
Money, in Nazi Germany, 282
Mongol(-ia), 52, 269
Morris, William, 4, 356

Moscow, 3, 10
Moscow-Volga Canal, 253, 254
Mrachovsky, 300-1
Muggeridge, Malcolm, 51, 57, 99, 298
Munich Settlement, 134, 313
Mussolini, 30, 220, 257, 343, 353

Napoleon, 337-8, 340, 355
Nation, The, 134, 222, 313, 329
National income, 70, 211-2, 220
National Socialism, 89, 256, 294 *et seq.*, 297-9, 322 *et seq.*, 335-9; in England, 335, 354 *et seq.*
Nazi Germany, 213, 239, 258, 277-312, 335 *et seq.*
Nazis, 56, 62, 121, 133-4, 139, 178, 222, 255, 273, 277 *et seq.*
Nazi system, the, 215 *et seq.*
Negro, 133, 344
New Deal, 100, 353
New Economic Policy (N.E.P.), 3, 15, 34, 35, 43, 45, 49, 53, 56, 58-9, 140, 151-2, 214, 225
New Moscow Hotel, 20, 57, 94, 114; life in, 95-7, 99
New Republic, 5, 134, 222, 313, 329, 342
News Chronicle, 329
New Statesman and Nation, 84, 273, 329, 331
New York Times, 57, 327
Newton, 11
Nicholas I, 21, 196
Norse sagas, 31
Note issue, 197, 201

O'Connor, Feargus, 4
Odessa, 86
O.G.P.U., 17, 21, 22, 40, 49, 50-2, 57, 68, 71, 72, 87, 90, 96-7, 102, 105, 150, 156, 166, 176, 178, 183, 187, 195, 198, 204, 213, 219, 228, 229, 238-59, 261 *et seq.*, 300-2
Oil production, 206, 208, 209
Old Bolsheviks, Society of, 256
Ottawa Conference, 346

Paassen, Van, 343
Pan-Slav, 331
Pares, Sir Bernard, 10
Parlor Bolsheviks, 9
Party: dictatorship, 136 *et seq.*, 348; inter-democracy, 142, 308; maximum, 69, 128, 223-5; privileges, 85, 87, 93, 145, 222-5; salaries, 222

Passport system, 104-6
Patriotism, 307
Peasants, 15, 34, 39, 40, 41, 43-58, 73-4, 88, 90, 101, 104, 110, 127, 136, 141, 147-71, 182, 184, 204, 209-10, 218, 285, 287-8, 292, 306; compulsory deliveries to state, 148 *et seq.*, 288; forced collections, 148 *et seq.*; individual allotments, 147, 157-62; income, 147, 152-6; livestock, 157-8, 163-4, 166; rebellion, 34
Peking, 22
Pensions, 187, 189, 194
Pericles, 4, 31
Persia, 232
Petrovsky, 13
Pharaoh, 51, 125
Planned economy, 43, 197 *et seq.*, 205, 220, 282, 290, 292
Plechanov, 143
Poland, 62, 102, 265, 285, 315, 325, 329
Poles, 218, 256, 322, 331
Politbureau, 143, 255
Politt, Harry, 30
Popular Front, 120, 287, 313-5, 318, 326
Postwar: Europe, 130, 132-3; Germany, 294
Power, 89, 125-6, 294; corruption by, 88-9, 144-5
Pravda, 52, 120, 152, 160, 164, 185, 194, 208, 211, 307
Preobrazjensky, 47
Press, freedom of, 41
Prices, 101-3, 152, 166, 189-93, 212; of export goods, 232-5; paid to peasants, 150; retail (tables), 192-3
Printers' Trade-Union, 40-1
Prison camps, 85, 98. *See also* Concentration camps
Prisons, 92, 200, 238-54, 285
Prisoners, 198, 204, 240 *et seq.*
Pritt, D. N., 267
Production, industrial, 199 *et seq.*
Promexport, 73, 78, 92, 94, 95, 116, 119, 226; my work at, 230-6
Prosecutor, Public, 104, 149, 266-7, 270
Prostitution (Prostitutes), 102, 105
Protestants, 5, 142
Purge, the great, 254-9, 299-302
Pyramids, 203

Racial theories, 341 *et seq.*
Radek, 114
Railways, condition of, 185, 213, 216, 320
Ransome, Arthur, 23

Rations, 79, 85-6, 100, 101
Rationing, 21, 214
Raushning, 278-80, 293-4, 296, 299, 303, 340-1
Red Army, 42, 63, 68, 197, 216, 220, 230, 246, 255-7, 306, 318, 320, 324, 329, 332; Political Commissars of, 257
Red Imperialism, 332
Reimann, Guenter, 282
Renting land, 47
Rents, 21, 76, 78, 194
Repairs, 110
Rest homes, 86-8, 187, 225
Retail trade, 199, 211
Revolution, 45, 49, 88, 90, 135 et seq., 172 et seq.; Bolshevik (November), 9, 21, 34-5, 42, 83, 140-1, 173, 255, 329, 347; (February), 34, 39, 142; celebrations of, 110; French 341, 356; world, 34-5, 45, 141, 217, 317, 349
Right opposition, 15, 45, 46, 48, 49
R.K.I. (Workers' and Peasants' Inspection), 229, 263
Roehm, 300
Roman Empire, 19, 181, 323, 344, 360
Rosenwald Foundation, 99
Rousseau, 131
Rumania, 322
Russell, Bertrand, 10-11, 14, 89, 273
Russian resources, 321
Russo-German: Pact, 205, 216, 221, 239, 257, 273, 312, 314-9, 328; relations, 213-59

Sanatoria, 88, 117, 187, 225
Saturday Evening Post, 316
Schacht, Dr., 282, 322
Schleicher, von, 300
Science, 305
Scissors Crisis, 57
Sedov, Leon, 90
Selassie, Haile, 343
Seredniaki, 53
Servants, 76-8, 97-9, 106-7, 117
Shanghai, 21-3, 59, 61
Shaw, Bernard, 273, 329
Shean, Vincent, 314, 327
Shelley, 4, 31
Siberia, 21, 51, 62, 65, 71, 98, 268, 272, 306
Siliga, 253-4
Skilled labor, shortage of, 208
Slave labor, 19
Sloutsky, 301-2

Smoot-Hawley Tariff, 346
Snobbishness, in Communists, 69
Social Democracy (-crats), 16, 35-6, 37, 38, 45, 135, 142-3, 287, 291, 294, 317, 348
Social Fascists, 313, 317
Social Revolution, 135
Social revolutionaries, 34, 40, 62, 174, 268
Social services, 187-8, 193-4, 197
Socialism, 40, 83, 88, 90, 103, 104; construction of, 16, 45, 52, 196, 202; democratic basis of, 37, 126 et seq.
Socialist Appeal, 258
Socialist competition, 205
Soermus, 96
Solovetsky Island, 239, 241-52
Soule, George, 222
South Seas, 30, 111, 115, 212
Souvarine, Boris, 137-8, 143-4, 196, 203, 253-4
Soviet: democracy, 33, 49, 138-9, 212; intelligentsia, 204, 278; Trade Delegation Representation, 9, 13, 16, 27, 67, 71
Soviets, 4, 39
Spain, 30, 315, 316
Spartacists, 104
Specialists, 59, 69, 71-3, 91, 172, 198, 201, 204, 219, 225-39, 278, 284, 301, 309
Spectator, The, 315
Stakhanovism (-ists), 184-5, 187, 190, 195, 204, 205
Stalin, 5, 6, 10, 11, 15, 21, 31, 36, 38-40, 45-50, 55-7, 63, 71, 74, 83, 89, 90, 93, 98, 128-34, 137, 139-44, 148, 151, 157, 164, 167, 172, 177, 180, 185-8, 199, 202, 204-5, 214, 216-27, 255-9, 267, 278, 283, 286, 293, 296-310, 312-62; foreign policy of, 312-34
Stalinism (-ists), 4, 30, 126-8, 130, 205, 221-2, 297, 313, 319, 322, 324, 328, 332, 334, 339
Starvation, 88, 90, 100; of children, 86, 90-1, 110-1; of Europe, 323; of Germany, 323, 327
State: capitalism, 5, 45, 140, 210, 218 et seq., 285; power, 130 et seq., revenue, 168-71, 215; withering away of, 144-5
Steel, production of, 92, 186, 200, 206, 208
Strength Through Joy, 286
Strikes, 178, 186, 204
Swedish Press, 333
Swinburne, 4-5, 31
Switzerland, 6, 17

Tabrisky, Jane, 69, 70, 81-4, 95, 97, 99, 111, 261
Tatar, 54, 323
Tax, turnover, 168-70, 209-12
Taxes on agriculture, *see* Peasants
Tchernavin, Professor, 239-53; Madame, 239
Tea, price of, 170
Technicians, 49
Terror, 71, 73, 98, 130, 195, 213, 238, 256, 296
Textile: industry, 199, 207, 231-7; specialist, my work as, 226, 231-7; workers, 85, 191, 236
Theodosius, 181
Thompson, Dorothy, 314, 327
Tientsin, 316
Timber export, 85. *See also* Concentration camps
Tolischus, Otto D., 287
Tomsky, 15, 49, 50
Torgsin shops, 102, 117, 204
Torture, 90
Totalitarian war, 336 et *seq.*, 357, 360
Tractor drivers, 165
Trade: barter, 345-6; private, 47
Trade-Union Congress: British, 40; Russian, 42, 173; Soviet, 143, 172 *et seq.*, 188; *cf.* Nazi Labor Front, 178, 286-7
Treason, 305
Trials, Moscow treason, 222
Troika, 174-5, 177, 196
Trotsky, 3, 11, 15, 21, 31-7, 39, 43, 45, 46-50, 54, 141-3, 172, 225, 315, 347
Trotskyism (-ists), 30, 83, 119, 121, 176, 185, 190, 255-8, 273, 303, 332
Troyanovsky, 27
Tsar (-ist), 35, 40, 52, 58, 59, 71, 98, 150, 152, 173, 181, 201, 203, 212, 230, 232, 269, 278, 285, 288, 295, 308, 330-1
Tsar, Iron, 21, 153, 155
Tukatchevsky, General, 254

Ukraine, 56, 85, 86, 175
Unemployed (-ment), 50, 74, 77, 103, 181-3, 194, 213-6, 285-6, 351

United States, 17, 63, 102, 134, 196, 203, 213, 218, 222, 240, 298, 307, 312, 313, 316, 318, 322, 324, 329, 331, 341, 346-50, 352
U.S.S.R., 3, 4, 10, 13, *passim.*
University Labour Federation, 10, 13
University of London, 8, 9
Utley, Temple, 9, 14, 24, 31, 111, 115, 117

Varga, 118, 119, 121, 260, 264
Veressayev, 51
Versailles Treaty, 344, 358
Voitinsky, 119-20
Volga, 162; Germans, 97-9, 104-5, 114

Wage earners, number of, 182, 201
Wages, 50, 85, 175, 178, 187-91, 194, 210, 212, 290; nominal average, 189
War(s): communism, 42, 43, 49; office, 8, 9; of religion, 5; World, 7, 37, 83, 129, 132-3, 290, 311, 322, 326, 336, 344, 348-50; Second World, 274, 307, 330, 335 *et seq.*
Washington, 100
Webb, Sydney and Beatrice, 4, 5, 27, 169, 189, 220-31, 273, 305
Weimar Republic, 283, 290, 347
Wells, H. G., 323
White Sea-Baltic Canal, 240, 254
Winter help, 287
Wise, E. F., 61
Woolf, Leonard, 132
Work Certificate, 172, 179-80
Workers' Educational Association, 19
Workers' control (management), 42, 128, 172 *et seq.*
Working class, 65; dictatorship, 136 *et seq.*, 172, 188; in Nazi Germany, 284-7, 289; Russian, 41, 48, 56, 172-95, 203, 204, 218, 268, 306, 309; standard of life, 100-4, 148, 184, 204, 285, as *cf.* pre-Revolution, 192-3, 205, 212

Yezhov, 266

Zhdanov, 177